D0617150

PETER THE VENERABLE
AND ISLAM

Princeton Oriental Studies

Number 23

Peter the Venerable and Islam

By JAMES KRITZECK

PRINCETON UNIVERSITY PRESS · 1964

PRINCETON, NEW JERSEY

TO

THE ABBOT AND MONKS

OF ST. JOHN'S ABBEY

PREFACE

In 1542 two swiss scholars found themselves seriously at issue with the city council of Basel. The scholars were Theodor Buchmann (or Bibliander, as he preferred to call himself after the fashion of the Humanists), Ulrich Zwingli's principal successor in Zurich, and Johann Herbst (or Oporinus), a gifted classicist and publisher in Basel. The cause at issue was the publication of a collection of translations from the Arabic, including a translation of the Koran, which Bibliander had just finished editing and which he regarded as a timely contribution to learning. Oporinus, who had been party to his friend's work, had agreed to publish the collection in Basel. Recalling that the city council had forbidden another publisher from undertaking a similar venture six years before, he chose to carry on his printing in secret, hoping either to bypass the council's censors or to present them with an accomplished fact. In any case, the council learned of the project. The uncompleted edition of Bibliander's volume was confiscated and Oporinus was forced to spend some time in prison for his crime.[1]

With the army of Sultan Suleyman the Magnificent on the eve of its successful conquest of Hungary, the timeliness of Bibliander's work could not easily have been and, in fact, was not disputed. The council of Basel, a body not given to reckless decisions (or, as Erasmus himself had discovered, to hasty patronage of the schemes of Humanists), entertained a loftier reservation about the matter. Until some worthy reason for doing so were forthcoming, the council decided, it could not assume the responsibility for permitting such a collection of "fables and heresies" to be placed on the market for the disturbance of Christian minds and consciences.

---

[1] The complicated story of this edition is told in detail by Emil Egli, *Analecta Reformatoria*, II (Zurich, 1901), 50-61, citing earlier work and, with additional information, by O. Cl[emen] and H. B[arge], "Vorrede zu Theodor Biblianders Koranausgabe, 1543," *D. Martin Luthers Werke*, LIII (Weimar, 1920), 561-68. See also Egli, "Biblianders Missionsgedanken," *Zwingliana*, III:2 (1913), 46-50, and Walther Köhler, "Zu Biblianders Koran-Ausgabe," *Zwingliana*, III:11 (1918), 349-50.

Fortunately for the scholars involved, such worthy reason was not long in coming forth, and from no less considerable a source than Martin Luther himself. Almost immediately Oporinus had won for his cause a great deal of measured sympathy and some open support from such widely differing quarters as the imperial court at Frankfort and the circle of young John Calvin. But it was a letter from Luther, read to the council on December 2, which settled the issue. In his opinion, Luther wrote, nothing more vexing to the Moslems could possibly be done than to publish translations of the Koran and their other books.[2] The council then approved the completion of the edition, provided that the names of Basel and Oporinus were in no way connected with it and that no copies were offered for sale within the city. The edition, with introductory essays by Luther and Philip Melanchthon, was released on January 11, 1543.[3]

An important fact about Bibliander's volume, while acknowledged, was not emphasized. The timely translations it contained were already, to the very year, four centuries old. They had been produced at the request and under the patronage of Abbot Peter the Venerable of Cluny. Yet Bibliander is not to be despised for his choice of material. On the contrary, it is a signal tribute to his scholarship that he had discovered and recognized the major source of informed European Christian knowledge of Islam since the twelfth century. His publication of the translations assured that their unique importance would be more widely and perma-

[2] See Karl Rudolf Hagenbach, "Luther und der Koran vor dem Rate zu Basel," *Beiträge zur vaterländischen Geschichte*, hrsg. von der historischen Gesellschaft in Basel, ix (1870), 291-326. Luther's letter, dated October 27, reads in part: "Mich hat das bewogen, dass man dem Mahmet [*sic*] oder Türken nichts verdriesslicheres thun, noch mehr Schaden zufügen kann—mehr denn mit allen Waffen—denn dass man ihren Alkoran bei den Christen an den Tag bringe, darinnen sie sehen mögen, wie gar ein verflucht, schändlich, verzweifeltes Buch es sei, voller Lügen, Fabeln, und aller Gräuel"; as cited in full in *ibid.*, 298-301.

[3] Under the title *Machumetis Saracenorum principis eiusque successorum vitæ ac doctrina, ipséque Alcoran*. There were three separate versions of the first edition, in one of which the *Præmonitio* of Melanchthon was erroneously attributed to Luther (such as Asia 84.20F* in the Houghton Library at Harvard). A second edition, embodying corrections made from a manuscript copied in Constantinople for John Cardinal Stokovič in 1437 and adding nine other works, was published in 1550.

nently recognized. They were often quoted and epitomized thereafter, and served as the basis for a number of vernacular translations during the following century.[4] In other words, the fruits of
a single scholarly enterprise of the twelfth century exerted a domi-
nant influence upon European Christian understanding of Islam
for more than half a millennium.

Because of errors and omissions in Bibliander's edition and in
the later manuscripts from which it derived and, one regrets to
note, because of the incomplete and inaccurate study of the available descriptive sources, many facts concerning this collection of
translations have only recently come to light.[5] Valuable preliminary work was done by Pierre Mandonnet, Moritz Steinschneider,
and Ugo Monneret de Villard.[6] It was not until the rediscovery
and study of MS 1162 of the Bibliothèque de l'Arsenal in Paris by
Marie-Thérèse d'Alverny, however, that the way was prepared
for a thorough investigation of the collection, of the circumstances
surrounding its production, and of the contemporary use to which
it was put.[7]

[4] See Régis Blachère, *Introduction au Coran* (Paris, 1947), ix-x, for examples.
[5] Typical of the obstructed state of scholarship on the subject was Marcel Devic,
"Une traduction inédite du Coran," *Journal Asiatique*, 8 série, 1 (April-June,
1883), 343-406, especially 368-76. There seems no point in calling attention to the
misreadings of and misinterpretations placed upon the sources of information in
innumerable articles and books of later date. Rather, I hope that the conclusions
reached in this book, which owe so much to Mlle d'Alverny's work cited below,
will gain acceptance.
[6] Mandonnet, "Pierre le Vénérable et son activité contre l'Islam," *Revue
Thomiste*, 1 (1893), 328-42; Steinschneider, *Die europäischen Übersetzungen aus
dem Arabischen bis Mitte des 17. Jahrhunderts*, iv Abhandlung, Sitzungsberichte
der philosophisch-historischen Klasse der kaiserlichen Akademie der Wissen-
schaften (Vienna, 1905); Monneret de Villard, *Lo studio dell'Islām in Europa
nel xii e nel xiii secolo*, Studi e Testi 110 (Vatican City, 1944).
[7] The MS will be cited hereafter as "A." Mlle d'Alverny's work was published
in "Deux traductions du Coran au Moyen Age," *Archives d'histoire doctrinale et
littéraire du Moyen Age*, 22-23 années (1947-48), 69-131, and "Pierre le Vénérable et la légende de Mahomet," *À Cluny, Travaux du Congrès scientifique en
l'honneur des saints abbés Odon et Odilon, 9-11 juillet, 1949* (Dijon, 1950),
161-70; see also note 12 below. Two articles by P. Manuel, "La première traduction latine du Coran," *En Terre d'Islam* (1945, fasc. 2), 98ff., and (1946, fasc. 1),
31ff.; one by Jean Leclercq, "Pierre le Vénérable et l'invitation au salut," *Bulletin
des Missions* (1947), 145ff.; an unpublished paper read by Dom Leclercq at

A short while after Mlle d'Alverny's articles appeared, Giorgio Levi Della Vida repeated to me a suggestion he had already made in print—that such an investigation of the collection, which had been dubbed the Toledan Collection by Mlle d'Alverny, should be accompanied by a new edition of the texts from the Arsenal manuscript.[8] With Mlle d'Alverny's permission and assistance, I began that task. As it progressed I was struck by the fact that none of the recent authorities who mentioned the collection seemed to be very much concerned with one substantial outcome of the project, the *Liber contra sectam sive hæresim Saracenorum* of Peter the Venerable.[9] After I had compared the printed versions of that work with what appears to be the sole surviving manuscript of it, MS 381 of the Bibliothèque municipale de Douai, it was clear that a new edition of the *Liber* was also an essential part of the study required.[10]

In 1956 Giles Constable and I edited a volume of studies and texts commemorating the eighth centenary of the death of Peter the Venerable.[11] In one of those studies I summarized the results of my research to that date and was able to identify the quotations from the Toledan Collection in the writings of Peter the Venerable; that volume contained three other studies which contributed

---

Puigcerdá in 1948 (mentioned by Darío Cabanelas in "Juan de Segovia y el primer Alcorán trilingüe," *Al-Andalus*, XIV:1 [1949], 157, note 1); and M. T., "Pietro il Venerabile tra i dissensi del suo tempo," *Unitas* (1954, no. 2, March-April), 51-58, add nothing more to the discussion.

[8] Levi Della Vida, "Nuova luce sulle fonti islamiche della Divina Commedia," *Al-Andalus*, XIV:2 (1949), 382, note 2.

[9] Besides those already cited I am thinking particularly of Enrico Cerulli, *Il "Libro della Scala" e la questione delle fonti arabo-spagnole della Divina Commedia*, Studi e Testi 150 (Vatican City, 1949), and José Muñoz Sendino, *La Escala de Mahoma* (Madrid, 1949).

[10] The MS will be cited hereafter as "D." The edition of Edmond Martène and Ursin Durand, *Veterum scriptorum et monumentorum historicorum, dogmaticorum, moralium, amplissima collectio*, IX (Paris, 1733), 1125A-1184D, none too reliable to begin with, was copied with new errors by J.-P. Migne, *Patrologiæ cursus completus, series prima [Latina]* (cited hereafter as "PL"), 189, 663D-720B. A new edition of this text is provided in this volume.

[11] *Petrus Venerabilis (1156-1956): Studies and Texts Commemorating the Eighth Centenary of his Death*, Studia Anselmiana 40 (Rome, 1956). This book will be cited hereafter as "PV."

much toward the solution of problems connected with my work.[12] Since then several other articles have shed further light on related topics, and recently Norman Daniel has published an excellent book treating the general subject of the Christian image of Islam in mediaeval times.[13] R. W. Southern's even more recent study may serve as an adequate introduction for the general reader.[14]

This present book is intended to initiate a series of publications in which I hope to put at the disposal of scholars new editions of the texts relevant to the project sponsored by Peter the Venerable and later projects of a similar nature. It will be followed by an edition of the Toledan Collection based on the Arsenal manuscript.

I wish to record my deep gratitude to the late Theodor E. Mommsen for having directed my work. My debt to Mlle d'Alverny, who not only waived her prior rights to the task in my favor but has provided me with constant advice and assistance ever since, is truly immense. Giles Constable kindly informed me of pertinent findings in his own research toward a new edition of the letters of Peter the Venerable; many problems raised in this book will undoubtedly be solved as a result of Professor Constable's work.

For help and encouragement of many kinds at various stages in my work I should like to thank, omitting their many titles, Georges Anawati, Louis Gardet, Charles Journet, Gerhart Ladner, Jean Leclercq, Jacques Maritain, the late Louis Massignon, Jean de Menasce, Jean Muller, the late Arthur Darby Nock, Guillaume

[12] Kritzeck, "Peter the Venerable and the Toledan Collection," PV, 176-201. I had previously published two short articles on the subject, "Robert of Ketton's Translation of the Qur'ān," *The Islamic Quarterly*, II:4 (December, 1955), 309-12, and "Peter the Venerable and Islam," *American Benedictine Review*, VII:2 (Summer, 1956), 144-49. The other studies in PV to which I refer are Virginia Berry, "Peter the Venerable and the Crusades," 141-62; Charles Julian Bishko, "Peter the Venerable's Journey to Spain," 163-75; and Marie-Thérèse d'Alverny, "Quelques manuscrits de la 'Collectio Toletana,'" 202-18.

[13] Daniel, *Islam and the West: The Making of an Image* (Edinburgh, 1960). His thorough bibliography of primary and secondary sources, 393-427, makes it unnecessary to append a special bibliography to this volume. My review article, "Moslem-Christian Understanding in Mediaeval Times," *Comparative Studies in Society and History*, IV:3 (April, 1962), 388-401, may also be consulted.

[14] *Western Views of Islam in the Middle Ages* (Cambridge, 1962).

Pijper, Anselm Strittmatter, Eugène Tisserant, and John Wright, as well as the members of my pro-seminars in Dunster House at Harvard and my colleagues in the Department of Oriental Studies at Princeton. The Society of Fellows of Harvard gave support to my work in its earlier stages, and I was greatly assisted by associates of the Bibliothèque Nationale, the Bibliothèque de l'Arsenal, and the Institut de Recherche et d'Histoire des Textes in Paris, the Bibliothèque municipale de Douai, and the Bibliotheca Apostolica Vaticana.

The miniature reproduced on the title page, representing Peter the Venerable disputing with the Jews, is from MS 381 of the Bibliothèque municipale de Douai, folio 131r. The colors are gold, blue, green, red, pink, brown, and white. The photograph is by the Institut de Recherche et d'Histoire des Textes in Paris.

J. K.

Lisbon, 1963

CONTENTS

I · PETER THE VENERABLE

*Solus enim vos estis
nostris temporibus.*
PETER OF POITIERS

*Il n'y a qu'un mot
pour le dire: Pierre le
Vénérable est parfait.*
ETIENNE GILSON

1 · THE JOURNEY TO SPAIN

AT THE TURN OF the twelfth century the abbey of Cluny in Burgundy was a place of enormous importance in Europe. Founded in 910 as a center for the reformation of monasticism, it had enjoyed entirely exceptional privileges, among them a status of exemption under the immediate protection of the Roman Pontiff and the right freely to affiliate other monasteries with itself as dependencies. In the course of the tenth and eleventh centuries, under a series of remarkably capable abbots, Cluny acquired great influence and wealth. It was, in effect, the capital of a monastic empire comprising some ten thousand monks in more than six hundred monasteries located throughout western Christendom. Its monks had become popes and cardinals, and its abbots were counsellors to emperors and kings.[1]

Pierre Maurice de Montboissier, known as Peter the Venerable, was only twenty-eight years old when he was elected abbot of Cluny in 1122.[2] He was not so startling a choice for that prelacy

[1] Works on the history of Cluny are very numerous and readily accessible by means of standard bibliographies. The most valuable collections of sources are *Bibliotheca Cluniacensis*, ed. M. Marrier and A. Duchesne (Paris, 1614; reprinted Mâcon, 1915), cited hereafter as "BC," and *Recueil des chartes de l'abbaye de Cluny*, ed. A. Bernard and A. Bruel, 6 vols. (Paris, 1876-1903), cited hereafter as "CC." Both the abbey and its greatly diminished order continued to exist until the time of the French Revolution. The monks were dispersed in October of 1791; in November the abbey was sacked by a revolutionary mob and its manuscripts and vestments were burned in the market place. Later the abbey was sold at auction and systematically destroyed between 1798 and 1823. See G. Charvin, "La fin de l'Ordre de Cluny (1789-1791)," *Revue Mabillon*, XL (1950), 29-41. Excavations of the abbey were carried out by the Mediaeval Academy of America under the direction of K. J. Conant between 1928 and 1938; see his many reports in *Speculum*, and Jean Virey, "Les Travaux du Professeur K. J. Conant à Cluny," *Revue Mabillon*, XXIV (1934), 65-80.

[2] Hereafter I shall call him Peter. The title "the Venerable" was evidently accorded him by his contemporaries; its use in addressing prelates of the time, and notably the abbots of Cluny, was not uncommon. Although Peter was honored as a saint by the Cluniac order, and is still considered such in Alfons M. Zimmermann, *Kalendarium Benedictinum*, III (Metten, 1937), 476-78, he was never canonized. His is an "approved cult" (by Pope Pius IX in 1862; Zimmermann, *op. cit.*, 478), giving him honors proper to a *beatus*; cf. The Benedictine Monks of St. Augustine's Abbey, Ramsgate, *The Book of Saints* (New York, 1947), 480, and D. Attwater, *A Dictionary of Saints* (London, 1938), 243. There

3

as the mere fact of his youth might seem to suggest. He was a grandnephew of Cluny's greatest abbot, Hugh I, and had been promised to the monastery, according to his official biography, even before his birth.[3] He had entered the Cluniac order at Sauxillanges at the age of sixteen. As the gifted son of a noble Burgundian family closely connected with Cluny, his rapid advancement to important priorates at Vézelay and Domène was only to be expected.[4]

Moreover, Cluny was in some straits in 1122. Peter's predecessor, who ruled only three months, had inherited a host of disciplinary and financial problems from Abbot Pontius. That conten-

---

is as yet no satisfactory scholarly biography of Peter, but a short descriptive analysis of the sources for his life may be found in Jean Leclercq, *Pierre le Vénérable* (Abbaye Saint-Wandrille, 1946), xiv-xvii, and a survey of the study of his works in Giles Constable, "Manuscripts of Works by Peter the Venerable," PV, 219-42. More detailed biographical information than it has been possible to include in this chapter may be obtained from Dom Leclercq's biography, and from the following other works: *Histoire littéraire de la France*, XIII (Paris, 1814), 240-67; C. A. Wilkens, *Petrus der Ehrwürdige, Abt von Clugny* (Leipzig, 1857); B. Duparay, *De Petri Venerabilis vita et operibus* (Chalon-sur-Saone, 1857); C. Dubois, *Pierre le Vénérable* (Geneva, 1862); J.-H. Pignot, *Histoire de l'Ordre de Cluny*, III (Autun and Paris, 1868), 49-609; J. d'Avenel, *Vie de Pierre le Vénérable, suivie de récits merveilleux* (Paris, 1874); M. Demimuid, *Pierre le Vénérable, ou la vie et l'influence monastiques au xiie siècle* (Paris, 1876); M. Manitius, *Geschichte der lateinischen Literatur des Mittelalters*, III (Munich, 1931), 136-44; P. Séjourné, "Pierre le Vénérable," *Dictionnaire de Théologie Catholique*, XII:2 (Paris, 1935), 2065-81; W. Williams, *Monastic Studies* (Manchester, 1938), 132-45; and the other studies in PV. *Selected Writings of Peter the Venerable*, ed. J. Kritzeck, is scheduled for publication in the Benedictine Studies series in 1964-65.

[3] PL 189, 17A.

[4] The Montboissier family had founded a Cluniac monastery. Peter entered Sauxillanges as an *oblatus*, i.e., a lay student who was a presumptive candidate for the novitiate; see *Sancti Benedicti Regula Monachorum*, ed. P. Schmitz (Maredsous, 1946), cap. 59, 83. He pronounced his vows before Abbot Hugh; BC 589A. He spent ten years at Vézelay with his elder brother Pontius, who became abbot of that monastery. His brothers Jordanus and Armannus became abbots of La-Chaise-Dieu (Casa Dei) and Manglieu respectively; PL 189, 28A-B. Another brother, Heraclius, a secular cleric (BC 817C), became archbishop of Lyons. Of the three other brothers one, Otto, died in youth (BC 614E); the second, Dissutus, married and had two daughters who became nuns at Marcigny, as did his mother (BC 939D-45A); the third and youngest, Eustachius, also remained a layman; Dissutus and Eustachius were knights. On the different types of Cluniac priorates, see G. de Valous, *Le monachisme clunisien dès origines au xve sciècle*, I (Paris, 1935).

tious and prodigal prelate had resigned the abbacy in Rome, after answering to charges of malfeasance, and departed on a pilgrimage to the Holy Land.[5] At the same time a rival and combative Cistercian (from Cîteaux) order had recently been approved by the Holy See. What Cluny needed, as its priors well knew, was a vigorous young abbot, mindful of tradition, who could maintain Cluny's greatness. "Would that they had chosen better!" was Peter's comment on his election.[6] The remark is more poignant and unintentionally ironic when one considers that during the thirty-four years of his abbacy he proved himself, against obstacles his predecessors had been spared, the last of Cluny's great abbots. His life and work involved almost every aspect of ecclesiastical history in the first half of the twelfth century. The overshadowing power of his contemporary, Bernard of Clairvaux, notwithstanding, Peter has always been regarded as one of the most admirable and captivating personalities of the Latin Middle Ages. This book is devoted to a study of one project, from among his numerous activities, which serves to justify and enforce the esteem of the centuries.

Peter the Venerable was a man formed by Cluny at the height of its magnificence and power, the Cluny that was building the largest church in Christendom, the Cluny that was fostering, almost uniquely in its age and environment, the values of the arts and sciences. Any attempt to explain him must make ample use of that fact. Much of the contemporary biographical material was given over to disarming enumerations of his virtues and accounts of miracles he is said to have performed.[7] The reader must deal with this hagiography according to his lights. It is possible, even easier, to form a portrait of Peter without it.

He was an astonishingly energetic man in spite of somewhat

[5] "Sua voluntate," it was said; PL 189, 17C. See A. Wilmart, "Deux pièces relatives à l'abdication de Pons, abbé de Cluny en 1122," *Revue Bénédictine*, XLIV (1932), 351-53, and H. White, "Pontius of Cluny, the 'Curia Romana,' and the End of Gregorianism in Rome," *Church History*, XXVII (1958), 197-219.

[6] "Utinam sibi melius consulentes," BC 1311A.

[7] PL 189, 21C-28A.

delicate health.[8] Throughout his life the essential occupation of each day was participation in liturgy, particularly in the solemn chanting of the Psalms, to which, as St. Benedict legislated, "nothing should be preferred," and to which Cluny, in the face of mounting criticism, did in fact prefer nothing.[9] As abbot he was daily called upon to preach and instruct; one concludes from the stress laid upon it in the sources and from its ubiquitous traces throughout his writings that his rhetorical talent was genuinely extraordinary.[10] He was obliged to travel often, to visit abbeys and priories dependent upon Cluny and to attend gatherings of spiritual and temporal magnates. Because of the large number and wide extension of his monastaries, some of Peter's journeys were necessarily of long duration. There is abundant evidence that his fidelity to his many and varied abbatial duties taxed him inordinately, and that his personal inclination ran, instead, toward activities of a scholarly nature.

Such an inclination would not be rare in a child of the mature Cluny. At the beginning, to be sure, the abbey was not known for its erudition. Like monastic reform movements before and since, Cluny's had had its anti-intellectual phase. Peter embodies the culmination of an eleventh-century development which removed the stigma from and provided the material means for sound scholarship, as it placed at the disposal of the Cluniac monk a large share of the store of extant pagan and early Christian writings.[11]

Peter has been singled out, more than once, as the most peaceful man of his age. In comparison with most of his contemporaries, not excluding his fellow prelates, he does indeed stand out as a man of peace. The first challenge to his pacific nature came soon

---

[8] See Henri Quentin, "Une correspondance médicale de Pierre le Vénérable avec Magister Bartholomaeus," *Miscellanea Francesco Ehrle*, I (Vatican City, 1924), 80-86.

[9] *Ed. cit.*, cap. 43, 64.

[10] His sermons may be found in BC 1231A-1248A, and Giles Constable, "Petri Venerabilis Sermones Tres," *Revue Bénédictine*, LXIV (1954), 224-72.

[11] Both Abbots Odo and Maiolus had studied the classics before coming to Cluny; see J. Evans, *Monastic Life at Cluny, 910-1157* (London, 1931), 101-02. On the library of Cluny, see below, part 4.

after his election and from a rather unexpected source. Ex-abbot Pontius, whose pilgrimage appears to have done him little good, took advantage of Peter's absence from Cluny while he was visiting monasteries in Aquitaine to attack the abbey with an army of mercenary soldiers. In his own words Peter has left us a record of this invasion. He did nothing to oppose the usurper by force during the months that Pontius terrorized Cluny, imprisoning monks and pillaging the treasury. When news of the situation reached the new pope, Honorius II, Pontius and "the Pontians" were swiftly excommunicated and captured.[12] Peter was frequently called upon, over the years, to mediate between warring lords. He played an important role in healing the schism of the anti-pope Anacletus II, and his many accomplishments in peacemaking are impressive.[13]

One of Peter's chief concerns throughout his abbacy was the reform of Cluniac monasticism.[14] The proximate causes for that concern are obvious enough, but its background is more complicated. One must take into account, for instance, the connection between Cluny and the wider reform movement in the Church during the later eleventh century, a connection which has frequently been exaggerated.[15] One has to recognize that the Cluniac

[12] BC 1311B-12A; cf. Odericus Vitalis, *Historia Ecclesiastica*, III, 12:15, PL 188, 894D 95D.

[13] Leclercq, *op. cit.*, 41. On the schism of Anacletus, who had been a Cluniac monk, see H. Bloch, "The Schism of Anacletus II and the Glanfeuil Forgeries of Peter the Deacon of Monte Cassino," *Traditio*, VIII (1952), 159-264.

[14] Leclercq, *op. cit.*, 107-13, and his "Pierre le Vénérable et l'érémitisme clunisien," PV, 99-120. Peter's efforts were crowned by the adoption of seventy-six reforms, listed, with the reasons for their adoption, in BC 1353B-76A; an analysis of these reforms was made by David Knowles, "The Reforming Decrees of Peter the Venerable," PV, 1-20. On the economic side, see G. Duby, "Économie domaniale et économie monétaire. Le budget de l'abbaye de Cluny entre 1080 et 1155," *Annales. Économies. Sociétés. Civilisations.*, VII (1952), 155-71, and "Un inventaire des profits de la seigneurie clunisienne à la mort de Pierre le Vénérable," PV, 128-40.

[15] See G. Tellenbach, *Church, State, and Christian Society at the Time of the Investiture Contest*, tr. R. F. Bennett (Oxford, 1940), esp. 82-85, 186-92; A. Fliche, *La réforme grégorienne et la reconquête chrétienne* (n.p., 1940), 427-45; J. Haller, *Das Papsttum: Idee und Wirklichkeit*, II (Basel, 1951). Caution in the matter had already been urged by L. M. Smith, *Cluny in the Eleventh and Twelfth*

monastic reform as such had come to a near standstill in Abbot Odilo's time and that soon afterward there were indications of a strong and persistent feeling that Cluny itself stood in need of reform. It was being argued, and not only by the unfriendly, that the collectivization which had made Cluny great ran boldly counter to both the letter and the spirit of the Rule of St. Benedict.[16] A few new orders had been founded, but the alternative of devising entirely different forms for the religious life did not take prominent shape until the rise of the mendicant orders later in the twelfth century. Reproving opinion in this earlier period generally sought a return to a stricter observance of St. Benedict's Rule. It was to recognize and satisfy this opinion that the Roman Pontiff approved the Cistercian order in 1119.[17]

Strong impetus for Peter's reforming efforts came from the Cistercian criticism of Cluny, a highly articulate reproach which reached a zenith of intensity in the early and middle years of his abbacy. The controversy between the "white" Cistercians and the "black" Cluniacs (so called because of the colors of their monastic robes), very largely but not entirely a battle of words with overtones of petty jealousies and broken friendships, was the most bitter in the history of western monasticism.[18] There were, of

---

Centuries (London, 1930), xxi, and E. Sackur, *Die Cluniazenser in ihrer kirchlichen und allgemeingeschichtlichen Wirksamkeit,* II (Halle, 1894), 445.

[16] K. Hallinger, *Gorze-Kluny: Studien zu den monastischen Lebensformen und Gegensätzen im Hochmittelalter,* 2 vols. (Rome, 1950-51).

[17] U. Berlière, "Les origines de Cîteaux et l'ordre bénédictin au xii⁰ siècle," *Revue d'histoire ecclésiastique,* I (1900), 448-71; II (1901), 253-90; J. O. Ducourneau, "Les origines cisterciennes," *Revue Mabillon,* XXII (1932), 133-64, 233-52; XXIII (1933), 1-32, 82-111, 153, 189. There has been a considerable advance in our understanding of the origins of the Cistercian order in recent years, but several scholarly controversies have been engendered in connection with it; see the articles cited by A. H. Bredero, "The Controversy between Peter the Venerable and St. Bernard of Clairvaux," PV, 54-55, note 5; 58-59, note 16.

[18] See "Dialogus inter Cluniacensem monachum et Cisterciensem," *Thesaurus Novus Anecdotorum,* ed. E. Martène and U. Durand, v (Paris, 1717), 1571A-1654E; J. Sturm, *Untersuchungen zum Dialogus duorum monachorum Cluniacensis et Cisterciensis* (Bocholt i. W., 1926), and the review by P. V. Redlich, in *Studien und Mitteilungen zur Geschichte des Benediktiner-Ordens und seine Zweige,* XLIV (1926); F. Cabrol, "Cluny et Cîteaux," *Saint Bernard et son temps,* I (Dijon, 1928), 19-28; E. Bishop, "Cluniacs and Cistercians," *Downside Review,*

course, genuine issues at stake; it was therefore incumbent upon the leaders of the two orders, Peter as abbot of Cluny and Bernard (who, though abbot of Clairvaux rather than Cîteaux, was acknowledged to be the chief spokesman for the Cistercians), to issue lengthy statements in defense of their respective positions.[19]

It is remarkable that in the very fury of the duel between their orders, when there were innumerable defections and signs of ill will on both sides, Peter and Bernard struck up and maintained a friendship. Each had won the other's respect and admiration and both were capable of seeing beyond the controversy. Their friendship did have its steep ups and downs. Peter, especially, desired peace between the orders, but not at the price of surrendering the charitable spirit of the Rule; Bernard, a different kind of man, was unwilling to compromise. Peter proceeded to reform Cluniac monasticism as rapidly and efficiently as he could, and he did so as a devout Cluniac.[20] He continued to regard many of the Cistercian positions, notably those opposing the study of the classics and philosophy and the fostering of the arts, as pharisaical and utterly unwarranted, even in the light of the common suppositions of both Cîteaux and Cluny.[21] Whenever, as they were bound to do,

---

LII (1934), 48-70, 209-30; D. Knowles, *Cistercians and Cluniacs* (Oxford, 1955); Giles Constable, "The Letter of Peter of St. John to Hato of Troyes," PV, 38-52; Bredero, *op. cit.*; C. H. Talbot, "The Date and Author of the 'Riposte,'" PV, 72-80; M. A. Dimier, "Un témoin tardif peu connu du conflit entre Cisterciens et Clunisiens," PV, 81-98.

[19] BC 657D-95B, 704E-06E, PL 182, 895A-918A, the most famous, among others. On the problem of dating them and for a detailed analysis, see Bredero, *op. cit.*

[20] In a *locus classicus*, BC 931D-E, Peter wrote to Bernard, "Si liceret, si Dei dispositio non obstaret, si in hominis potestate esset via eius, maluissem, charissime, beatitudini tuæ nexu indissolubili adhærere, quam vel principari inter mortales alicubi, vel regnare." That expression of affection disturbed Bernard enough for him to write to Pope Eugene: "Si enim petierit, quod suspicor vereorque, dimitti a regimine monasterii, quis illum noscens in nomine Jesu petere putet? . . . Quanquam pene ab introitu suo in multis ordinem illum meliorasse cognoscitur" (BC 602C). But Bernard was imputing a meaning to Peter's sentiment (which was preceded, after all, by three important conditional clauses) which is not necessarily to be found there. It is impossible to believe that Peter was ready to abandon Cluny, whose principles he defended and embodied to the end of his life. He had said the same things to the Carthusians, for example; BC 651D-E.

[21] E. Mâle rather overstates the two positions in *Religious Art* (New York,

implications of the controversy spilled over into nonmonastic ecclesiastical and even secular affairs, Peter acted with decision and consistency. In 1140, to cite a famous example, when Peter Abelard fell victim to Bernard's hounding zeal, it was Peter the Venerable who saved his life and soul by granting him sanctuary at Cluny, in one of whose neighboring priories the philosopher ended his troubled life in peace two years later.[22]

Early in 1142 Peter the Venerable left Cluny on a journey to Spain.[23] He was still a young man and accustomed to travel, but there are many indications that this journey represented something quite unusual for him. He obviously expected to be gone for a considerable length of time, because he felt it necessary in his absence to entrust the care of all the Cluniac monasteries to Archbishop Geoffrey of Bordeaux.[24] It was his first visit to Spain, and,

---

1949), 17: "At the very time when Saint Bernard was despoiling his churches of all their ornaments, Peter the Venerable was ordering the chiseling of capitals and the sculpture of tympana. The eloquence of the ardent apostle of austerity did not convince Peter that beauty was dangerous; he saw in it, rather, as Saint Othon had taught, a prefiguring of heaven." See also Leclercq, *Pierre le Vénérable*, 262-64, and K. J. Conant, "Cluniac Building during the Abbacy of Peter the Venerable," PV, 121-27. For an interesting account of another quarrel of Bernard's on the same questions, see E. Panofsky, *Abbot Suger* (Princeton, 1946), 1-37.

[22] Peter's warmly sympathetic letters about Abelard to Heloise (BC 850C-54B, 920A-D) are justly numbered among the most humane documents in mediaeval literature. He arranged for Abelard's body to be transported to Heloise's convent for burial, accompanied the body himself, later sent his own sacerdotal absolution of Abelard's sins in a sealed charter which Heloise hung on the tomb, and composed an epitaph for the philosopher. See the classic study, F.-A. Gervaise, *La Vie de Pierre Abélard* (Paris, 1720), and, among many modern works, E. Gilson, *Héloïse et Abélard* (Paris, 1948).

[23] C. J. Bishko's illuminating study, "Peter the Venerable's Journey to Spain," PV, 163-75, has been used extensively in the following account. Peter himself gave the date as 1141: "Hoc anno illo factum est quo Hyspanias adii, et cum domno Aldefonso uictorioso Hyspaniarum imperatore colloquium habui, qui annus fuit ab incarnatione Domini mcxli.us," D f. 18ord, PL 189, 671D. But the year could have extended, in one French style, to Easter of 1142. All other evidence points to 1142 as the correct date.

[24] BC 824A-25B; "Ago quas possum gratias quia non imparem in mutui amoris constantia uos inueni, quem de amici ad remotas Hispaniarum partes et uelut ad peregrina tendentis mandatis et precibus tam deuotum conseruatorem habui. Commendaui ei monasteria nostra abbatias prioratus et cellas; et ecce non eius

indeed, only the third time that an abbot of Cluny had crossed the Pyrenees.[25] He travelled with a large entourage and elaborate panoply. Something out of the ordinary had clearly motivated the trip.

Peter himself mentioned only the purpose of visiting the Cluniac monasteries in Spain, although one passage could be made to suggest that he intended to go on a pilgrimage to the shrine of Santiago de Compostella.[26] Considering the nature and number of demands on the abbot of Cluny in 1142, neither of these reasons strikes one as sufficiently compelling to have warranted so long and arduous a journey. A recent study has brought to light another and far more satisfying reason for it: Emperor Alfonso VII had invited Peter to meet with him on Spanish soil.[27]

Such an invitation would have commanded Peter's eager attention and ready compliance for a special reason. The emperor's grandfather, Alfonso VI, had pledged to Cluny an annual census donation of two thousand *metcales* (Arabic *mithqāl*). Once a major source of income for the abbey, the donation was now far in arrears. Inasmuch as Cluny's financial situation had been steadily worsening, any favorable settlement of this matter could only have appealed to its abbot. The emperor's invitation was probably borne by Bishop Stephen of Osma, who is mentioned in Peter's entourage and who may even have conveyed immediately his temporal sovereign's proposed *quid pro quo*: Peter's support of

---

tantum sed et omnium nostrum uoce attestante fidissimum etiam in hoc commisso reperi," interpreted by Bishko, *op. cit.*, 165, note 10.

[25] In 1090 Abbot Hugh went as far as Burgos, and in 1113 Abbot Pontius visited Compostella; *ibid.*, 163. Some authorities were misled in thinking that Peter had visited Spain in 1126.

[26] "Cum in Hispaniis pro uisitatione locorum nostrorum quae ibi sunt," A 3vs; "ad remotas Hispaniarum partes et uelut ad peregrina tendentis," in the passage cited above in note 24, "which may point to an original, but unfulfilled, intention of proceeding all the way to the Apostle's tomb," Bishko, *op. cit.*, 172.

[27] *Ibid.*, 164; CC 5, 423-26. On the Spanish use of the imperial title, see P. E. Schramm, "Das kastilische König- und Kaisertum während der Reconquista (11 Jahrh. bis 1252)," *Festschrift für Gerhard Ritter*, ed. R. Nürnberger (Tübingen, 1950); C. Erdmann, *Forschungen zur politischen Ideenwelt des Frühmittelalters*, ed. F. Baethgen (Berlin, 1951), 31ff. See also P. Rassow, *Die Urkunden Kaisers Alfons VII von Spanien* (Berlin, 1929), 89.

Alfonso's candidate, Bishop Berengarius of Salamanca, for the archbishopric of Santiago.[28]

There are many problems connected with Peter's itinerary in Spain, some of which may never be solved. It would seem that he travelled by the direct route through Lyons, Le Puy, and Moissac toward Roncesvalles and Pamplona, and moved westward along the pilgrims' *camino francés* toward Compostella, stopping at Estella in southern Navarre and then at the monastery of Santa María de Nájera, the first great Cluniac possession he would have encountered in Spain. By June or early July, however, he must have been en route to Salamanca for his meeting with the emperor. The time and choice of site for that meeting were determined by Alfonso's siege of the Almoravid (Arabic *Al-Murābiṭ*) stronghold at Coria, which ended victoriously for the emperor in June.[29] It is probable that Peter remained at the monastery of San Zoil at Carrión de los Condes, the principal Cluniac center in western Spain, while awaiting word from the emperor as to the time and place of the conference.

No detailed account of their negotiations was written down, but they can be reconstructed, through charters and other evidence, from their results. In a diploma issued on July 29, 1142, Alfonso ceded to Cluny the great Castillian abbey of San Pedro de Cardeña near Burgos, along with certain minor properties in Burgos and an annual stipend from the royal revenues of that city's public baths.[30] That was a respectable compensation to mark the

---

[28] On the members of Peter's entourage, see Bishko, *op. cit.*, 165-66. Alfonso was determined "to obtain a friendly, financially generous metropolitan in a Galicia threatened by the rising power of the new Portuguese monarchy and torn ecclesiastically, as well as politically, by pro-Portuguese, pro-Castilian and pro-independence factions. It should be remembered also that Compostella's suffragan sees, located in the Luso-Hispanic borderlands of the old Visigothic ecclesiastical province of Merida, added to the political importance of the Gallegan metropolitanate," *ibid.*, 170-71.

[29] *Ibid.*, 166-69; *Chronicon Adefonsi imperatoris*, ed. H. Flórez and M. Risco, XXI (Madrid, 1747-1879), 380-81.

[30] CC 5, 423-27. Special privileges were accorded to San Zoil at Carrión, and in October of 1143 the church of San Vincente at Salamanca was ceded for conversion into a Cluniac priory; *ibid.*, 428-30. L. Serrano, *El obispado de Burgos y Castilla primitiva*, II (Madrid, 1935), 26, note 1, emphasized, somewhat caus-

end of the census donation. Peter, on his part, interested himself in the details of the disputed archiepiscopal election at
Compostella. There is a possibility that he actually visited Galicia,
but it is quite as likely that he collected his testimony on the matter
from witnesses who were summoned to meet with him at Carrión
or elsewhere.[31] At any rate, he was still there in August, and
travelled with the emperor eastward to Burgos at the end of the
month. Two documents affirm their presence in Burgos in early
September.[32] Very likely both men felt that the abbey of San
Pedro de Cardeña (which was associated in the national mind
with the exploits of El Cid and the ancient Castilian kings) could
more gracefully be transferred to Cluny in their presence.

It is no less difficult to date precisely Peter's return to France.
Some of the problems connected with his return journey will be
discussed in a more appropriate context later. From Burgos, it
would appear, he returned to Nájera and Pamplona toward
Roncesvalles; there is some reason to believe that he may have
stayed at Pamplona for a time. However, he received reports of serious conditions at Cluny requiring his immediate return, and he
abandoned plans to visit the archbishops of Bordeaux and Nar-
bonne on his way.[33] Whether these reports reached him before
or after he had crossed the Pyrenees is impossible, from present
evidence, to ascertain. He could certainly have been prevented from
crossing the mountains by the winter snows. His official biographer
states that he celebrated Mass at Le Puy, on his way back from
Spain, on Ascension Day (May 13) in 1143.[34] That would not seem
to indicate any particular haste in returning, and it is always
possible that his letters to the archbishops (who themselves may
not have been resident in their sees at the time) were in the

tically, the economic motivations for Peter's visit. Yet Cluny was able to hold San
Pedro de Cardeña less than four years, and most of its Spanish dependencies de-
serted it for the Congregation of St. Benedict of Valladolid later in the century.

[31] Bishko, op. cit., 173; such testimony is mentioned in BC 821D-E.

[32] Rassow, op. cit., 88-89; F. de Berganza, Antigüedades de España propug-
nadas en las noticias de sus reyes y condes de Castilla la Vieja (Madrid, 1719-21),
2, 76.

[33] BC 823C-25B.

[34] PL 189, 27B.

nature of social regrets. Be that as it may, Peter's whereabouts in the winter and early spring of 1142-43 remain, in the absence of further evidence, something of a mystery.

Soon after he returned to Cluny, at any rate, Peter sent the monk Natalis (a former royal chancellor of France and abbot of Saint-Pierre de Rebais) as an envoy to Pope Innocent II for the purpose of urging the pontiff to recognize Bishop Berengarius as archbishop of Santiago de Compostella.[35] As important as the financial results of Peter's journey undoubtedly were for Cluny, it produced an infinitely more important result, totally incidental to the others and probably also unpremeditated, which marks that journey as a momentous event in the intellectual history of Europe. For in its course Peter conceived, planned, and sponsored his project to study, comprehensively and from original sources, the religion of Islam.

[35] BC 797A-C, 821B-22B. Bernard, who was visited by Berengarius on his way back to Spain, also urged the translation (PL 182 377A-D); but the contending claimant, Pedro Helías, was finally recognized.

2 · THE CRUSADE: A MISSING GOAL

IT REQUIRED a measure of both originality and heroism on the part of Peter the Venerable to initiate the study of Islam in Europe. Although the Islamic empire was hewn out of Christian lands to a very large extent, and encroached upon both the Eastern Roman empire and southern Europe in short order, "the Christian world was slow to recognize Islam for what it was, viz., not another outgrowth of the familiar Arian sectarianism, but an independent religion of considerable appeal."[36] Byzantium, forced to deal with Islam first, could hardly have been expected to view it otherwise than as a military power of astounding force, since in a matter of a few decades after its emergence out of the Arabian peninsula most of the Byzantine lands along the south-eastern littoral of the Mediterranean were in the hands of its followers. A state of sporadic conflict endured for so long a time that it was left to a few Christians within the Islamic empire to discover the nature of Islam and to risk polemicizing against it. St. John of Damascus and his successor Theodore Abu-Qurrah were the first and greatest of them.[37] Although some worked with a fairly complete and accurate knowledge of Islamic doctrine, their works cannot be said to have enlightened Christendom proper very much. Theophanes, the first Byzantine historian to deal with the origins of Islam,[38] or simple hearsay long remained

[36] G. von Grunebaum, *Medieval Islam* (Chicago, 1946), 12.

[37] J.-P. Migne, *Patrologiae cursus completus, series Graeca* (cited hereafter as "PG"), 96, 1335-48; 94, 1585-98. I have translated most of the *Debate between a Christian and a Saracen* in *A Treasury of Early Christianity*, ed. Anne Fremantle (New York, 1953), 321-24; PG 97, 1461-1602; C. Bacha, *Un traité des oeuvres arabes de Théodore Abou Ḵurra* (Rome, 1905); A. Guillaume, "A Debate between Christian and Muslim Doctors," *Centenary Supplement of the Journal of the Royal Asiatic Society* (1924), 233-44; G. Graf, *Die arabischen Schriften des Theodor Abu Qurra* (Paderborn, 1910). See also F. Nau, "Un colloque du Patriarche Jean," *Journal Asiatique*, xi:5 (1915), 225-79; A. Mingana, "The Transmission of the Ḵur'ān," *Journal of the Manchester Egyptian Oriental Society* (1916), 35-47; *ibid.*, "The Apology of Timothy the Patriarch before the Caliph Mahdi," *Bulletin of the John Rylands Library*, xii (1928), 137-298; L. E. Browne, "The Patriarch Timothy and the Caliph al-Mahdi," *The Moslem World*, xxi (1931), 38-45.

[38] Von Grunebaum, *op. cit.*, 43; *Theophanis Chronographia*, ed. C. de Boor, 2 vols. (Leipzig, 1883-85)

the sources of Byzantium's meager knowledge of these matters.

Europe, at the time of Islam's rise, was still culturally dependent upon Byzantium; "from 685 to 752 . . . the oriental influence was at its height, not only in Rome, but throughout the West."[39] Then came the pressure of new barbarian invasions and the Iconoclastic controversy of the eighth century, which had the effect of destroying that dependency. At the precise time of the first direct contact between western Christendom and Islam, therefore, when the Islamic empire was piercing well into Europe's center before settling to include Spain and Sicily and generally forming Europe's southern boundary, Europe itself was reorienting its gaze and energies toward the northeast and northwest, a process which had been in fact underway since the time of Pope St. Gregory the Great.[40] Had the Carolingian empire, certainly the most ambitious attempt at uniting Europe in this period, not proven itself premature, there might have been much greater contact between the two cultures than there was.[41] As it happened, the pagan lands in northern Europe furnished as great a challenge to Christian missionaries as they were prepared, at that time, to deal with. As Christian monks from Italy, southern France, and Ireland, the principal agents in turning the tide of barbarism, went their apostolic way, one by one the lands of the north adopted the faith of these men who, like their founder St. Benedict, "found a world in ruins and restored it by creating a Christian culture."[42]

It is not surprising, in this atmosphere of building atop paganism, that the task of refuting heresy proved to be not a particularly urgent one. The burning theological issues of the eighth and ninth

[39] C. Dawson, *The Making of Europe* (New York, 1932), 207.

[40] The most extreme statement of Islam's part in that reorientation is that of H. Pirenne, *Mohammed and Charlemagne*, tr. B. Miall (New York, 1939); but see R. S. Lopez, "Mohammed and Charlemagne: A Revision," *Speculum*, XVIII (1943), 14-38; D. C. Dennett, "Pirenne and Mohammed," *Speculum*, XXIII (1948), 181-85; A. R. Lewis, *Naval Power and Trade in the Mediterranean, A.D. 500-1100* (Princeton, 1951). Oscar Halecki, *The Limits and Divisions of European History* (New York, 1950), 27-29, gives a balanced judgment.

[41] See F. W. Buckler, *Harunu'l-Rashid and Charles the Great* (Cambridge, 1931).

[42] J. H. Newman, *Historical Sketches*, II (London, 1890), 433-87.

centuries centered around controversies in the Eastern Church, notably Iconoclasm and Photianism. Such heresies as did arise in Europe at the same time, some Adoptionism and Predestinationism, and a later neo-Manichaean movement and one of neo-Nicholaitism, were without exception associated with individuals or small groups, and were not of a size or importance to command concerted polemical activity.[43] In the eleventh century certain errors of Berengarius of Tours, especially on the modality of Christ's presence in the Eucharist, hung fire.[44] Then one must come to the Petrobrusians, against whom Peter the Venerable wrote, or to the nascent philosophical controversies, for anything comparable.[45]

What scraps of information about Islam Europeans possessed, usually centered about the figure of Mohammed, were utterly or in large part false.[46] Mohammed was sometimes thought to be the god of the Moslems, but a more current view was that he was only one god in a pantheon worshipped by them; the *Chanson de Roland,*

[43] F. Cayré, *Manual of Patrology,* II (Paris, Tournai, and Rome, 1940), 381-82; S. Runciman, *The Mediaeval Manichee* (Cambridge, 1955).

[44] C. E. Sheedy, *Eucharistic Controversy of the Eleventh Century* (Washington, 1947), esp. 64-79; G. Ellard, *The Mass of the Future* (Milwaukee, 1948), 92.

[45] J. H. Blunt, *A Dictionary of Sects* (London, 1874), v-vi, lists forty-six "medieval sects and heresies," most of which postdate the beginning of the twelfth century. See F. Tocco, *L'eresia nel medio evo* (Florence, 1884); G. Volpe, *Movimenti religiosi e sètte ereticali nella società medioevale italiana* (Florence, 1926); I. da Milano, "Le eresie popolari del secolo xi nell'Europa occidentale," *Studi Gregoriani,* II (Rome, 1947), 43-89; R. Manselli, *Studi sulle eresie del secolo xii* (Rome, 1953).

[46] Daniel, *op. cit.,* is now the indispensable work on this subject. But see also A. d'Ancona, "La leggenda di Maometto in Occidente," *Giornale storico della letteratura italiana,* XIII (1889), 199-281, reprinted with additional information in his *Studii e critica e storica letteraria,* II (Bologna, 1912), 165-306; A. Graf, "Spigolature per la leggenda di Maometto," *Giornale storico della letteratura italiana,* XIV (1889), 204-11; R. Renier, "Ancora un appunto sulla leggenda di Maometto," *ibid.,* XVII (1891), 444-46; D. C. Munro, "The Western Attitude toward Islam during the Period of the Crusades," *Speculum,* VI (1931), 329-43; A. Mancini, "Per lo studio della leggenda di Maometto in Occidente," *Rendiconti della Reale Accademia Nazionale dei Lincei,* VI:10 (1934), 325-49; S. C. Chew, *The Crescent and the Rose* (New York, 1937), 387-451; A. Eckhardt, "Le Cercueil Flottant de Mahomet," *Mélanges Ernest Hoepffner* (Paris, 1949), 77-88. M.-T. d'Alverny is preparing several studies on the subject.

for instance, placed both Mohammed and the Koran in this pantheon.[47] Those who knew that Mohammed was regarded by Moslems merely as a prophet often confused him with the heretic Nicholas condemned in the Apocalypse (2:6) or contented themselves with spurious tales about his sinful excesses. He was variously viewed as a drunkard, an epileptic, and a pupil of a heretical monk. Since Peter the Venerable was to mention some of these charges, they will be discussed in a later chapter. It is amusing to note that one bizarre variation of the widespread legend that Mohammed had been taught by a heretic eliminated the interlocutor completely and made of Islam's prophet a renegade cardinal from Rome who had set up his heretical religion in Arabia in a fit of pique after having failed to be elected pope.[48]

"The development of the conception of Mahomet [sic] is, then, from that of a heretic to that of a fraud."[49] Some legends, such as that to the effect that Mohammed had tricked a wealthy widow into marriage, turn out to be unflattering interpretations of the true facts. There were many curious legends about his death. One of them had him poisoned by his followers in order to test his powers of resurrection; another had his body thrown into a ditch and devoured by dogs and swine (occasionally mentioned to explain the fact that Moslems do not eat pork); a very popular legend narrated that his followers had placed Mohammed's body in an iron coffin, attached lodestones to the "temple" in Mecca, and left him suspended in mid-air.[50] Some of the later legends were

[47] P. Casanova, "Mahom, Jupin, Apollon, Tervagant, dieux des Arabes," *Mélanges Hartwig Derenbourg* (Paris, 1909), 391ff.; E. Dreesbach, *Der Orient in der altfranzösischen Kreuzzugsliteratur* (Breslau, 1901), 4-6. See the work of F. Viré in *Cahiers de Tunisie* and the study of Charles Pellat presented at Cordova in 1962.

[48] E. Doutté, "Mahomet Cardinal," *Mémoires de la Société d'agriculture, commerce, sciences, et arts de la Marne*, 2 ser., 1:2 (1898-99), 233-43. Later he was identified as a member of the Colonna family; d'Ancona, "Il Tesoro di Brunetto Latini versificato," *Atti della Reale Accademia dei Lincei*, 4 ser., IV (1888), 111-274.

[49] Chew, *op. cit.*, 398.

[50] B. Ziolecki, *A. du Pont's Roman de Mahomet* (Oppeln, 1887), 58-59; for material on the origins of this legend and similar ones concerning the Ptolemies, Aristotle, and St. Thomas the Apostle, see Chew, *op. cit.*, 414-16.

consciously contrived and circulated as propaganda to incite Christians to warfare against Moslems.[51]

When a more vital, consolidated Christian Europe did ponder the extension of Christendom into the Islamic world, it did so with an impatient and bellicose persuasion that by their indocility, however untried, the Moslems had forfeited all inheritance in the Christian household. The tactic, therefore, was one of pushing back the Islamic frontiers, expelling the Moslems, and "liberating" whatever Christians remained. If there were Moslems ready to abandon their faith out of immediate expediency or in the face of greater force, well and good. But Christian knights had no intention of forgoing military success by pausing to engage in theological disputation. The results of eleventh-century expeditions to drive the Moslems out of Sicily and Spain encouraged prospects for an even more ambitious and visionary endeavor—the deliverance of the Holy Places in Palestine. These prospects were carefully considered as early as the pontificate of Gregory VII.[52] It was not until the Cluniac Pope Urban II delivered his famous sermon at Clermont in 1095, however, that the Crusade was formally launched.[53]

Of course, one must allow for divers less sublime motivations and purposes which impelled the crusaders to this warfare in the Orient, and for the evident economic and political rearrangements that it assisted. The success of the First Crusade, nonetheless, which saw the capture of Jerusalem and the establishment of a quite spacious Latin enclave within the Islamic world, raised the

---

[51] Daniel, *op. cit.*, 109-33; Munro, *op. cit.*, 330.

[52] C. Erdmann, *Die Entstehung des Kreuzzugsgedankens* (Stuttgart, 1935), 149-53. See also M. Villey, *La Croisade: Essai sur la formation d'une théorie juridique* (Paris, 1942), and Paul Alphandéry (and Alphonse Dupront), *La chrétienté et l'idée de croisade*, 2 vols. (Paris, 1954-59).

[53] D. C. Munro, "The Speech of Urban II at Clermont, 1095," *American Historical Review*, XI (1905), 231-42, gives an analysis of the recorded versions of the sermon. There is no mention in any of them of converting the Moslems to Christianity. On all aspects of the First Crusade, see *History of the Crusades, I: The First Hundred Years*, ed. M. W. Baldwin (Philadelphia, 1955); A. C. Krey, *The First Crusade* (Princeton, 1921).

pitch of optimism and enthusiasm in Europe. It also gave rise to further compromises in the crusading ideal. Divine sanction of this use of the sword was now taken as established, and the powerful authority of Bernard of Clairvaux was lent to a strange new form of monasticism—the Military Order of the Temple.[54] More fundamentally even than that, however, Christianity triumphant in the land of its birth did not manifest its universality by becoming native.[55]

There was at least one man in Europe who was not entirely satisfied with the direction which the crusading movement was taking. That man was Peter the Venerable. In spite of the fact that during the course of the eleventh century the general decision had swung in the other direction, and Cluny itself may have helped weight the pendulum,[56] in Peter's mind the idea of "holy war," or at least many of its implications, remained somewhat problematical. While attempting to measure Peter's reactions to it, however, one must not forget that the Holy Places meant as much to him as they did to any Christian (or Moslem) in his age, that the aim of winning access to them was, for him, a perfectly legitimate and even sacred aim, and that his abhorrence of pagan-

[54] PL 182, 921A-40B; see Américo Castro, *The Structure of Spanish History*, tr. E. King (Princeton, 1954), 219-21, on the possible Islamic origins of the military order.

[55] Raymund of Agiles relates that a few Saracens, baptized "either out of zeal or from fear of our law," were in the crusading armies in 1099, *Historia Francorum, Recueil des historiens des Croisades, Historiens Occidentaux*, III (Paris, 1866), 278, but their conversion was certainly no motive for the expedition. By the time of the Second Crusade "the conversion of the infidels" had at least become a sorry second half of double-*aut* clauses; Odo of Deuil, *De Profectione Ludovici VII in Orientem*, ed. and tr. V. Berry (New York, 1948), 70, and Berry, "Peter the Venerable and the Crusades," PV, 146.

[56] The contention that the Crusade was a Cluniac idea is totally unwarranted in the light of Pope Gregory VII's monastic origins and of Erdmann's results, *op. cit.*, 60ff. Cluny did have a special interest in the pilgrimage to Compostella, which its monks had helped to popularize, possibly to some extent in support of the Spanish *Reconquista*; see E. Petit, "Croisades bourguignonnes contre les Sarrazins d'Espagne au xiie siècle," *Revue Historique*, XXX (1886), 259-72; P. Boissonnade, "Cluny, la papauté, et la première grande croisade internationale contre les Sarrazins d'Espagne," *Revue des questions historiques*, LX (1932), 257-301; Monneret de Villard, *op. cit.*, 8-9.

ism and heresy was if anything, as will be demonstrated, greater than that of his contemporaries.[57]

Whenever Peter wrote to crusading leaders, as, for example, to the king of Jerusalem, "defender of [Christ's] faith, enemy of His enemies," he did not hesitate to identify the "Turks, Saracens, Persians, and Arabs" as "enemies of the Cross of Christ." And yet he added that they might be considered enemies only insofar as they rejected "His salvation."[58] They would, of course, cease to be enemies when they ceased to reject. The remedy was ready; Christ, "the eternal Sun, brighter by far than the morning sun, illumined the darkness of our west from your east," Peter reminded the patriarch of Jerusalem, "and wanted the Gospel of the eternal kingdom preached to all nations (Matt. 28:19)."[59] Peter could even perceive cogent reasons for the Templars, "monks in virtues and soldiers in deeds," proceeding to "not a single but a double warfare," but he could not bring himself to tolerate warfare for its own or some doubtful sake.[60] In a letter to King Louis VII he emphasized what was, for him, the point: "God does not will[61] cold-blooded murder or outright slaughter."[62] To be sure, he wrote that of the persecution of the Jews, but it was also expressive of his attitude toward the Moslems, since, as he understandably informs or at least reminds the king in the same passage, the Moslems are in a sense better than the Jews; at least they do not deny "that Christ was born of a Virgin, and agree with us concerning many

[57] Berry, op. cit., 141-62. Against my thin argument to follow, I am well aware, there might be cited a large amount of material written to express encouragement for the Crusade, much of which is referred to in Mrs. Berry's article. But I am inclined to regard most of it as somewhat forced, and less expressive of Peter's deeper feelings on the matter than those passages in which he concerns himself directly with the moral issues or speaks to the Moslems themselves. I would sooner be at pains to explain his apparent inconsistencies along the lines developed below than to seem to accept the view that he was a conventional and uncritical supporter of the Crusade. See also P. A. Throop, Criticism of the Crusade: A Study of Public Opinion (Amsterdam, 1940).

[58] BC 785D-86A.

[59] Ibid., 786C-D.

[60] Ibid., 925A-B.

[61] Reminiscent of, and pertinent to, the rallying cry of the Crusade, "Deus vult!"

[62] "Non vult enim Deus prorsus occidi, non omnino extingui," BC 867A.

things about Him."[63] He cites the example of the fratricide Cain, on whom God "set a mark, to warn the chance-comer not to kill him (Gen. 4:15)" in the hope of his repentance, in Peter's view. Interpreted in terms of the Crusade, he was calling for the conversion rather than the extermination of the Moslems.

Peter wrote to St. Bernard in words even more direct: "But someone may say, 'The Church has no sword. Christ took it away when he said to Peter, "Put back thy sword into the scabbard; for all those who take the sword will perish by the sword (Matt. 26:52)."' This is true, true indeed. The Church does not have the sword of a king, but the staff of a shepherd, of which the Apostle [of the Gentiles, St. Paul; cf. Rom. 11:13] had this to say: 'What is your wish? Shall I come to you with a staff, or in love and in the spirit of meekness (I Cor. 4:21)?' . . . Yet it may also be said to have a sword, according to him, 'And take unto you the helmet of salvation and the sword of the Spirit, which is the Word of God (Eph. 6:17).'"[64] Peter seemed to hold out for some punitive powers for the Church, but insisted that the only manner in which the Church might wield her rightful "sword" was by preaching the Gospel.[65]

Peter's exception to aspects of the Crusade was not of a nature to take the form of overt or active opposition to it. It was manifested, predictably, in praise of peace and in persistent exhortation of the crusading leaders to the more upright purposes of their

[63] "Christum de Virgine ut nos natum fateantur, multaque de ipso nobiscum sentiant," *ibid.*, 866E.

[64] "Sed dicet quispiam: Ecclesia non habet gladium. Christus illum abstulit cum Petro dixit, 'Converte gladium in vaginam. Omnis qui acceperit gladium, gladio peribit.' Verum est, inquam, verum est. Non habet Ecclesia gladium regis, sed habet virgam pastoris, de qua Apostolus, 'Quid vultis? In virga veniam ad vos an in spiritu mansuetudinis?' Et . . . immo habet et gladium, secundum eumdem, 'Et galeam salutis assumite, et gladium spiritus, quod est verbum Dei,'" *ibid.*, 954C. On the history of the controversy over the two swords mentioned in Luke 22:38, see J. Lecler, "L'argument des deux glaives," *Recherches de science religieuse*, XXI (1931), 299-339; XXII (1932), 151-77, 280-303; H.-X. Arquillière, "Origines de la théorie des deux glaives," *Studi Gregoriani*, I (Rome, 1947), 501-21; W. Levison, "Die mittelalterliche Lehre von den beiden Schwertern," *Deutsches Archiv*, IX (1951), 14-42.

[65] For the quite different interpretation of Pope Gregory VII, see A. Stickler, "Il 'gladius' nel Registro di Gregorio VII," *Studi Gregoriani*, III (Rome, 1948), 89-103.

expedition, those to which he felt he could promise "devotion, prayer, counsel, and assistance of such a kind and quality" as a monk could give to the "militia of the Eternal King."[66] There had grown in his mind a strong conviction that the avowed purposes and goals of the Crusade had omitted entirely what should have been the most central Christian concern, namely, the conversion of the Moslems; that it had squandered an opportunity and had sacrificed something in favor of military and political considerations which by its very nature transcended them.[67] His most important activity in this connection was his project to study Islam, which will be discussed in detail in the following chapters.

It would entirely miss the point of Peter's position to feel disappointment that his exception did not take stronger or more influential forms. "His essential attitude to the Crusade had not changed over the years. In its ideal meaning as an unselfish, sacrificial journey to faraway lands to combat the enemies which were threatening the shrines of the Christian faith, the Crusade attracted his admiration and support. . . . Undoubtedly, however, some disillusionment and modification had crept in."[68] He participated in the preparations for the Second Crusade and, with a dampened enthusiasm by no means unique to himself, in the unsuccessful attempts to launch a Third Crusade.[69] It was hardly to be expected that he would oppose the wishes of the papacy in these matters. He was willing to allow for the manias of his friends. Being a man of optimism and courage as well as intelligence, he must sincerely have believed that he could remedy what was, in his opinion, wrong with the Crusade by providing it with the goal it lacked, a goal which might ultimately have justified it.

[66] BC 865E-68C.

[67] See above, notes 53 and 55.

[68] Berry, op. cit., 162.

[69] Ibid., 159-62; cf. Constable, "The Second Crusade as Seen by Contemporaries," Traditio, IX (1953), 213-79.

3 · THE PROJECT TO STUDY ISLAM

✣ SUCH WAS THE STATE of western Christendom in the times of Peter the Venerable that by his insistence, on the familiar grounds of the Gospels and patristic tradition, that the Moslems of his day were as specifically intended as any of the Gentiles to participate in Christian salvation, he was in fact a pioneer. The fact that his view was unique caused Peter some surprise and agitation. With his disposition and background it was inevitable that his interest should first take the form of study.

It will not escape the student who approaches the writings of Peter the Venerable with probity and at least such sympathy as is essential for understanding them that in his mind "his function as abbot and head of his order was itself only a part of his function as a man of the Church."[70] The then less impeded practice of the liturgy, nourished by singularities of his education and temperament, had developed in Peter a mastering sense of the catholicity and apostolicity of the Church. That sense certainly played its part in his efforts as pacifier, reformer, and monastic partisan. It influenced his relations with the Holy See. But it was most strikingly manifested in his apologetical and polemical writings.

Peter's major apologetical works are four in number. The first was written before 1132 to an unnamed monk of his order who had been teaching certain errors concerning salvation.[71] Another answered three theological questions about the Virgin Mary posed by the monk Gregory.[72] A third, written toward the year 1140 "against those who assert that Christ never openly called Himself God in the Gospels," was addressed to Peter of St. John.[73] The *Tractatus contra Petrobrusianos Haereticos,* the most ambitious work in this category, was probably written before 1134.[74]

---

[70] Leclercq, *Pierre le Vénérable,* 187.

[71] BC 707B-13D; Séjourné, *op. cit.,* 2069-70.

[72] BC 797E-814C; Séjourné, *op. cit.,* 2070-71.

[73] BC 965C-84A; Séjourné, *op. cit.,* 2071; on the identity of Peter of St. John, see below, chapter 2, section 3.

[74] BC 1117C-1230D; Séjourné, *op. cit.,* 2073-74. A short study of the theology of this treatise is contained in an appendix to Leclercq, *Pierre le Vénérable,* 357-

Against the views of the heresiarch Peter de Bruis and a follower of his named Henry, Peter defended infant baptism, "baptism by blood," veneration of the Cross, the efficacy of the Sacrifice of the Mass and prayers for the dead, and the use of chant and musical instruments in liturgical worship.

It is on the basis of Peter's two large polemical works, however, one addressed to the Jews and the other to the Moslems, that one is compelled to agree with the abbot's *notarius* that he stood "alone in his times."[75] These fruits of the over-riding responsibility he felt toward non-Christians have never been given anything more than passing consideration in the history of Christian polemics. Yet they would seem, even at first glance, to merit serious study, for they represent the first European books dealing with these faiths in which talmudic and koranic sources are cited verbatim within a carefully structured Christian argument.

The *Liber adversus Judaeorum inveteratam duritiem* is the longest of Peter's works.[76] It may have been begun before 1140, but I have cited internal evidence which establishes that it could not have been completed before 1143, perhaps much later.[77] It differs considerably from most patristic works on the Jews. The first and major portion of the book sets about to prove a few basic theses: that the Hebrew prophets had foretold that the Messiah was to be the Son of God and God himself, and that his kingdom would not be an earthly kingdom, and that these prophecies were fulfilled in Christ. But the true originality of the work lies in its lengthy appendices. The first of them discusses the credibility of Christ's miracles and those connected with his cross and sepul-

---

67. Manselli, *op. cit.*, 1-67, provides an excellent exposition of the Petrobrusian doctrine and a careful analysis of Peter's *Tractatus*.

[75] D 177rd; PL 189, 661C.

[76] BC 983B-1108B; Séjourné, *op. cit.*, 2074-76; Manitius, *Geschichte der lateinischen Literatur des Mittelalters*, III, 137-38; Leclercq, *Pierre le Vénérable*, 234-41.

[77] "Peter the Venerable and the Toledan Collection," PV, 192-95. It is also possible that a second redaction of the work, with the addition of the crucial quotations in D 157vs-d, PL 189, 591A-92A, was prepared in or after 1143.

chre.[78] The second analyzes a selection of stories culled from the Talmud by Peter with the assistance of certain converts from Judaism.[79] Peter attempts to refute the contents of these stories from the writings of the prophets; he chides the Jews for having added these books to the canon of their scriptures and for accepting unsound doctrine. It might also be noted in passing that this book contains "one of the earliest references to true paper in the West."[80]

Peter has been criticized for his attitudes toward the Jews, especially on the basis of a letter to King Louis VII, but also in connection with the book we are presently considering.[81] The charges fail to take into account several pertinent facts. First, one can expect charity of Peter, but one cannot demand that he cease speaking as a Christian. He had a marked predilection for irony and sarcasm, neither of which must be confused with hatred. The letter to King Louis was instrumental in halting the murder of Jews which was a partial, albeit unintentional result of Bernard of Clairvaux's preaching of the Second Crusade. One authority, concluding a study of the *Liber,* wrote, "If there is any illusion there, it has but one excuse, and that is [Peter's] love for the Jews."[82] Surely one who made it a point to verify his quotations and obtain the exact literal sense of the Hebrew texts he was quoting, who sought out talmudic scholars and familiarized himself with these sources, who, in sum, developed in himself a profound knowledge of the Jewish mind, was already well beyond the bounds which could (even optimistically) be set down for a

[78] BC 1038B-66B; see also P. C. Grossbölting, *De miraculo in scriptis Petri Venerabilis* (Limbourg, 1937).

[79] BC 1066B-1108B.

[80] G. Sarton, *Introduction to the History of Science,* III:1 (Baltimore, 1947), 174; see also A. Blum, "Les origines du papier," *Revue historique,* 170 (1932), 441-42. The passage is PL 189, 606: "ex rasuris ueterum pannorum."

[81] For example, H. Graetz, *Popular History of the Jews,* tr. A. B. Rhine, III (New York, 1919), 207-08; A. L. Sachar, *A History of the Jews* (New York, 1953), 191; and Bloch, *op. cit.,* 167, note 3. Cf. Guido Kisch, *The Jews in Medieval Germany* (Chicago, 1949), 470, note 14.

[82] Leclercq, *Pierre le Vénérable,* 241; cf. Séjourné, *op. cit.,* 2075. See also A. L. Williams, *Adversus Judaeos* (Cambridge, 1935), and O. S. Rankin, *Jewish Religious Polemic* (Edinburgh, 1956).

Christian prelate in the first half of the twelfth century. Further, the very nature of the book, seen as part of a full cycle of apologetical and polemical activity, which chose to consider the Jews in terms of their religious faith alone, abandoning all the customary Christian invective, represented a signal advance over most Christian polemics against the Jews in mediaeval times. The one attempt known to me to locate Peter's talmudic sources has established beyond question the interest of the book in this connection.[83] It is to be hoped that a more thorough investigation of these sources and a proper evaluation of the argumentation in the *Liber* will be undertaken by some biblical and talmudic scholar.

Such a study of the second of Peter's polemical works, the *Liber contra sectam sive haeresim Saracenorum,* is one of the principal parts of the present volume.

Peter's journey to Spain was the proximate occasion, as has already been indicated, of his inaugurating a project to study Islam. We are fortunate in possessing several accounts by Peter himself of the circumstances surrounding the inception of this project and of the purposes which inspired him to undertake it. Five texts claim our careful attention in a study of these accounts: (1) *Epistola de translatione sua,* a letter addressed to Bernard of Clairvaux which is contained in the original manuscript of the translations of the Toledan Collection, MS 1162 of the Bibliothèque de l'Arsenal in Paris;[84] (2) *Summa totius haeresis Saracenorum,* a summary of Islamic doctrine written by Peter as an introduction to the Toledan Collection, likewise contained in the Arsenal manuscript;[85] (3) Letter 17 of Book Four of Peter's letters, a long letter to Bernard which contains, toward the end, the entirety of the *Epistola de translatione sua* (with a few different readings) and the central portion of the *Summa totius haeresis*

[83] S. Lieberman, *Shkiin, A Few Words on some Jewish Legends, Customs, and Literary Sources Found in Karaite and Christian Works* (Jerusalem, 1939), 27-42; "his sources seem to have been the *Dialogue* of Peter Alphonsi, which he used almost word for word, and probably a collection of tales embodied in a French version of a booklet known as the *Alphabet of Ben Sira,*" *ibid.,* iv.

[84] A 3v-4v; for a description of the manuscript, see chapter III, part I.

[85] A 1r-3v.

Saracenorum;[86] (4) a version of the beginning of the *Summa totius haeresis Saracenorum* containing several variant readings, included in two late manuscripts, one belonging to the Chapter of Le Puy and the other MS 2261 of the Bibliothèque municipale de Troyes;[87] (5) the *Prologus* to the *Liber contra sectam sive haeresim Saracenorum,* an introduction for Christian readers to Peter's refutation of Islamic doctrine addressed to the Moslems, contained in MS 381 of the Bibliothèque de Douai.[88]

These texts pose some difficult chronological problems. Since we know that the entire *Liber contra sectam sive haeresim Saracenorum* postdates the other texts by "several years,"[89] we may, for present purposes, disregard it. There remain the problems of the relationship of the *Epistola de translatione sua* to Letter 17 of Book Four and that of both letters and the short *Summa* to the whole *Summa totius haeresis Saracenorum.*

It appears at first glance that the *Epistola de translatione sua* is a letter written "not long" after Peter's return from Spain, accompanying the gift of one translation from the Toledan Collection and requesting Bernard to write a refutation of Islamic doctrine.[90] The very wording with which Peter refers to the translation in question, which in the *Epistola de translatione sua* he "is sending" and in Letter 17 he "has sent" to Bernard, seems to suggest that the former is older than the latter.[91] Yet there is good reason to doubt whether the *Epistola de translatione sua* is really a separate letter at all. Its salutation, for example, is identical with that of Letter 17,[92] and its variants from the longer letter[93] point to its

---

[86] BC 828A-47D; the portion of the *Summa totius haeresis Saracenorum* is *ibid.*, 843E-47B. This letter is not contained in MS 381 of the Bibliothèque de Douai, which is the oldest and most authoritative manuscript of the letters.

[87] Le Puy, unnumbered, 55v; Troyes, 2261, 27v-28r. I am grateful to G. Constable for having called my attention to these manuscripts. The text stops with the words "intercessores aderunt et auxiliatores," A 1vs.

[88] D 178v-181r.   [89] PL 189, 685D.   [90] A 3vd.   [91] *Ibid.*; BC 843E.

[92] "Singulari ueneratione colendo, totis karitatis brachiis amplectendo, indiuiduo cordis mei hospiti, domno Bernardo Claraeuallis abbati, frater Petrus humilis Cluniacensis abbas, salutem ad quam suspirat aeternam," A 3vd; cf. BC 828A. Note that the Arsenal manuscript confirms the reading "cordis mei."

[93] Especially the important variants, such as the omission of the entire section on Mohammed's life which was, if my view is correct, copied into the *Summa,*

having been excerpted from it, probably to give readers of the Toledan Collection additional information about the project and possibly, in its original form, to accompany the gift of the translation.

I tend to agree with Mlle d'Alverny that Letter 17 represents an archetype from which both the *Epistola de translatione sua* and the *Summa totius haeresis Saracenorum* (the latter only in part, of course) were derived.[94] It seems to me that this can be more easily demonstrated in the case of the *Summa*. Peter evidently considered it more appropriate to commence the *Summa* with a discussion of the Islamic view of the nature of God than with a sketch of Mohammed's life such as Letter 17 provided. Therefore he both prefixed and suffixed material to that basic text to produce the *Summa,* and in the process of doing so duplicated, as will be shown later, points which were made within the basic text itself. But there is even more compelling reason for regarding the *Summa* as postdating Letter 17. At the end of the *Summa* Peter states that he had waited "a long time" for someone to refute Islamic doctrine, "and there was not one who would open his mouth . . . and speak up with zeal for holy Christianity."[95] Whether or not this is a personal reference to Bernard is not important for the problem at hand. What is important is that he adds: "I myself have determined to take up the problem at some time or other, at least if my great occupations will allow me to do so. Nevertheless, in any case, I should be grateful to have this task performed well by someone else rather than poorly by myself."[96] It is scarcely likely that Peter would have announced his intention to write a refutation of Islam (still less made a general appeal for others to consider

---

and the addition of the names of the two most important translators, Robert of Ketton and Herman of Dalmatia, which seems the type of information that would be added to rather than subtracted from such an account.

[94] D'Alverny, "Deux traductions du Coran au Moyen Age," 73, note 2.

[95] "Expectaui enim diu, et non fuit qui aperiret os et zelo sanctae Christianitatis moueret pennam et ganniret," A 3vs.

[96] "Ego ipse saltem, si magnae occupationes meae permiserint, quandoque id aggredi Domino adiuuante proposui. Semper tamen a quocumque altero melius, quam a me deterius hoc fieri, gratum haberem," *ibid.*

doing so) before he had given Bernard sufficient time to consider
his request.

The very brevity of the short *Summa* reduces its importance
in the context under consideration. Its inclusion after Letter 17
in both manuscripts confirms the connection between the two
texts. Although it stops short of the point at which material from
Letter 17 is introduced into the *Summa,* it could be an earlier
draft of the information Peter wished to prefix to the other.

These texts reveal in some detail and in his own words the
plan of Peter's project. In the *Prologus* to the *Liber contra sectam
sive haeresim Saracenorum* he diagnosed the ailment he set out to
remedy: "Because the Latin-speaking peoples, and most particularly those of recent times, losing their ancient zeal, according to
the maxim of the Jews,[97] have not known the various languages of
the former wonderful Apostles, but only their own language into
which they were born, in that condition they could not know what
such an error [as Islam] was or, consequently, put up any resistance to it. For this reason 'my heart glowed within me and a
flame was enkindled in my meditation' (Ps. 38:4). I was indignant
that the Latins did not know the cause of such perdition and, by
that ignorance, could not be moved to put up any resistance;
for there was no one who replied [to Islam] because there was
simply no one who knew [about it]."[98] Given the abysmal state
of knowledge about Islam in Europe, which Peter recognized and
of which he did not hesitate to accuse himself, and given the ob-

[97] The words "iuxta Iudeorum uocem" in the text admit of several interpretations. Perhaps Peter was giving Hebrew as one of the forgotten apostolic languages,
although the words seem to mean "according to the maxim of the Jews," referring to some biblical passage, or "as the Jews say to us," referring to the
contemporary Jewish charge mentioned in the *Liber adversus Judaeorum inveteratam duritiem,* PL 189, 527B-C, and especially 617D.

[98] "Sed quia Latini et maxime moderni, antiquo studio pereunte, iuxta Iudeorum uocem, uarias linguas apostolorum olim mirantium, non nisi linguam suam
nouerunt, in qua nati sunt, cuiusmodi tantus error esset agnoscere, ne dicam tanto
errori obuiare non poterant. Vnde 'concaluit cor meum intra me et in meditatione mea exarsit ignis.' Indignatus sum causam tantae perditionis Latinos ignorare, et ipsa ignorantia nullum ad resistendum posse animari. Nam non erat
qui responderet, quia non erat qui agnosceret," D 18ord.

vious fact that Peter himself knew no Arabic,[99] it was clear that informants and translators would have to be sought to provide trustworthy information about Islam before anything further could be done.

Just how much Peter had thought about this matter before his journey to Spain is anyone's guess. It is possible, but not probable, that it had been forward in his thinking. It would seem far more likely that his wider convictions and concerns simply disposed him to act quickly and decisively as soon as he realized how favorable the possibilities were for such activity in Spain. At any rate, Peter learned of the existence of a Christian Arabic book "disputing" Islamic doctrine, and set a certain "Master Peter of Toledo" to work translating it into Latin for him; "but because the Latin language was not as familiar or known to him as the Arabic," he told Bernard of Clairvaux later: "I gave him as an assistant the learned man, our beloved son and brother, the notary Peter. . . . This man polished and set in order the Latin words, which had for the most part been set forth by him [Peter of Toledo] in an unpolished and confused fashion, and thus he produced an epistle, indeed a little book, of much use to many, I believe, on account of the knowledge it communicates of things unknown."[100] Even if one allows for the fact that this translation was omitted from many later manuscripts, it is still difficult to understand why so many scholars believed that Peter was speaking of the Koran in this passage. The translation of which he was speaking was that of the *Risālat ʿAbdillāh ibn-Ismāʿīl al-Hāshimī*

[99] Only the *Chronicon Cluniacensis*, BC 591C, written several centuries later, reads as though Peter did the translating himself: "Idem ipse Petrus noster Cluniacensis abbas ipso existente in Hispaniis cum imperatore, transtulit de Arabico in Latinam Alchoranum de lege Mahometici haeretici."

[100] "Mitto uobis carissime nouam translationem nostram, contra pessimam nequam Mahumet heresim disputantem, quae dum nuper in Hispaniis morarer, meo studio de Arabica uersa est in Latinam. Feci autem eam transferri a perito utriusque linguae uiro, magistro Petro Toletano. Sed quia lingua Latina non adeo ei familiaris uel nota erat ut Arabica, dedi ei coadiutorem doctum uirum, dilectum filium et fratrem Petrum, notarium nostrum, reuerentiae uestrae ut aestimo bene cognitum. Qui uerba Latina impolite uel confuse plerumque ab eo prolata poliens et ordinans, epistolam immo libellum multis ut credo propter ignotarum rerum noticiam perutilem futurum, perfecit," A 3vd.

ila 'Abd-al-Masīḥ ibn-Isḥāq al-Kindi wa-Risālat al-Kindi ila al-Hāshimi, perhaps the most celebrated of early Christian Arab apologetical works.

"Apart from that," Peter continued to Bernard, "I had translated from the Arabic into the Latin language also all the unholy sectarian doctrine,[101] the life of the nefarious man [Mohammed], and the law, which he called the Koran, that is, 'a collection of precepts,'[102] and which he led the most miserable folk to believe was brought down to him from heaven by the angel Gabriel. [In the case of the latter translations] the translators were men skilled in both languages, Robert of Ketton from England, who is now archdeacon of the church of Pamplona, and Herman of Dalmatia, a scholar[103] of the most incisive and literary genius. I found them in Spain around the Ebro River studying the art of astrology, and brought them to do this by means of a large remuneration."[104]

In the *Prologus* to the *Liber contra sectam sive haeresim Saracenorum* a substantially similar account is given, although there is no mention of the first translation (doubtless because Peter's own

[101] Thus I have translated the word "secta" whenever it is applied to the body of Islamic doctrine.

[102] It is clear from Letter 4:17 ("si e verbo verbi expressa translatio fiat," BC 844C) that Peter was not giving a description of the book's contents, but rather following an inexact translation of the Arabic words *Al-Qur'ān* given more than once in marginal notations to the Arsenal manuscript. The words mean "the recitation" or "the discourse"; E. W. Lane, *An Arabic-English Lexicon*, 1:6 (London, 1874), 2504; A. J. Wensinck and J. H. Kramers, *Handwörterbuch des Islam* (Leiden, 1941), 347.

[103] I translate "scholasticus" as "scholar," following d'Alverny, "Deux traductions du Coran au Moyen Age," 74, note 1, on the authority of A. Brunet, G. Paré, and P. Tremblay, *La Renaissance du xiie siècle. Les Écôles et l'Enseignement* (Paris, 1933), 69-72. M. Alonso, "Hermann de Carinthia, *De Essentiis*," *Miscelánea Comillas*, v (1946), 13, felt that the technical term "scholastic" could already be applied.

[104] "Sed et totam impiam sectam, uitamque nefarii hominis ac legem quam Alchoran id est collectaneum preceptorum appelauit, sibique ab angelo Gabrihele de caelo allatam, miserrimis hominibus persuasit, nichilominus ex Arabico ad Latinitatem perduxi, interpretantibus scilicet uiris utriusque linguae peritis, Rotberto Ketenensi de Anglia, qui nunc Pampilonensis ecclesiae archidiaconus est, Hermanno quoque Dalmata, acutissimi et litterati ingenii scolastico, quos in Hispania circa Hiberum astrologicae arti studentes inueni, eosque ad hoc faciendum multo precio conduxi," A 3vd-4rs.

work was meant to supersede it), the word "origin [of Moham-
med]" is added to the description of the texts, and another member
of the translating group is mentioned: "In order that the translation[s] should not lack the fullest fidelity, nor anything be
taken away by deceit from our attention, I also added a Saracen
to the Christian translators. . . . The name of the Saracen was
Mohammed."[105] Although it might appear that this passage in-
corporates an insult to his Christian translators, I believe it is more
properly to be explained as a strong statement of Peter's desire for
absolute accuracy, a most creditable concern. Peter repeats with
some feeling that "monetary remuneration" had been required to
engage the translators in their tasks. "These men, examining that
most secret library of the barbaric people, put together not a small
book for Latin readers from the aforementioned material."[106]

The four translations described by Peter in these passages are as
follows: (1) "the sectarian doctrine," *Masā'il Abī-al-Ḥārith 'Abdillāh ibn-Salām*; (2) "the origin," *Kitāb Nasab Rasūl Allāh*, by
Sa'īd ibn-'Umar; (3) "the life," a compendium of Islamic traditions (Arabic *aḥādīth*); (4) "the law," the Koran. The first two
were translated by Herman of Dalmatia, the others by Robert of
Ketton.[107]

The following chapters will furnish more detailed information about the translators and their translations. Unfortunately,
the sources do not provide specific information as to how the
project was carried out. There has been, as a result, a wide difference of opinion on the subject among the authorities who have
considered it.[108] Most recently it has been suggested that Peter

[105] "Et ut translationi fides plenissima non deesset, nec quicquam fraude aliqua
nostrorum notitiae subtrahi posset, Christianis interpretibus etiam Sarracenum
adiunxi. . . . Sarraceni Mahumeth nomen erat," D 18ord.

[106] "Qui intima ipsa barbarae gentis armaria perscrutantes, uolumen non
paruum ex praedicta materia Latinis lectoribus ediderunt," *ibid.*

[107] Peter's mention of both Robert and Herman as the translators of the four
last-named works led many authorities to believe that the two had collaborated
on all of them, but the titles in the Arsenal manuscript, and Robert's prefaces
to his own translations, strongly support these individual attributions; cf. d'Alverny, "Deux traductions du Coran au Moyen Age," 85.

[108] See, for instance, *ibid.*, 77-89, 102-04; Monneret de Villard, *op.cit.*, 11-14;

encountered his translators, who were travelling between Toledo and Pamplona, at Santa María de Nájera soon after he arrived in Spain, that it was Peter of Toledo who whetted or actually inspired Peter the Venerable's interest in the project, and that the group thereafter travelled in the abbot's entourage.[109] Those suggestions have merit, but relate the various pieces of evidence so closely as to seem, in detail, improbable.

Nájera, located in the Castilian Rioja below the Ebro, qualifies for the site identified by Peter only as *circa Iberum* ("around the Ebro River"). Peter does not make it clear, however, that he met all of his translators there or at the same time. Herman and Robert had been close associates for many years and may be presumed to have been together when Peter met them. That Peter of Toledo was with them is far from certain. On the other hand, Peter of Toledo must have been instrumental in planning the collection (rightly dubbed, for that reason, Toledan), for Herman and Robert, influenced by the school of Chartres, had devoted themselves exclusively to the study of Arabic mathematics and astronomy. If he was also able to provide all of the necessary Arabic manuscripts, that would almost suggest that he had proposed to the abbot a ready-planned project, a notion at variance with Peter the Venerable's own accounts. The Moslem Mohammed must have been hired to join the group or some part of it, as Peter's verb *adiunxi* clearly implies, sometime after the project was already planned.

It may be assumed that there were three or more distinct phases in the production of the Toledan Collection. There are some reasons for believing that the translation and "polishing" of the Christian Arab apology of Al-Kindi may have been regarded as a separate project, and that the collection may actually have been planned around it.[110] The conjoint work of Herman and Robert,

---

J. Muñoz Sendino, "La Apologia del Cristianismo de al-Kindi," *Miscelánea Comillas*, XI-XII (1949), 339-460; Bishko, *op. cit.*, 166-68.

[109] *Ibid.*

[110] Peter mentioned it first in his accounts, and clearly regarded it as the most valuable translation in the collection; the sentiment is repeated in the rubric "Si uis" preceding the collection in the Arsenal manuscript (see chapter 3, note 10).

assisted by the Moslem Mohammed, might then have been a second phase, the result, perhaps, of more careful consideration of the needs to be met by such source material. But the period of the completing of Robert's translations, certainly that of the Koran, which is the only translation in the collection capable of being dated precisely, would seem to mark yet another phase, since at that time Herman and Robert were no longer working together and Peter the Venerable was back at Cluny.[111]

Certain signs suggest that some, if not all, of the translators accompanied Peter the Venerable during his travels in Spain. There is mention of *sapientes* ("wise men") in his company.[112] Peter of Poitiers, the abbot's notary, certainly worked along with Peter of Toledo on the translation of Al-Kindi, and mentions conversation with Robert of Ketton.[113] Herman completed one of his translations at Leon, through which city Peter must twice have passed, on his way to and from Astorga, the junction point for Salamanca. The possibility of such works going on in the course of the journey is incidentally attested by the fact that Peter himself was collecting material which he subsequently incorporated into his *Liber de miraculis*.[114]

Naturally the translations were not completed simultaneously. It would appear that those assigned to Herman were completed first, followed by that of Peter of Toledo and Peter of Poitiers.[115] Robert's translations were added to the collection later; his trans-

---

[111] Kritzeck, "Peter the Venerable and the Toledan Collection," 182-83.

[112] PL 189, 904; cf. Robert of Ketton's description, BC 1116C.

[113] D 177rd.

[114] BC 1290B-96C.

[115] Herman's translation of the *Kitāb Nasab Rasūl Allāh* was completed "apud Legionensem Hyspanie ciuitatem," A 11rs, quite likely in the abbot's company. Muñoz Sendino, "La Apologia del Cristianismo de al-Kindi," 372, contends that the translation of the apology of Al-Kindi was completed last because Peter spoke of it as "nouam translationem nostram" (A 3vd), but overlooked the rubric which precedes the translation in many manuscripts (now missing, unfortunately, from the Arsenal manuscript): "Hunc librum fecit dominus Petrus Cluniacensis abbas transferri de Arabico in Latinum a Petro magistro Toletano, iuuante Petro monacho scriptore, cum esset idem dominus ac uenerabilis abbas in Hispaniis constitutus cum glorioso imperatore Adefonso, eo anno quo idem gloriosus imperator Choriam ciuitatem cepit et Sarracenos inde fugauit." As has been noted, Alfonso captured Coria in June of 1142.

lation of the Koran was not finished until June or July of 1143.[116] That explains why they are the only ones preceded by letters of introduction and why something of Robert's subsequent career, namely, his appointment to the archdeaconate of Pamplona, was known to Peter the Venerable.[117] Ultimately the translations were brought together in a single volume, quite likely under the general editorship of Peter of Poitiers, which survives to us (less a few folios) as MS 1162 of the Bibliothèque de l'Arsenal in Paris.

[116] The *explicit* in A, 138rd, reads, "Illustri glorios[is]simoque uiro, Petro Cluniacensis abbate precipiente, suus angligena Rodbertus Ketenesis [*sic*] librum istum transtulit, anno Alexandri millesimo quàdragentesimo tercio, anno Al-higere quingentesimo tricesimo septimo, anno Persarum quingentesimo undecimo." The Alexandrian year should read 1453, not 1403, which I judge to represent an omission in copying rather than an error in calculation. This permits us to establish the date of its completion between June 16 and July 16, 1143, the be-ginnings of the Persian year 511 and the year of the Hijrah 538 respectively.

[117] Most likely through Peter of Poitiers, D 177rs.

PETER THE VENERABLE was explicit in stating the authority and precedents for his project. "My intention in this work," he told Bernard of Clairvaux, "was to follow that custom of the Fathers [of the Church] by which they never silently passed by any heresy of their times, not even the slightest (if I may speak in these terms), without resisting it with all the strength of faith and demonstrating, both through writings and discussions, that it is detestable."[118]

He developed the point at great length in the *Prologus* to the *Liber contra sectam sive haeresim Saracenorum*: "The reason for my writing these things was precisely the reason which the many great Fathers had. They could not suffer any or the slightest rejection of the Christian faith, nor did they tolerate the insane raving of all manner of heretics against sound doctrine."[119] Peter then enumerates, by way of illustrating his point, many early heretics and their opponents among the Church Fathers. He summarizes the tenets of the major heresies, which he identifies as Manichaeanism, Arianism, Macedonianism, Sabellianism, Donatism, Pelagianism, Nestorianism, and Eutychianism.[120] These summaries are not only accurate, which is, of course, the least one might expect, but also remarkably clear and sensibly organized. One could doubt whether modern encyclopedias achieve the purpose any more effectively.

Peter lists, virtually without comment, the patristic apologists and polemicists against them. He cites, against the Manichaeans, the works of Archelaus of Mesopotamia, Serapion, and St. Augus-

[118] "Fuit autem in hoc opere intentio mea, ut morem illum patrum sequerer, quo nullam umquam suorum temporum uel leuissimam ut sic dicam heresim silendo preterierunt, quin ei totis fidei uiribus resisterent, et scriptis atque disputationibus esse detestandam ac dampnabilem demonstrarent," A 4rs.

[119] "Causa plane scribendi haec michi fuit, quae multis et magnis patribus extitit. Non potuerunt illi pati quamlibet uel paruam iacturam fidei Christianae, nec aduersus sanam doctrinam insanientem multiformium hereticorum uesaniam tolerarunt," D 178rd.

[120] *Ibid*. The summaries continue through 178vs.

tine, "younger than those in time, but far greater in perception and eloquence";[121] against the Arians, the works of Eustathius of Antioch, Marcellus of Ancyra, St. Athanasius of Alexandria, St. Hilary of Poitiers, Marius Victorinus, Didymus of Alexandria, and Maximus;[122] against the Macedonians, besides the works against the Arians, those of Didymus, St. Basil, St. Gregory Nazianzen, and St. Ephraem;[123] "although I have not discovered special works against the Sabellians, all those who fight the Arians and deny the Macedonians disagree with the Sabellians as well";[124] against the Donatists, the works of Optatus of Milevis and St. Augustine;[125] against the Pelagians, the works of "the same greatest and highest doctor of the Latin [Church], Augustine";[126] against the Nestorians, the decrees of the Council of Ephesus;[127] against the Eutychians, the works of Pope St. Leo I and the decrees of the Council of Chalcedon.[128]

Peter then draws the conclusion aimed at throughout the maze of foregoing examples: "The Church of God always did and does this, and, by the zealous hands of her husbandmen, roots out the brambles and thorns which are detrimental to the Lord's sowing. At no time has the unwearied strength of the saints ceded to hateful missiles; but, overcoming powers with virtue and cunning with wisdom, it has both protected its own, by the shield of faith, from the fury of their enemies, and by vehement force has turned back the thundering missiles to the enemies' destruction...

---

[121] "Hiis tempore iunior, sed longe sensibus et eloquio maior," *ibid.*, 178vd.

[122] *Ibid.*; see P. Hughes, *A History of the Church*, 1 (New York, 1949), 187-213.

[123] D 178vd-79rs.

[124] "Contra Sabellium licet specialia opera non inuenerim, quicunque tamen resistunt Arrianis, quicunque repugnant Macedonianis, uniuersi pariter contradicunt et Sabellianis," *ibid.*, 179rs. This heresy was also called Modalism, Monarchianism, and Patripassianism. Peter might have mentioned the works of St. Hippolytus, Tertullian, and Dionysius of Alexandria. See Hughes, *op. cit.*, 1, 100ff.

[125] D 179rs. For all of these heresies many more patristic references and vast bibliographies are supplied by the standard reference works.

[126] *Ibid.*

[127] *Ibid.*

[128] *Ibid.*; Eutychianism was actually a radical form of Monophysitism, a denial of the two natures in Christ.

[The defense of] heavenly decrees [and] the way of right faith . . . was the whole and only reason those saints had for writing and for attacking the enemies of Christian salvation."[129]

Peter realized that, once this much was established, his case was as good as won. He goes on to tell his readers that what motivated and inspired the efforts of the Fathers devolves upon the Christians of his own time, and on himself: "It is the same for me. Nor must I, though by far inferior and unequal to them, be less zealous for the Church of God, the Spouse of Christ, than they."[130] Finally, lest there remain any doubts in their minds that the Church intends all, and not merely certain, heresies to be brought to light and resisted, he cites the authority of several of the Fathers who attempted summary refutations of all the heresies of their times.[131]

Peter's views on the nature of Islam will be discussed in detail in a later chapter. But, to anticipate slightly, he reaches no certain conclusion as to whether the Moslems are more properly to be regarded as heretics or pagans. "If you call them heretics, it has been proven that they are to be opposed beyond all [other] . . . heresies; if you call them pagans, I shall demonstrate, by the authority of the Fathers, that they are to be resisted nonetheless."[132] His list of Fathers who wrote against pagans and Jews includes St. Justin, Apollinarius the Senator, Arnobius, Methodius of Tyre,

---

[129] "Fecit hoc semper et facit aecclesia Dei et uepres spinasue satis dominicis inimicas, studiosa ruricolarum suorum manu exstirpat. Non cessit quolibet tempore hostilibus iaculis indefessum robur sanctorum, sed uires uirtute, astutiam sapientia superans, et scuto fidei suos ab hostium furore protexit, et in eorum perniciem fulminantia spicula uehementi nisu intorsit. Non potuit pati uenenosi sibilos serpentis, caelestibus oraculis praeualere, nec rectae fidei uiam ad beatam aeternitatem ducentem, prauis errorum semitis ad inferos retorqueri. Haec inquam haec plane tota ac sola sanctis illis causa fuit scribendi, pro qua in hostes Christianae salutis non solum uerbis librisque inuecti sunt, sed nec suis nec sibi, nec ipsi tandem uitae propriae pepercerunt," *ibid.*, 179rd.

[130] "Haec eadem est et michi. Nec debeo licet longe illis inferior et impar minus zelari pro aecclesia Dei, sponsa Christi, quam ipsi," *ibid.*

[131] D 179rd-vs.

[132] "Si hereticos dixeris, probatum est supra, omnibus hereticis uel heresibus obuiandum. Si paganos uocaueris, probo idque patrum auctoritate ostendo, non minus et illis resistendum," D 180rs.

Apollinarius of Laodicea, St. Athanasius, St. Eusebius, St. Irenaeus, Miltiades, Apollonius, and, once again, St. Augustine.[133]

Since this section of the *Prologus* was provided more in illustration of patristic zeal against heresy, Judaism, and paganism than in the nature of a readily usable bibliography, Peter can be forgiven for having included works of whose existence he could only have been made aware from reading standard compilations such as Eusebius' *Ecclesiastical History* and, for later authors, Rufinus' supplement to it, St. Jerome's *About Illustrious Men*, and St. Isidore's *Etymologies*.[134] It cannot be ascertained how many of the extant items in the lists Peter had actually studied, but quotations throughout his works demonstrate that he was intimately acquainted with a wide range of patristic writings.[135]

Certainly Peter had ample opportunity to familiarize himself with these works. Besides the private reading prescribed by St. Benedict's Rule,[136] there was at Cluny in his time a good deal of reading aloud in the abbey church, the refectory, and the chapter house. The library of Cluny, moreover, was one of the better ones of the age. It was particularly strong in patristics, although its collections of monastic literature, canon and civil law, historical works, and Roman literature were also notable.[137] At the beginning of the eighteenth century Mabillon was shown a catalogue of the library of Cluny, made about 1200, comprising some eighteen hundred entries.[138] With two thirds that number it would still

[133] D 18ors-rd. Peter apparently confused Eusebius of Emesa with Eusebius of Caesarea, whose works against pagans and Jews are extant (PG 21, 21-1408, 22, 13-792).

[134] Half of the fifty-two works cited by Peter in this section are mentioned in these sources and the same number, coincidentally, are extant.

[135] M. Manitius, "Zu Petrus' von Cluni patristischen Kenntnissen," *Speculum*, III (1928), 582-87.

[136] *Ed. cit.*, cap. 48, 69-71.

[137] L. Niepce, "Bibliothèque de l'ancienne abbaye de Cluny," *Revue Lyonnaise*, I (1881), 215-33; L. Delisle, *Inventaire des manuscrits de la Bibliothèque Nationale, Fonds de Cluni*, II (Paris, 1884), 458-81; A. Bénet and J. Bazin, *Archives de Cluny* (Macon, 1884); A. Wilmart, "Le convent et la bibliothèque de Cluny vers le milieu du onzième siècle," *Revue Mabillon*, XI (1921), 89-124.

[138] J. Evans, *op. cit.*, 99, note 3.

have been the richest library in France in the latter half of the twelfth century.[139]

There are, of course, omissions in Peter's admittedly selective list of heresies and patristic writings, but few that one would be inclined to class as important as those he identifies.[140] This particular section of the *Prologus* to the *Liber contra sectam sive haeresim Saracenorum* represents an outstanding scholarly tour de force and goes far toward proving Manitius' contention that Peter's knowledge of patristics was in all probability greater than that of all the other abbots of Cluny.[141] It must be granted that the simple but, for him and his Christian readers, crucial points he set out to establish there were, in fact, well established.

[139] Leclercq, *Pierre le Vénérable,* 264.

[140] He might, for example, have mentioned the heresies of Adoptionism, Novatianism, Photianism, Millenarianism, and Origenism; and, against Manichaeanism, the works of Alexander of Lycopolis, Titus of Bostra, Didymus of Alexandria, and Prudentius; against Arianism, those of Alexander of Alexandria, Hosius of Cordova, Eusebius of Vercelli, Zeno, and St. Gregory of Nyssa; against Pelagianism, those of Paulus Orosius, St. Jerome, and St. Leo; against Nestorianism, those of St. Cyril of Alexandria; against Jews and pagans, those of St. Hippolytus, Tertullian, Aristo of Pella, St. John Chrysostom, Prudentius, and Orosius.

[141] Manitius, "Zu Petrus' von Cluni patristischen Kenntnissen," 582.

41

Just as Peter the Venerable's "indignation" that European Christians "did not know" Islam and "by that ignorance could not be moved to put up any resistance" was twofold, so was the purpose of his project. To remedy that ignorance he intended to supply his coreligionists with trustworthy information about Islam. Hence he made available the whole of the Toledan Collection for copying; and, shortly afterwards, finding its contents "prolix, and for the most part difficult to understand because of the barbarism of the language,"[142] provided a brief handbook of Islamic doctrine, with what accuracy I shall indicate later, in the *Summa totius haeresis Saracenorum.*

But, haunted as he admittedly was by the shades of patristic zeal in combating doctrinal error, a second purpose—that of refuting those elements in Islam which a Christian would consider false—was present in his mind from the very outset. Thus he could write, toward the end of the *Summa:* "I have briefly noted down these facts beforehand so that whoever will read [the Toledan Collection] may understand [it]. And if there is such a one who wishes to and can write against the whole of this heresy, he may recognize with what kind of enemy he will have to struggle. For perhaps there will yet be one whose spirit the Lord will arouse to free the Church of God from the great shame it suffers from this source. Although it has refuted all the heresies up to our time, whether ancient or modern, through replying to them, it not only has not replied to this heresy alone, which above all others has brought widespread destruction upon the bodies as well as the souls of the human race, but it has not applied itself greatly or even slightly to looking into the nature of this pestilence or its origin.[143] . . . I made it come thus bare to our attention so that it might be known how foul and worthless this heresy was, and in order that

---

[142] "Sed quia res diffusa est, et propter linguae barbariem ex magna sui parte ad intelligendum difficilis," BC 844C.

[143] Literally, "what this pestilence was and from whence it came."

some servant of God should be incited with the inspiration of the Holy Spirit to refute it in writing."[144]

There can be no doubt that as the project was first and long conceived by Peter his own role was meant to cease with the accomplishment of the first purpose—that of providing the information; refutation would be left to another. The man Peter would like to have left it to was, equally without doubt, Bernard of Clairvaux. "I have made known all these things to you especially," Peter told him in the *Epistola de translatione sua,* "[for two reasons:] that I may communicate our zealous studies to such a friend, and that I may animate that magnificent learning of yours, which God has so singularly granted to you in our days, to write against so pernicious an error. . . . This task is yours, and that of all learned men: to combat, destroy, and crush by every study, through word and writing, 'all knowledge that exalts itself against the height of God.'[145] . . . Therefore if there is, by the inspiration of God, any willingness on the part of Your Reverence to work on these things (for the ability will not fail to be there through His Grace), reply, and we will send the book which we have not yet sent,[146] that through your mouth, filled with praise of Him, the benign Spirit (I Wis. 1:6) may reply to the spirit of

---

[144] "Ista breuiter prenotaui, ut qui legerit intelligat, et si talis est, qui contra totam heresim istam scribere et uelit et possit, cum quali hoste pugnaturus sit agnoscat. Erit fortasse adhuc, cuius spiritum Dominus suscitabit, ut ecclesiam Dei a magna quam inde patitur ignominia liberet, quia scilicet cum omnes siue antiquas siue modernas hereses usque ad nostra tempora, respondendo confutauerit, huic soli quae super omnes alias tam in corporibus quam in animabus infinitam humani generis stragem dedit, non solum nichil respondit, sed nec quid tanta pestis esset, aut unde processerit, inquirere saltem uel tenuiter studuit. . . . Denudatam ad nostrorum noticiam uenire feci, ut quam spurca et friuola heresis esset sciretur, et aliquis Dei seruus, ad eam scripto refellendam, Sancto inflammante Spiritu incitaretur," A 3vs.

[145] II Cor. 10:5 reads, "Omnem altitudinem extollentem se adversus scientiam Dei." Peter of Poitiers made the same erroneous inversion of "altitudo" and "scientia" in his letter accompanying his *Capitula,* D 177rd, a fair indication that it is not a scribal error but faulty memory on one or the other's part. Peter the Venerable had corrected it, for his part, later in the *Liber contra sectam sive haeresim Saracenorum,* D 178rd.

[146] That is, all of the Toledan Collection except the translation of the apology of Al-Kindi.

iniquity, and fill up the treasuries of His Church with the wealth of your wisdom."[147]

Of course, the primary use for such a refutation would consist in winning converts to Christianity. But Peter showed himself subject to no illusions about the reception Moslems might give it when he added, in the same letter: "Although I think this might not be of much use to the lost ones, nevertheless it would be proper to have a really suitable reply as a Christian armory[148] against this pestilence. . . . If anyone should consider this [latter purpose] to be superfluous, since there is no one fortified with such weapons with which he ought to put up resistance, he should know that in the commonwealth of a great king, [for example,] some things are done for safeguard, some for propriety, [and] some for both. Arms were made by the peace-loving Solomon for safeguard, although in his time they were less necessary (II Para. 8:2-6). Large expenses were made by David, and decorations were prepared and allotted by him for the building of the Holy Temple (I Para. 18:7-11); although they were not of any use in his time, they passed into divine use after his time. They remained, therefore, for some time idle; but when necessity came, these things which were sterile for a long time became manifestly fruitful."[149] It may be taken for granted, I believe, that Peter's use

---

[147] "Specialiter autem uobis haec omnia notificaui, ut et tanto amico studia nostra communicarem, et ad scribendum contra tam perniciosum errorem, illam uestram quam nostris diebus Deus uobis singulariter contulit doctrinae magnificentiam animarem. . . . Vestrum est et omnium doctorum uirorum, 'omnem scientiam extollentem se aduersus altitudinem Dei,' omni studio uerbo et scripto impugnare, destruere, conculcare. . . . Si igitur reuerentiae uestrae in his laborandi Deo aspirante uoluntas fuerit, nam facultas per eius gratiam desse non poterit, rescribite, et mittemus librum quem nondum misimus, ut per os uestrum ipsius laude repletum, spiritui nequitiae 'Spiritus benignus' respondeat, et ecclesiae suae thesauros gazis uestrae sapientiae suppleat," A 4rd-vd.

[148] I have frequently translated "armarium" as "library," which it often means in this period and may, indeed, mean here; but the literal meaning seems appropriate to the general military terminology.

[149] "Nam licet hoc perditis illis ut aestimo prodesse non possit, responsionem tamen condignam sicut contra alias hereses, ita et contra hanc pestem, Christianum armarium habere deceret. Quam si superfluam quilibet causatus fuerit, quoniam quibus resistere debeant talibus armis muniti non adsunt, nouerit in republica magni regis quaedam fieri ad tutelam, quaedam fieri ad decorem, quaedam etiam ad utrumque. Nam ad tutelam facta sunt a Salomone pacifico

of military terminology in this passage and many others signifies no more than an attempt to speak the language best calculated to make sense and produce the desired result. Peter's warfare was single-mindedly against false doctrine, not against men.

He was at pains to encourage Bernard to consider the possible future utility of a refutation of Islamic doctrine. "And yet," he continues, "it seems to me that I might not call this work idle even in this present time. . . . If thereby those in error cannot be converted, at least a learned man, or a teacher,[150] if he has zeal for justice, should look after and provide for the weak ones in the Church, who are inclined to be tempted to evil or to be obscurely shaken by slight causes, and not to neglect them."[151] He cites the example of his favorite St. Augustine in this connection.

Peter could scarcely have summoned up more respect and praise for Bernard, or more cogent and compelling reasons for undertaking the work he describes, than this letter contains. Yet it appears that Bernard replied, if at all, negatively.[152] By the time

---

arma, licet tempore suo minus necessaria. Preparati sunt a Dauid sumptus, parata et ornamenta, templi diuini constructioni et ornatui deputata. Sed nec illa eius tempore alicui usui profecerunt, sed in usus diuinos post eius tempora transierunt. Manserunt itaque ista aliquanto tempore ociosa, sed incumbente necessitate apparuerunt quae diu uacauerant fructuosa," A 4rd-vs.

[150] The Arsenal manuscript gives "doctor" rather than the "doctior" of later editions.

[151] "Nec tamen ut michi uidetur opus istud etiam hoc tempore ociosum uocare debeo. . . . Quod si hinc errantes conuerti non possunt, saltem infirmis ecclesiae qui scandalizari uel occulte moueri leuibus etiam ex causis solent, consulere et prouidere, doctus uel doctor si zelum habet iusticiae, non debet negligere," A 4vs.

[152] A more generous view would be that his reply has not been preserved, though it must still have been a refusal; cf. Leclercq, *Pierre le Vénérable*, 243-44, who is unquestionably more understanding of Bernard than I. It would seem that a high point in the estrangement between Bernard and Peter was reached about this time, because of the rivalry between their orders, disputed elections, and the controversy over tithes; see G. Constable, "Cluniac Tithes and the Controversy between Gigny and Le Miroir," *Revue Bénédictine*, LXX (1960), 591-624; Bredero, *op. cit.* Bernard claimed that Peter did not answer two of his letters (PL 182, 397A) and asked, "Are you therefore surprised that I did not presume to trouble you with my trifles when you got back from Spain?" That cannot refer to Peter's request, for Letter 4:17 is Peter's reply. In later letters

Peter was concluding the *Summa,* probably during or just after the time Bernard was engaged in preaching the Second Crusade, it must have been abundantly evident to him that Bernard did not intend to interest himself in the project, for he wrote: "But since —for shame!—there is no one to do this task on account of the fact that everywhere in the Church the zeal for such kind of sacred studies has grown lukewarm (for I have waited a long time, and there was not one who would open his mouth and move his pen and speak up for holy Christianity), I myself have determined to take up the problem at some time or other, at least if my important occupations will allow me to do so. Nevertheless, in any case, I should be grateful to have this task performed well by someone else rather than poorly by myself."[153]

Eventually Peter did write the refutation himself. One's doubts as to the type of refutation Bernard might have produced need not blind one to the tragedy inherent in his refusal to write it. Pope Eugene's commission to Bernard to preach the Second Crusade was more than fraternal friendliness (Eugene was a Cistercian); it was a frank recognition of Bernard's extraordinary powers to entrance and direct.[154]

The fact that Peter himself gave even more of his time, thought, and energy to carrying out his project to its desired and logical

---

Bernard refers to his "many great occupations" (PL 182, 591C) and "many daily duties" (PL 182, 595B) as responsible for his silences, although they do not appear to have prevented him from directing his epistolary talents in a variety of other directions. Cf. J. B. Auniord, "L'ami de Saint Bernard. Quelques textes," *Collectanea Ordinis Cisterciensium Reformatorum,* XVIII (1956), 88-99.

[153] "Quod quia proh pudor, iam paene toto huiusmodi studiorum sanctorum ubique in ecclesia tepefacto feruore, non est qui faciat, expectaui enim diu, et non fuit qui aperiret os et zelo sanctae Christianitatis moueret pennam et ganniret, ego ipse saltem, si magnae occupationes meae permiserint, quandoque id aggredi Domino adiuuante proposui. Semper tamen a quocumque altero melius, quam a me deterius hoc fieri, gratum haberem," A 3vs.

[154] The pope himself had been a novice under Bernard, who once told him, "People are saying that you are not the pope, but I am" ("Aiunt non vos esse papam sed me," PL 182, 431A). Bernard very correctly did not regard that as a jest. His singular powers could no more be documented concisely than they could be denied. The first half of the twelfth century was "his time." Even one of Peter the Venerable's epitaphs begins, "Tempore Bernardi Clareualis floruit olim," BC 602B.

conclusion is eloquent evidence of the importance it had for him, and of the depth of his engagement to it. Quite apart from his unusual knowledge of Islamic doctrine at this stage, he was in an especially favorable position to "take up the problem" himself. He was one of the few ecclesiastics of his age whose office was so exalted as to render him virtually immune from any charges of dabbling in scandalous and dangerous matters. The heirs to his ideas were not to be so fortunate.

The greatest share of credit for this project to study Islam, therefore, from start to finish, is rightfully Peter's own. It is, above all, the testimony of one man's intelligence and zeal and fervent conviction that the Moslems were not to be approached, "as our people often do, by arms, but by words; not by force, but by reason; not in hatred, but in love."[155] Whatever weaknesses there are in the *Summa* and in the *Liber contra sectam sive haeresim Saracenorum* are, as will be demonstrated in due course, limitations imposed by the sources of his information, not deficiencies in his understanding or intention. But before examining in detail the manner in which the purposes of his project were accomplished, it will be necessary to identify both the translators and their translations more closely.

[155] "Non ut nostri sepe faciunt armis sed uerbis, non ui sed ratione, non odio sed amore," D 181rs. Peter died on Christmas Day in 1156.

II · THE TRANSLATORS

Contuli ergo me ad
peritos linguæ Arabicæ.
PETER THE VENERABLE

Ego peditis tantum
officio prævii functus,
vias et aditus
diligentissime patefeci.
ROBERT OF KETTON

1 · THE SCHOOL OF TOLEDO

꧁ One of the most interesting phenomena attending the revival of learning in the twelfth century, which is sometimes spoken of as a "renaissance,"[1] was the immense concern with the fund of knowledge which had accumulated during the centuries when "Arabic-speaking peoples were the main bearers of the torch of culture and civilization throughout the world,"[2] and which had been, save to exceptional individuals like Gerbert (afterward Pope Sylvester II),[3] closed to Europe's ken. It was especially to the works of mathematics, the physical sciences, and philosophy, in which ancient thought had been synthesized and markedly advanced, that the European scholars turned to make up their own deficiencies. Many of them spent their entire lives in transmitting this learning from Arabic into Latin.[4]

An African monk of Monte Cassino seems to have begun this process. Adelard of Bath, who probably learned Arabic in Sicily or the Holy Land, was one of the earliest translators. He translated Euclid's *Elements,* the astronomical tables of Al-Khwārizmi as revised by Al-Majrīṭi, and a mathematical encyclopedia ascribed to the same Al-Khwārizmi.[5] Early in the century Salerno became a center for the dissemination of Greek and Arabic medical treatises.

---

[1] C. H. Haskins, *The Renaissance of the Twelfth Century* (Cambridge, 1927). The free use of the word "renaissance" to describe this movement (and others at other times) is regrettable, since it involves or leads to many basic confusions and a notable lack of precision in employing the sources in support of extravagant and far-reaching conclusions. See E. Panofsky, "Renaissance and Renascences," *The Kenyon Review,* vi:2 (Spring, 1944), 201-36; W. A. Nitze, "The so-called Twelfth Century Renaissance," *Speculum,* xxiii (1948), 464-71; E. M. Sanford, "The Twelfth Century—Renaissance or Proto-Renaissance?" *Speculum,* xxvi (1951), 635-42; U. T. Holmes, "The Idea of a Twelfth-century Renaissance," *Speculum,* xxvi (1951), 643-51; Brunet, Paré, and Tremblay, *op. cit.*

[2] P. K. Hitti, *History of the Arabs* (London, 1951), 557.

[3] J. Leflon, *Gerbert* (Abbaye Saint-Wandrille, 1946). Although there can be no doubt of the ultimate Arabic sources of much of his scientific learning, the story of Gerbert's education in Cordova, "si séduisante qu'elle paraisse, en réalité ne repose sur rien," *ibid.,* 24.

[4] Haskins, *op. cit.,* 278-302.

[5] Haskins, "Adelard of Bath," *English Historical Review,* xxvi (1911), 491-98; Sarton, *op. cit.,* ii:1, 167-69. See also D. O'Leary, "Constantine the African," *The Islamic Literature,* viii (1956), 29-35.

51

Sicily under its Norman ruler likewise saw an important exploration and extension of Arabic learning by European Christians.[6]

The greatest center for this work was Toledo, which "for a time became equal to Paris and Bologna as a factor in mediaeval culture."[7] It was uniquely situated for this purpose; it was in the middle of Spain, had been the Visigothic capital, and had remained in the hands of the Moslems for nearly four centuries, from its capture in 712 to its "liberation" by Alfonso VI in 1085.[8] Its episcopal see had functioned throughout those centuries, and Pope Urban II made it the primatial see of the Spanish Church in 1088. The city still contained libraries of Arabic books; but also, what was just as important, a large segment of its population, which included Jews and Moslems as well as Christians (the latter two designated as Mozarabs and Mudejars[9]), still used Arabic as its common language.[10] The man who recognized the great opportunity which history was offering to Toledo, and

[6] Haskins, *The Normans in European History* (Boston, 1915); "Michael Scot and Frederick II," *Isis*, no. 11 (1921), 250-75; "Science at the Court of Emperor Frederick II," *American Historical Review*, xxvii (1922), 669-94.

[7] Dawson, *Religion and the Rise of Western Culture* (London, 1950), 231. See P. G. Théry, *Tolède, grande ville de la renaissance médiévale, point de jonction entre les cultures musulmane et chrétienne* (Oran, 1944).

[8] "As thank-offering for the capture of Toledo" Alfonso contributed generously toward the construction of the new abbey church at Cluny and "received honors suitable to the founder," Conant, "The Apse at Cluny," *Speculum*, vii (1932), 25.

[9] Mozarabs (Arabic *al-musta'ribūn*) were Christians who adopted the Arabic language under Moslem domination; Mudejars (Arabic *al-muta'akhkhirūn*), Moslems under Christian domination; see A. González Palencia, *Los Mozárabes de Toledo en los siglos xii y xiii*, 4 vols. (Madrid, 1926-30); Hitti, *op. cit.*, 551. Chew, *op. cit.*, 434, is incorrect in saying that Peter the Venerable observed the "growing power" of the Moslems in Spain; he could only have observed the opposite.

[10] "There were, in fact, four languages in use in Muslim Spain: 1) Classical Arabic, the language of men of letters; 2) Colloquial Arabic, the language of administration and government; 3) Ecclesiastical Latin, a merely ritual language associated with a particular form of worship; and 4) a Romance Dialect, mainly derived from Low Latin, but destined to become (under the name of Romance *castellano* or Spanish) one of the great international languages of the world," *The Legacy of Islam*, ed. T. Arnold and A. Guillaume (Oxford, 1931), 7. Most Toledans were at least bilingual (numbers 2 and 4) long after the Reconquista; d'Alverny, "Deux traductions du Coran au Moyen Age," 71, note 1.

acted on it, was the city's archbishop, Raimundo.[11] He had been bishop of Osma before being elected to the see of Toledo, succeeding a Cluniac abbot named Bernard, in 1125. During the quarter century of his rule, which ended with his death in 1151, he gathered around him a "school" of translators whom he patronized—the first such enterprise in European history.

Archbishop Raimundo's "school" was not a school such as the nascent universities of Paris, Salerno, Bologna, and Oxford.[12] The scholars of Toledo came and went very much as they pleased, or rather as the progress of their education dictated. The fact that the reputation of their labors and of the archbishop's patronage spurred men in other parts of Europe to devote themselves to this work and avail themselves of the same or similar patronage testifies, perhaps as much as the actual output of translations, to the importance of the school of Toledo.

The early translators were seldom men for whom what we now call linguistics was of much importance. They were interested in the subject matter of Arabic works, not in the niceties and subtleties of language differences. As one would expect from such an attitude, their translations are rarely as precise or as elegant as they might have been. When one takes that into consideration, it is remarkable that they are as accurate as they are. That may be accounted for by the fact that many of the translators found it to their advantage to work with dragomans or in pairs.[13]

Among the most famous pairs of translators was that of Domingo González, archdeacon of Segovia, and John of Seville (or "of Spain"), a converted Jew, who were commissioned by Archbishop Raimundo about 1133.[14] Together they translated

---

[11] González Palencia, *El Arzobispo Don Raimundo de Toledo* (Barcelona, 1942); "Noticias sobre D. Raimundo, Arzobispo de Toledo (1125-1152)," *Moros y Cristianos en España Medieval* (Madrid, 1945), 101-76.

[12] Haskins, *The Renaissance of the Twelfth Century*, 363-97; *The Rise of the Universities* (New York, 1923).

[13] Sarton, *op. cit.*, II:1, 114-15. The same methods had been used to great advantage in the translation of Greek and Syriac works into Arabic some centuries before.

[14] L. C. Karpinski, *Robert of Chester's Latin Translation of the Algebra of*

many works, including Al-Farghāni's astronomy, the neo-Platonic treatise *De Causis*,[15] and philosophical writings of Al-Fārābi, Ibn-Sīna, and Al-Ghazzāli.[16] Other translators were Hugh of Santalla, who worked under the patronage of Bishop Michael of Tarazona, Plato of Tivoli, who worked at Barcelona with Abraham bar-Ḥiyya, and Gerard of Cremona, who is credited with no less than seventy-one translations, including works of Ptolemy, Euclid, Galen, Hippocrates, Aristotle, and Al-Fārābi. These translators, and many others, seem to have obtained their knowledge of Arabic in Spain.[17]

The cosmopolitan character of the school of Toledo is obvious from the names of the translators. At the time of Peter the Venerable's visit, of course, the school was still in its infancy, but it had already produced a creditable number of translations and trained many translators. Despite its growing reputation "as the true center for the study of magic and the black arts,"[18] Toledo remained such a citadel for these studies that in 1250 the Dominicans chose it as the site of the first formal school of oriental studies in Europe.[19] By the time its importance began to fade, at the close of the thirteenth century, it had furnished scholars with Latin versions of many of the principal works of Greek and Arabic science and philosophy. There was no intellectual center in Europe that was not touched in some way by, that did not owe some debt to, the school of Toledo.[20]

There is no evidence that Archbishop Raimundo had a part in Peter the Venerable's project, and one authority has argued strongly against it.[21] But Peter is known to have met Raimundo at

---

al-Khowarizmi (New York, 1915), 23; Alonso, "Traducciones del Arabe al Latin por Juan Hispano (Ibn Dāwūd)," *Al-Andalus*, XVII (1952), 129-51.

[15] Alonso, "El 'Liber de Causis,'" *ibid.*, IX (1944), 43-69.

[16] Alonso, "Traducciones del arcediano Domingo Gundisalvo," *ibid.*, XII (1947), 295-338.

[17] Sarton, *op. cit.*, II:1, 115, 338-44.

[18] Holmes, *Daily Living in the Twelfth Century* (Madison, 1952), 240.

[19] Hitti, *op. cit.*, 588.

[20] *Ibid.*, 590; see also Aldo Mieli, *La science arabe et son rôle dans l'évolution scientifique mondiale* (Leiden, 1938).

[21] Bishko, *op. cit.*, 167-68, note 21. J. M. Millás Vallicrosa, "La corriente de las

Salamanca in late July of 1142,[22] and it would be difficult to believe that the subject was not discussed. Whether or not the archbishop influenced the project directly, he certainly influenced it indirectly through the three main translators, all of whom can be associated in one way or another with his school.

---

traducciones cientificas de origen oriental hasta fines del siglo xiii," *Journal of World History,* II (1954-55), 416-17, posits a Pyrenean and "Ebro River" school of translators.

[22] CC 5, 425, 429.

2 · PETER OF TOLEDO

NEXT TO NOTHING is known with certainty about the man whom Peter the Venerable identified as "Master Peter of Toledo." The cartularies and *pergaminos* of the cathedrals of Toledo and other cities through which the abbot's entourage passed may yield more information about him. The tempting possibility of identifying him with Peter Alphonsi, a learned Toledan with whose work the abbot became acquainted while in Spain, must be rejected.[23]

Because Peter the Venerable calls him "Master Peter," Muñoz Sendino suggests that he had acquired this title at a university, probably that of Paris.[24] But, in a passage from the *Epistola de translatione sua* already quoted, Peter also remarked that, "the Latin language was not as familiar or known to him as the Arabic,"[25] which would have been an unbelievable state of affairs for a master from Paris. In the simpler sense of "teacher" it might have been a title he was accustomed to receiving in Toledo. Almost certainly its use by the abbot indicates a particular respect for the man's erudition and, perhaps, age.

Peter of Poitiers confirmed the fact that he had assisted Peter of Toledo in translating the apology of Al-Kindi and remarked on his knowledge of Islamic customs in a letter to Peter the Venerable: "The chapter about using wives dishonorably which is also there should not scandalize you in any way, for it really is in the Koran and, as I heard for certain in Spain, both from Peter of Toledo, whose associate I was in translating, and from Robert, now archdeacon of Pamplona, all of the Saracens do this freely, as if by Mohammed's command."[26]

[23] Monneret de Villard, *op. cit.*, 14; see above, chapter I, note 83.

[24] *La Escala de Mahoma*, 14.

[25] See above, chapter I, note 100; his difficulty with Latin should probably not be exaggerated in light of the fact that the abbot also says he was "skilled in both languages."

[26] "Capitulum etiam quod est ibi de uxoribus turpiter abutendis, non uos ullo modo scandalizet, quia uere ita est in Alchorano, et sicut ego in Hyspania pro certo, et a Petro Toletano, cuius in transferendo socius eram, et a Roberto Pampilonensi

Blachère thought that Peter of Toledo was a convert from Islam to Christianity.[27] Although it is a plausible conjecture, the facts that he knew Arabic better than Latin and had some acquaintance with Islamic customs are inconclusive proof.[28] It is fully as possible that he came from a Mozarab family and was as conversant with Islam as any Toledan Christian of his time could have been, given the intelligence, interest, and pains.

In later manuscripts and scholarship Peter of Toledo is often credited with the translation of the Koran as well as that of the apology of Al-Kindi. That was one result of the general confusion over the identity of the work mentioned by the abbot as "disputing" Islamic doctrine, since the apology of Al-Kindi was omitted in one manuscript tradition. Muñoz Sendino, however, disturbed by a single use of the pronominal adjective "our" in Robert of Ketton's prefatory letter to Peter the Venerable,[29] devised a theory that Peter of Toledo may have revised a "primitive translation" of Robert's.[30] That theory does not seem likely or even called for.

It is highly probable that Peter of Toledo not only planned the Toledan Collection for Peter the Venerable, but also annotated it.[31]

---

nunc archidiacono audiui, omnes Sarraceni hoc licenter quasi ex praecepto Mahumeth faciunt," D 177rd. See Kritzeck, "Peter the Venerable and the Toledan Collection," 191, and Daniel, op. cit., 320-22.

[27] Op. cit., vii.

[28] Still less are they proof that he was a Moslem, which has also been suggested; see below, note 70.

[29] "Translationis nostrae," BC 1116D.

[30] "La Apologia del Cristianismo de al-Kindi," 363-70; cf. La Escala de Mahoma, 145. D'Alverny, "Deux traductions du Coran au Moyen Age," 85, also rejected the notion.

[31] See above, chapter I, part 3. The Arsenal manuscript is annotated unevenly throughout. The Koran is annotated most heavily; the first ten folios, for example, contain three hundred and sixty-four marginal and interlinear notes, ranging from an outraged "O quantum mendacium" to informed commentaries, hundreds of words in length, on Islamic beliefs and customs. Since Peter the Venerable utilized those notes in the composition of the Summa totius haeresis Saracenorum and the Liber contra sectam sive haeresim Saracenorum, they must have been made while the collection was being put together or shortly thereafter. Although I once thought differently ("Peter the Venerable and the Toledan Collection," 183, note 30; "Moslem-Christian Understanding in Mediaeval Times," 397), I

He would thus have been recognized as the dean of the translating group, and it is more the pity that even conjecture must stop there.

---

am now convinced that Peter of Toledo (perhaps in consultation with Moham-med) was the only member of the translating group capable of annotating in this way. The fact that the translation of the apology of Al-Kindi is similarly heavily annotated would seem to eliminate Robert of Ketton. Daniel, *op. cit., passim,* emphasizes the influence of this annotator; see also R. W. Southern, *The Making of the Middle Ages* (London, 1953), 40.

3 · PETER OF POITIERS

❦ PETER OF POITIERS was a monk of Cluny.[32] There is reason to believe that he was also known as Peter of St. John.[33] He served as his abbot's *notarius* or, as we might say, secretary, and there was a strong bond of friendship between them. He seems to have shared Peter the Venerable's scholarly enthusiasms and to have collaborated with him on some of them. He attributed his "passion for reading" to the abbot's inspiration.[34]

By accepting some of Lecointre-Dupont's theories (which are, however, full of problems), it is possible to construct a career for Peter of Poitiers which may not be altogether hypothetical. According to this construction, he was first a monk of St.-Jean de Montierneuf (hence, "of St. John").[35] He wrote a panegyric praising Peter the Venerable on the occasion of his visitation to Aquitaine in 1134, to which the abbot replied in verse.[36] He was obliged to defend himself in a letter "ad calumniatorem" against a charge of having praised the abbot too highly.[37] Besides the letters

[32] None of the other translators had any known connection with the Cluniac order. He should not be confused with the Peter of Poitiers who was chancellor of Paris or the Canon Regular of St. Victor; P. Moore, *The Works of Peter of Poitiers* (Washington, 1936), 1-24.

[33] *Histoire littéraire de la France*, XII (Paris, 1830), 349; A. Franklin, *Dictionnaire des Noms, Surnoms, et Pseudonymes latins de l'Histoire littéraire du Moyen Age* (Paris, 1875), 455; and, in particular, M. Lecointre-Dupont, "Notice sur Pierre de Poitiers, grand prieur de Cluni, abbé de Saint-Martial de Limoges," *Mémoires de la Société des Antiquaires de l'Ouest*, IX (1842), 371 and 377-78; see the references in BC 630C, 861C, 862A, 965C; PL 189, 27. An alternate candidate for some of these references is Prior Peter of the Augustinian house of St. John at Sens; V. Rose, *Verzeichniss der lateinischen Handschriften*, I (Berlin, 1893), 411; G. Constable, "The Letter from Peter of St. John to Hato of Troyes," PV, 42-43. Professor Constable has promised to take up this difficult matter in the introduction to his edition of the letters of Peter the Venerable.

[34] "Dum semper omnia more uestro philosophice agitis, satis competenter michi et patienti et multis passionibus digno, passionem legendam misistis," D 177rs-rd.

[35] Lecointre-Dupont, *op. cit.*, 371.

[36] BC 607A-15E, 1337B-44A. See Wilmart, "Le poème apologétique de Pierre le Vénérable et les poèmes connexes," *Revue Bénédictine*, LI (1939), 53-69; E. R. Curtius, *European Literature and the Latin Middle Ages*, tr. W. R. Trask (New York, 1953), 164.

[37] BC 616A-17B.

to Peter the Venerable preserved in the *Bibliotheca Cluniacensis* and elsewhere, there are attributed to him two epitaphs, one for Pope Gelasius II and the other for Alfonso, a bishop of Salamanca.[38] He may have served as a prior, even the grand prior of Cluny, and been elected abbot of St.-Martial at Limoges a few months before Peter the Venerable's death in 1156.[39] After the abbot's death he was charged with collecting his correspondence, and is therefore responsible for the customary arrangement of the letters.[40]

Although Peter the Venerable first associated his notary with Peter of Toledo only in order to "polish and set in order" the "confused" translation of the apology of Al-Kindi, Peter of Poitiers' role in the accomplishment of the entire project was probably one of great importance. His collaboration with Peter of Toledo may well have extended to editing and arranging the Toledan Collection,[41] and he may have been delegated to provide the digest of information for the *Summa totius haeresis Saracenorum*. Certainly Peter the Venerable relied on him to prepare a list of possible chapter headings for a book of refutation of Islamic doctrine. They seem to have been completed while the abbot was in England.[42] A first copy had been lost "on the way" by a certain John, most likely a monk sent to join the abbot's retinue.[43]

"I believe they are set in order," Peter of Poitiers wrote of the chapter headings, "more distinctly than before. . . . If it pleases you thus, let what I have presumed to add or change remain; if not, it is yours to correct what we do wrong. . . . For you, alone in our times, are the one who cuts to pieces by the sword of the divine Word the three greatest enemies of holy Christianity; I speak of the Jews and the heretics and the Saracens. And you

[38] See above, note 33; BC 617B-18B.
[39] Lecointre-Dupont, *op. cit.*, 384; see BC 861C, 862A; M. Chaume, "Les Grand Prieurs de Cluny. Compléments et rectification à la liste de la *Gallia Christiana*," *Revue Mabillon*, xxviii (1938), 147-52. This abbot travelled to Rome in 1158 and died in 1161; Lecointre-Dupont, *op. cit.*, 385-88.
[40] BC *Notae*, 102C.
[41] D'Alverny, "Deux traductions du Coran au Moyen Age," 102-03.
[42] D 177rd; cf. Mandonnet, *op. cit.*, 340, note 1.
[43] "Mitto uobis capitula quae Iohannem perdidisse mandastis," D 177rd.

have shown that Mother Church is not so deprived of good sons. ... Excuse my tardiness and weakness, I pray you, for the Lord knows I have been unable to send these before, though I much wanted to, since I was confined by the infirmity of my whole body, and especially the usual lameness of my feet. But I have copied all these [chapters] also into a large book, fearing that they also might be lost on the way, as the first ones were lost, because it was extremely wearisome [work]."[44]

From this letter it becomes clear that we must be grateful to the plaudits and constancy of Peter the Venerable's notary, as well as to the unwillingness of Bernard of Clairvaux to devote himself to the task, for the eventual composition of the *Liber contra sectam sive haeresim Saracenorum*.

[44] "Credo quod multo distinctius ordinata sint, quam ante . . . siquid addere uel mutare praesumpsi, et hoc uobis ita placuerit, maneat. Sin autem, uestrum est corrigere quod erramus. . . . Solus enim uos estis nostris temporibus, qui tres maximos sanctae Christianitatis hostes, Iudeos dico et hereticos ac Sarracenos, diuini uerbi gladio trucidastis, et matrem aecclesiam non ita orbatam uel desolatam bonis filiis ostendistis. . . . Ignoscite queso traditati et infirmitati meae, quia nouit Dominus cum multum uoluissem, graui totius corporis et maxime solita pedum debilitate constrictus, non ante potui uobis haec mittere. Scripsi enim haec omnia etiam in maiore libro, timens ne et ipsa perdantur in uia, sicut perdita sunt capitula. Quod ualde laboriosum fuit," D 177rd-vs.

IT IS POSSIBLE that the Englishman Robert of Ketton[45] had travelled extensively before settling in Barcelona, by July of 1136, to study with Plato of Tivoli.[46] He was chiefly interested in astronomy and geometry, as he told Peter the Venerable in so many words in his preface to the translation of the Koran. He had been willing, he said, "to overlook, in the meantime, my principal study of astronomy and geometry" in order to participate in Peter's project, but in the next breath he announced his intention to prepare a *summa astronomica* which would "penetrate . . . all the heavenly orbits, and their quantities, orders, and habits, and especially all manner of movement of the stars, and their effects and natures."[47]

After finishing his translations for the Toledan Collection and perhaps in some manner as a result of them, he was appointed archdeacon of Pamplona, an ecclesiastical position of consequence, which may indicate that he was a priest.[48] In 1144 he translated

[45] He is usually called Robert of Chester, and sometimes Robert of Reading, because of misspellings of his name in many manuscripts. The oldest manuscripts, and notably the Arsenal manuscript, read "Ketenensis," which is evidently "Ketton" in Rutlandshire; E. Ekwall, *The Concise Oxford Dictionary of English Place-Names* (Oxford, 1936), 261; d'Alverny, "Deux traductions du Coran au Moyen Age," 71, note 2; Muñoz Sendino, "La Apologia del Cristianismo de al-Kindi," 373-74. See L. Leclercq, *Histoire de la médicine arabe*, II (Paris, 1876), 380-87; A. M. Clerke, *s.v.* "Chester, Robert," *Dictionary of National Biography*, x (London, 1887), 203; T. A. Archer, *s.v.* "Robert the Englishman, etc.," *Dictionary of National Biography,* XLVIII (New York, 1896), 362-64; Sarton, *op. cit.,* II:I, 175-77.

[46] Archer, *op. cit.,* 362; Karpinski, *op. cit.,* 28, note 1. A. Clerval, *Les Écoles de Chartres au Moyen Age* (Paris, 1895), 191, says Robert knew Thierry of Chartres (cf. below, note 61), but cites no evidence for the statement. It is possible that both Robert and Herman were his pupils.

[47] "Sed ne proemium fastidium generet ipsi finem impono, tibique celesti celum omne penetranti, celestes munus uoueo, quod integritatem scientie in se complectitur. Quæ secundum numerum, et proportionem, atque mesuram, celestes circulos omnes, et eorum quantitates, et ordines et habitudines, demum stellarum motus omnimodus et earumdem effectus atque naturas et huiusmodi cetera diligentissime diligentibus aperit, nunc probabilibus, nonnumquam necessariis argumentis innitens," A 29rs.

[48] "These archdeacons were generally priests. . . . The authority of the archdeacons culminated in the eleventh and twelfth centuries. At that time they exer-

a book on alchemy.[49] His translation of the algebra of Al-Khwā-rizmi, completed the following year, was "the beginning of European algebra" and became a widely used textbook.[50] Indications are that he returned to England for some time, possibly permanently. He completed a revision of an earlier translation of a work on the astrolabe in London in 1150. He compiled a set of astronomical tables for the longitude of London, based on those of Al-Battāni and Al-Zarqāli, and revised the tables of Al-Khwā-rizmi as translated by Adelard of Bath. Several other works are attributed to him with less certainty.[51] His long friendship and association with Herman of Dalmatia is well established by their own words.[52] Both the date and place of his death are unknown.

Robert's dedicatory letter to the translation of the *Fabulae Saracenorum* and his prefatory letter to that of the Koran are pretentious, almost pompous bits of rhetoric, replete with biblical and classical allusions. "It is beneficial and appropriate [only] to touch," he wrote in the former letter, "rather than to hold onto a foul and poisonous thing, and preferable to pass by Sirens with ample and hasty ways rather than with slow and numerous footsteps. . . . I exposed the law of the aforementioned [Mohammed] by my own hand, and brought it into the treasury of the Roman tongue, in order that, once its baseness became known, the Corner-stone [Christ; cf. Eph. 2:20], the most precious Redemp-

---

cised within the province of their archdiaconates a quasi-episcopal jurisdiction. They made visitations, during which they were empowered to levy certain assessments on the clergy; they conducted courts of first instance, and had the right to punish clerics guilty of lapses; they could also hold synodal courts"; J. P. Kirsch, s.v. "Archdeacon," *The Catholic Encyclopedia*, 1 (New York, 1907), 693-94. But cf. S. Kuttner, "Cardinalis: The History of a Canonical Concept," *Traditio*, III (1945), 159, 178, 180, where it is shown that archdeacons frequently were not priests.

[49] Karpinski, *op. cit.*, 30; Sarton, *op. cit.*, II:1, 176. The work was published in Paris in 1546, and again in J. J. Manget, *Bibliotheca Chemica Curiosa*, 1 (Geneva, 1702), 509-19.

[50] Sarton, *op. cit.*, II:1, 176.

[51] *Ibid.*

[52] See below, notes 62-64. Robert dedicated a translation of an astronomical work by Ya'qūb ibn-Isḥāq ibn-Ṣabbāḥ al-Kindi to "my friend Herman, second to no astronomer of our time, of those who speak Latin," Karpinski, *op. cit.*, 30-31.

tion of the human race, might send forth His splendors farther and wider."[53]

He remarks that Peter the Venerable, "the venerable man whom the church of Cluny chose for itself as bridegroom, truly seeing in him the same thing that Christ saw in [the Apostle] Peter," is especially to be praised for his efforts to bring Islamic doctrine to light, since "the Doctors of the Church allowed . . . that greatest heresy of all . . . to come forth into immensity and superabundance for five hundred and thirty-seven years.[54] For it is manifestly a pernicious thing that the flower of that perverse sectarian doctrine, covering up a scorpion, fails to draw the attention of, and destroys by trickery, ministers of the law of the Christian faith, to whom alone the law can be afforded truly and absolutely—which, alas, we have very often seen already."[55] More than that, he says, there are Christian priests so overcome with hatred that they declare that the conversion of the Moslems is not even desirable: "They say in the presence of all, either by ignorance or negligence, that His beautiful portion of the human race [the Moslems] should hear nothing of His nuptials, or should be held fast in the chains of darkness and by the songs of Sirens, ignorant that His redemption has been accomplished."[56] This passage is extremely interest-

[53] "Est enim salubrius commodiusque rem friuolam et uenenosam tangere quam tenere, potiusque Sirenes spaciosis cursibus ac festinis, quam lentis et numerosis passibus preterire . . . legem predicti manu propria detexi, et in linguae Romanae thesaurum attuli, ut illius uilitate notata, lapis angularis, redemptio generis humani preciosissima, longius magisque suos fulgores emittat," A 5rs. "Lex" is sometimes translated as "law" and sometimes as "religion"; cf. Daniel, *op. cit.*, 14.

[54] Why Robert chose the year 605/06 is a mystery; the date of Mohammed's first revelation is usually given as ca. 610.

[55] "Cum igitur domno Petro uiro uenerabili, . . . quem aecclesia Cluniacensis sibi sponsum elegit, idem in ipso uere perspiciens quod Christus in Petro . . . ut illam heresim omnium maximam per me denudatam, quam inter rudes origine sumpta, omnes etiam ecclesie doctores in immensum et nimium crescere, per dxxxvii. annos passi sunt, ipse fortiter improbet et omnino destruat. Visum est enim perniciosum, ut Christianae fidei legisque quae sola ueraciter et absolute lex perhiberi potest, ministros, flos illius praue secte scorpionem operiens, alliciendo falleret, fallendoque perimeret, quod sepius proh dolor, iam contigisse uidimus," A 5rs-rd.

[56] "Qualem quidem uocis uultusque gestum ferent, quidue dicent coram sponso cunctos inuitante sui precones atque ministri, si sua uel negligentia generis humani pulcra portio uel de nuptiis nichil audiat, uel in tenebrarum

ing not merely for its criticism of contemporary clerical attitudes toward Islam, but also as an indication of the spirit in which Peter the Venerable's project was executed, a spirit very different from that in which the Crusade was being conducted, and with quite another end in view.

The theme of the prefatory letter to the Koran is much the same. "When I learned . . . in what manner and to what extent your soul, assiduous for each and every good, longed to make fruitful the unproductive swamp of Saracen doctrine . . . I exposed the ways and means very diligently, performing this in the capacity of a foot-soldier, leading the way."[57] A great deal may be gathered from this letter about the thoughts in Robert's mind as he performed this service. He, too, saw his task in providing accurate information as but a preliminary stage in the total project. He must have stood in awe of the boldness and strength of purpose in the man who had conceived it. "Selecting nothing, altering nothing in the sense except for the sake of intelligibility, I have brought stones and wood so that your beautiful building may hereafter be raised up all joined together and imperishable. I have uncovered Mohammed's smoke so that it may be extinguished by your bellows."[58]

It is ironic that this Englishman, recruited by accident to work on a project far afield from his lifelong interests and acknowledged competency, achieved by means of it a unique place at the beginning of a new chapter in the intellectual history of Europe. He is less often recognized as Robert of Ketton, the astronomer and geometrician, the first to use "sinus" (sine) "in its trigonometrical acceptation,"[59] than as Robert of Ketton, the first translator of the Koran.

---

uinculis Sirenumue cantibus detenta, turpiterque lusa, non accedat, suam redemptionem factam esse nesciens," A 5rd.

[57] "Vbi sepius atque serio percepi qualiter quantumue tuus animus solius et totius boni studiosus sitiuit sterilem paludem sarracene secte nondum uise fertilem efficere . . . ego peditis tantum officio preuii functus uias et aditus diligentissime patefeci," Paris, Bibliothèque Nationale, MS 3390, 28rd; BC 1116B.

[58] "Lapides igitur et ligna ut tuum deinde pulcherrimum et commodissimum edificium coagmentum et indissolubile fugat, nil excerpens, nil sensibiliter nisi propter intelligentiam tantum alterans, attuli. Machometique fumum, ad ipsius tuis follibus extinctum . . . patefeci," MS 3390, 28vd; BC 1116E.

[59] Sarton, op. cit., II:1, 176.

5 · HERMAN OF DALMATIA

PETER THE VENERABLE singled out Herman of Dalmatia, in his account of the translators, as "a scholar of the most incisive and literary genius."[60] Herman had been a pupil of Thierry of Chartres and was in contact with the Chartrain school.[61] It is possible that he was a priest. He lived and travelled in Spain during the 1130's and at least until 1142; there is, in fact, no certain evidence that he ever left Spain after that time.

Herman and Robert worked together for many years and were close friends. Herman mentions the fact in his translation of Ptolemy's *Planisphere*[62] and in the preface to his treatise *De Essentiis* calls Robert "my sole, special, and inseparable comrade in studies."[63] It appears from this preface that their studies were at first carried on in secret, very likely to avert false suspicion as to their motives, and these studies involved the pair in long and arduous labors.[64]

Sarton lists four of Herman's translations from the Arabic, apart from those in the Toledan Collection: an astronomical treatise of Sahl ibn-Bishr, completed in 1138; astronomical tables of Al-Khwārizmi and Abu-Ma'shar, both completed in 1140; and Al-Majrīṭi's translation of and commentary on Ptolemy's *Planisphere*.[65] This latter work was completed at Tolosa de

[60] See above, chapter I, note 104. He is to be distinguished from Herman "the Lame," a monk of Reichenau, and Herman "the German," a bishop of Astorga; see Clerval, "Hermann le Dalmate," *Compte rendu du Congrès scientifique international des Catholiques,* II (1891), 163-69; A. A. Björnbo, "Hermannus Dalmata als Üebersetzer astronomischer Arbeiten," *Biblioteca Mathematica,* IV (1903), 130-33; H. Bosmans, "Hermann le Dalmate, traducteur des traités arabes," *Revue des questions scientifiques,* LVI (1904), 669-72; P. Duhem, *Système du monde,* III (Paris, 1915), 171-76; Haskins, *Studies in the History of Medieval Science,* 43-66; Sarton, *op. cit.,* II:1, 173-74.

[61] Haskins, *Studies in the History of Medieval Science,* 54-55; Alonso, "Hermann de Carinthia, De Essentiis," *Miscelánea Comillas,* V (1946), 11. On Thierry, see M. B. Hauréau, "Mémoires sur quelques chanceliers de l'église de Chartres," *Mémoires de l'Institut de France, Académie des Inscriptions et Belles-lettres,* XXXI (1884, 63-122; Clerval, *Les Écoles de Chartres au Moyen Age,* 191.

[62] Karpinski, *op. cit.,* 32, note 2.

[63] *Ibid.,* 32, note 1; Alonso, "Hermann de Carinthia, De Essentiis," 24:3-10.

[64] *Ibid.*   [65] *Op. cit.,* II:1, 174.

Guipúzcoa on June 1, 1143.[66] Alonso, in the introduction to his edition of Herman's *De Essentiis,* identifies eleven additional works ascribed to him.[67]

Herman must have spent some time at Toledo, for he uses it in geographical illustration in the *De Essentiis.*[68] Since his translation of the *Liber generationis Mahumet* was completed in 1142 in Leon and that of Ptolemy's *Planisphere* at Tolosa the following spring, it would appear that he and Robert had parted company by that time. We are certain of the identity of one disciple of Herman's, Rudolph of Bruges, who, as "Hermanni secundi discipulus," dedicated a description of the astronomical instrument of Al-Majrīṭi to John of Seville.[69]

Nothing of Herman's later life is known.

[66] Alonso, "Hermann de Carinthia, *De Essentiis,*" 14; previously the place name had been thought to refer to Toulouse; cf. Muñoz Sendino, "La Apologia del Cristianismo de al-Kindi," 367.

[67] Alonso, "Hermann de Carinthia, *De Essentiis,*" 13-16; Sarton's are numbers 1, 2-3, and 6.

[68] *Ibid.,* 99:11ff.

[69] Haskins, *Studies in the History of Medieval Science,* 56, 66.

6 · MOHAMMED

THE LAST-NAMED TRANSLATOR of the Toledan Collection, the Moslem who bore the singularly undistinctive name of Mohammed, is even more impossible to identify than Peter of Toledo.[70] He is mentioned, in fact, only once in connection with the project—by Peter the Venerable in the passage from the *Liber contra sectam sive haeresim Saracenorum* already cited and translated in full.[71]

Mohammed's role in the project is not to be judged by the recognition he received, however. Peter the Venerable explicitly stated that it was his duty to see to it that the translations "should not lack the fullest fidelity, nor anything be taken away by deceit." That was a position of trust which is astounding not only in terms of the plan and sponsorship of this particular project but also in the wider context of the twelfth-century translating activities in Spain.[72] Mohammed's duty would therefore have involved giving information to the other translators on the exact meanings of Arabic words and, very likely, on Islamic doctrine in general. Since Peter the Venerable explained that Peter of Toledo's difficulty was with Latin, not Arabic, it would seem that Mohammed's offices were utilized principally or only by Robert and Herman, who translated the four Islamic works.[73]

It is not out of the question that Mohammed himself may have suggested works to be translated and provided manuscripts of them. Certainly his position implies some measure of learning.

[70] Devic, *op. cit.*, 373, note 2, made the startling suggestion, "Je soupçonne que le prétendu Sarrazin n'est autre que Pierre de Tolède"; but it is clear from context, *ibid.*, 376, that he did not know of the existence of the *Liber contra sectam sive haeresim Saracenorum*, the origin of the reference. It is absolutely clear that Mohammed was a Moslem.

[71] See above, chapter I, part 3, and note 105.

[72] No known Moslems participated in the schools of translation, and it is customarily assumed that the translators from northern Europe who learned Arabic there learned it from Mozarabs and converts. The situation was, of course, different in Sicily and the Holy Land.

[73] Muñoz Sendino, "La Apologia del Cristianismo de al-Kindi," 367, holds the same view.

If he provided the manuscript of the Koran, which it is not necessary to assume, he committed a sin in the view of his coreligionists, since Islamic law ruled that the Koran should be withheld from the hands of unbelievers. The very fact that he was party to a translation of the Koran at all, of course, would indicate that he had few if any qualms deriving from the Islamic legal prescriptions under this rubric.[74] Peter the Venerable does not mention that any special inducement was required to persuade him to undertake his work; probably the "multum pretium" he so often mentions was in this case, too, sufficient. That may do the Moslem an injustice. It would be nice to think that he knew and approved of the project's worthy aim and assisted with conviction in advancing Moslem-Christian understanding.

The omission of Mohammed's name in the *Epistola de translatione sua* may or may not be significant. It could conceivably have been a device to protect him, or merely indicate a desire on Peter's part to conceal Mohammed's cooperation from Bernard of Clairvaux and others whom it might have scandalized. It seems highly unlikely that he could have been a member of the abbot's entourage for much of the duration of the journey in Spain. It is easier to imagine that he was hired somewhere in the south, at a later stage of the project's development, travelled north with the group to a site (perhaps Pamplona) which became a fixed editorial headquarters, and there discharged his duties through the completion of Robert's translation of the Koran and possibly also Peter of Toledo's annotation of the collection. In all events, Mohammed lives in history, like Peter of Toledo, in this one connection only, and he cannot be identified more closely from any evidence known at the present time.

[74] See below, chapter III, part 5.

III · THE TRANSLATIONS

*Libellum multis, ut
credo, propter ignotarum
rerum notitiam perutilem
futurum perfecit.*

PETER THE VENERABLE

*Lapides igitur et ligna
ut tuum deinde pulcherrimum
et commodissimum ædificium
coagmentatum et indissolubile
fugat, nil excerpens, nil
sensibiliter nisi propter
intelligentiam tantum
alterans, attuli.*

ROBERT OF KETTON

1 · MS 1162 OF THE BIBLIOTHÈQUE DE L'ARSENAL

❧ Although MS 1162 of the Bibliothèque de l'Arsenal in Paris was carefully and correctly described by H. Martin in 1886, it was Mlle Marie-Thérèse d'Alverny who first recognized its unique importance for the study of the Toledan Collection.[1] The manuscript belonged to the Collège de Navarre-Champagne before becoming a part of the Arsenal collection. It is written on parchment and contains one hundred and seventy-eight folio pages, plus one half-folio twenty-five *bis* and minus folio one hundred and thirty-nine. The folios all have double columns, with red and green initials and red titles. On folio eleven, at the beginning of the *Liber generationis Mahumet,* there is a representation of Mohammed in the form of a fish with a human head,[2] and on folio one hundred and forty-six, at the beginning of the *Rescriptum Christiani ad Saracenum,* the initial "I" is formed by a monk with bowed head, holding a book in his hands. The manuscript is bound in purple morocco executed for the Bibliothèque de l'Arsenal.[3]

Martin identified the script as from the twelfth century.[4] Mlle d'Alverny established from palaeographic and artistic evidence that nearly all of it had been transcribed in Spain before the middle of the twelfth century.[5] There is a variation of script in the separate sections of the manuscript. The foliation is mediaeval, in Arabic numerals, on the reverse side of each of the folios, excepting that of the last portion of the manuscript.[6] The Koran

---

[1] Martin, *Catalogue général des manuscrits des bibliothèques publiques de France: Paris, Bibliothèque de l'Arsenal,* II (Paris, 1886), 315-17; d'Alverny, "Deux traductions du Coran au Moyen Age," 77-78.

[2] The figure was copied by M. J. Baltrusaitis and printed in *ibid.,* 82. It is similar to certain Mozarabic initials; see A. Huntingdon, *Initials and miniatures of the 9th, 10th, and 11th centuries from the Mozarabic manuscripts of S. Domingo of Silos in the British Museum* (New York, 1904).

[3] Martin, *op. cit.,* 317. [4] *Ibid.*

[5] "Deux traductions du Coran au Moyen Age," 78.

[6] See D. E. Smith and L. C. Karpinski, *The Hindu-Arabic Numerals* (Boston, 1911), 99-127.

has traces of a special foliation, largely effaced, and there are traces of erasure on the foliation of the translations which precede it. There are many deletions and interlinear additions by the scribal hands as well as the heavy annotation previously referred to.[7]

There is no alternative but to conclude from these facts that the Arsenal manuscript is the original collection, transcribed by or for the translators in Spain and put together in this form at Cluny.[8] Its preservation is a rare stroke of fortune.[9]

In this chapter the order of exposition of the translations of the Toledan Collection will follow the order of the Arsenal manuscript, with the exception of the *Epistola de translatione sua,* which has already been discussed, and the *Summa totius haeresis Saracenorum,* which is the subject of the next chapter. The short rubric which opens the Arsenal manuscript was not copied into other manuscripts of the collection.[10] It was probably written by Peter of Poitiers, possibly by Peter the Venerable himself.

[7] See above, chapter II, note 31.

[8] D'Alverny, "Deux traductions du Coran au Moyen Age," 77. On the manuscript tradition, see *ibid.,* 108-13, and d'Alverny, "Quelques manuscrits de la 'Collectio Toletana,'" PV, 202-18.

[9] See above, chapter I, note 1, and d'Alverny, "Deux traductions du Coran au Moyen Age," 77.

[10] "Si uis scire quis fuerit, uel quid docuerit maximus precursor Antichristi, et electus discipulus diaboli Mahumet, prologum istum intente lege, in quo breuiter continentur omnia, quae liber iste continet, siue de genealogia eius turpissima et mendosissima, siue de uita ipsius uel doctrina incestissima et nefanda, siue de fabulis tam ab ipso quam a sequacibus eius confictis, omni ridiculositate et deliramento plenis. Sane in fine codicis huius, legere non omittas librum utilem et necessarium, epistolas scilicet duas, quas ibi inuenies, unam cuiusdam Sarraceni quendam sanctum Christianum et doctum ad legem suam inuitantis, alteram uero eiusdem Christiani ei plenissime respondentis, et quam detestabilis uitae simul atque doctrinae fuerit Mahumet, ueracissime atque luculentissime ostendentis," A 1rs.

THE FIRST TRANSLATION of the Toledan Collection, entitled *Fabulae Saracenorum* and unfairly subtitled *Chronica mendosa et ridicula Saracenorum,* is a typical potpourri of Islamic traditions.[11] Many thousands of examples of the genre exist in collections of Arabic manuscripts throughout the world. The Arabists whose advice Mlle d'Alverny sought on the identity of the Arabic original of the work failed to identify it; I could not join more distinguished company.[12]

There are several reasons why the Arabic text of this work is especially difficult to locate. In the first place, the chain of authority (Arabic *isnād*) with which the original is known to have begun, and which would identify both the author and his sources, was deliberately omitted by the translator, Robert of Ketton, on the grounds that the Arabic names would mean nothing to his Latin readers: "God, at the beginning of His creation, created four things with His own hands, as the testimony and authority of many Arabs and other Saracens assign and attest. But I, the Latin translator, have passed their names by in silence, for inasmuch as they are absolutely foreign to the rules of the Latin language, to make them all known diligently would remain wholly devoid of all fruit, unless one esteems as fruit the prolixity of words and augmentation of folios."[13] Moreover, the work

---

[11] A 5r-10v (and margin of 11); Bibliander, *op. cit.,* 213-23. Annotation of these translations could go on almost indefinitely. Fuller references will be provided in the forthcoming edition of the collection; but the reader will want to consult Wensinck *et al., Concordance et Indices de la Tradition Musulmane* (Leiden, 1936-), and Wensinck, *A Handbook of Early Muhammadan Tradition* (Leiden, 1927), throughout.

[12] *Sc.,* M. Marçais, H. Massé, J. Sauvaget, L. Massignon, and G. Vajda; "Deux traductions du Coran au Moyen Age," 69, note 1. Portions of the text are similar to descriptions in J. Ribera and M. Asín, *Manuscritos Árabes y Aljamiados de la Biblioteca de la Junta* (Madrid, 1912).

[13] "In creationis sue primordio Deus manu propria .iiii.or condidit, prout multorum Arabum ceterorumque Sarracenorum plurimum, testimonium perhibet, et auctoritas asserit. (Ego uero Latinus interpres, eorum nomina silentio commendaui. Ut enim a Latinitatis regulis prorsus sunt aliena, sic illi licet diligenter annotata, penitus manerent frugis omnis experta, nisi quis uerborum prolixitatem et foliorum augmentum, fructum estimet)," A 5rd-vs.

lacks structural unity. It is composed of many parts of unequal length, treating unconnected subjects within a broad historical framework. In the Arsenal manuscript the last folio of the translation appears to have been cut off, and the end of the text was copied by a contemporary annotator in the right margin of the eleventh folio. The original text may, therefore, have been considerably longer.

I would be prepared to believe, on the basis of these facts, that the work is the first and major part, perhaps even a partial condensation, of a longer book.[14] It is possible but unlikely that it is a compilation of several books. Fortunately, however, there exists so rich a literature in Arabic on each of the subjects treated in the *Fabulae Saracenorum* that it is not difficult to determine in a general manner where and how it fits into Islamic thought, the nature of its information, and its utility for Peter the Venerable's purposes. In the very titles of the translation Robert of Ketton showed himself to have lacked even a slight sympathetic interest in the fascinating and noteworthy rabbinical and historical elements which the book preserves.[15] This is especially noticeable in the dedicatory letter he wrote for it, wherein he refers to its contents in contemptuous and mocking figures of speech.

The work begins by enumerating the four things which God is said to have created "with His own hands": the Pen, whose function is to "set down . . . all things from the beginning of the world to its end," Adam, the Throne, and Paradise.[16] In the

---

[14] Perhaps, as Mlle d'Alverny suggests, the ninth-century chronicle attributed to Ibn-Ḥabīb, which is, however, much more developed; see R. Dozy, *Recherches sur l'histoire et la littérature de l'Espagne pendant le moyen âge*, I (Paris, 1881), 28-29; C. Brockelmann, *Geschichte der arabischen Litteratur*, I (Leiden, 1943), 105, and Supplementband I (Leiden, 1937), 165. It also resembles the *Kitāb al-Iktifā'* of Abu-al-Rabī' Sulaymān ibn-Mūsā (ibn-Sālim) al-Kilā'i, MS 639, Garrett Collection, Princeton University Library.

[15] A 5rs-rd.

[16] A 5vs. On the Pen, see Koran 68:1; Al-Tabari, *Tafsīr*, xxix (Būlāq, A.H. 1329), 107; Fakhr-al-Dīn al-Rāzi, *Mafātīh al-Ghayb*, vi (Cairo, A.H. 1278), 330; L. Ginzberg, *Legends of the Jews*, tr. H. Szold and P. Radin, 7 vols. (Philadelphia, 1913-38) (cited hereafter as "LJ"), I, 5, 83. In confining myself very largely to this work for references to Jewish legends, I assume that the rich annotations

creation of Adam, the author goes on to say, God gathered "multi-colored dust" in his fist, and that is the reason why some men are white, some black, and some "in between," as well as why some partake of evil, some of goodness and other qualities.[17] Mohammed is quoted as having told the Arabs of his time that they were the sixty-first generation from Adam and that they "surpass all peoples in uprightness and goodness." Even before Adam was created, we are told, God named man.[18] A curious account of human gestation follows. For forty days, it is said, the human foetus continues as sperm; during the next forty days it joins with the blood, then takes on flesh and the features of the body are formed.[19] When the time for birth comes, an angel is sent by God to breathe in the soul and to prescribe "four necessary things" about it, notably, whether it is destined, on the basis of future "works or merits," for heaven or hell.[20]

The chronology of the patriarchs and prophets, a subject of enduring interest for Semitic exegetes, is then taken up. From Adam to Noah, the author bravely states, 1242 years elapsed; from Noah to Abraham, 1080 years; from Abraham to Moses, 515 years; from Moses to David, 569 years; from David to Christ, 350 years;

---

and references which it contains will also be consulted. The remarkable article by Haim Schwarzbaum, "The Jewish and Moslem Versions of Some Theodicy Legends," *Fabula*, III (1959), 119-69, is a mine of further information. For Islamic legends concerning the creation of Adam, see M. Seligsohn, *s.v.* "Adam," *Encyclopaedia of Islâm* (cited hereafter as "EI"; a new edition of the work is in progress), I, 127; cf. Gen. 1:26-31; 2:7-25; ch. 3-5:4; LJ I, 54-55, 59, 60, 83; V, 64, 71, 72-73, 78, 79, 106, 107, 108, 117, 126, 127, 136, 162. On the Throne, see Koran 2:256; Al-Ṭabari, *op. cit.*, III, 7; LJ I, 281; III, 321, 401. On Paradise, see Koran 55:54, 72; 56:15-22, 27-33; Gen. 2:8 says God had already created it; Jewish legend had it created on the third day, LJ I, 19-23.

[17] A 5vs. Koran 15:26 mentions only "dried clay of black mud"; this is a Jewish legend, LJ I, 55.

[18] A 5vs. Cf. Gen. 1:26; LJ I, 69; V, 90.

[19] A 5vs. To this point the exposition closely follows Jewish legend, LJ I, 163; V, 81, 106, except that the formation of the female embryo was said by the rabbis to require eighty days, LJ V, 106. There was also a notion that prophets were seven-month children, LJ V, 397; VI, 217.

[20] A 5vs-vd. On predestination in Islam, see A. J. Wensinck, *The Muslim Creed* (Cambridge, 1932), 51-56, 142, 157, 214, 234ff.; W. M. Watt, *Free Will and Predestination in Early Islam* (London, 1948).

from Christ to Mohammed, 620 years.[21] Thus more than five millennia separated Mohammed from creation.[22] Between Moses and Christ one thousand prophets "from the sons of Israel" are said to have existed, while there were only four between Christ and Mohammed.[23] Mary, the mother of Christ, is said to have died at the age of fifty-three, five years after her son's crucifixion.[24] Seth, the chronicle continues, recited ninety-five prayers over his dead father, Adam; the opening of his prayers was, of course, *Allāhu Akbar* ("God is most great"), the Islamic formula.[25] The total number of the prophets is set at one hundred and twenty thousand, that of the "messengers" (Arabic *rusul*) at three hundred and fifteen, of whom five were Jews and five Arabs; Moses is cited as the first Jewish prophet and Christ as the last.[26] One hundred and four scriptures are said to have been revealed by God to the prophets.[27] The Arabs, Persians, Romans, and Jews are identified as the four wisest races, "compared to whom all the rest put together rate [as] nothing."

Mohammed is reported to have appeared in a dream with the information that the world would endure for seven millennia, during the sixth of which he (and after him no other prophet) would live. The sign of the end of the world would be the rising

[21] A 5vd. This is more or less the traditional chronology, except for the interval between David and Christ. Needless to say, modern biblical scholars do not credit or attempt such chronologies.

[22] A 5vd. Either the author or the translator seems to have made an error in addition, but it is likely that the numbers were subjected to various changes and I do not consider it worth while to digest the many other attempts at calculating these periods.

[23] A 5vd.

[24] *Ibid.* Christian mystical tradition usually sets Mary's age at death as sixty-three, fifteen years after Christ's ascension; see R. Brown, *The Life of Mary as Seen by the Mystics* (Milwaukee, 1951), 274-81; J. M. Abd-el-Jalil, *Marie et l'Islam* (Paris 1950).

[25] A 5vd. This may correspond to a Jewish benediction; see Wensinck, *s.v.* "Ṣalāt," EI iv, 99, and "Takbīr," EI iv, 627.

[26] A 5vd-6rs. Adam was often regarded as the first prophet by Jews and Moslems alike; cf. LJ v, 83.

[27] A 6rs. *Sc.*, ten to Adam, fifty to Seth, thirty to Enoch, ten to Abraham, and one each to Moses, David, Christ, and Mohammed; cf. T. P. Hughes, *A Dictionary of Islam* (London, 1885), 475.

of the sun in the west and its setting in the east.[28] As for the progeny of the sons of Noah, the Arabs, Romans, and Persians are assigned to Shem, the Ethiopians and Egyptians to Ham, and Gog and Magog, with "the other peoples believing in God least," to Japhet.[29] Mohammed is said to have known that he was to become a prophet "between the creation of Adam's body and the inspiration of his soul."[30] God forechose Qaydar from Ishmael's sons, and Quraysh from Qaydar's, "among whose sons was Mohammed."[31] Although Quraysh came forth "naturally from the womb of his mother," yet a miraculous circumstance attended it. A light "which, as many think, came from the hands of the Creator two thousand years before the making of Adam," surrounded him, as it had Adam, Noah, Abraham, and the other heirs of "that seed" up to the birth of Mohammed.[32] An ascendant paternal genealogy of Mohammed follows this, with a maternal genealogy of four generations. The date of Mohammed's birth is discussed and a short account given of the Ka'bah in Mecca, the shrine which was to become the center of Islam.

Before Mohammed's birth his father died at Medina.[33] At the

---

[28] A 6rs. This does not appear among the traditional signs of the end of the world, but cf. LJ i, 25,154.

[29] A 6rs. Cf. Gen., ch. 10; LJ i, 169-70, 175; ii, 289; v, 192-97.

[30] A 6rs. "The predestined essence of the last of the prophets is said to have been created first of all, in the form of a dense and luminous point"; Massignon, s.v. "Nūr Muḥammadi," EI iii, 961; see below, part 3.

[31] A 6rs-rd. See T. Hughes, op. cit., 216-20. Certain Arabic proper names have been changed back to their more customary spellings, since all but the most familiar biblical names are garbled in the Latin translations.

[32] A 6rd. This is the subject of the *Liber generationis Mahumet*; see below, part 3.

[33] A 6rd-vs. This account of Mohammed's life accords in the main with Islamic history and tradition. However, the tradition itself is subject to criticism by scholars, so the following works should be consulted: F. Buhl, s.v. "Muḥammad," EI iii, 641-57; L. Caetani, *Annali dell'Islam*, 10 vols. (Milan, 1905-26); W. Muir, *Life of Mahomet*, ed. T. Weir (Edinburgh, 1923); Buhl, *Das Leben Muhammeds*, tr. H. H. Schaeder (Leipzig, 1930); T. Andrae, *Mohammed, sein Leben und Glaube* (Göttingen, 1932); K. Ahrens, *Muhammed als Religionsstifter* (Leipzig, 1935); W. M. Watt, *Muhammad at Mecca* (Oxford, 1953); Watt, *Muhammad at Medina* (Oxford, 1956). The semiofficial biography of Ibn-Ishāq (d. 767) has been translated by A. Guillaume, *The Life of Muhammad* (London, 1955), and will be cited extensively below; references to the Arabic text are given in the margins of the translation.

age of six Mohammed accompanied his mother on a journey there; she fell ill and died on the return trip, and he was placed in the custody of his grandfather 'Abd-al-Muṭṭalib. The angel Seraphael,[34] "always heard but never seen," was given charge over him; later the angel Gabriel took over the task. At forty Mohammed began to receive the Koran through Gabriel and won a few followers. Then he was taken on a miraculous nocturnal journey to Jerusalem and to heaven.[35] He publicly taught that he was a prophet and converted many. One of Mohammed's sermons is recorded in which he admonishes abstention from evil and proclaims holy warfare (Arabic *jihād*) in the name of God. "And for such works," he is made to say, "I promise you paradise." Several of the first Moslems are mentioned by name; 'Umar, who became the second caliph, is given special mention.

The author then goes on to recount the famous Hijrah, Mohammed's emigration from Mecca to Medina. Later the direction of prayer was changed from Jerusalem to Mecca and Mohammed began armed conflict with unbelievers. His battles are recounted in some detail. They are followed by accounts of the delegations sent to secure the allegiance and tribute of the Arabian tribes, as well as those sent to the emperor Heraclius, the kings of Persia and Abyssinia, and the governor of Egypt.[36] The "Farewell Pilgrimage" to Mecca is described. A few months after Mohammed's return to Medina he took sick and died. He was buried in the place "which God had foreordained for his burial," namely, the chamber of his wife 'Ā'ishah.

Mohammed's son-in-law 'Ali is quoted in a description of the prophet as having possessed a rather large head, with a light and rosy complexion and a thick beard. Other descriptions and characterizations supplement 'Ali's, together with a tradition concern-

[34] Confused by Robert, and by Herman also, with the Seraphim, a choir of the angelic host.

[35] A 6vs-vd. See J. Horovitz, *s.v.* "Mi'rādj," EI III, 505-08; Muñoz Sendino, *La Escala de Mahoma*; Cerulli, *op. cit.*; Levi Della Vida, *op. cit.*

[36] A 7rs-vs. See Guillaume, *The Life of Muhammad*, 652; M. Hamidullah, *Documents sur la diplomatie musulmane à l'époque du Prophète et des khalifes orthodoxes* (Paris, 1935).

ing the inscription on the prophet's seal and a list of his pilgrimages to Mecca. Several traditions relating alleged prophecies concerning his successors close this section. The first of them says that Mohammed himself named the first three caliphs. A speech to 'Uthmān is quoted, including the words "it is no more difficult for a camel to go through a needle's eye than to enter paradise."[37] The speech concludes with an admonition to all his successors to observe the law and precepts of Islam. According to another tradition, Mohammed promised paradise to the first three caliphs; the rest of the caliphs would attain it, the tradition continues, only if they were properly commissioned by the Islamic community and distinguished themselves by just works. Still another tradition foresees the caliphs' wearing the humblest clothing for thirty years and then turning to personal adornment. A final tradition quotes Mohammed as having said that his work would be completed by Abu-Bakr and 'Umar.[38]

The last section of the *Fabulae Saracenorum* comprises seven biographical sketches of the first caliphs. The ordering of information in these sketches is close to the settled forms adopted by many later Islamic historians; for that reason detailed references are unnecessary.

The genealogies of Abu-Bakr trace him back four generations on both sides. It is said that he reigned "by common consent" and that, "by warring, he converted the wicked and unbelievers to the law of Islam." Several victims of his severe punishment are mentioned. He died of consumption and was buried near the prophet.[39] The second caliph, 'Umar, was "of the same branch of the tribe [of Quraysh] as the prophet." It was he who ordered special prayers to be said during the month of Ramaḍān and the whole of the Koran to be recited during that month. He was assassinated at the age of sixty-three after reigning for more than ten

[37] A 7vd; cf. Koran 7:38; Matt. 19:24.
[38] A 7vd-8vs. References to the traditions in this section are given by Wensinck, *A Handbook of Early Muhammadan Tradition*, 5-7, 234-36, 239-40.
[39] A 8vs-vd.

81

years. He had ordered his successor to be chosen from among seven men whom he named.[40] 'Uthmān "was beloved by all both before his conversion and even more greatly afterwards." He was known for his magnanimity and munificence. He is credited with having collected the Koran and established its text. After conquering many lands for Islam, he was assassinated; he had lived eighty-seven years, twelve of them as caliph. Several traditions about him are recorded, as well as the stated motive for his assassination—the restoration of a more godly rule—which the chronicler clearly does not credit.[41]

'Ali was chosen as caliph on the day of 'Uthmān's death, although there were "many dissenters," among whom was 'Ā'ishah. Her forces were defeated in the Battle of the Camel, after which 'Ali moved to Al-Kūfah. Soon afterward Mu'āwiyah and the son of 'Uthmān, "to avenge his father's blood," met 'Ali's forces for battle and the rebel forces called for arbitration. A treaty was concluded, but later, in his fifth year as caliph, 'Ali was assassinated. The eulogy at the end of this biographical sketch describes him as Mohammed's "Aaron." Many other traditions testify to his virtue.[42] 'Ali's son Al-Ḥasan, it is said, bore a close resemblance to the prophet. "Moved by piety," the chronicler states, he placed himself in Mu'āwiyah's hands and resigned the caliphate after five months. Mohammed is said to have predicted that "through this boy God will restore peace to two armies." A dream of Al-Ḥasan's concerning the caliphal succession is also recorded.[43]

The unity of the Islamic empire was preserved by Mu'āwiyah, the founder of the Umayyad dynasty. He won its allegiance and extended it farther into Christian territory. The chronicler describes him as "the firmest tutor of justice and good habits." His death came after a convulsion at the end of the eighteenth year of his reign, and he was buried in Damascus, the Umayyad capital. The stories which conclude the sketch emphasize 'Ali's unwillingness to appoint a successor, thereby rationalizing Al-Ḥasan's resignation. One person is quoted as saying that he had not seen,

[40] A 8vd-9rs. [41] A 9rs-vs. [42] A 9vs-10rs.
[43] A 10rs-rd.

"after the prophet," a better man than Mu'āwiyah, although another, more cautious, authority said, "Abu-Bakr was better."[44]

Yazīd, Mu'āwiyah's son, had been appointed his successor while the father was still alive, which marked the beginning of the dynastic caliphate. He is said to have had a paralytic ailment and reigned only a little more than three years. The traditions included in this sketch all point to the same moral: obedience to authority. They are meant to justify Yazīd's quelling of the rebellion led by 'Ali's son Al-Ḥusayn, aided by the citizens of Al-Kūfah, of which an account is given. The chronicle does not remark on the tremendous significance of this action of Yazīd's, which solidified the most important and enduring rift between Moslems.[45] Instead, it comes, at this point, to an abrupt end.

[44] A 10rd-vs. See H. Lammens, *Études sur le règne du calife omeyyade Mo'âwiya Ier* (Beyrouth, 1908).

[45] A 10vd-11rd. See Lammens, *Le califat de Yazîd Ier* (Beyrouth, 1921).

3 · THE *LIBER GENERATIONIS MAHUMET*

᛭ THE SECOND TRANSLATION bears the title *Liber generationis Mahumet et nutritia eius.*[46] Like the *Fabulae Saracenorum,* it contains a great many Judaeo-Islamic legends about creation and the lives of the patriarchs and prophets. The main purpose and theme of the book, however, is the tracing of a miraculous light through all the generations from Adam to Mohammed. Several stories of miraculous events connected with Mohammed's birth and childhood, some of which have Christian parallels, are appended to it. It apparently escaped the notice of scholars that Herman did not follow Robert's example in omitting the *isnād* at the beginning of the book. The first authority named is Ka'b al-Aḥbār; the last, Sa'īd ibn-'Umar. The Arabic original may thus be identified as the *Kitāb Nasab Rasūl Allāh,* of which we have at least two manuscripts of Spanish provenance.[47]

The work is clearly bound up with the doctrine of prophetic light (Arabic *nūr*) and an abundant *mawlid* ("birth") literature in Islam. The former made its appearance early in the eighth century, and is customarily attributed to "meditation on the Ḳur'ān, Persian stimuli, gnostic-Hermetic writings, [and] lastly and most tenaciously, Hellenistic philosophy."[48] Thus it is water from the same streams as some Christian uses of light.[49] The poet Kumayt (d. 743) was among the first to sing of a light emanating from Adam to Mohammed, and then into the family of 'Ali.[50] This notion found fertile ground among the Shī'ites, who explained it "either as 'spirit' transmitted from age to age

---

[46] A 11r-18r; Bibliander, *op. cit.,* 201-12.

[47] J. Ribera and M. Asín, *op. cit.,* 44, 50.

[48] T. de Boer, *s.v.* "Nūr," EI III, 955-56. See also Massignon, *op. cit.,* 961; Andrae, *Die Person Muhammads* (Stockholm, 1918), 313-26; W. Ivanow, "Notes sur l'*Ummu 'l-Kitâb* des Ismaëliens de l'Asie Centrale," *Revue des Études Islamiques,* VI (1932), 444-51.

[49] "It certainly required for its development the stimulus of Christian gnostic and Manichaean antecedents," Massignon, *op. cit.,* 961. See also E. Josi, *s.v.* "Nimbo," *Enciclopedia Cattolica,* VIII (Vatican City, 1952), 1884-87; H. Leclercq, *s.v.* "Nimbe," *Dictionnaire d'archéologie chrétienne et de liturgie,* XII, 1272-1312.

[50] De Boer, *op. cit.,* 955; see *Die Hāšimijjāt des Kumait,* ed. J. Horovitz (Leiden, 1904).

and from elect to elect, or as spermatic germ [Traducianism] inherited from male to male."[51] Later the primogeniture of a "luminous shadow" (Arabic *ẓill*) transmitted through the prophets was also taught.[52] The notion also had a place among the Sunnites, where it appeared less coherently among the mystics of the ninth century and later came "to dominate popular worship."[53]

The *mawlid* genre as such, "panegyrical poems of a very legendary character" devoted to Mohammed's birth and childhood, did not appear at so early a date.[54] Of course, there was a deep interest among Moslems in the details of the prophet's life from the very beginning, but the embellishments in the *mawlid* form were made possible by the celebration of the prophet's birthday, a festival instituted by the Shī'ite Fāṭimids of Egypt.[55] This festival reached Spain "sooner or later," but may not have been celebrated there when the *Liber generationis Mahumet* was written.[56] At any rate, works of the same genre found favor with the Ṣūfis and many Sunnites generally.

The book is introduced with the story of Ka'b al-Aḥbār, a Yemenite Jew who converted to Islam.[57] Ka'b knew, the work tells us, that the scriptures and astrology concurred in predicting that a new prophet was to arise. Having heard of Mohammed's birth, he went to him, observed his "manner and conversation," and recognized him as that promised prophet. In order to testify to that fact, he explained Mohammed's descent from Adam in the following manner.

When God created Adam, He told him of his "seed of light" which "shone like the sun in the round of its orb or the moon on a

[51] Massignon, *op. cit.*, 961.   [52] *Ibid.*   [53] *Ibid.*

[54] H. Fuchs, *s.v.* "Mawlid," EI III, 419-22.

[55] *Ibid.*, 421. See also A. Mez, *Die Renaissance des Islams* (Heidelberg, 1922), 403; I. Goldziher, *Vorlesungen über den Islam*, II (Heidelberg, 1925), 257; Goldziher, "Neuplatonische und Gnostische Elemente im Ḥadīth," *Zeitschrift für Assyriologie*, XXII (1908), 317-44.

[56] Fuchs, *op. cit.*, 421.

[57] See B. Chapira, "Légendes bibliques attribuées à Ka'b al-Aḥbār," *Revue des Études Juives*, LXIX (1919), 86-107; LXX (1920), 37-43; M. Perlmann, "A Legendary Story of Ka'b al-Aḥbār's Conversion to Islam," *The Joshua Starr Memorial Volume* (New York, 1953), 85-99.

bright moon-lit night." When Eve conceived Seth, the account continues, the light moved to him, and "God placed a limit between
the child and Satan."[58] When Adam felt death approaching, he
took Seth to his customary place of prayer and explained the
meaning of the light to him. Then Adam prayed to God to seal
a testament between them, and this was done in the presence of
seventy thousand angels. After Adam's death, Seth's wife (his
sister) gave birth to Enos, whom Seth warned of the divine command "to preserve the light and propagate it with dignity and
reverence."[59]

The light then descended from Enos to Chainan, and through
Enoch and Methuselah, Noah, and Shem, to Abraham, to whom
God said, "From your seed will come forth my friend and messenger, whose soul was mingled with your soul in the first creation of
souls,[60] whose word is in my virtue, whose name in heaven is
Aḥmad, on earth Muḥammad, [and] in paradise Abu-al-Qāsim."[61]
The light then descended to Ishmael, Abraham's son by Hagar,
which angered his other wife Sarah.[62] Ishmael's son Cedar
(Qaydar) was granted seven gifts: he was "powerful, courageous,
handsome, swift, equanimous, and a hunter and archer."[63] He
left his fatherland after having been commanded in a dream to
marry the only daughter of an Arabian king. His son accompanied
him to the "sanctuary of Abraham" at Mecca, but before they
reached their destination "the angel of death came and took out
[Cedar's] soul through the ear."[64]

After various other miraculous occurrences which the book
recounts in some detail, the light descends to men whose names
can be recognized from the *Fabulae Saracenorum* as the imme-

---

[58] A 111rs-vs. For Jewish legends on the birth of Seth, see LJ I, 121; v, 268, 273.

[59] A 111vd. See LJ I, 101, 102; v, 125-27, 162, 169.

[60] See above, note 30.

[61] A 111vd-12rd.

[62] A 12rd. At this point the account departs from the biblical story, of course;
cf. Gen. 16:15-16; 21:9-21.

[63] A 12rd; cf. Gen. 25:13.

[64] A 12rd-vd. See LJ I, 60.

diate ancestors of Mohammed. The first of them is ʿAbd-Manāf, "a powerful king over the four parts of the earth," whose son Hāshim was offered the daughters of "all the kings and princes in the world," but, "not unmindful of the divine admonition," chose an Arab woman as his wife. Hāshim's son ʿAbd-al-Muṭṭalib was fifteen years old when his father died, and was forthwith invested with the religious and political offices of his father. The miraculous light plays a central role in two long stories concerning him which the *Liber generationis Mahumet* includes. The first has to do with a prolonged drought which was relieved by rain after the light shone from ʿAbd-al-Muṭṭalib's face. The second concerns the attempted invasion of Mecca by Abrahah, the Abyssinian viceroy of Yemen.[65]

At the birth of ʿAbdallāh, ʿAbd-al-Muṭṭalib's youngest son, several miraculous signs indicated that the child was destined to be Mohammed's father. One of them was the liquefaction of a cloth "stained with the blood of Yaḥya ibn-Zakariyyā [John the Baptist]."[66] There were several attempts on ʿAbdallāh's life; one by seventy Jewish rabbis was thwarted when certain beings "who seemed to be men but were not" came to his aid. ʿAbdallāh married Āminah, and, on the night when Mohammed was conceived, God is said to have ordered the gates of heaven opened "in order that I may transfer the light of my messenger from the loins of ʿAbdallāh into the womb of Āminah."[67]

The book enumerates seven marvels which allegedly attended Mohammed's birth: idols were toppled, Lucifer plunged into the depth of the sea, the earth around Mecca was replenished, sorcerers and soothsayers lost their power, the thrones of kings were swept down, and God acknowledged the birth of "a faithful and blessed friend."[68] Āminah is said to have attested that the birth was pain-

---

[65] A 12vd-14vs. See Muir, *op. cit.*, cxvi-vii; Guillaume, *The Life of Muhammad*, 21-30.

[66] A 14vs. There is a considerable body of legend about the liquefaction of John the Baptist's blood; see Carra de Vaux, *s.v.* "Yaḥya," EI IV, 1148-49, who connects it with the liquefying blood of St. Januarius in Naples.

[67] A 14vd-15rs.

[68] A 15rs-vs.

less. Many miracles followed the delivery. Among others, three men with faces "radiant as the sun" came to him with gifts.[69] The first offered him an emerald basin with four pearl handles; the second presented him with a pitcher and bathed him seven times; the third either had nothing to offer or the compiler or translator omitted it. At the same time 'Abd-al-Muṭṭalib saw a vision which told him about his grandson, and he lost his speech for a week.[70] Even the angels are reported to have been jealous over the grace and power given to Mohammed.[71]

The *Liber generationis Mahumet* concludes with a long and famous tradition attributed to Ḥalīmah, a woman of the Saʿd tribe who is said to have nursed and cared for Mohammed until he was five years old.[72] According to this tradition, Ḥalīmah was commanded in a vision to go to Mecca and was greeted by name when she entered Āminah's chamber. When she took the child out of the house, a donkey prostrated itself before him and exclaimed, "This is the seal of the prophets, the lord of the messengers, better than those who went before, a friend of Almighty God." Some years later, the account goes on, Ḥalīmah was summoned by one of her sons to witness the curious spectacle of the opening and cleansing of Mohammed's breast by three more mysterious strangers. Then she was ordered by a soothsayer to return him to Mecca. There Mohammed disappeared while she stopped to talk with an elder at the main gate. He was later discovered in the midst of a vast multitude of evil spirits who were accusing him of having been born "for our ruination."[73] Ḥalīmah ran to 'Abd-al-Muṭṭalib, who girded on his sword and dispelled the spirits. When he had located his grandson, he took him into his house, and Ḥalīmah returned to her tribe.

[69] A 15vs-vd; cf. Matt. 2:1-12.
[70] A 15vd-16rs; cf. the story of Zachary, Luke 1:8-25.
[71] A 16rd. See Seligsohn, *op. cit.*, 127.
[72] A 16rd-18rd. See Guillaume, *The Life of Muhammad*, 70-73.
[73] A 18rs; cf. Luke 2:41-50; 4:34; Mark 1:24.

4 · THE *DOCTRINA MAHUMET*

HERMAN OF DALMATIA's second translation, the *Doctrina Mahumet*, is known in Arabic as the *Masā'il 'Abdillāh ibn-Salām*, the *"questions"* of 'Abdallāh ibn-Salām.[74] Manuscripts of the original work are very numerous, although they are sometimes listed under deceptively different titles.[75] There is at least one printed text,[76] an English translation which is very rare and not very useful,[77] and a study of the work in Dutch.[78] The work is, by its very nature, a marvellous seedbed for variants and a catchall for ad libitum comments by scribes. The task of preparing an edition of the Arabic text might well prove an impossibility.[79]

The work takes the form of an imaginary didactic dialogue, a form which enjoyed considerable success in both Islamic and Christian mediaeval literatures.[80] Even Herman's addition to the

---

[74] A 19r-25v (and half-folio 25 *bis*); Bibliander, *op. cit.*, 189-200.

[75] A number is often attached, e.g., "One hundred questions," "Fourteen hundred and four questions." See Steinschneider, *Polemische und apologetische Literatur in arabischer Sprache* (Leipzig, 1877), 110-14; Steinschneider, *Die arabische Literatur der Juden* (Frankfurt-am-Main, 1902), 8-9; and the ample bibliography in J. Horovitz, *s.v.* "'Abd Allāh ibn Salām," EI I, 31. I have relied chiefly upon MSS 2003/16 (1148 H) of the Garrett Collection and 2658 (ELS 3018) of the Yahuda Collection in the Princeton University Library.

[76] Cairo, 1867. The class mark in the New York Public Library is *OGC; this may be the only copy in the United States.

[77] N. Davis, *The Errors of Mohammedanism Exposed: or, A Dialogue between the Arabian Prophet and a Jew, translated from the Arabic* (Malta, 1847). As is clear from the title, it mistakes the character of the text; it has remained unknown to all bibliographical sources, and is not even listed in Davis' bibliography in the *Dictionary of National Biography*, v (London, 1921-22), 620-21.

[78] G. F. Pijper, *Het boek der duizend vragen* (Leiden, 1924); see the review by J. Horovitz in *Der Islam*, xvi (1927), 296-98. I am grateful to Professor Pijper for having called my attention to several important facts concerning this work.

[79] The edition is being considered by the *Corpus Scriptorum Christianorum Orientalium* of Louvain.

[80] W. Suchier, *L'Enfant sage* (Dresden, 1910); Suchier, *Altercatio Hadriani Augusti et Epicteti Philosophi* (Urbana, 1939); Islamic examples cited by Horovitz, *Der Islam*, xvi (1927), 297-98, and Perlmann, *op. cit.*, 88. I have noted parallels with the "Questions of the Queen of Sheba to Solomon"; LJ iv, 145. See also M. Grünbaum, *Neue Beiträge zur semitischen Sagenkunde* (Leiden, 1893); L. Blau, *s.v.* "Sheba, Queen of," *Jewish Encyclopaedia*, xi (1905), 235-36.

title, which portrays the work as possessing "great authority" among the Moslems, is an exaggeration, but Bibliander's gloss to the effect that it was written by "another prophet of the same spirit [as Mohammed's]" and "accepted among the authentic books" of Islam is, of course, quite false.[81] It is entirely true that quotations from the work are frequent throughout Arabic literature, but it can safely be assumed that Islamic theologians of any age would have regarded it as nothing better than a highly suspicious repository of predominantly rabbinical legend. Many of the questions are no more than riddles or tricky catechism questions.

The book opened as Mohammed was sitting among his companions in Medina. He was visited by Gabriel, who informed him that four "leaders of the Jews and teachers in Israel," headed by Abdia (who became 'Abdallāh), were coming to question him. Mohammed ordered 'Ali to go out to meet them, "having described each of the persons by name and appearance." The visitors were understandably impressed. Approaching the prophet, 'Abdallāh greeted him and explained his mission. He and his companions had come "to enquire of you the explanation of matters which are not clear to us from our own law." Being assured that they had come for serious inquiry and not merely to trick him, Mohammed gave permission for as many questions as they might wish to pose. Taking him at his word, 'Abdallāh produced "one hundred[82] principal questions which had been carefully chosen out of all of his law" and began the fascinating, if at times rather tedious and mechanical, questioning.[83]

To the first question, "Are you a prophet or a messenger?" Mohammed replied that he was, in fact, both, supporting himself with koranic quotations. In response to further questions he as-

[81] Bibliander, *op. cit.*, 189; "glossa tipica dell'idea che in occidente si facevano dei libri compresi nella Collectio Toletana," Cerulli, *op. cit.*, 391, note 5.

[82] According to my count, there are one hundred and twenty-five; it is probably fruitless to speculate as to which questions are meant to be subsumed by which others.

[83] A 19rs-rd. Herman reproduces the tone of the original Arabic very well in his translation. After each of Mohammed's replies, 'Abdallāh utters some phrase of assent.

serted that he preached the law of God, which is faith in God's unity and his own prophethood, final judgment, and the resurrection of the flesh. There is, he added, only one law of God. "What, then, do you say about the prophets who have gone before you?" 'Abdallāh asked. "The law or faith of all of them was one," Mohammed replied, "but the rites of different ones were certainly different." Mohammed then discoursed on the requirements for reaching heaven, emphasizing that true faith is the basic requirement.

"Tell us, if you please," 'Abdallāh then asked, "has God sent you a book?" Mohammed replied that God indeed had. The book is called "Al-Furqān"[84] because "its thoughts and images are divided into sections," and it did not come down to him "all at once, as the Law was given to Moses, the Psalms to David, and the Gospel to Christ." He mentioned the opening of the Koran and explained the *abjad*, a word symbol for God.[85] 'Abdallāh asked him to enumerate the four things which God had created with his own hands, which Mohammed proceeded to do: the highest paradise, the tree of Ṭūba, Adam, and the tablets of Moses.[86] "Who explained these things to you?" 'Abdallāh asked. "Gabriel, who was sent from the Lord of the Universe," was the prophet's reply, and he went on to say that the angel had come to him in the form of a man, "[standing] erect, never sleeping, eating, or drinking."

Mohammed was then asked to explain the symbolic meaning of the numerals up to one hundred.[87] One, he said, was God; two,

[84] A 19rd-vs. A synonym for *Al-Qur'ān, Al-Furqān* means "separation, distinction, proof," hence Mohammed's explanation. Within the Koran it is often used simply as "revelation," as in 3:2, 21:49, and 25:1; in the meaning "salvation," as in 8:42, Wensinck (EI II, 120) says it is "certainly an Aramaic loanword."

[85] A 19vs. *Abjad* ("alphabet") is a word compounded of the first four letters of the Arabic alphabet according to its original order; to each of the letters there corresponded a name of God, and eight such words designated the entire symbol; "on the basis of this mutual relationship of numeral and letter on the one side, and the symbols corresponding to them on the other, a whole system of practical mysticism has been erected," Weil, *s.v.* "Abdjad," EI I, 68-69.

[86] A 19vs; cf. above, note 16, and LJ I, 83; III, 119, 120.

[87] A 19vd-20rd. See E. Bischoff, *Die Mystik und Magie der Zahlen* (Berlin, 1920); V. F. Hopper, *Medieval Number Symbolism* (New York, 1938).

Adam and Eve; three, Michael, Gabriel, and Seraphael; four, the Law of Moses, the Psalms of David, the Gospel, and the Koran; five, the Islamic daily prayers; six, the days of creation; seven, the heavens; eight, the angels who will bear God's throne on Judgment Day; nine, the miracles of Moses; ten, the days of fasting. From eleven on, as might be supposed, things were considerably more strained; fourteen, for instance, was the number of candles around God's throne, and twenty-one was the day of the month of Ramaḍān when Solomon was born. When the number of thirty was reached, 'Abdallāh requested (not a moment too soon for the reader's peace of mind) that Mohammed might be a trifle more brief. Accordingly, he proceeded by tens to one hundred, which turned out to be the number of blows "inflicted as a scourging upon those found in adultery."

Mohammed then explained how the slime from which Adam was created emanated from the divine command, "Be!" Two angels, he said, are set over each individual to inscribe their good and evil deeds. God himself has a tablet of green emerald on which "everything that was or will be in heaven and on earth" is inscribed in words of pearl by a pen as long as "a journey of five hundred years" and as wide as "a journey of eighty years."[88] Heaven was created from smoke; there are, in fact, seven heavens beneath six seas which support a surprisingly varied hierarchy of things (including "spaces of light" and mountains) with God at the top. The sun and moon were created with equal brilliance, but Gabriel happened once to touch the moon with his wing when he was flying by, "and after that the moon was darkened."[89]

At 'Abdallāh's request Mohammed continued in this vein with a description of night, the winds, the sun, and the stars. He said that strange birds traverse the upper heavens; they are like "white snakes with horses' manes, hair like women's hair, and birds' wings" and "lay eggs on their tails." Several questions concerning

[88] A 2ord-vs. These are common rabbinical measurements; see LJ I, 11, 12, 70; II, 307-09; IV, 334; V, 17, 20; VI, 46, 423.

[89] A 20vs-21rs. On the heavens, see LJ I, 9, 10, 23; II, 194, 260; V, 9-11, 34, 36. Gabriel is also connected with light in rabbinical literature, LJ V, 70, and with the phases of the moon, LJ V, 164.

the differences between this world and "the other" followed. "Now," 'Abdallāh said, "I will bring up something else for you to start with." He asked a riddle: "What son is stronger than his father?" Mohammed's answer was "iron," indicating that it is stronger than the ore from which it is made. And fire is stronger than iron, water stronger than fire, and wind stronger than water.[90]

The next subject was Adam, the meaning of his name and the method of his creation.[91] Mohammed recounted the story of the forbidden fruit and traced the journeys of Adam and Eve after their expulsion from paradise.[92] Eve is said to have been created from Adam's left rib.[93] It was Adam who commenced the pilgrimage to Mecca; Gabriel shaved his head, and he circumcised himself.[94] Abraham was the next patriarch to be circumcised.[95]

A number of riddles followed. Typical of them were: "What land did the sun see once, but will never again see to the end of time?" Answer: "The bottom of the Red Sea." "What woman came forth only from a man, and what man only from a woman?" Answer: "Eve from Adam and Christ from the Virgin Mary." In response to a question about "two whose graves were lost," Mohammed recounted stories concerning the graves of "a certain Arab" and of Moses.[96]

[90] A 21rs-vs.

[91] A 21vs; see above, note 16.

[92] A 21vd; cf. LJ v, 97.

[93] A 21vd; cf. LJ v, 88.

[94] A 21vd; shaving is one of the requirements for the pilgrimage, and circumcision, while not mentioned in the Koran, is universally practiced as a religious rite among Moslems.

[95] A 21vd. The koranic material on Abraham, like most koranic material, is highly repetitive. A. Sprenger, *Das Leben und die Lehre des Mohammed* (Berlin, 1862), and C. Snouck Hurgronje, *Het Mekkaansche Feest* (Leiden, 1880), were among the first to point out that the koranic Abraham changes somewhat from the Meccan to the Medinese periods. See Kritzeck, "Jews, Christians, and Moslems," *The Bridge*, ed. J. M. Oesterreicher, III (New York, 1958), 87-91; LJ I, 239, 240, 262; IV, 360; v, 233, 234, 240, 245; VI, 151; Y. Moubarac, *Abraham dans le Coran* (Paris, 1958).

[96] A 25vd, 25²r; cf. the sixth and seventh questions of the Queen of Sheba, LJ IV, 147, and LJ III, 471-73; VI, 163, 410. Hitti, *op. cit.*, 182, refers to a Shī'ite tradition concerning 'Ali's grave which is similar to the first story.

Mohammed then explained why Jerusalem is the true center of the earth, how Noah's ark was built, and what happened at the end of the Deluge.[97] He told 'Abdallāh that a child resembles its father "when the sensual pleasure of the man is greater than that of the woman [in sexual intercourse]."[98] He denied that God had ever punished anyone without cause. He related that infidels will be permitted to enter heaven only if they obey God's command to leap into the river of hell on Judgment Day, and that the same opportunity will be afforded to those born blind, deaf, or mute. Ultimately, he said, the earth will be reduced to ashes by fire.[99]

"What stands under the seven earths?" 'Abdallāh asked. A bull, Mohammed answered, standing on a white stone resting on a mountain; beneath the mountain lie a succession of lands and seas, a fish "whose head is pointed toward the east," a litany of virtues followed by the Throne, the Tablet, the Pen, and the "greater name" of God. "And what is below that?" 'Abdallāh wanted to know. "You continue asking about the infinite," Mohammed replied. "What can be beyond? Beyond is the omnipotence of God."[100] 'Abdallāh then asked him to measure the world, and was surprised to hear that it measures only "the journey of one day," the journey of the sun.

'Abdallāh was curious to know about paradise and "the life of its inhabitants." Mohammed obliged him with an account of its golden floor ornamented with gems and cooled by rivers of milk, honey, and wine. 'Abdallāh seemed inclined to accept that account as sufficient, but Mohammed continued to explain that the blessed have everything they desire in paradise. They all have the proportions of Adam and the beauty of Christ. They eat a certain species of fish liver which is "more delectable than you can ever marvel

[97] A 22rs-rd. See LJ i, 171, 285; iii, 166; v, 117, 162, 186, 187, 208, 226, 253; vi, 68, 242, 245.

[98] A 22rd; cf. Lucretius, *De Rerum Natura*, lib. iv.

[99] A 22vs.

[100] A 22vs-23rs. Much of this view of the underworld is peculiarly Islamic, but there are some parallels in Indian legends; see J. Meyer, *Die Hölle im Islam* (Basel, 1901); M. Reinaud, *Géographie d'Aboulfeda*, i (Paris, 1848), clxxxi-ii.

about," as well as the fruits of trees, and they drink from the rivers. ʿAbdallāh was rather anxious about that answer, and timidly asked how the food was eliminated. Irrelevantly pointing out that the embryo in the womb does not eliminate food, Mohammed went on to admit that the excrement of the blessed is in the form of fragrant perspiration.[101]

He was careful to add that the blessed will have no desire for "forbidden things" like the flesh of swine. "Why, bless me, most excellent Mohammed," ʿAbdallāh exclaimed, "God has also forbidden that to us Jews, and I know it is not without reason." Indeed not; Mohammed then embarked on an unsavory tradition concerning the prohibition of pork, the substance of which is that a problem of sanitary engineering had arisen in Noah's ark and was exacerbated by the presence of a large pig. Even the indefatigable ʿAbdallāh was quick to grant that "this is enough, lest we digress any further from our subject." He was interested to know whether the blessed copulate, and Mohammed insisted that they do, since "if any kind of pleasure were missing, beatitude would not be complete." ʿAbdallāh then asked how it is that wine can be drunk in paradise. Mohammed told the story of the angels Hārūt and Mārūt, who permitted themselves to be seduced by the most beautiful woman on earth after having drunk wine.[102] Apparently that established the taste and redeemed the vintage.

In reply to a request from ʿAbdallāh "to run briefly over" the description of hell, Mohammed delivered himself of a grisly and genuinely fearsome account of the punishments awaiting the damned. An account of Judgment Day followed that. The Angel of Death, he said, would be ordered to slay all living creatures and then himself; the suicide would be accomplished by suffocation

---

[101] A 23rs-vs.

[102] A 23vs-24rd. See Koran 2:96; Wensinck, *s.v.* "Hārūt and Mārūt," EI II, 272-73, who mentions this legend; LJ v, 160; J. de Menasce, "Une légende indo-iranienne dans l'angélologie judéo-musulmane, à propos de Hārūt et Mārūt," *Etudes Asiatiques*, I (1947), 10-18; H. C. Puech, "De la mythologie indo-iranienne à la légende juive et musulmane des anges Azael et Semhazzai ou Hārūt et Mārūt," *Revue d'histoire des religions*, CXXXIII (1947-48), 221-25; Leo Jung, *Fallen Angels in Jewish, Christian, and Mohammedan Literature* (Philadelphia, 1926), 124-39.

with his wings.[103] Then the earth would remain empty for four hundred years, during which time God would deliver several speeches to himself concerning the ephemeral nature of earthly empires. After that the trumpet would sound, "the souls will put on their bodies," and all would repair to Jerusalem for judgment.[104]

Mohammed assured his questioner that the appeals which frightened souls might make to the patriarchs and prophets on Judgment Day would be to no avail. God would place a bridge over hell, and at the head of the bridge a scale; "all the acts of each man having been weighed, they will walk over the bridge. The saved will go across, the damned will fall." 'Abdallāh asked the number of the saved and damned. Of the one hundred and twenty legions of men, Mohammed replied, only three would comprise the saved. 'Abdallāh's final question was: "What will become of death?" Mohammed replied: "Death will be changed into a ram,[105] and they will lead it out between heaven and hell. And there will be a great struggle between the inhabitants of both regions. . . . The people of heaven, for fear of death, will plot its destruction; the people of hell, in the hope of dying, will desire it to survive. The people of heaven will win, and will kill death between heaven and hell."[106]

With the questioning finished, only a suitable flourish was needed by way of conclusion. What more inevitable flourish than the conversion of 'Abdallāh? "At this point the Jew, exclaiming, said, 'You have been victorious, most excellent Mohammed. Stop, and receive me as one professing faith [in Islam]. I believe, as I see, that there are no gods but God the One, whose messenger and prophet you truly are.' "[107]

---

[103] A 24rd-vd. See Meyer, *op. cit.* This account follows Jewish legend closely; see LJ I, 101, 102, 320; III, 31, 98-99, 302, 443, 460; IV, 66, 70; V, 77, 204, 242; VI, 104, 237. On the Angel of Death, see LJ I, 306; II, 308; III, 475; V, 16, 26, 56, 57, 123, 312; VI, 153, 162.

[104] A 24vd-25rs.   [105] See LJ V, 312.

[106] A 25rd-vs.   [107] A 25vs-vd.

5 · THE KORAN

❦ Robert of Ketton's translation of the Koran has proven itself the most famous item in the Toledan Collection.[108] It is by far the longest of the translations, and evidently required the greatest period of time to complete—rather more than a year.[109]

It is not the purpose of this part of the chapter to summarize the contents of the Koran, or even to dwell on the problems connected with it which are claiming (some, indeed for the first time) the attention of scholars today.[110] It must suffice to indicate the Koran's unique right to a place in the collection and to discuss two particular questions which have a bearing on its place there: the question of the prohibition of koranic translations in Islam and the question of this translation's claim to have been the first.

The Koran is the title of the scripture which is believed by Moslems to constitute divinely revealed truth. They hold that this revelation was transmitted to Mohammed through the instrumentality of the angel Gabriel, and that it is, word for word, the dictation of God. Thus Mohammed was in no sense, according to the Moslems, the author of the book; he merely memorized the words and recited them to the people. Although much of the book may have been written down during the lifetime of the prophet, its text was arranged and canonized only after his death. It comes down to us in that same form of one hundred and fourteen chapters (called *sūrahs*), arranged (except for the first) in an order roughly determined by length, with the longest second and one of the shortest last. Although it had rabbinical precedents, that would seem to have been a singularly unsuitable method for

---

[108] A 25v (copied from Bibliander, *op. cit.*, 8) -138r; Bibliander, *op. cit.*, 8-188.

[109] See above, chapter I, note 116.

[110] T. Nöldeke, F. Schwally, G. Bergsträsser, and O. Pretzl, *Geschichte des Qor'āns*, 3 vols. (2nd ed., Leipzig, 1909-38), is still, and will doubtless long remain, the best history of the Koran. See also A. Jeffery, *Materials for the History of the Qur'ān* (Leiden, 1937), and R. Blachère, *Le Coran*, 3 vols. (Paris, 1947-50), particularly the first volume, which contains the best summary of work on the text and a valuable bibliography, xliii-ix; it is regrettable that the information about the Toledan Collection (vii-ix) is so faulty.

ordering the chapters of the Koran, inasmuch as the shorter ones are generally held to have preceded the longer ones in revelation or composition. Each chapter has a title, usually derived from some striking reference within it, an indication of its place of revelation (Mecca or Medina), and all but the ninth begin with the invocation, "In the name of God, the merciful, the compassionate."[111] At the beginning of twenty-nine chapters there are certain mysterious initial letters which have been explained in a variety of ways.[112]

Scholars have long applied themselves to reclassifying the chapters, insofar as possible, according to the evidence for the dates of composition; but the systematic study of the history of the text —no easy mater—is far from finished.[113] The question of the sources of the Koran, which, of course, is not posed by Moslems, is also a complicated one. A good deal of biblical material is included, sometimes with differences or embellishments which are traceable to rabbinical or Christian apocryphal literature; references to events in Arabian history lend themselves to study in relation to other types of historical evidence.[114]

Robert of Ketton indicated in his preface to the translation that he had experienced considerable difficulty with it.[115] Among the many liberties he took with the text was a redivision of the chapters, which he began by dividing the second chapter into three separate parts and continuing that policy wherever he thought it necessary; he ended with nine more chapters than the traditional number. On the basis of his occasional biting remarks concerning the Koran's style and content it might be thought that Peter the Venerable underestimated its place among Moslems; but he was

---

[111] The number of verses is also given, and there are separate methods of division based upon the liturgical use of the text.

[112] Nöldeke *et al., op. cit.,* II, 68-78.

[113] See Blachère, *op. cit.,* I, 240-63.

[114] See especially J. Fück, "Die Originalität des arabischen Propheten," *Zeitschrift der deutschen morgenländischen Gesellschaft,* N.F. xv (1936), 509-25; and J. Obermann, "Islamic Origins: A Study in Background and Foundation," *The Arab Heritage,* ed. Nabih A. Faris (Princeton, 1946), 58-120. A summary of the questions is given in Kritzeck, "Jews, Christians, and Moslems," 92-102.

[115] MS 3390. 28vs; BC 1116D.

fully aware, as will be demonstrated in its proper context, that the Koran was the unique and divinely authored scripture of Islam. His recommendations of the apology of Al-Kindi do not cancel out that recognition; rather the apology, which was to form the basis for his own *Liber contra sectam sive haeresim Saracenorum,* was being recommended for quite another reason.

Because of the peculiarly stringent notion of revelation in Islam, assisted by the success of the Islamic armies and the spread of the Arabic language, there has been and remains in Islam a strong prohibition against translating the Koran into other languages.[116] The Koran itself emphasizes that Arabic was specifically chosen as the language of God's final revelation, and the Arabs have understandably taken great pride in the fact. In the early years of Islam, and even after Arabic was imposed by conquest, the question of translation seldom arose. Eventually, however, it was bound to arise, and the orthodox view of Islamic theologians and legists, adhered to with striking uniformity, was that the Koran was incapable of being translated because of the inimitability (Arabic *i'jāz*) of its language, but that paraphrase (especially in connection with commentary) or interlinear annotations in foreign languages were acceptable.[117] To this day most Moslem leaders consistently refuse to authorize or recognize the accuracy of any translation, although many translations have been published and a few groups no longer seem inclined to obey the prohibition.[118] It is therefore

[116] To my knowledge, the prohibition was never made the subject of special treatises, nor have the sources for it been gathered together; it is therefore impossible to arrive at certain conclusions regarding its strength and persistence.

[117] See W. Woolworth, "A Bibliography of Koran Texts and Translations," *The Moslem World,* v (1915), 244-61; S. Zwemer, "Translations of the Koran," *The Moslem World,* xvii (1927), 279-89; Zwemer, *Studies in Popular Islam* (London, 1939), 80-99.

[118] *Al-Manār,* xxvii, 160, 794. M. Pickthall, a convert to Islam and the most popular English translator of the Koran, wrote: "The Koran cannot be translated. That is the belief of the old-fashioned Sheykhs and the view of the present writer. The Book is here rendered almost literally and every effort has been made to choose befitting language. But the result is not the Glorious Koran," *The Meaning of the Glorious Koran* (New York, 1953), vii. No traditional legist could have condoned so fine a distinction. Compare B. M. Ahmad, *Introduction to the Study of the Holy Quran* (London, 1949), 440-41.

particularly interesting that a Moslem took part in the translating of the Koran for Peter the Venerable.[119]

Robert's translation of the Koran has customarily been regarded
as the first complete translation in any language. Mingana discovered evidence for the existence of an early Syriac translation,
but that may have been only a partial translation.[120] Claims made
for early Berber and Turkish translations have not been substan-
tiated; if genuine, they would antedate Robert's version, but it
appears likely that they were no more than commentaries or
fragmentary annotations. The claim for a Persian translation, on
the other hand, is quite firmly established.[121] The Sāmānid ruler
Abu-Ṣāliḥ Manṣūr ibn-Nūḥ (961-76) is known to have sponsored
a Persian translation of the famous commentary on the Koran by
Al-Ṭabari. If one assumes that this would qualify as a translation
of the Koran, the claim is considerably weakened by the fact that
this translation was also, and to a large extent, an abridgement.[122]
There do not seem to be other contenders prior to the twelfth
century. It would seem perfectly proper, therefore, on the basis of
present evidence, to continue to accord to Robert of Ketton the
honor of having been the first translator of the entire Koran.[123]

[119] See above, chapter II, part 6.
[120] A. Mingana, "An Ancient Syriac Translation of the Ḳur'ān Exhibiting New
Verses and Variants," *Bulletin of the John Rylands Library, Manchester,* ix (1925),
188-235.
[121] C. A. Storey, *Persian Literature: A Bio-bibliographical Survey,* 1:2 (London,
1935), 61.
[122] *Ibid.*; see also R. Paret, *s.v.* "Al-Ṭabari," EI iv, 578-79; Nöldeke *et al., op. cit.,*
ii, 139-42, 171-73; Goldziher, *Die Richtungen der islamischen Koranauslegung*
(Leiden, 1920), 85-98, 101ff.
[123] Hitti, *op. cit.,* 126, 127, note 1; von Grunebaum, *op. cit.,* 50.

6 · THE *EPISTOLA SARACENI* AND *RESCRIPTUM CHRISTIANI*

THE LAST TRANSLATION of the Toledan Collection is that of the work known in Arabic as *Risālat ʿAbdillāh ibn-Ismāʿīl al-Hāshimi ila ʿAbd-al-Masīḥ ibn-Isḥāq al-Kindi wa-Risālat al-Kindi ila al-Hāshimi.*[124] Peter the Venerable considered this fruit of the collaboration of Peter of Toledo and Peter of Poitiers as the most valuable of the translations for the Christian reader, an opinion given unrelated support by the fact that the work has come to be the best-known Christian apology in Arabic.[125] The Arabic text was edited by Anton Tien for the Turkish Mission Aid Society,[126] but better manuscripts have been discovered and collated.[127] Muñoz Sendino published an edition of the Latin translation in 1949, but did not make use of the Arsenal manuscript, which provides better readings throughout and supplies many passages omitted entirely in that edition.[128] Muir paraphrased and translated portions of the work into English in 1882,[129] and it has been studied in detail by many other scholars, including Casanova, Massignon, and Graf.[130] Armand Abel has indicated that he will publish a book or series of articles on the

---

[124] A 140r-178r; omitted by Bibliander.

[125] See H. P. Smith, "Moslem and Christian Polemic," *Journal of Biblical Literature*, XLV (1926), 243-45; E. Fritsch, *Islam und Christentum im Mittelalter* (Breslau, 1930); P. Kraus, "Beiträge zur islamischen Ketzergeschichte," *Rivista degli studi orientali*, XIV (1933-34), 335-41.

[126] London, 1880; reprinted in Cairo in 1885 and 1912.

[127] L. Cheikho, "Catalogue raisonné des manuscrits de la Bibliothèque Orientale. VI: Controverses," *Mélanges de l'Université Saint-Joseph*, XIV (1929), 43-48 (nos. 663-69), and G. Graf, *Catalogue de manuscrits arabes chrétiens conservés au Caire* (Vatican City, 1934), 204 (no. 542).

[128] "La Apologia del Cristianismo de al-Kindi," *Miscelánea Comillas*, XI-XII (1949), 339-460.

[129] *The Apology of Al-Kindy* (London, 1882).

[130] Casanova, *Mohammed et la fin du monde*, 2 vols. (Paris, 1913), especially I, 110ff.; II, 228-29; Massignon, *s.v.* "Al-Kindi," EI II, 1021; Graf, *Geschichte der christlichen arabischen Literatur*, II (Vatican City, 1947), 135-45. Graf considered Al-Kindi a Nestorian, but Mlle d'Alverny disagreed, "Deux traductions du Coran au Moyen Age," 88; "Pierre le Vénérable et la légende de Mahomet," 168.

work; therefore, discussion here will be limited to those aspects of the work which bear directly upon the main subjects of this study and the summary of the contents will be correspondingly brief.

The work consists, as both its Arabic and Latin titles indicate, of two letters. The first purports to have been written by a Moslem closely related to the caliph Al-Ma'mūn (regn. 813-33); the second, a reply to the first, by a Christian in the service of that caliph. Al-Ma'mūn is said to have heard of these letters and ordered them read to him by their authors.[131] It is highly probable that both of the authors are fictionary, although a few elements in the work suggest that they are not.[132] Al-Bīrūni (973-1048) testifies that the work was current in his time,[133] and Massignon has dated it from the beginning of the tenth century.[134] The many koranic passages included in this translation of the work differ entirely from Robert of Ketton's version.

The first letter, that of Al-Hāshimi, opens with a salutation of peace and mercy upon the Christian, for which Mohammed's authority is cited. There follow various expressions of esteem and references to Al-Kindi's noble birth, his piety, culture, and learning.[135] Forthwith Al-Hāshimi invites his friend to faith in Islam and, as a preliminary step in that direction, since they are both familiar with each other's creeds, to an orderly exposition of the two religions. The Moslem makes something of a point of the added strength his invitation takes on in the light of his apprecia-

[131] Such an action would not have been out of character for Al-Ma'mūn, who was jokingly called *amīr al-ḳāfirīn* ("the commander of the unbelievers") because of his fondness for theological and philosophical disputation with non-Moslems.

[132] Their names, for example, too perfectly mirror their positions, and do not appear in other sources; see Massignon, "Al-Kindi," 1021.

[133] *Chronologie*, ed. E. Sachau (London, 1878), 205.

[134] "Al-Kindi," 1021; cf. Muir, *The Apology of Al-Kindy*, v; Graf, *Geschichte der christlichen arabischen Literatur*, II, 141; d'Alverny, "Deux traductions du Coran au Moyen Age," 88-91; Muñoz Sendino, "La Apologia del Cristianismo de al-Kindi," 344-55; Kraus, *op. cit.*, 335.

[135] The opening of the *Epistola Saraceni* is missing from the Arsenal manuscript. The tribe of Kindah was indeed a very distinguished one in pre-Islamic times; see W. Caskel, "Die einheimischen Quellen zur Geschichte Nord-Arabiens vor dem Islam," *Islamica*, III (1927), 336-41.

tion of Christianity's many good points; in his view, Al-Kindi has only to renounce his errors and return to the faith of their common father, Abraham. He recounts the major tenets of Islamic doctrine, including prayer, fasting, the pilgrimage, and holy war, and dwells on the delights of heaven according to the Islamic view. If Al-Kindi were to accept Islam, Al-Hashimi says, he would acquire the privilege of marrying four wives liable to divorce and could expect advancement at court. Having completed his invitation, he concludes with an affectionate appeal to his friend to consider it carefully, adding an assurance that he might reply to it without fear, if he wished to do so, "under royal guarantee of absolute security."[136] The case for Islam is undersold and even purposely weakened in Al-Hashimi's letter—a fact which suggests a Christian author or editor.

Al-Kindi's reply is fully six times longer than the Moslem's letter, and leaves the desired impression that the latter got the worst of the argument. It begins with a complimentary address expressing gratitude for Al-Hashimi's interest and including a prayer for the caliph. Al-Kindi asks the guidance of Christ, who promised help when his servants were brought before kings and governors (Matt. 10:18-19). The dogma of the Trinity is the first to be defended by Al-Kindi; he outlines certain metaphysical demonstrations and Old Testament prefigures of that dogma, insisting that the Koran misrepresents it completely by following the ideas of Jews and Christian heretics.[137]

Turning then to Mohammed, Al-Kindi assures his correspondent that he will say nothing offensive against Al-Hashimi's prophet, but only scrutinize his claim to prophethood. He summarizes the facts concerning Mohammed's life, praising his desire to reform the religious beliefs and moral lives of the Arabs but decrying his sanction of raids and plundering to achieve that end. He includes rather lengthy accounts of the prophet's military expeditions; in some details, as Muir pointed out, these accounts are

[136] A 145vd-46rs; Muir, *The Apology of Al-Kindy*, 2.
[137] A 147rs-49vd.

erroneous.[138] "Still stranger and more flagrant," Al-Kindi adds, "were the assassinations, banishments, and robberies" which Mohammed sanctioned.[139] He then alludes to the injuries which Mohammed suffered at the Battle of Uḥud, suggesting that God would have delivered a genuine prophet from injury.[140] Finally he mentions Mohammed's custom of "taking many beautiful women to wife" and accuses him of having neglected God in favor of his wives; "I am sure that no prophet in olden times resembled him in this respect."[141]

Al-Kindi then raises the subject of prophecy. Because his distinctions in the matter are repeated by Peter the Venerable in the *Liber contra sectam sive haeresim Saracenorum*, they will be discussed in a later chapter. Al-Kindi himself makes shorter work of the Islamic claims in this regard than Peter was to do, insisting that most of Mohammed's pronouncements "tell us what we already knew, and what even our children read at school," while the traditions about him are "witless fables and old wives' tales, such as we Arabs hear night and day, and are no proof whatever of a divine mission."[142]

As for the evidence of miracles, Al-Kindi reminds the Moslem that Mohammed himself disavowed them in the Koran, and he is inclined to believe that the reason for that disavowal was "because he did not have the power of performing them."[143] The success of the Islamic conquest cannot be interpreted as proof of miraculous intervention, he says, inasmuch as it may only have been God's way of punishing ungodly people. He quotes and discusses several alleged miracles of Mohammed as related in the traditions. It was Mohammed himself, the apologist says, who cut the ground out from under such fables by asserting that those not in accord with the Koran were to be considered false.[144] Mohammed's claim was enforced by the sword, he charges, not by miracles; and it had been precisely their miracles that had justified some of the proph-

[138] A 150rs-51rd; Muir, *The Apology of Al-Kindy*, 5, note 1.
[139] A 151rd; Muir, *The Apology of Al-Kindy*, 5-8.
[140] A 151vs; Muir, *The Apology of Al-Kindy*, 8.
[141] A 151vd-52vs.   [142] A 153rs.
[143] A 153vs.   [144] A 153vs-54rd.

ets of the Old Testament in their use of the sword. Al-Kindi recapitulates this argument by contrasting the miracles and spread of Christianity with those of Islam.[145]

The Christian apologist then turns to the Koran, quoting stories about the assistance supposedly rendered Mohammed by a Nestorian monk and by two Jews, 'Abdallāh and Ka'b.[146] He accuses the Moslems of disregarding the variants and discrepancies "which are known to have existed" in the versions of the Koran which preceded the canonized text of the caliph 'Uthmān. All of this, he insists, "is drawn from your own authorities." He scoffs at the claim that the language of the Koran is unsurpassed in beauty, since he has found that every nation considers its own language to be the most beautiful, and "Arabic is regarded by other nations as barbarous." Moreover, if the Arabic of the Koran is perfect, why are there so many loanwords in it? For his own part, he considers the Arabic of Amru' al-Qays, one of the pre-Islamic poets, as superior to that of the Koran, and in a breach of good manners reminds the Moslem that his own ancestors were Arabian princes when Mohammed's were only merchants.[147]

It was the material inducement, Al-Kindi claims, and the promise of the pleasures of an entirely sensual paradise that tempted the Arabs to join Islam. Its armies were full of hypocrites, renegades, and apostates. He ridicules the notion that Mohammed's name is inscribed on God's throne and has no time for the claim that Ishmael inherited prophethood from Abraham.[148] He does, however, take up the ceremonies of Islam in some detail. The pilgrimage to Mecca he views as idolatrous, and Islamic legislation respecting marriage and divorce as downright pagan, while the holy war is purely and simply "the work of Satan." He throws into the argument several sets of contradictory passages

[145] A 154rd-55vs.

[146] A 156rs; no doubt 'Abdallāh ibn-Salām and Ka'b al-Aḥbār, the alleged authorities for the *Doctrina Mahumet* and the *Liber generationis Mahumet*, which again suggests a skilled polemical hand (Peter of Toledo's?) behind their inclusion in the collection.

[147] A 157vs.

[148] A 157vs-59rs; see LJ v, 67; vi, 272.

from the Koran. He says he knows that the Moslem's reply will be that some of these texts were abrogated, but he is moved to ask how it can be known with certainty "which one cancels and which is cancelled."[149]

Although he does so with some hesitancy, Al-Kindi then contrasts the ministry of Christ with that of Mohammed, and attempts to demonstrate that the latter's intention was not, like Christ's, to redeem and perfect man, but rather, "like other conquerors, to extend his empire." He illustrates the difference with several stories of Christian conversions and martyrdoms. At this point he seems to fear that he has gone too far. He apologizes for the warmth of his expressions, but emphasizes the need for freedom of expression in these matters, expressing gratitude to the caliph for the guarantee of security. He states further that advancement at court holds nothing for him if, to secure it, he must deny Christ. There is likewise nothing appealing to him in the representation of Islam as an "easy" way of faith and practice.[150]

The apologist reviews several of the points he has sought to establish, by way of conclusion. In doing so, he pays special attention to the remnants of Christian truth which he has perceived in Islam. He identifies Christianity with "the upright path" mentioned in the first chapter of the Koran, verse 5, and urges Al-Hāshimi to study it more closely. To assist his friend, he gives a brief account of the life of Christ, beginning with an analysis of the Old Testament prophecies concerning him. He defends the Jewish and Christian scriptures against the Islamic charges that they were corrupted and falsified and cites passages from the Koran which appear to have been derived from them. He then explains the Christian doctrine of inspiration and once again contrasts the spread of the "good tidings" of Christianity by "the wonderful works and signs of the Apostles, and their lives and conversation," with the spread of Islam.[151]

The *Rescriptum* proper has reached an end. Al-Kindi urges Al-Hāshimi to "consider what you will of what I have set before you . . . and judge between us righteously." He reminds the

[149] A 159rs-62vs.   [150] A 162vs-70vd.   [151] A 170vd-76rs.

Moslem that nothing is more important than truth and salvation. For his part, he feels that he has replied to the best of his ability; it remains for God to bring the work to fruition in his friend's soul.[152] At the end of the text is a brief anecdote, missing from most manuscripts and in part imperfectly deleted in the Arsenal manuscript, relating Caliph Al-Ma'mūn's curious judgment on the presentations—that Christianity is the faith "of this world" and Islam that "of the other."[153] There is also a poetic scribal finis, of customary form and sentiment, to the collection as a whole.[154]

[152] A 176rd.

[153] A 176rd-77vd; the anecdote appears in some of the Arabic manuscripts, but not in all.

[154] A 178rd. "Omnis honor mundi fluit ut maris unda profundi:
  Ubertas rerum, formae decor, ordo dierum,
  Es, lapis, argentum, vis, gloria, legata parentum,
  Ut flos arescunt, ut nixque gelusque liquiescunt."
For "legata," Martin, *op. cit.*, 317, read "legma."

7 · THE CHOICE AND ACCURACY
OF THE TRANSLATIONS

PETER THE VENERABLE had every reason to be satisfied that the fund of information in the Toledan Collection was sufficient to provide a more complete and accurate picture of Islam than had hitherto been available to most European Christians. Naturally he was too occupied to learn Arabic himself, and therefore had to rely altogether upon the integrity and ability of his translators in the matter of the accuracy of the translations. The presence among them of a Moslem certainly increased the probability that no major error or misinterpretation of fact would occur, though it could not guarantee it.

It would be difficult to say whether Peter had much to do with the choice of the texts to be translated. As has already been suggested, the apology of Al-Kindi may well have sparked the project and Peter of Toledo probably proposed the other works and won the abbot's approval.[155] There can be no doubt whatever that all of the works are what they are represented to be and that what is contained in them, however heterodox or fabulous, has at least some basis in Islamic scripture, theology, law, history, or legend. In attempting to determine the value of the choice for Peter's purposes, however, we are greatly handicapped by the paucity of exact information as to which Arabic books were available in Christian Spain at this time.[156] It would not seem an extravagant assumption, in light of the known translations, that quite a large store of such books had fallen into Christian hands.

Certainly the Koran, as the supreme source of Islamic doctrine, was an obvious and fundamental choice; the value of its presence in the collection, especially when one considers the number of times it is quoted directly in the other works, can hardly be

---

[155] See above, chapter II, part 2.

[156] See F. Pons Boïgues, *Ensayo bio-bibliográfico sobre los historiadores y géografos arábigo-españoles* (Madrid, 1878); H. Derenbourg, *Les manuscrits de l'Escurial,* 2 vols. (Paris, 1884-1903); and J. M. Millás Vallicrosa, *Las traducciones orientales en los manuscritos de la Biblioteca Catedral de Toledo* (Madrid, 1942).

overemphasized. The material on the lives of Mohammed and the early caliphs in the *Fabulae Saracenorum* was an excellent addition because of its fairly representative selection of traditions and its general accord with historical facts almost entirely unknown in Europe at the time. No doubt, Ibn-Isḥāq's biography of the prophet and some such detailed history as Al-Ṭabari's would have been better choices, if they had been available, but their length has discouraged translators even up to our own times.[157] Herman's translations, the *Liber generationis Mahumet* and the *Doctrina Mahumet,* were decidedly the weakest selections. The former, by arranging so much *spurii* and trivia in a context subject by its very nature to scorn by Christian readers, proved an almost total washout in terms of providing accurate information (though it gave Peter of Poitiers a chuckle), and the latter was at best of doubtful orthodoxy and at worst completely silly. Practically any works of systematic theology would have been preferable to them. Still, even they had the advantage of repeating a great deal of Judaeo-Islamic legend and manifesting popular Islamic lore, thereby communicating at least Islam's essential connection with the main stream of Semitic religion, an indisputable boon to readers unfamiliar with this side of Islam's nature. The presence of the apology of Al-Kindi was a master stroke. It is surely one of the more perceptive and comprehensive of the Christian apologies against Islam, and probably one of the very few available to the translators.[158] Not only did it set Islamic doctrine in some perspective for the Christian reader, but it supplied Peter the Venerable with a ready-made approach for his own works of summary and refutation—a fact which saved him endless time and protected him from going far astray in the evaluation and interpretation of the other translations in the collection.

Much of the Toledan Collection, as one would expect, was doomed to become mere jetsam, scraps of truth and legend never

[157] Guillaume, *The Life of Muhammad; Annales quos scripsit . . . At-Ṭabari,* ed. M. de Goeje, 15 vols. (Leiden, 1879-1901).

[158] See, however, D. M. Dunlop, "A Christian Mission to Muslim Spain in the 11th Century," *Al-Andalus,* XVII (1952), 259-310.

to be cited by any writers and never to appear in any other form.[159] Peter's motivation and talent were evidenced in what he selected and what he rejected from all of this material. It should also be remarked that although he confined himself very largely to the information provided by the translations, he did not rely on it exclusively. He consulted other sources, notably Theophanes, and utilized some information presumably acquired as a result of inquiry while he was in Spain.

The question of the accuracy of the translations is, of course, a central one. However, no final pronouncements on the subject can or should be made until the translations are carefully and completely compared with the Arabic texts, some of which will have to be reconstructed, at least in part. The problems concerning the relationship of the Arabic texts to the Latin translations are obviously entirely different from those concerning the origin and character of the works themselves. I have been inclined to leave the former to scholars more interested in them and better equipped to deal with them than I. Nevertheless, a few remarks on the subject are called for.

When one considers the word-for-word accuracy of the translations, the situation appears to be completely reversed from that of their value as sources. Both of Herman's translations, the *Liber generationis Mahumet* and the *Doctrina Mahumet,* are so literal and precise that the Arabic texts from which they were translated could probably be reconstructed without difficulty. Robert's translations, on the other hand, tend to be florid, wordy, and often obscure. Just how much this difference is to be attributed to their respective abilities in the languages and how much to the texts themselves defies comment at this stage of the study. One might assume, since they learned Arabic together and since Robert's weakness for rhetorical bombast carried over into his Latin prose, that that constitutes a genuine stylistic difference between them.[160]

[159] Daniel, *op. cit.*, 229-307.
[160] See above, chapter II, parts 4 and 5.

The translation of the Koran poses a special problem, since the style of the original itself is by no means easy to comprehend. Robert's solution to this difficulty, as he explained to Peter the Venerable, was to sacrifice absolute accuracy for comprehension. In the process of doing so, he took liberties which produced some almost comic results.[161] Darío Cabanelas, who has studied the translation carefully, distinguished two classes of imperfections, the external and the internal.[162] As examples of the former, Robert misunderstood the divisions of chapters and verses, changed the number of the former, and rearranged the latter.[163] Internally, he tended to use superlatives instead of positives, expressed causes and conclusions left unexpressed in the original, and occasionally made rather bad mistakes in translating terms.[164] His translation compares unfavorably, for example, with that of Mark of Toledo a century and a half later.[165] Only the translation of the apology of Al-Kindi, it appears, escapes the sometimes stilted literalism of Herman and the unscrupulous flights of fancy of Robert—a fact which vindicates once again the method of collaboration which was employed with similar success by so many other translators of the time.[166]

Much, however, can be forgiven the translators of the Toledan Collection in consideration of the utter dearth of lexicographical materials available to them.[167] If we must censure Robert of Ketton for frequent lack of precision and all of the translators for many

[161] D'Alverny, "Deux traductions du Coran au Moyen Age," 86; Daniel, *op. cit.*, 19, 142.

[162] "Juan de Segovia y el primer Alcorán trilingüe," *Al-Andalus*, XIV (1949), 158; see also Cabanelas, *Juan de Segovia y el Problema Islámico* (Madrid, 1952).

[163] See above, part 5; Cabanelas, "Juan de Segovia y el primer Alcorán trilingüe," 158-60.

[164] *Ibid.*, 159, note 2, and 160.

[165] D'Alverny, "Deux traductions du Coran au Moyen Age," 113-19; d'Alverny and Vajda, "Marc de Tolède, traducteur d'Ibn Tūmart," *Al-Andalus*, XVI (1951), 99-140, 259-308; XVII (1952), 1-56.

[166] See above, chapter II, part 1.

[167] See E. Schiaparelli, *Vocabulista in arabico pubblicato &c.* (Florence, 1871); P. de Alcalá, *Vocabulista arabigo en letra castellana* (Granada, 1505; ed. P. de Lagarde, Göttingen, 1883); C. F. Seybold, *Glossarium latino-arabicum*, ed. C. Bezold (Berlin, 1900).

little inaccuracies, we cannot gainsay the more important fact that they admirably and expeditiously fulfilled their contracts with Peter the Venerable by providing him with the library of information he sought and with an acceptable and sufficiently rigorous terminology with which to deal with it.

IV · THE SUMMARY

Infirmis ecclesiæ qui
scandalizari vel occulte
moveri levibus etiam ex
causis solent, consulere
et providere doctus vel
doctor, si zelum habet
iustitiæ, non debet
negligere.

Nam non erat qui
responderet quia non
erat qui agnosceret.

PETER THE VENERABLE

1 · THE *SUMMA TOTIUS HAERESIS SARACENORUM*

❦

PETER THE VENERABLE's first purpose in sponsoring his project to study Islam—to provide European Christians with accurate information about that religion—was accomplished by means of the Toledan Collection and a short summary of Islamic doctrine entitled *Summa totius haeresis Saracenorum*.[1] This latter text will be analyzed in this chapter, supplemented by parallel passages from the *Epistola de translatione sua* and the *Prologus* to the *Liber contra sectam sive haeresim Saracenorum*.[2]

Mandonnet,[3] followed by Monneret de Villard[4] and others, believed that the *Summa* was the book translated from the Arabic by Peter of Toledo and Peter of Poitiers and mentioned in the *Epistola de translatione sua* as "disputing against that very bad, worthless heretical doctrine of Mohammed." Both of these scholars recognized that Peter the Venerable could not have been referring to the translation of the Koran in this passage, and thus avoided an error into which many others fell. The *Summa* was chosen as the only plausible substitute for it, despite the clear statement at the end of the text that it had been prepared by Peter the Venerable himself.[5] Mlle d'Alverny was the first to solve the problem correctly when she discovered, on the basis of her study of the Arsenal manuscript, that the work referred to in the disputed passage was the apology of Al-Kindi.[6]

The preparation of the *Summa* must have required a considerable amount of work and thought on the part of the abbot (possibly with the assistance of his notary), for there was no single translation in the Toledan Collection which, of itself, would have provided him with an easy summation of Islamic doctrine. He

---

[1] A 1rs-3vs. It is called a *Summula* in BC 1111A and PL 189, 651B.

[2] In several of Peter's letters, such as that to King Louis (BC 865E-68C), some of the information contained in the *Summa* is repeated, but nothing is added to it.

[3] *Op. cit.*, 331-32.

[4] *Op. cit.*, 9-11.

[5] A 3vs. See above, chapter I, parts 3 and 5.

[6] "Deux traductions du Coran au Moyen Age," 77.

relied heavily upon the translations of the Koran and the apology of Al-Kindi, as will become evident in the course of this chapter, but in addition made use of the *Chronicon* of Theophanes in the Latin translation of Anastasius Bibliothecarius.[7]

It must be emphasized that the *Summa* was intended for the use of Bernard of Clairvaux (in its initial form within Letter 17 of Book Four) in particular, and Christian clerics in general. Its superior tone, fits of impatience, and frankly derogatory adjectives represent an attempt at conveying in the most direct, meaningful, and effective manner at once both the "sum and substance" of the Islamic creed and instilling the proper attitude which, in Peter's opinion, a Christian should assume toward it.

Although Peter was deeply concerned about the accuracy of his sources, and intended the *Summa* (in its final form) as an introduction to them, one cannot expect him to have written as a Moslem. A completely sympathetic presentation of Islam's case to Christians was never a principal aim of his, nor any aim at all. Peter's tone changed, as will be demonstrated, when he came to address the Moslems themselves, and this change is not devoid of significance. In the *Summa,* however, as a devout Christian speaking to other Christians, he chose "rather to tremble than dispute."[8]

[7] Ed. C. de Boor, 2 vols. (Leipzig, 1883-85). See also E. W. Brooks, "The Sources of Theophanes and the Syriac Chroniclers," *Byzantinische Zeitschrift*, xv (1906), 578-87; E. Perels, *Papst Nikolaus I und Anastasius Bibliothecarius* (Berlin, 1920).

[8] A 3rd-vs.

2 · GOD, CHRIST, AND THE
LAST JUDGMENT

❧ PETER THE VENERABLE began his summary, as Al-Kindi had begun his reply to Al-Hāshimi,[9] with what is indisputably the most fundamental point of difference between Moslems and Christians—the nature of God: "Their first and greatest error to be cursed is that they deny the Trinity [of persons] in the unity of the Godhead; and so, shunning number in unity, they do not believe that there exists in the single essence of the deity the number of three Persons. While they do not accept, as I say, a Trinity,[10] the beginning and end of all forms, and consequently the cause and origin and end of all formed things, they may be confessing God with their mouths, [but] they do not know Him fully."[11]

It might seem that this was an obvious point of departure; yet, when one reflects that the most common European view still saw Islam as a variety of polytheism and persisted in the identification of Mohammed with the Islamic god or gods, it can be appreciated what an immense advance was, in fact, being made when the matter was posed in these exact terms. Peter's reading of the Koran could not have failed to make this difference abundantly clear. There is more than a little reason to believe that Mohammed had no notion of what the Christian doctrine of the Trinity really was (or at best understood it in a consciously heretical sense); but, if one puts that aside, Peter is absolutely correct in affirming that it has at no time been accepted as Islamic doctrine that there is any division of persons in God.[12]

[9] A 147rs-49vd.

[10] Literally, "the ternary number."

[11] "Primus et maximus ipsorum execrandus est error, quod trinitatem in unitate deitatis negant, sicque dum in una diuinitatis essentia trinum personarum numerum non credunt, in unitate numerum euitantes, dum ternarium inquam omnium formarum principium atque finem, sicque rerum formatarum causam et originem atque terminum, non recipiunt, Deum licet ore confitentes, ipsum penitus nesciunt," A 1rs-rd.

[12] R. Bell, *The Origin of Islam in its Christian Environment* (London, 1926), 100-33; H. Massé, *Islam* (New York, 1938), 129; W. C. Smith, "Some Similarities

"Moreover," he continues, "these same devious people, these same changeable ones, acknowledge a principle of change and of all altering, clearly only a binary principle in this unity, which is [1] the divine essence itself, and [2] its soul. Thus it is that the Koran, by which name they call their law, always presents God speaking in the plural."[13] One's first impression upon reading this passage, if it is not to observe that God often speaks in the plural in the Bible, is to imagine that Peter has already begun to misrepresent Islamic doctrine. There is no single point on which the Koran speaks with greater insistence, and Mohammed reiterates with greater feeling, than the doctrine of the unity of God.[14] *Shirk,* the Arabic term denoting the act of associating other beings with God, is the gravest, and indeed the only unforgivable, sin in Islam.

But it should not be forgotten that Islamic theology, in the course of its historical development, fell heir to many a problem seemingly not directly provided for by the Koran.[15] Two important problems which touched on the unity of God—one the problem of the "creation" of the Koran and the other that of the definition of the divine essence—exercised the theologians for many centuries. On both of these questions there was much difference of opinion.[16] The position that the Koran was "uncreated" achieved such support that it became the orthodox view.[17] But the view that the divine soul (Arabic *nafs* or *rūḥ*) was distinguishable from the divine essence analogously to two states in the human condition, on the other hand, was too sophisticated for the believers

---

and Differences between Christianity and Islam," *The World of Islam,* ed. J. Kritzeck and R. B. Winder (London, 1960), 47-59.

[13] "Ipsi autem deuii, ipsi uariabiles, principium uarietatis et alteritatis omnis, uidelicet binarium solum in unitate confitentur, scilicet ipsam diuinam essentiam, et eius animam. Vnde Deum pluraliter loquentem, introducit semper Alchoran, quo nomine legem suam nuncupant," A 1rd.

[14] See Louis Gardet, *s.v.* "Allāh," EI², 1, 406-17.

[15] L. Gardet and M.-M. Anawati, *Introduction à la théologie musulmane* (Paris, 1948), 94-101, 208-37.

[16] *Ibid.,* 48-49; J. W. Sweetman, *Islam and Christian Theology,* 1:1 (London, 1945), 113, note 3; Wensinck, *The Muslim Creed,* 58-101.

[17] Gardet and Anawati, *op. cit.,* 59.

and too suspect for the theologians to become accepted as a perma-
nent credal distinction.[18] Peter the Venerable, following Al-Kindi,
was evidently alluding to this latter problem in the passage quoted
above.[19] Quite obviously he was not in a position to detail this
controversy, and so cited the only indication of the distinction of
which he had any knowledge.

"Furthermore," the *Summa* continues "these blind ones deny that
God the creator is Father, for, according to them, no one becomes
a father without sexual intercourse. And consequently they do not
believe that Christ, though conceived of the Holy Spirit, is the
son of God, or God, but [only that he is] a good prophet, most
true, free from all falsehood and sin, the son of Mary, born without
a father, [and] never having died, because it was not fitting that
he should die. On the contrary, [they believe that] when the Jews
wanted to kill him, he ascended to the heavens,[20] having escaped
out of their hands, and [that] he lives there now in the flesh in the
presence of the creator until the coming of the Antichrist."[21] In
this passage Peter establishes other basic points of difference
between the two creeds: the Moslem denies the incarnation, the
redemption, and the resurrection of Christ, but accepts the virgin
birth and the ascension. The Koran contains numerous denials
of the fatherhood of God and the sonship of Christ;[22] never is it
more starkly stated than in 112:1, 3: "He is God, One. . . . He did

[18] Sweetman, *op. cit.,* 1:1, 103, 113, 114, 137; Wensinck, *The Muslim Creed,* 58-82.
The problem was a more natural, and hence easier, one for Christianity, which
had to define the humanity of Christ. St. John Damascene was one of the
Christian theologians who treated it very fully; *ibid.,* 68-72.

[19] A 147vs-48rd.

[20] Literally, "the stars."

[21] "Illi item caeci, Deum creatorem patrem esse negant, quia secundum eos
nullus fit pater sine coitu. Christum itaque licet ex diuino Spiritu conceptum, Dei
filium esse non credunt, nec etiam Deum, sed prophetam bonum, ueracissimum,
omnis mendacii atque peccati immunem, Mariae filium, sine patre genitum,
nunquam mortuum, quia morte non est dignus, immo cum illum Iudei interficere
uellent, de manibus eorum elapsum, ascendisse ad astra, ibique nunc in carne
uiuere in presentia Creatoris, usque ad aduentum Antichristi," A 1rd.

[22] For example, 2:116; 6-102-04; 10:68; 17:111; 18:4-5; 19:35-36, 91-92; 23:91;
37:151; cf. Sweetman, *op. cit.,* 1:2, 11-47.

not beget and was not begotten." God is called the creator (Arabic *khāliq*) in the Koran, and there are scores of anthropomorphisms and anthropopathisms; but even though there were troublesome compensational concepts such as the "indwelling" (Arabic *ḥulūl*) and "union" (*ittiḥād*), Islam persisted in its protest that the incarnation was plain *shirk* and blasphemy.[23] "Later, when Islam had more accurate information, protests were strengthened against the attribution of Sonship to Jesus Christ."[24]

Nevertheless, as Peter knew well and wished to emphasize, Christ was always reverently regarded by Moslems as one of the prophets of God. They held that he was sinless, as were other prophets and some who were not prophets. Among the latter, according to one tradition, was the Virgin Mary.[25] There was not the same unanimity on the subject of Christ's death. Some Islamic theologians, not the oldest, arguing from two passages in the Koran (3:55 and 5:117) variously interpreted, held that he did die a natural death. Others placed a more literal value upon 4:157-58: "[The Jews] declared: 'We have put to death the Messiah, Jesus the son of Mary, the apostle of God.' They did not kill him, nor did they crucify him, but they thought they did. . . . God took him up to Himself." The notion that Christ himself did not die

[23] *Ibid.*, 27-38, 98-115; Wensinck, *The Muslim Creed*, 66, 85, 92.

[24] Sweetman, *op. cit.*, 1:2, 98.

[25] Since Islam does not profess a doctrine of original sin, however, it is surprising to find often repeated, even by so eminent an authority as H. A. R. Gibb, *Mohammedanism* (London, 1949), 45, that Moslems believe in the Immaculate Conception of the Virgin Mary. There is one passage in the Koran (3:37) and a tradition rated as "most reliable" by Al-Bukhāri and Muslim which refer to the Virgin Mary, as well as to Christ, as being (uniquely, in the case of the tradition) exempted at their births from any association with Satan. Although it seems likely that these passages represent a direct borrowing from Christian doctrine, they nevertheless did not serve as the basis for any dogma of original sin or of the Immaculate Conception in Islamic theology, since the koranic treatment of Adam would have contradicted such dogmas. As Sweetman says, *op. cit.*, 1:2, 186: "The usual explanation of the story of the temptation of Adam [in the Koran 2:33-37; 7:18-24] is that Adam really did not wilfully sin, but was deceived by Satan and was immediately pardoned. Thus there can be no thought that Adam's fault involved his descendants. . . . Man was created weak [cf. Koran 4:32] rather than sinful in the Muslim conception." See also Anawati, "Islam and the Immaculate Conception," *The Dogma of the Immaculate Conception*, ed. Edward D. O'Connor (Notre Dame, 1958), 447-61.

was a popular doctrine among the Ebionitic and Gnostic sects; Bell quotes Roesch as finding in this doctrine "the mythic precipitation of the Corinthian heresy and the Nestorian separation of the two natures in Christ: the higher Christ being exalted to heaven and the man Jesus being crucified."[26] The important thing for present purposes, however, is that Moslems commonly held the view, founded upon the Koran, that Christ did not die, "because it was not fitting that he should die," but, instead, that he "ascended to the heavens . . . and lives there now in the flesh in the presence of the creator until the coming of the Antichrist."[27]

"When [the Antichrist] comes," the *Summa* continues, "Christ himself will slay him by the sword of his virtue, and will convert the Jews who have been left to his law; and further, he will teach his law perfectly to the Christians, who have now for quite a while lost his law and his Gospel on account of his departure and the death of his apostles and disciples, by which then all Christians and those first disciples of his will be saved. Christ himself will die with them and all creatures when Seraphim [Seraphael], whom they say is one archangel,[28] sounds the trumpet, and afterwards he will rise with the rest and will lead his own [followers] to judgment, and will help them and pray for them, but will not judge them. For God alone will judge. The prophets, however, and the individual messengers,[29] will be present with them and will be on hand as intercessors and helpers for them."[30] Many (in

---

[26] *Op. cit.*, 154.

[27] A 1rd.

[28] Or, "the one archangel," but Peter knew from the *Doctrina Mahumet* that the Moslems believe in other archangels; see above, chapter III, note 34.

[29] "Legati," translating the Arabic *rusul*.

[30] "Quem uenientem, Christus idem gladio suae uirtutis interficiet, et Iudeos residuos ad legem suam conuertet. Christianos autem, qui iam a longo tempore legem eius atque Euangelium perdiderunt, tum propter eiusdem discessum, tum etiam propter apostolorum atque discipulorum mortem, legem suam perfecte docebit, in qua tunc omnes Christiani, sicut et illi primi sui discipuli, saluabuntur. Cum quibus simul et omnibus creaturis, Seraphim quem ipsi dicunt archangelum unum, sonante buccinam, morietur et ipse Christus, postea resurrecturus cum ceteris, et ad iudicium suos ducturus, eisque auxiliaturus et pro eis oraturus, sed nequaquam iudicaturus. Deus enim solus iudicabit. Prophetae uero et legati singuli, cum suis et pro suis intercessores aderunt, et auxiliatores," A 1rd-vs.

Peter's time perhaps most) Moslems believed in the coming of the Antichrist (Arabic *al-Masīḥ al-Dajjāl*).[31] Although he is not mentioned in the Koran, the traditions abound in references to him.[32] The similarities between these traditions and those concerning the Mahdi and "Hidden Imām" which may have developed out of them are striking.[33]

Because preoccupation with eschatology has become so much less important a factor in later Semitic theology, it is easy to underemphasize its former importance. Peter had had a good sampling of Islamic eschatology in the *Doctrina Mahumet*.[34] He discussed the accusation of the loss of the Christian scriptures at great length in the *Liber contra sectam sive haeresim Saracenorum*.[35] The conversion of the Jews was a common Christian "sign" of the end of the world, though its belief by Moslems was, of course, less common.[36] The sounding of the trumpet, Christ's death and resurrection with the rest of mankind, as well as the other echoes of rabbinical teaching about the details of the Last Judgment, have a time-honored place in Islamic eschatology.[37]

Christian theology would not only insist upon judgment by Christ,[38] but would deny the efficacy of intercession after the end of the world. However, the koranic notion of intercession is scarcely to be identified with that of Christianity anyway, as God

[31] "Dajjāl is sometimes represented as a monster . . . but in the Traditions [he] is mostly represented as a man. . . . Remembering the source of the figure of Dajjāl, it will not surprise us so much that according to these traditions he is to be overthrown by Jesus. . . . Jesus will appear according to one version at the white minaret on the east of Damascus; according to another at Jerusalem. He will pursue the Dajjāl, and overtaking him at the gate of Ludd or Lydda, will slay him," Bell, *op. cit.*, 202-03.

[32] See Wensinck, *A Handbook of Early Muhammadan Tradition*, 50-51.

[33] See D. B. Macdonald, *s.v.* "al-Mahdi," EI III, 111-15; T. Hughes, *op. cit.*, 204; Bell, *op. cit.*, 206.

[34] See above, chapter III, part 4.

[35] See below, chapter V, part 4.

[36] See Rom. 11:25-26; Wensinck, *A Handbook of Early Muhammadan Tradition*, 113, 117.

[37] *Ibid.*, 78-79. According to other legend, it is the archangel Gabriel who will sound the trumpet.

[38] Cf. the Nicene Creed: "Iterum venturus est cum gloria judicare vivos et mortuous, cujus regni non erit finis."

himself is spoken of as an "intercessor."[39] The intercession of the Islamic traditions, limited to the prophets and angels, more closely approximates the Christian concept.[40]

Peter concludes this first section of the *Summa* by remarking, "For thus the very wretched and wicked Mohammed has taught them who, by denying all the mysteries of the Christian religion[41] whereby particularly men are saved, has condemned almost a third of the human race by some unknown judgement of God and by unheard-of, raving-mad tales, to the devil and eternal death."[42]

[39] Koran 6:51.

[40] Wensinck, *A Handbook of Early Muhammadan Tradition*, 111-12.

[41] Literally, "holiness."

[42] "Sic enim docuit eos miserrimus atque impiissimus Mahumet, qui omnia sacramenta Christianae pietatis, quibus maxime homines saluantur, abnegans, iam pene terciam humani generis partem, nescimus quo Dei iudicio, inauditis fabularum deliramentis, diabolo et morti aeternae contradidit," A ivs.

"IT SEEMS NECESSARY to speak about [Mohammed]," the *Summa* continues, "who he was and what he taught, for the benefit of those who will read this book,[43] so that they may better understand what they read, and may know how detestable both his life and his doctrine appear. Some[44] indeed think that he was that Nicholas, one of the seven first deacons, and that the sectarian doctrine of the Nicholaites, a group named after him, a doctrine which is condemned in the Apocalypse of John, is this law of the modern Saracens."[45] Thus Peter began his account of Mohammed's life by disabusing his readers of the view, apparently widely held, that Mohammed was to be associated with the heresiarch Nicholas, "a proselyte from Antioch" (Acts 6:5) who was chosen as one of the first deacons of the Christian Church, or his doctrine with that of the Nicholaites. Little is known about the nature of this particular heresy, which Eusebius says was short-lived.[46] There is an interesting version of this legend identifying Mohammed with Nicholas in the *Liber Nicholay*.[47] Peter is impatient with these legends. "Others too conjure up other individuals," he adds, "and, as they are indifferent to reading and unacquainted with the history of events, so also in the other cases they hold certain false opinions."[48]

He turns without delay to the facts he accepts. "As the chron-

[43] That is, the Toledan Collection, which the *Summa* prefaces.

[44] The section in Letter 17 of Book Four of Peter's letters (BC 844C) begins here.

[45] "De quo quis fuerit, et quid docuerit, propter eos qui librum istum lecturi sunt, ut scilicet quod legerint melius intelligant, et quam detestabilis tam uita quam doctrina illius extiterit sciant, dicendum uidetur. Putant enim quidam hunc Nicholaum illum unum e septem primis diaconibus extitisse, et Nicholaitarum ab eo dictorum sectam, quae et in Apochalipsi Iohannis arguitur, hanc modernorum Sarracenorum legem existere," A ivs.

[46] *Ecclesiastical History*, iii:29; see also d'Alverny, "Pierre le Vénérable et la légende de Mahomet," 165-66.

[47] Mlle d'Alverny intends to publish this text, based on two Vatican manuscripts, in *Cahiers de civilisation médiévale*; Daniel, *op. cit.*, vi.

[48] "Somniant et alii alios, et sicut lectionis incuriosi, et rerum gestarum ignari, sicut et in aliis casibus, falsa quaelibet opinantur," A ivs.

icle translated from the Greek into Latin by Anastasius the librarian of the Roman Church also most openly relates,[49] [Mohammed] lived in the time of the emperor Heraclius, and a little after the times of the great and first Gregory, the Roman Pontiff, almost five hundred and fifty years ago. He was an Arab by race, of low birth, at first a supporter of the old idolatry, as also the other Arabs still were at that time, unschooled in practically any learning."[50] The date Peter assigns to Mohammed is substantially correct. We are not certain of the date of his birth, but it is usually given as 570/71; he died in 632. Heraclius was born about 575 and ruled as emperor from 610 to 641. Pope St. Gregory I was born about 540 and ruled as pope from 590 to 604; so he was actually a contemporary of Mohammed's.

Mohammed was, it is true, an Arab of humble birth. Some branches of his tribe, the Quraysh, had means, but his immediate family did not. It is well attested that he was an orphan, raised by his grandfather 'Abd-al-Muṭṭalib and later by his paternal uncle Abu-Ṭālib.[51] He was "at first a supporter of the old idolatry" by his own admission, and a branch of his family served as custodians of the shrine of the Ka'bah in Mecca.[52] Peter is incorrect in implying that all of the Arabs were idolaters at this time, however. There were Jewish and Christian communities, and at Mecca itself a mysterious little group called the *Ḥunafā'* ("the pure ones") which favored monotheism and with which Mohammed was associated.[53] Mohammed is called *ummi* in the Koran (e.g., 7:157-

[49] *Ed. cit.*, i, 333; ii, 209.

[50] "Fuit autem iste, sicut etiam chronica ab Anastasio Romanae ecclesiae bibliothecario de Greco in Latinum translata, apertissime narrat, tempore imperatoris Heraclii, paulo post tempora magni et primi Gregorii Romani pontificis, ante annos fere .d.tos et quinquaginta, Arabs natione, uilis genere, antiquae primum ydolatriae cultor, sicut et alii Arabes tunc adhuc erant, ineruditus, nullarum pene litterarum," A ivs.

[51] Guillaume, *The Life of Muhammad*, 73-79.

[52] *Ibid.*, 35-56, 84-89.

[53] See the Koran 2:135; 3:67, 95; 4:125; 6:79, 161; 10:105; 16:120, 123; 22:31; 30:30; 98:5; Bell, "Who were the Hanifs?" *The Moslem World*, xx (1930), 120-24; N. A. Faris and H. W. Glidden, "The Development of the Meaning of the Koranic *Ḥanīf*," *Journal of the Palestinian Oriental Society*, xix (1939), 1-13. Watt, *Muhammad at Mecca*, 162-64, points out that three of the four most famous *Ḥunafā'* mentioned in the traditions eventually became Christians.

58), a word usually translated as "illiterate" or "unlettered" and variously interpreted as meaning that he was at first one of the Arab polytheists to whom no divine scripture had yet been sent[54] or simply that he was unable to read.[55] When it became a polemical necessity to assert the wholly miraculous character of the Koran, particularly since the prophet had claimed no other miracles, the exegetes favored the latter interpretation.[56] But whether or not Mohammed was illiterate, it is safe to say, as Peter does, that he was "unschooled."

There follows the most serious misconstruction in the *Summa*: "[Because Mohammed was] very active in worldly affairs, and extremely clever, he advanced from low birth and poverty to wealth and renown. Having raised himself up little by little, and frequently attacking all those who were near to him, and particularly close blood-relatives, with wiles, robberies, and invasions, killing whomever he could by stealth, or whomever he could publicly, he increased the terror of his [name]. And when time and again he came out on top in contests, he began to aspire to the kingship of his people; and when, with everyone equally offering him opposition and spurning his low birth, he perceived that he could not attain for himself his desire in this way, since his power by the sword availed nothing, he tried to become king under the cloak of religion and by the name of 'divine prophet.' "[57]

[54] Especially on the basis of the Koran 2:74; 3:19; and 62:2; cf. Al-Ṭabari, *op. cit.*, III, 142. It corresponds to *ethnikós* or *gentilis*, later interpreted as *vulgaris*.

[55] See J. Horovitz, *Koranische Untersuchungen* (Berlin, 1926), 51-53, and R. Paret, *s.v.* "Ummī," EI IV, 1016. Incidentally, it is unlikely that there were any Arabic translations of the Bible for Mohammed to have read; cf. Guillaume, "The Meaning of *Amānīyᵃ* in Sūrah 2:73," *The World of Islam*, ed. J. Kritzeck and R. B. Winder, 43, 46, note 3.

[56] Normally the Koran is called Mohammed's only miracle (Arabic *āyah*) by Moslems on the basis of 29:42, but some exegetes have adduced three others: the clefting of the moon in 54:1-2, the assistance of angels at Badr in 3:13, and the night journey in 17:1. Tradition, of course, has added many more.

[57] "Strenuus in secularibus, et calliditate multa, de ignobili et egeno, in diuitem et famosum prouectus. Hic paulatim crescendo, et contiguos quosque ac maxime sanguinis propinquos, insidiis, rapinis, incursionibus frequenter infestando, quos poterat furtim, quos poterat publice occidendo, terrorem sui auxit, et sepe in congressionibus factus superior, ad regnum suae gentis aspirare caepit. Cumque uniuersis pari modo resistentibus, eiusque ignobilitatem contempnentibus, uideret

Peter went wrong by following Al-Kindi,[58] and his essential error consisted in regarding Mohammed's prophethood as postdating his first battles and merely as an outcome of his desire for political authority over his people.

Mohammed's advance from poverty to wealth is historical, but was the result of his marriage, at the age of about twenty-five, to a wealthy widow named Khadījah, some years his senior.[59] There is no evidence that he aspired to the kingship of the Arabs before or apart from his role as prophet, and certainly none that he began his career as a murderer. His sanction of the use of the sword came long after he had won his first converts—a fact which might have shocked Peter even more if it had been made clear to him.[60] Detailed accounts of his later raids and battles abound.[61] Inasmuch as Theophanes gives a different version of the story, having Mohammed invent his prophethood in an effort to explain his epileptic attacks to his wife,[62] it must be concluded that Peter here accepted Al-Kindi too slavishly and to the detriment of his *Summa*'s accuracy.

"And since he lived as a barbarian among barbarians," the text goes on, "and himself an idolater among idolaters, and among those who, as he knew, above all people were unacquainted with and ignorant of both the divine and the human law, and therefore could easily be led astray, he began to give his attention to the evil he had conceived. And since he had heard that the prophets of God were great men, saying that he was His prophet to make the feint of some good, he tried to lead them bit by bit from idolatry: not, however, to the true God, but to the error of his own heresy, which he had now begun to bring to fruition."[63] It is

---

se hac uia non posse consequi quod separabat, quia ui gladii non potuit, religionis uelamine, et diuini prophetae nomine, rex fieri attemptauit," A 1vs-vd.

[58] A 159rs-62rs.

[59] Guillaume, *The Life of Muhammad*, 82-84. Both Theophanes, *ed. cit.*, I, 333; II, 209, and Al-Kindi, A 152rs, had mentioned Khadījah.

[60] See Watt, *Muhammad at Medina*, 1-77; Majid Khadduri, *The Law of War and Peace in Islam* (London, 1941).

[61] Guillaume, *The Life of Muhammad*, 219-659.   [62] *Loc. cit.*

[63] "Et quia inter barbaros barbarus, inter ydolatras et ipse ydolatra habitabat,

unquestionably true that Mohammed had heard of the Jewish prophets and Christ before he declared his prophethood and that he intended, above all, to lead the Arabs away from idolatry. The Moslem interprets these facts in a totally different manner, of course.

---

atque inter illos, quos utpote pre cunctis gentibus, tam diuinae quam humanae legis expertes, et ignaros, faciles ad seducendum esse nouerat, conceptae iniqui-tati dare operam caepit. Et quoniam prophetas Dei, magnos fuisse homines audierat, prophetam eius se esse dicens, ut aliquid boni simularet, ex parte illos ab ydolatria, non tamen ad Deum uerum, sed ad suae quam parturire iam caeperat heresis fallaciam traducere conabatur," A IVd.

4 · THE KORAN AND ITS SOURCES

PETER THE VENERABLE rejected Mohammed's prophethood and asserted that the Koran had sources. "Satan gave success to the error and sent the monk Sergius, a follower of the heretical Nestorius who had been expelled from the Church, across to those regions of Arabia, and joined the heretical monk with the pseudo-prophet. And so Sergius, joined with Mohammed, filled in what was lacking to him, and explaining to him also the sacred scriptures, both the Old Testament and the New, [in part] according to the thinking of his master Nestorius, who denied that our Saviour was God, [and] in part according to his own interpretation, and likewise completely infecting him with the fables of the apocryphal writings, he made him a Nestorian Christian."[64]

There is a considerable body of literature concerning the legend of the monk Sergius. The legend is of Islamic origin, but has Christian forms.[65] According to the most usual Islamic version, Mohammed, when he was twelve years old, accompanied his uncle Abu-Ṭālib on a caravan journey into Syria.[66] A monk, later given the name Baḥīra, saw the caravan shaded by a cloud as it approached; he invited the travellers into his cell for refreshments and asked if all were present. The camel boy Mohammed was then brought in and Baḥīra recognized him as "the prophet to come."[67] A related story has it that Khadījah's cousin Waraqah,

---

[64] "Dedit Sathan successum errori, et Sergium monachum, heretici Nestorii sectatorem, ab ecclesia expulsum, ad partes illas Arabiae transmisit, et monachum hereticum pseudoprophetae coniunxit. Itaque Sergius coniunctus Mahumeth, quod ei deerat suppleuit, et scripturas sacras tam Veteris Testamenti quam Noui secundum magistri sui Nestorii intellectum, qui Saluatorem nostrum Deum esse negabat, partim prout sibi uisum est, ei exponens, simulque apochriphorum fabulis eum plenissime imbuens, Christianum Nestorianum effecit," A ivd-2rs.

[65] Wensinck, *s.v.* "*Baḥīrā,*" EI i, 576-77; A. Abel, "L'Apocalypse de Baḥīra et la notion islamique du Mahdi," *Annuaire de l'Institut de philologie et histoire orientales*, iii (1935), 1-12; R. Gottheil, "A Christian Baḥīra Legend," *Zeitschrift für Assyriologie*, xiii (1898), 189-242; xiv (1899), 203-68; J. Odier-Bignami and G. Levi Della Vida, "Une version latine de l'Apocalypse syro-arabe de Serge-Baḥīra," *Mélanges de l'Ecole Française de Rome*, 1950, 128ff; Daniel, *op. cit.*, 88-90.

[66] Guillaume, *The Life of Muhammad*, 79-81.

[67] *Ibid.*, 80.

one of the *Ḥunafā'*, had convinced Mohammed of the validity of his revelations.[68] A Christian monk (Nestorian or not) who was on the lookout for "the prophet to come" would have been a curious specimen, but the story of Waraqah is not difficult to believe. There is also a story mentioned by Al-Bukhāri about a Christian "who used to write for the Holy Prophet. He then went back to Christianity and used to say, 'Mohammed does not know anything except what I wrote for him.' "[69]

The version of the story which Peter the Venerable adopted, culled from Theophanes and Al-Kindi, seems to have been a combination of the Waraqah story and a Syriac version of the Baḥīra legend wherein the monk is identified as a Nestorian named Sergius.[70] In several of the Christian versions the monk is distinguished from a hermit (more plausibly the Baḥīra figure) who had hailed Mohammed's appearance as a prophet. In separate versions he is identified as a Nestorian, Arian, Nicholaite, or anything else that suited the telling; and though he is usually named Sergius, he is sometimes Nicholas (which probably led to the confusion mentioned by Peter) or nameless.[71]

There is an impressive amount of evidence that Mohammed had some knowledge of the apocryphal literature of Christianity, probably not directly but by hearsay.[72] Recent scholarship tends to minimize direct Christian influences on Mohammed, but some specifically Nestorian elements have been detected.[73] To say that

---

[68] *Ibid.*, 83.   [69] *Al-Ṣaḥīḥ*, 61:25.

[70] Theophanes, *ed. cit.*, I, 334; II, 209; Theophanes does not call Sergius a Nestorian, but Al-Kindi does; cf. d'Alverny and Vajda, "Marc de Tolède, traducteur d'Ibn Tūmart," 118-19.

[71] Daniel, *op. cit.*, 4-5, 88-89, 93, 235-37, 241, 281, 286, 290, 344, 345, 347.

[72] Bell, *The Origin of Islam in its Christian Environment*, 110, 112; Kritzeck, "Jews, Christians, and Moslems," 91-102.

[73] J. Wellhausen, *Reste arabischen Heidenthums* (Berlin, 1897), 204-12; Nöldeke *et al.*, *op. cit.*, I, 7, and *passim*; H. P. Smith, *The Bible and Islam* (New York, 1897); W. Rudolph, *Die Abhängigkeit des Qorans von Judentum und Christentum* (Stuttgart, 1922), 63-71; C. H. Becker, *Islamstudien* (Leipzig, 1924), I, 386-431, 450-71; T. Andrae, *Der Ursprung des Islams und das Christentum* (Uppsala, 1926); K. Ahrens, "Christliches im Qoran," *Zeitschrift der deutschen morgenländischen Gesellschaft*, N.F. IX (1930), 15-68, 148-90; C. Brockelmann, *Geschichte der islamischen Völker und Staaten* (Munich, 1939), 15.

Mohammed actually became a Nestorian, however, is to press the matter entirely too far. Some koranic stories—for example, Christ's speaking in the cradle (19:30-34, 5:109) and fashioning a live bird out of clay (3:43, 5:110)—echo apocryphal writings such as the Protoevangel of James the Less, the Gospels of Thomas the Israelite and of Nicodemus, and the so-called "Infancy Gospels" known to have existed in Coptic, Syriac, and even Arabic.[74]

"And in order that the whole fullness of iniquity should come together in Mohammed, and that nothing should be lacking for his damnation and that of others, Jews were joined to the heretic. And lest [Mohammed] become a true Christian, the Jews, craftily providing for this man eager for novelties, whispered[75] to Mohammed not the truth of the scriptures, but their own fables in which they abound even now."[76] Al-Kindi's mention of these Jews, whom he names, must have been considerably strengthened for Peter by the translation of the *Doctrina Mahumet* and by his own familiarity with the Talmud.[77] The evidence for abundant and far-reaching Jewish influences on early Islam is overwhelming.[78]

Some of the Nestorian influences are discussed by T. O'Shaughnessy, *The Koranic Concept of the Word of God* (Rome, 1956); cf. Bell, *The Origin of Islam in its Christian Environment*, 10, 25ff., 38, 212.

[74] *Ibid.*, 110.

[75] Literally, "hissed."

[76] "Et ut tota iniquitatis plenitudo in Mahumet conflueret, et nichil ei ad perditionem sui uel aliorum deesset, adiuncti sunt Iudei heretico, et ne uerus Christianus fieret dolose precauentes, homini nouis rebus inhianti non scripturarum ueritatem, sed fabulas suas quibus nunc usque abundant, Mahumet Iudei insibilant," A 2rd.

[77] He repeated some of the Talmudic stories in his *Liber adversus Judaeorum inveteratam duritiem*, BC 1066B-1008B.

[78] A. Geiger, *Was hat Mohammed aus dem Judenthum aufgenommen?* (Bonn, 1833), stimulated much of the modern discussion. See H. Hirschfeld, *Jüdische Elemente im Koran* (Berlin, 1878) and *Beiträge zur Erklärung des Koran* (Leipzig, 1886); I. Schapiro, *Die haggadischen Elemente im erzählenden Teil des Korans* (Leipzig, 1907); E. Mittwoch, *Zur Entstehungsgeschichte des islamischen Gebets und Kultus* (Berlin, 1913); D. S. Margoliouth, *The Relations between Arabs and Israelites prior to the Rise of Islam* (London, 1924); Guillaume, "The Influence of Judaism on Islam," *The Legacy of Israel*, ed. E. R. Bevan and C. Singer (Oxford, 1928), 129-71; E. Rosenthal, "Islam," *Judaism and Christianity*, ed. H. Loewe (London, 1937), II, 147-85; C. C. Torrey, *The Jewish Foundation of Islam* (New York, 1933); A. Katsh, *Judaism in Islām* (New York, 1954). Cf. Gardet and Anawati, *op. cit.*, 30, note 4.

It is likewise true that such influences are not only evident in the Koran and Islamic ritual and legislation, but pervade the traditions and popular legend as well.[79]

Such, then, is Peter's explanation of the production of the Koran. "Thus Mohammed," he says, "instructed by the best Jewish and heretical doctors, produced his Koran and wove together, in that barbarous fashion of his, a diabolical scripture, put together both from the Jewish fables and the trifling songs of heretics. Lying that this collection was brought to him chapter by chapter by Gabriel, whose name he already knew from sacred scripture, he poisoned with a deadly poison that people that did not know God, and in the manner of such [poisoners], coating the rim of the goblet with honey and letting the death-dealing poison follow afterwards, he destroyed, alas, the souls and bodies of the wretched people. That wicked man did so plainly when, praising both the Christian and the Jewish law, asserting nevertheless that neither one was to be upheld, the reprobate, [although] taking it over, [at the same time] rejected it."[80] It is perfectly true that Mohammed asserted that the Koran was revealed to him in separate portions by Gabriel and that he appeared ambivalent, as the revelations continued, on the role of the scriptures which antedated the Koran. On the one hand, he praised the former scriptures and acknowledged them to have been, at least in their original forms, divinely revealed; on the other, he warned that the Koran was intended to supersede them all, thereby relieving the Moslems (or so it was, in effect) of any obligation to read them.[81]

[79] Torrey, op. cit., 28-61.

[80] "Sic ab optimis doctoribus, Iudeis et hereticis, Mahumet institutus, Alchoran suum condidit, et tam ex fabulis Iudaicis, quam ex hereticorum neniis confectam nefariam scripturam, barbaro illo suo modo contexuit. Quod paulatim per thomos a Gabrihele cuius iam nomen ex sacra scriptura cognouerat, sibi allatum mentitus, gentem Deum ignorantem, letali haustu infecit, et more talium, oram calicis melle liniens, subsequente mortifero ueneno, animas et corpora gentis miserae proh dolor, interemit. Sic plane impius ille fecit, quando et Christianam et Iudaicam legem collaudans, neutram tamen tenendam esse confirmans, probando reprobus reprobauit," A 2rs.

[81] See below, chapter V, parts 3 and 4.

Peter then summarizes the Islamic views of Christ, resurrection, and judgment, as they are found in the Koran, and in doing so repeats several points he had already made in the first section. "Thence it is that he asserts that Moses was the best prophet, and Christ our God was greater than all. He proclaims that [Christ] was born of a virgin. He acknowledges [that he was] the messenger of God, the word of God, [and] the Spirit of God; but he does not understand or acknowledge [that he was] the messenger, Word, or Spirit as we do. He absolutely ridicules [the Christian doctrine] that he is to be called or believed to be the Son of God. And the beastly[82] man, measuring the eternal birth of the Son of God in terms of the likeness of human generation, denies and derides with every effort at his command that God could either beget or be begotten. He advocates by constant repetition the resurrection of the flesh. He does not deny a universal judgment at the end of time, although not to be conducted by Christ, but by God. However, he insanely believes that at that judgment Christ, as the greatest of all after God, and he himself will be present as a source of defense for all his people."[83]

Most of this information represents Islamic doctrine fairly and has already been discussed.[84] Christ is called both "Spirit" (Arabic *rūḥ*) and "Word" (*kalimah*) in the Koran, although "Messiah" (*masīḥ*) is his usual title.[85] It is no longer customary for Moslems to regard Christ as in any sense "greater" than Mohammed, but

[82] Literally, "cow-like."

[83] "Inde est, quod Moysen optimum prophetam fuisse, Christum Dominum maiorem omnibus extitisse confirmat, natum de uirgine predicat, nuncium Dei, uerbum Dei, spiritum Dei fatetur, nec nuncium uerbum aut Spiritum ut nos aut intelligit aut fatetur. Filium Dei dici aut credi, prorsus deridet. Et de humanae generationis similitudine uaccinus homo filii Dei eternam natiuitatem metiens, uel gignere uel generari Deum potuisse, quanto potest nisu denegat et subsannat. Resurrectionem carnis sepe replicando astruit, iudicium commune in fine seculi, non a Christo sed a Deo exercendum esse non negat. Illi tamen iudicio, Christum ut omnium post Deum maximum, ac seipsum ad gentis suae presidium affuturum, uesanit," A 2rs-rd.

[84] See above, part 2.

[85] Koran 4:171; 16:102; cf. 2:87; 5:110. See also G. Gabrieli, "Gesù Cristo nel Qorano," *Bessarione*, ix (1901), 32-60; J. Robson, *Christ in Islam* (London, 1929); C. J. Ledit, *Mahomet, Israel, et le Christ* (Paris, 1956).

there is good reason to believe that this was once a widely accepted view, particularly among the Ṣūfis.[86] The general resurrection and last judgment have always been cardinal tenets of the Islamic creed.[87]

[86] Sweetman, *op. cit.*, 1:2, 110ff; Daniel, *op. cit.*, 316-17.
[87] Wensinck, *The Muslim Creed*, 130, 178, 274.

THE *Summa* continues with a description of the Islamic heaven and hell. "[Mohammed] describes the torments of hell," Peter says, "such as it pleased him [to describe them], and such as it was becoming to a great pseudo-prophet to devise. He painted a paradise not of angelic society, nor of the vision of God, nor of that highest good which neither eye has seen, nor ear heard, nor has it entered into the heart of man [Isa. 64:4; I Cor. 2:9], but actually in such a way as he wished it to be prepared for himself. He promises to his followers there the eating of meats and all kinds of fruits, there rivers of milk and honey and gleaming waters, there the embrace and sensual satisfaction of the loveliest women and virgins, in which things his whole paradise is comprehended."[88]

The koranic descriptions of heaven are precisely as Peter presents them.[89] A few of the commentators and nearly all of the mystical schools in Islam rejected the literal interpretation of these passages in favor of a less sensual and more intellectual paradise.[90] Some of the early Christian writers, notably St. Ephraem (d. 373), had described paradise in terms approximating those of the Koran.[91] However, paradise in the sense of "the Garden of Eden" (which is, roughly speaking, the Islamic sense, derived directly from Judaism) was sharply and speedily distinguished from para-

[88] "Inferni tormenta, qualia sibi libuit, et qualia ad inuenire magnum pseudoprophetam decuit, describit. Paradysum non societatis angelicae, nec uisionis diuinae, nec summi illius boni quod nec oculus uidit, nec auris audiuit, nec in cor hominis ascendit, sed uere talem, qualem caro et sanguis, immo fex carnis et sanguinis concupiscebat, qualemque sibi parari optabat, depinxit. Ibi carnium et omnigenorum fructuum esum, ibi lactis et mellis riuulos, et aquarum splendentium, ibi pulcherrimarum mulierum et uirginum amplexus et luxus, in quibus tota eius paradysus finitur, sectatoribus suis promittit," A 2rd.

[89] Koran 2:35; 3; 7:40ff.; 13:23; 15:45ff.; 18:32, 108; 19:61ff.; 22:23ff.; 25:15ff.; 36:54ff.; 37:42ff.; 38:51ff.; 43:70ff.; 44:51ff.; 47:15; 52:17ff.; 55:46ff.; 56:12ff.; 76:12ff.

[90] See A. J. Arberry, *Sufism* (London, 1950); T. Izutsu, *The Structure of the Ethical Terms in the Koran* (Tokyo, 1959).

[91] Andrae, *Der Ursprung des Islams und das Christentum*, III, 53-54; von Grunebaum, *op. cit.*, 13.

dise in the sense of "the Beatific Vision," which is the Christian's (and thus Peter's) unique doctrine.[92]

"Vomiting back among these things," the text goes on, "almost all the dregs of the ancient heresies, which he had sopped up by the devil's infection, he denies the Trinity with Sabellius, he rejects the divinity of Christ with his Nestorius, [and] he disavows the death of the Lord with Mani, although he does not deny His return to the heavens."[93] Much more will be said of Peter's notion of Islam as a summation of Christian heresies a little later in this chapter.

"Infecting the people with these and similar doctrines, not of a profitable but of a harmful nature, he turned them away from God most fully. And lest the word of the Gospels be able to have any further place among them, as though they were acquainted with everything that pertained to the Gospel and Christ, he stopped up the access of their hearts by the iron barrier of impiety. He determined, moreover, that circumcision was to be maintained, just as it had been taken up by Ishmael, the first of that people."[94] As has already been mentioned, circumcision is not specifically commanded in the Koran, but is practiced by Moslems as a religious rite.[95] The Arab claim of descent from Ishmael, itself a rabbinical notion, is the cornerstone of the Islamic inheritance of faith, for in the koranic view the Arabs were the true descendants of the chosen people and the true heirs of Abraham's covenant.[96] Hence Islam was seen not as a new covenant but as an urgently needed

[92] See the reference in H. Denziger, *Enchiridion Symbolorum*, ed. C. Rahner (Rome, 1957), [54-55].

[93] "Inter ista, omnes pene antiquarum heresum feces, quas diabolo imbuente sorbuerat, reuomens, cum Sabellio trinitatem abnegat, cum suo Nestorio Christi deitatem abicit, cum Manicheo, mortem Domini diffitetur, licet regressum eius non neget ad caelos," A 2rd.

[94] "His et similibus non adquisitionis sed perditionis populum imbuens, a Deo plenissime auertit, et ne euangelicus sermo ultra in eis posset habere locum, uelut omnia quae sunt Euangelii et Christi scientibus, cordium eorum aditum ferrero impietatis obice obturauit. Circumcisionem insuper, uelut ab Hismahele gentis illius patre sumptam, tenendam esse decreuit," A 2rd-vs.

[95] See above, chapter III, note 94.

[96] See Kritzeck, "Jews, Christians, and Moslems," 88-91; S. D. Goitein, *Jews and Arabs* (New York, 1955), 22; Y. Moubarac, *op. cit.*

restoration of the old; the Koran was thought to have been sent down to reestablish a "pure religion" that had been defiled.

"And in addition to all these things, in order that he could more easily attract to himself the carnal minds of men, he loosed the reins on gluttony and impurity, and he himself having at the same time eighteen wives, including the wives of many others, committing adultery as if by divine command, he added to himself a larger number of damned ones by his example, as it were, as a prophet."[97] There is no proof of any kind that Mohammed approved of gluttony, unless Peter is using the word in a somewhat different sense than usual, but polygamy is definitely sanctioned in the Koran.[98] A man may have as many as four wives (but is not, of course, obliged to have more than one or, for that matter, any) and may keep concubines. Mohammed claimed, on the authority of the Koran, that he was permitted to have more wives than the rest of the believers.[99] The exact number of his wives is somewhat difficult to determine, but he certainly had at least eleven wives and six concubines.[100] It has been traditional to distinguish between those whose marriage with the prophet was consummated and those whose marriage was left in a state of treaty or verbal agreement.[101] Unquestionably some of Mohammed's wives had been married before and divorced (for Peter the same thing as "committing adultery," in any case). Although divorce is a relatively easy thing to accomplish according to koranic law, punishment of adulterers is proportionately more severe.[102]

"And in order that he might not appear disgraceful in everything," Peter concludes, "he urges zeal for almsgiving and certain

[97] "Et super haec omnia, quo magis sibi allicere carnales mentes hominum posset, gulae ac libidini frena laxauit, et ipse simul decem et octo uxores habens, atque multorum aliorum uxores uelut ex responso diuino adulterans, maiorem sibi uelut exemplo prophetico numerum perditorum adiunxit," A 2vs.

[98] Koran 4:12, 20ff., 129; 33:4, 37.

[99] Ibid., 33:6, 28ff., 50ff., 55.

[100] See G. H. Stern, Marriage in Early Islam (London, 1939); N. Abbott, Aishah: The Beloved of Mohammed (Chicago, 1942). Mohammed lived monogamously with Khadījah until her death.

[101] Stern, op. cit., 151-57.

[102] Koran 4:15ff., 19; 17:32; 24:2ff.; 33:30.

works of mercy, [and] he praises prayer."[103] Thus the abbot admits that almsgiving and prayer, two of Islam's five "pillars," together with "certain works of mercy," do ameliorate the otherwise shocking nature of Mohammed's doctrine. However, he doubts Mohammed's intentions in proclaiming them, quoting his favorite poet Horace: "And thus, utterly unnaturally, as a certain one says, he 'joined to the human head a horse's neck and the feathers of birds.' "[104]

[103] "Et ne ex toto inhonestus proderetur, studium elemosinarum et quaedam misericordiae opera commendat, orationes collaudat," A 2vs.

[104] "Et sic undique monstruosus, ut ille ait, 'humano capiti ceruicem equinam, et plumas' auium copulat," *ibid*. The reference is to the *Ars Poetica*, 1:1-2.

PETER THE VENERABLE says very little in the *Summa* about the spread of Islam or the historical development of its doctrine. The former concerned him principally insofar as it was the extension of theological error, and he possessed such scant information about the latter that he could not treat it adequately.

"Since, at the persuasion of the aforesaid monk and the aforementioned Jews, [Mohammed] himself left idolatry completely and also persuaded whomever he could that it must be abandoned, and since he taught that one God was to be worshipped, a multiplicity of gods having been abandoned, he seemed to say unheard of things to the simple and uninstructed men. And because this preaching accorded with their reason, he was first believed by them to be a prophet of God."[105] For some time Mohammed's followers were limited to a few relatives and friends; later, as one branch of the Quraysh fought what could only appear to them as a dangerous new religious movement, Islam's recruits came "mainly from among the slave and lower classes."[106] It was not until some citizens of Yathrib (afterward called Medina) invited the prophet to their city to mediate between feuding tribes in 622 that Islam assumed the importance of a powerful and cohesive social force.[107]

"Hence, in the progress of time and error, he was elevated by them to the kingship which he sought. Thus mingling good things with evil things, mixing truth in with falsity, he sowed the seed of error, and in part in his own time, in part and very especially after his time, he produced a devilish crop, to be consumed by

[105] "Qui quoniam suadente iam dicto monacho, ac prefatis Iudeis, ydolatriam ex toto et reliquit, et reliquendam quibus potuit persuasit, atque unum Deum, deorum multiplicitate relicta colendum esse predicauit, hominibus, agrestibus et imperitis inaudita dicere uisus est. Et quia rationi eorum hec predicatio concordabat, propheta Dei primo ad eis creditur," A 2vs.

[106] Hitti, *op. cit.*, 113.

[107] Gibb, *op. cit.*, 29-35; B. Lewis, *The Arabs in History* (London, 1950), 41-42; Watt, *Muhammad at Medina, passim.*

everlasting fire."[108] If one overlooks its angry bias, this passage shows at least that Peter's sense of time in the spread of Islam was correct. During Mohammed's lifetime Islam did not succeed even in uniting all of Arabia; its remarkable conquests came later.[109] As for the prophet's "elevation to kingship," he was never regarded as a king, but rather as a "prophet, lawgiver, religious leader, chief judge, commander of the army, and civil head of the state."[110]

"Forthwith," the *Summa* continues, "while the Roman Empire was declining, nay nearly ceasing, with the permission of Him through whom kings rule [Prov. 8:16; Eccles. 24:9], there arose to power the dominion of the Arabs or Saracens, who were infested with this plague. And occupying by force of arms little by little the greatest parts of Asia, with all of Africa and a part of Spain, just as it transferred its rule upon its subjects, so also did it transfer its error."[111]

[108] "Dehinc processu temporis et erroris, in regem ab eis quod concupierat, sublimatus est. Sic bona malis permiscens, uera falsis confundens, erroris semina seuit, et suo partim tempore, partim et maxime post suum tempus segetem nefariam igne aeterno concremandam produxit," A 2vs.

[109] Brockelmann, *Geschichte der islamischen Völker und Staaten,* 41; see also the bibliography in J. Sauvaget, *Introduction à l'histoire de l'Orient musulman* (Paris, 1961), 126-33.

[110] Hitti, *op. cit.,* 139.

[111] "Nam statim Romano languescente immo pene deficiente imperio, permittente eo per quem reges regnant, Arabum uel Sarracenorum hac peste infectorum surrexit principatus, atque ui armata maximas Asiae partes cum tota Africa ac parte Hispaniae paulatim occupans, in subiectos sicut imperium sic et errorem transfudit," A 2vd.

7 · ISLAM AS A CHRISTIAN HERESY

MATERIAL FROM the *Epistola de translatione sua* and the *Prologus* to the *Liber contra sectam sive haeresim Saracenorum* should be introduced at this point in order to explain what follows in the *Summa*. Peter has two major theses to uphold concerning the relationship of Islamic to Christian doctrine. The first of them, already stated in the *Summa,* is that Islam may be considered as a summation of Christian heresies.

"I wanted to [follow patristic example]," Peter told Bernard of Clairvaux, "concerning that foremost error of errors, concerning those dregs of all the heresies into which all the remnants of the diabolical doctrines have flown together, which came into existence since the very coming of the Savior."[112] In the *Prologus,* after stating the general principle that "every error is to be refuted, everything wicked and against the mind of faith is to be attacked and, if possible, corrected," he goes on to say: "If therefore no heresy sprung up at any time could be immune from the sword of the Spirit, which is the word of God [Eph. 6:17], do you think that the Mohammedan error will be safe from it? Or that the Christian tongue will perhaps pass it by as nothing or little? Or that it will spare it as harmless or of slight harm? What heresy yet, O reader, has so injured the Church of God? Which error yet has so vexed the Christian republic? What has broken down its boundaries by so much? What has increased the number of the damned by such a mass of lost ones?"[113]

[112] "Hoc ego de hoc precipuo errore errorum de hac fece uniuersarum heresum, in quam omnium diabolicarum sectarum quae ab ipso Saluatoris aduentu ortae sunt reliquiae confluxerunt, facere uolui," A 4rs.

[113] "Confutandus est omnis error, omnis prauus et fidei aduersus intellectus corripiendus, et si potest fieri, corrigendus. . . . Si ergo nulla heresis quolibet tempora orta, immunis a gladio Spiritus, quod est uerbum Dei esse potuit, nunquid tutus ab illo Mahumeticus error erit? An forte ut nullum aut paruum Christiana lingua transibit? An forte ut innoxio uel minus noxio parcet? Et quae unquam o lector heresis adeo aecclesiae Dei nocuit? Quis unquam error adeo rem publicam Christianam uexauit? Quis in tantum terminos eius rescidit? Quis tanta massa perditorum numerum infernalem adauxit?" D 179vs.

Peter thinks his reader, in reply to these questions, might suggest Arianism, which he himself regarded as the most devastating of the early heresies. He therefore gives a short history of the spread of Arianism.[114] "But the Mohammedan fury," he continues, "taking its beginning from the Arab Ishmaelites, ravished the Persians, the Medes, the Syrians, the Armenians, the Ethiopians, the Indians, and the rest of the kingdoms of the East, and [did] the same in the three parts of the world: [1] it corrupted the greatest part (almost all) of Asia, and either turning [its inhabitants] away from Christianity or converting them to the sectarian doctrine of that lost man by means of certain errors, it took away Christ and substituted the devil; [2] from here, not by gentle reason but by violent invasion, it subjected to the profane religion (since almost all the armies of the East were subjected, as was said) Egypt, Libya, and all of Africa; [3] and having thus occupied two parts of the world, it did not leave the third (which is called Europe) whole to Christ or his Christians, but broke through into Spain."[115] Peter's assertion that the conquest of Asia preceded that of Egypt and North Africa is not completely sound, but his general conception of the geography of the Islamic world appears to have been more exact than was usual in his time.[116]

"And what shall I say beyond this?" Peter asks. "Not if you were to enumerate all the heresies that sprang up by the diabolical spirit through a thousand and one hundred years from the time of Christ and place them all together as on a scale, could they equal this one, nor could you find all [of them] to have thrown

[114] *Ibid.*

[115] "At Mahumeticus furor ab Hysmaelitis Arabibus sumens exordium, Persas, Medos, Syros, Armenios, Ethiopes, Indos, ac reliqua orientis regna ipsamque in tribus orbis partibus maximam Asiam pene totam corrupit, et uel a Christianismo auertans, uel a quibuslibet antiquis erroribus ad perditi hominis sectam conuertens, subtraxit Christo, substrauit diabolo. Hinc non miti ratione, sed uiolenta incursione, toto fere ut dictum est armis oriente subacto, Egyptum, Lybiam, Affricamque uniuersam prophane religioni subiecit, et sic duabus mundi partibus occupatis, nec tertiam quae Europa uocatur, Hyspania peruasa Christo uel Christianis suis integram dereliquit," D 179vs-vd.

[116] See J. K. Wright, *The Geographical Lore of the Time of the Crusades* (New York, 1925).

such matter equally into the everlasting flames. Therefore, will the Christian tongue, which passed by no (or even little) heresy intact, being sluggish, greatly overlook this greatest error of all errors?"[117]

Peter then faces the important objection that Islam should perhaps not be regarded as a Christian heresy at all. Taking the part of an antagonist, he questions whether any body of doctrine which did not originate within the Church could properly be termed "heresy."[118] He counters the objection first with a definition of heresy: "Christians acting persistently against any part of right faith are, already from ancient usage, to be called by the name 'heretics,' and what they basely think or say is to be called 'heresy.' "[119]

But Peter realizes that the objection is both cogent and potent. "I cannot clearly decide," he feels bound to admit, "whether the Mohammedan error must be called a heresy and its followers heretics, or whether they are to be called pagans. For I see them, now in the manner of heretics, take certain things from the Christian faith and reject other things; then—a thing which no heresy is described as ever having done—acting as well as teaching according to pagan custom. For in company with certain heretics (Mohammed writes so in his wicked Koran), they preach that Christ was indeed born of a virgin, and they say that he is greater than every other man, not excluding Mohammed; they affirm that he lived a sinless life, preached truths, and worked miracles. They acknowledge that he was the Spirit of God, the Word—but not the Spirit of God or the Word as we either know or expound. They insanely hold that the passion and death of Christ were not

---

[117] "Et quid dicam ultra? Nec si uniuersas a Christi tempore per mille et centum annos diabolico spiritu suscitatas hereses numeraueris, simulque collectas uelut in statera appenderis, adaequari huic poterunt, nec pariter omnes tantam aeternis ignibus materiem iniecisse inuenies. Quae ergo nullam uel paruam heresim intactam praeteriit, nunquid hunc omnium errorum maximum errorem, torpens uel multa Christiana lingua transibit?" D 179vd.

[118] *Ibid.*

[119] "Fateor hoc inquam et ipse, Christianos pertinaciter contra quamlibet rectae fidei partem agentes, iam ab antiquo usitato nomine dici hereticos, et id quod praue sentiunt uel fatentur, uocari heresim," *ibid.*

mere fantasies (as the Manichaeans [had held]), but did not actually happen. They hold these and similar things, indeed, in company with heretics. With pagans, however, they reject baptism, do not accept the Christian sacrifice [of the Mass, and] deride penance and all the rest of the sacraments of the Church."[120]

Peter concludes this discussion in the *Prologus* by inviting his reader to form his own decision on the question. "Choose, therefore, whichever you prefer: either call [the Moslems] heretics on account of the heretical opinion by which they agree with the Church in part and disagree in part, or call them pagans on account of the surpassing wickedness by which they subdue every heresy of error in evil profession."[121] For his own part, Peter usually chose to call them heretics.[122]

Returning to the text of the *Summa,* we discover the gist of the expanded discussion in the *Prologus.* "Though I named them heretics," Peter says, "because they believe some things in common with us, yet in many things disagree with us, perhaps I should call them pagans or heathens, which is worse. For although they say some true things about the Lord, they preach even more false things, and share [with Christians] neither baptism, nor the

[120] "Sed utrum Mahumeticus error heresis dici debeat, et eius sectatores heretici uel aethnici uocari, non satis discerno. Video enim eos hinc hereticorum more de fide Christiana quaedam suscipere, quaedam abicere, hinc ritu pagano quod nulla unquam heresis fecisse scribitur, facere pariter et docere. Nam cum quibusdam hereticis, scribente sic in Alchorano suo impio Mahumeth, Christum quidem de uirgine natum praedicant, maiorem omni homine ipsoque Mahumeth dicunt, sine peccato uixisse, uera praedicasse, mira fecisse affirmant, spiritum Dei, uerbum Dei fuisse fatentur, sed nec Spiritum Dei aut Uerbum ut nos aut intelligunt aut exponunt. Christi passionem aut mortem non solum ut Manichei phantasticam, sed nullam prorsus extitisse uesaniunt. Haec quidem et similia cum hereticis sentiunt. Cum paganis autem baptisma abiciunt, sacrificium Christianum respuunt, paenitentiam cunctaque reliqua aecclesiae sacramenta derident," D 179vd-8ors.

[121] "Elige igitur quod malueris. Aut uoca hereticos propter hereticum sensum, et quo partim cum aecclesia sentiunt, partim dissentiunt, aut dic paganos propter excellentem impietatem, qua omnium heresum errores professione impia uincunt," D 18ors.

[122] He did so also in his letters and the *Liber adversus Judaeorum inveteratam duritiem*, BC 1055B-56A. See Daniel, *op. cit.,* 184-88. It is interesting to note that Dante elevated Mohammed to the comparatively high rank of schismatic, *Inferno,* XXVIII:35.

sacrifice [of the Mass], nor penance, nor any other Christian sacrament, a thing which no one besides these heretics ever did."[123]

Peter is now prepared to advance his second thesis concerning Islam, namely, that it may be viewed as a part of a satanic scheme to harm the Christian Church and that Mohammed himself may be viewed as a kind of "mean" between Arius and Antichrist: "The highest purpose of this heresy is to have Christ the Lord believed to be neither God nor the Son of God, but (though a great man and one beloved of God) simply a man—a wise man and the greatest prophet. Indeed, that which was once conceived by the device of the devil, first propagated through Arius, then advanced by that satan, namely Mohammed, will be fulfilled completely, according to the diabolical plan, through the Antichrist. For since the Blessed Hilary said that the origin of the Antichrist arose in Arius,[124] then what [Arius] began by denying that Christ was the one true Son of God and calling him a creature, the Antichrist will finally bring to its completion by asserting that he was not only not God or the Son of God, but not even a good man. This most wicked Mohammed seems to have been appropriately provided and prepared by the devil as the mean between these two, so that he became both a supplement, to a certain extent, to Arius, and the greatest sustenance for the Antichrist, who will allege even worse things before the minds of unbelievers."[125]

[123] "Hos licet hereticos nominem, quia aliqua nobiscum credunt, in pluribus a nobis dissentiunt, fortassis rectius paganos aut ethnicos quod plus est, nominarem. Quia quamuis de Domino uera aliqua dicant, plura tamen falsa predicant, nec baptismati, sacrificio, paenitentiae, uel alicui Christiano sacramento, quod numquam ullus preter hos hereticus fecit, communicant," A 2vd.

[124] J. Kinnaney, *The Vocabulary of St. Hilary of Poitiers* (Washington, 1935), *s.v.* "Antichrist," lists nineteen references; Peter's statement seems to refer to *De Trinitate*, 6:43; but cf. 2:23.

[125] "Summa uero huius heresis intentio est, ut Christus Dominus neque Deus, neque Dei filius esse credatur, sed licet magnus Deoque dilectus, homo tamen purus, et uir quidem sapiens, et propheta maximus. Quae quidem olim diaboli machinatione concepta, primo per Arrium seminata, deinde per istum Sathanan scilicet Mahumet, prouecta, per Antichristum uero, ex toto secundum diabolicam intentionem complebitur. Cum enim dicat beatus Hylarius, Antichristi originem

Because this notion was original in the history of the Christian-Islamic polemic, it is fortunate that Peter went on to explain it in some detail.[126] "Surely nothing is so contrary to the enemy of human nature [Satan]," he states, "as faith in the incarnate God, through which particularly we are moved to a life of holiness, renewed as we are by the sacraments of heaven through the operative grace of the Holy Spirit, [and through which] we hope to return again to that place from which [Satan] took glory in having us cast forth, namely to the vision of our King and fatherland. . . . He tried to eradicate this [faith] also in the beginning of the still nascent Church, if it had been permitted then, by very ingenious subtlety, and in almost the same way by which afterwards he was allowed to lead that unhappy race [the Moslems] astray."[127]

Peter has in mind an illustration from St. Augustine. "The Blessed Augustine also says that the philosopher Porphyry, after he had wretchedly apostatized from Christianity, had related in his books which he put forth against the Christians that he consulted the oracle of the gods and asked about Christ, what he was; that, however, the reply of the devils had been that Christ was a man and that his disciples had sinned gravely when, by ascribing divinity to him, they had feigned something which he himself

---

in Arrio extitisse, dum quod ille caepit, uerum filium Dei Christum esse negando, et creaturam dicendo, Antichristus tandem nullo modo illum Deum uel Dei filium, sed nec etiam bonum hominem fuisse asserendo consummaturus est, merito impiissimus Mahumeth inter utrumque medius a diabolo prouisus ac preparatus esse uidetur, qui et Arrii quodammodo supplementum, et Antichristi peiora dicturi, apud infidelium mentes maximum fieret nutrimentum," A 2vd-3rs.

[126] Daniel, *op.cit.*, 184-86; later the notion was a common one among Christian polemicists.

[127] "Nichil quippe ita contrarium est humani generis inimico, sicut fides incarnati Dei, per quam precipue ad pietatem excitamur, et sacramentis caelestibus renouati Spiritus Sancti gratia operante, illuc unde nos deiecisse gloriabatur, ad uisionem scilicet regis et patriae nostrae, ipso rege et conditore Deo ad nostrum exilium descendente, nosque ad se misericorditer reuocante, iterum redire speramus. Hanc pietatis et diuinae dispensationis fidem pariter et amorem, semper ab initio in cordibus hominum molitur extinguere, hanc etiam in principio adhuc nascentis ecclesiae, si tunc permittetur, subtilitate uersutissima, et pene hoc eodem modo quo postea gentem istam infelicissimam seducere permissus est, eradicare temptauit," A 3rs.

had not said.[128] This opinion is found very often, in almost the same words, in those fables [of the Moslems]. How great, though, was this subtlety of the devil that he said something good about Christ, for he knew that he would not be believed at all if he spoke only evil of him. He did not care what Christ was thought to be as long as divinity, which particularly brings salvation to men, was not believed to be in him."[129] Peter adds a few specific references to the subject: "If anyone wishes to understand more fully, he should read the eighteenth and nineteenth books of *The City of God,* by the same Father Augustine,[130] and the first [book] of *The Concordance of the Evangelists.*[131] For there, if he is of good and scholarly talents, he should be able to infer for certain both what the devil then had planned to do, but was not allowed, and what he did effect, by a hidden judgment, in that most wicked race alone [the Moslems] when he was let loose."[132]

The connection between Mohammed and Satan is charged even more explicitly in the passage with which Peter ends his treatment of this matter: "For in no way could anyone of the human race, unless the devil were there helping, devise such fables

[128] *De Civitate Dei,* XIX:23, ed. M. Dods (New York, 1950), 701-06. It may be recalled that Peter the Venerable had himself written a treatise on Christ's claims to divinity in the Gospels; see above, chapter 1, note 73.

[129] "Dicit enim beatus Augustinus, Porphirium philosophum postquam a Christianitate miserabiliter apostatauit, hoc in libris suis quos aduersus Christianos aedidit, retulisse, quod scilicet oracula deorum consuluerit, et de Christo quid esset interrogauerit. Responsum uero sibi a demonibus fuisse, quod Christus, bonus quidem uir fuerit, sed discipulos eius grauiter peccasse, qui ei diuinitatem ascribentes, rem quam ipse de se non dixerat, confinxissent. Quae sententia, pene eisdem uerbis, in istis fabulis inuenitur sepissime. Quanta autem haec diaboli subtilitas extiterit, ut de Christo aliquid boni diceret, de quo si ex toto male dixisset, nullatenus iam sibi credi sciebat, non curans quicquid Christus putaretur, dummodo diuinitas quae maxime saluat homines in illo non crederetur," A 3rs-rd.

[130] *Ed. cit.,* 609-709.

[131] Tr. S. D. F. Salmond, *Nicene and Post-Nicene Fathers,* First Series, VI (New York, 1888), 77-101.

[132] "Si quis plenius uult intelligere, legat octauum decimum eiusdem patris Augustini librum, et nonum decimum De Ciuitate Dei, et primum De Consensu Euangelistarum. Ibi enim si boni ac studiosi ingenii est, coniciet pro certo, et quid diabolus tunc machinatus sit facere sed non permissus, et quid tandem occulto iudicio permittente, in hac sola miserrima gente fecerit relaxatus," A 3rd.

as the writings which here follow.[133] By means of them, after many ridiculous things and the maddest absurdities, this Satan had as his object particularly and in every way to bring it about that Christ the Lord would not be believed to be the Son of God and true God, the creator and redeemer of the human race. And this is truly what he then attempted to induce through Porphyry, but through the mercy of God was blown away from the Church, which even up to that time was fervent with the first-fruits of the Holy Spirit. But finally, employing that most wretched man Mohammed (and, as is said by some, a man possessed [by the devil] and an epileptic), using him as an instrument and tool very suitable for him, alas, he plunged with himself into everlasting damnation a very numerous race, which can be considered to constitute almost one-half of the world."[134]

The notion that Mohammed was "possessed" had been developed at length by Al-Kindi and was, not unnaturally, a popular Christian view.[135] Theophanes repeated or perhaps originated the story of Mohammed's epilepsy.[136] As suggestive as the descriptions of Mohammed's actions during his "revelations" undoubtedly are, the diagnosis of epilepsy is not, for many reasons, as deserving of consideration as it once seemed.[137]

To the single remaining question which Peter feels may lurk

[133] That is, the Toledan Collection.

[134] "Nullo enim modo tales fabulas quales hic scriptae secuntur, aliquis mortalium nisi diabolo presentialiter cooperante, fingere potuisset, per quas multa ridicula et insanissima deliramenta, hoc precipue omnimodo Sathanas intendit perficere, ne Christus Dominus, Dei filius et uerus Deus, humani generis conditor et redemptor esse credatur. Et hoc est uere, quod per Porphirium tunc persuadere uoluit, sed per Dei misericordiam ab ecclesia eo adhuc tempore, Spiritus Sanctu feruente primitiis, exsufflatus, tandem miserrimo homine isto Mahumet, et ut fertur a multis, arreptico et cadente, quasi instrumento et organo sibi aptissimo usus, proh dolor, gentem maximam et quae iam pene dimidia pars mundi reputari potest, secum in aeternam preditionem demersit," A 3rd.

[135] Daniel, *op. cit.*, 30-31, 69-70, 81, 246, 328, 339, 344.

[136] *Ed. cit.*, I, 334; II, 209; Daniel, *op. cit.*, 28-29, 90, 104-05, 239, 280, 287, 327-28.

[137] See J. C. Archer, *Mystical Elements in Mohammed* (New Haven, 1924), 14-23. O. Temkin, *The Falling Sickness* (Baltimore, 1945), does not include Mohammed in its references to known epileptics, although less reliable works such as J. E. Bryant, *Genius and Epilepsy* (Concord, 1953), 57-61, do.

in his reader's mind—why, if Arius and Porphyry were prevented from accomplishing their nefarious aims, was Mohammed permitted to accomplish his?—the abbot has but few words to say: "As to why it was permitted to him, He alone knows to whom no one can say, 'Why did you act this way?' and who has also said that 'of the many called, few are chosen' [Matt. 22:14]. On that account I choose rather to tremble than dispute."[138]

Although Peter offered no explanation for the vexing presence of this widespread heretical doctrine beyond the inscrutable design and economy of a divine providence, it is abundantly clear from the last few sentences of the *Summa,* which have been quoted to greater advantage in another context,[139] that he did not therefore hold himself or his fellow Christians excused from studying it closely and pointing out its errors.

---

[138] "Quod quare illi permissum sit, ille solus nouit cui nemo potest dicere, 'Cur ita facis?' et qui 'de multis etiam uocatis, paucos electos esse' dixit. Vnde ego magis eligens contresmiscere, quam disputare, ista breuiter prenotaui," A 3rd-vs.

[139] See above, chapter I, parts 3 and 5.

IN ATTEMPTING to evaluate the *Summa totius haeresis Saracenorum,* it is necessary first to distinguish sharply between the facts presented in the text and the interpretations which Peter gave to them. It must be granted that European ignorance of the subject was such as to render any even moderately informed statement of fact an advance.

No part of the Toledan Collection, naturally Peter's main source for the summary, is cited directly in the text, and yet the general references to it are sufficiently self-assured as to convince the reader that Peter had at very least scanned the translations with care. The information contained in the *Summa* bears this out. Peter had evidently consulted the *Fabulae Saracenorum* on the descent of the Arabs from Ishmael, on Mohammed, and on the spread of Islam; the *Liber generationis Mahumet* on Ishmael and Mohammed; the *Doctrina Mahumet* on Jewish influences, the retention of circumcision, and the Islamic eschatological beliefs; the Koran on its own composition, on the nature of God, the place of Christ, and moral precepts; and the *Rescriptum Christiani,* or apology of Al-Kindi, on the Islamic denial of the Trinity, on Christ and the Koran, and on special subjects such as Mohammed's polygamy.

In connection with the last-named translation, it is interesting to note that, although Peter missed a few opportunities to improve his information from it, he also avoided a great many of Al-Kindi's barbed and sometimes scurrilous remarks. To the material from the Toledan Collection must be added that obtained from the *Chronicon* of Theophanes, which Peter apparently consulted partly to confirm and partly to supplement the other. Most of the historical chronology is that of Theophanes, as are the suggestions of the diabolical possession and epilepsy of Mahommed, which Peter mentions merely in passing.

There are four undoubted errors of fact in the *Summa*: the establishment of the time of Mohammed's aspiration to kingship and use of the sword before his claim to prophethood; the relative dating of the conquests of Asia and Africa; the statement that Mohammed had once become a Nestorian; and, finally, his alleged approval of gluttony. Six other subjects treated by Peter in the text could be singled out as weakly presented, either because of disputes about them within Islam or some deficiency in Peter's own analyses: the distinction between the essence and soul of God, the death of Christ, the eventual conversion of the Jews, the Baḥīra-Sergius legend, the superiority of Christ to Mohammed, and the charge of epilepsy.

One should not make light of or attempt to explain away these errors and weaknesses, for they were to persist and exert influence for five centuries. On the other hand, they pale considerably in face of the tremendous advance in knowledge inherent in Peter's scrupulously accurate clarification of the Islamic denial of the Trinity; the portrayal of Christ in Islam; the disassociation of Mohammed from other heresiarchs; the precise dating of his life; the establishment of the ideological connections between Islam and the early Christian heresies, the apocryphal literature, and Judaism; the analysis of Islamic eschatology; and the outline of the geography of Islam.

Before facing the question of Peter's interpretations, it should again be stressed that he was a Christian cleric writing especially for other Christian clerics. That is, of course, the definition of a bias, a bias which explains why throughout, but particularly in cases of doubt, Peter's interpretations are set down in terms of the exigencies of Christian theology. Thus the idea that Islam as a religion was "founded" to realize Mohammed's political ambitions must now be discarded. The same holds true for the interpretation of the spread of Islam by the sword. With a tendency not to believe all of the meager store of facts at hand, Peter sometimes drew hasty and faulty conclusions.

The marked understatement of the good points (by Christian standards) in Islamic doctrine is less easily forgiven, while the quotation from Horace after the discussion of polygamy is almost vicious. Such interpretations as the diabolical possession of Mohammed and the providential explanation of Islam's rise do not, of course, fall within the historian's province and hence do not yield to comment here. Peter did put forward two original, vivid, and somewhat daring interpretations in his theses concerning Islam as a summation of Christian heresies and itself a heresy (though, owing to its denial of the sacramental system, a heresy bordering on paganism) and Mohammed as a "mean" between Arius and the Antichrist—the latter an idea nurtured more by his reading of St. Hilary of Poitiers and St. Augustine, one tends to conclude, than of the Toledan Collection.[140]

Both in its historical and theological content, then, the *Summa* set down by Peter for his fellow Christians had a great potential educational value. It would be unfair to him to draw any more stringent conclusions before examining his own method of employing this information in the very manner he intended, that is to say, in the refutation of Islamic doctrine which he himself composed.

[140] Cf. Daniel's verdict, *op. cit.*, 229-30: "The *summula* . . . contains little that it would have been altogether hopeless to maintain in public debate before a sympathetic or even neutral audience; clearly an editorial effort was made which is remarkable at least for excluding wilder elements. Treatment and substance in the *summula* are traditionally Christian, but it is characteristically Western in presentation; there is nothing that an Oriental Christian could have written."

V · THE REFUTATION

*Aggredior inquam vos non
ut nostri sæpe faciunt
armis sed verbis, non vi
sed ratione, non odio
sed amore.*

*Vos diligo, diligens vobis
scribo, scribens ad
salutem invito.*
PETER THE VENERABLE

1 · MS 381 OF THE BIBLIOTHÈQUE MUNICIPALE DE DOUAI AND THE *CAPITULA* OF PETER OF POITIERS

☙ MS 381 of the Bibliothèque municipale de Douai appears to be the only surviving manuscript of Peter the Venerable's *Liber contra sectam sive haeresim Saracenorum*.[1] This manuscript belonged to the abbey of Anchin before becoming the property of the municipal library of Douai, and so is unquestionably the manuscript from which Martène prepared his edition, which Migne copied.[2] It dates from the twelfth century, possibly within ten years of the lifetime of the abbot. There are one hundred and ninety-five folios on parchment, and the unusually perfect script is in double columns of forty-eight lines throughout. The titles are in red and green, and there are several fine initials recognized as the work of the scribe Siger, a monk of Anchin.[3] The bulk of the manuscript is taken up with Peter's letters[4] and the *Liber adversus Judaeorum inveteratam duritiem;*[5] the *Liber contra sectam sive haeresim Saracenorum* is the last item in the manuscript.[6]

The *Liber* survives in two books, preceded by a lengthy *Prologus* addressed to Christian readers. The work as it was projected by Peter of Poitiers in a set of chapter headings, prepared at his abbot's request, was to have contained four books.[7] Most authorities, following, no doubt, the careful and talented scribe of the Douai manuscript, have assumed that the two books represent only one half of Peter's original refutation.[8] I am of a contrary

---

[1] *Catalogue général des manuscrits des bibliothèques publiques des départements, VI: Douai* (Paris, 1878), 214-15.

[2] *Ibid.*, i-ix, 215; Martène and Durand, *op. cit.*, ix, 1119-20.

[3] *Catalogue général*, 215. Mandonnet's conjecture that the manuscript was sent from Cluny, *op. cit.*, 340-42, based on Peter of Poitiers' letter, is therefore inadmissible. Constable, "Manuscripts of Works by Peter the Venerable," 237, calls it "the largest and most authoritative manuscript collection of the works of Peter the Venerable."

[4] D 13r-120v.　　[5] D 131r-77r.　　[6] D 177r-95r.　　[7] D 177vs-78rs.

[8] There is a marginal notation by the scribe, "Desunt duo libri quos inuenire non potui," on D 195rd.

mind, believing that what remains to us is the entirety of the work completed by Peter. I suspect that the Anchin scribe and his followers went astray in taking Peter of Poitiers' *Capitula* to constitute an index to the work; whereas the fact of the matter is that these divisions were not followed by Peter the Venerable, and all the subjects which they propose, with some exceptions the omission of which is quite easy to account for, are amply treated in the two books.[9]

The only other evidence I have found for the existence of more books is the statement in the *Chronicon Cluniacensis* that there were, in fact, five books.[10] I have already had occasion to remark that this chronicle is not always a trustworthy source.[11] On this point its stature is further weakened by the addition of the words "qui libri diuiduntur per capitula," inasmuch as the *Liber* has no chapter divisions at all and the reference is obviously to the *Capitula*. It might be allowed that the ending of the second book is rather abrupt. This fact could support the view that the work was originally envisioned on a larger scale, but could not of itself require belief that more was actually written.

If more had been written, indeed, a great deal of entirely new material would have had to be introduced; and this seems to me, from Peter's fairly evident faltering toward the end of the second book, completely unlikely.

[9] The following items from the *Capitula* appear in the *Liber*: I, 1-7; II, 1, 8; III, 2-5, 7-8; IV, 1-4. Some of the items appear in the *Summa*: II, 2-3, 5, 7; IV, 5. Those eliminated altogether are mainly unsavory attacks on Mohammed. On the quotations from the Toledan Collection in the *Capitula*, see Kritzeck, "Peter the Venerable and the Toledan Collection," 190-92. On II, 6, see Daniel, *op. cit.*, 320-22.

[10] BC 591C.

[11] See above, chapter I, note 99.

✣ Most of the *Prologus* to the *Liber contra sectam sive haeresim Saracenorum* concerns itself with the origins of and patristic authority for the project to study Islam and a discussion of the nature of that religion with reference to Christianity—topics which it has seemed more appropriate to treat in the foregoing chapters. There are, however, a few other points considered in the *Prologus* which should be mentioned.

It opens with the customary invocation to the Holy Spirit and a statement of purpose replete with scriptural quotations. Peter then embarks at once on his elaborate justification for the work, summarizing the doctrines of early heresies and citing the patristic books of refutation.[12] He takes up the nature of the Islamic creed, discussing its spread and its "heretical" and "pagan" aspects, with appropriate citations of patristic books against the Jews and pagans.[13] Then he outlines the history of the project to study Islam and states its aims.[14]

Peter seems to have been worried by the possible objection that a book of refutation of Islamic doctrine, written in a foreign language to an obstinate people, would serve no useful purpose whatsoever. "Perhaps someone now [would ask]: 'What will it profit to pour out a fare to those who refuse it? . . . For the men against whom you are disposed to act are foreigners, are barbarians not only in customs but also in their language, manifesting nothing that is common to them and to the Latins. How, then, will the Arab hear, to say nothing of understanding, the Latin? . . . It must be considered, lest work is expended in vain . . . [and] time is unnecessarily wasted.' "[15] He puts the objections so ex-

---

[12] D 178rs-79vs; see above, chapter I, part 4.

[13] D 179vs-8ord; see above, chapter IV, parts 6-7.

[14] D 18ord; see above, chapter I, parts 3, 5.

[15] "Sed forte adhuc aliquis: 'Quid proderit fastidientibus cibos ingerere . . . ? Nam homines contra quos agere disponis, alieni sunt, barbari sunt, non solum moribus, sed et lingua ipsa, nil sibi Latinisque commune esse fatentur. Quomodo igitur audiet ne dicam exaudiet Arabs Latinum. . . . Videndum est ne frustra labor insumatur, . . . superfluo tempus teratur,' " D 18ord-vs.

plicitly and with such feeling that one might be tempted to imagine that he had already heard them, perhaps from fellow prelates (Bernard of Clairvaux?) or his own monks.[16] His reply, however, is ready: "It can happen, after all, that the book will be translated into their language, [for] Christian truth can be put into Arabic letters or any others, just as the deplorable error could come across to the knowledge of the Latins by my own zeal. Thus the Latin work, when translated into that strange language, may possibly profit some others whom the Lord will wish to acquire life by the grace of God."[17] There is no doubt that Peter hoped and at least vaguely planned that his work would be translated into Arabic so that the Moslems could read it.[18]

In order to strengthen his point Peter cites further examples of scriptural and patristic translations, remarking on the obvious need for translations from the Hebrew and Greek and the "reciprocity of sermons" between the Greek and Latin Fathers. But even if his book "will find no interpreters or produce no translations," he continues, "at least the Christian armory will also have arms against those enemies."[19] There may even be another use for the book, Peter believes—"to counteract the concealed thoughts of some of us, by which they may be led into scandal."[20] It sets one to wondering whom Peter had in mind; perhaps it was those

[16] See above, chapter I, note 152.

[17] "Poterit inquam quod scriptum fuerit in eorum linguam transferri, poterit Christiana ueritas in litteras Arabicas uel quaslibet alias commutari, sicut potuit nefandus error ad Latinorum noticiam meo studio transmigrare. Sic Latinum opus in peregrinam linguam translatum proderit forsitan aliquibus, quos ductrix ad uitam gratia Deo lucrari uoluerit," D 180vs.

[18] See below, part 7. To the best of my knowledge, the work has been translated only into German, *Zwei Bücher gegen den Muhammedanismus . . . von Petrus dem Ehrwürdigen, Abt von Clugny,* tr. J. Thomä (Leipzig, 1896). On pp. 131-36 the translator makes several emendations of the text, and on 135-36, note 95, discusses the question of the completeness of the work. The only copy of this translation I have ever seen is in the library of the American University in Cairo.

[19] "Quod si forte haec de qua agitur scriptura aut interpretes non habuerit, aut translata non profuerit, habebit saltem Christianum armarium etiam aduersus hos hostes arma," D 180vs.

[20] "Occurret fortasse uolumen editum cogitationibus occultis nostrorum, quibus scandalizari possunt," *ibid.*

people in Spain of whom Robert of Ketton had made mention in his dedicatory letter to the translation of the *Fabulae Saraceno-rum*,[21] or others in Sicily and the Holy Land.[22]

Peter concludes by attacking these objections in a more general manner. Although the Church Fathers did not know precisely whom their works would benefit, he insists, "they did not on that account leave the spirit to be unoccupied with study, or the tongue with speaking, or the hand with writing. The Greek writer did not pay attention to the Latin whom Greek could not profit, nor did the Latin [writer pause to] think that the Greek would read Latin in vain. . . . They knew, they were certain, that 'the Holy Spirit breathes where He wills,' [John 3:8] but they could not know on whom, when, or how much He breathes."[23] Peter had written in much the same terms to Bernard of Clairvaux concerning St. Augustine's efforts to convert the heretics of his own day.[24] "He who will wish to follow them, I think—indeed I affirm—will not err. If I myself shall have done it, I am certain that I shall not err. . . . Certainly it will not be possible for the work, undertaken for the cause of God, to escape completely without fruit; whether that may be to make converts, to resist enemies, or to fortify those at home, at least the peace promised 'to men of good will' [Luke 2:14] will not fail the writer of these [pages]."[25]

As a kind of afterthought Peter concludes the *Prologus* with an apology for its length: "In conclusion, I add that I knew and was certain that I would exceed a little, by unaccustomed great

---

[21] See above, chapter II, note 55.

[22] See Kritzeck, "Jews, Christians, and Moslems," 112-13.

[23] "Cumque nec elegissent neque praescissent, quorum saluti labores proprii inseruire deberent, non tamen idcirco uel animum a studendo, uel linguam a dictando, uel manum a scribendo uacare permiserunt. Non attendit Grecus scriptor Latino non posse prodesse Grecitatem, non cogitauit Latinus Greco frustra legi Latinitatem. . . . Nouerant, certi erant, quod Spiritus ubi uult spirat, sed scire non poterant, quos, quando, uel quantum inspirat," D 180vd.

[24] A 4rd-vs.

[25] "Hos qui sequi uoluerit, aestimo, immo affirmo, quia non errabit. Quod si et ipse fecero, certus sum quia non errabo. . . . Non poterit certe non poterit omnino labor causa Dei assumptus euadere absque fructu, si autem conuersis profuerit, aut hostibus obstiterit, aut domesticos munierit, aut saltem horum scriptori pax bonae uoluntatis hominibus repromissa non defuerit," D 180vd.

length in such matters, the customary limits of a prologue. But that the reader may hold me excused, let him know that it touched upon the troublesome objections of disputers. Lest I seem brief to them, I have appeared, I hope rightfully, more comprehensive to others."[26]

[26] "In fine addo, quia noui et certus sum, insolita in talibus prolixitate me consuetas prologi metas aliquantulum excessisse. Sed ut excusatam me lector habeat, sciat hoc importunis obiectionibus disputantium contigisse, quibus ne breuis uiderer, forte iusto prolixior aliis extiti," *ibid*.

THE WORDS with which Peter the Venerable begins his address to the Moslems set the tone for the entire work: "A certain Peter, by nationality a Frenchman, by faith a Christian, by profession an abbot of those who are called monks, to the Arabs, the sons of Ishmael, who observe the law of that one who is called Mohammed. It seems strange, and perhaps it really is, that I, a man so very distant from you in place, speaking a different language, having a state of life separate from yours, a stranger to your customs and life, write from the far parts of the West to men who inhabit the lands of the East and South, and that I attack, by my utterance, those whom I have never seen, whom I shall perhaps never see. But I do not attack you, as some of us often do, by arms, but by words; not by force, but by reason; not in hatred, but in love."[27]

By contrasting his own approach with that of many of his fellow Christians, Peter clearly implies a criticism of the Crusade and seeks to win the friendly attention of the Moslems.[28] He addresses all of the Moslems as "Arabs," not singling out any in particular but pointedly including those in the East. He goes on to relate his love to that of the Apostles and, indeed, of God for men.[29] He cites two authorities for his attitude—Christ's commands and human reason, illustrating the latter in some detail. Even lower animals, he says, are drawn together within their species; but man is "endowed with reason, which no other species of animals has," and hence "is known to love what is like himself,

[27] "Petrus quidam, Gallus natione, Christianus fide, abbas officio eorum qui monachi dicuntur, Arabibus Hysmahelis filiis, legen illius qui Mahumeth dicitur, seruantibus. Mirum uidetur, et fortassis etiam est, quod homo a uobis loco remotissimus, lingua diuersus, professione seiunctus, moribus, uitaque alienus, ab ultimis occidentis hominibus in orientis uel meridie partibus positis scribo, et quos nunquam uidi, quos nunquam forte, uisurus sum, loquendo aggredior. Aggredior inquam uos, non ut nostri sepe faciunt armis sed uerbis, non ui sed ratione, non odio sed amore," D 181rs.

[28] See above, chapter I, part 2.

[29] D 181rs. Where the text is paraphrased, summarized, or only very partially quoted in the following sections, reference will be given to the loci.

led by reason, far more than [the animal] which is motivated [only] by nature."[30]

"These are the reasons for which the Christian loves you," Peter says in summation, "one of them divine, the other human. In the former he is obedient to divine instruction; in the latter he satisfies his own nature. In the same way I, of the innumerable ones, and the very least among the numberless servants of Christ, love you; loving, I write to you; writing, I invite you to salvation."[31] It is not Peter's intention to keep the purpose of his book hidden. He reveals it at the outset. It consists of an invitation to salvation, the nature of which is in part explained by three quotations from the Psalms.[32]

He allows himself to digress for a short time in order to explain why he feels free to quote the Psalms in establishing his points: "I hear from your Mohammed that the Psalms were given to David by God. For, speaking to Abdia the Jew, he said so: 'One, indeed, is God; two are Adam and Eve; three, indeed, are Gabriel, Michael, and Seraphael; four are the Law of Moses, the Psalms of David, the Gospel, and Al-Furqān.'[33] And again: 'For the Word of God did not come down upon me all at once, as the Law was given all at once to Moses, the Psalms to David, and the Gospel to Christ.' "[34] The two quotations in the passage are from the *Doctrina Mahumet*.[35] Attention has been called to the many heterodox elements in this particular text. Fortunately for Peter's argument, however, the quotations he selected from it can be

[30] D 181rd.

[31] "Hee sunt causae, quibus uos Christianus diligere. . . . Harum altera diuina, altera humana est. In illa praecepto diuino obaedit, in hac naturae propriae satisfacit. Hoc modo ego de innumeris et inter innumeros seruos Christi minimus, uos diligo, diligens uobis scribo, scribens, ad salutem inuito," *ibid*.

[32] Ps. 145:3, 59:13, 36:39; *ibid*.

[33] See above, chapter III, note 84.

[34] "Quae Psalmorum uerba ea uobis de causa propono, quia Psalmos a Deo Dauid fuisse datos, a uestro Mahumeth audio. Loquens enim Abdiae Iudeo, sic ait: 'Vnum quidem, Deus. Duo uero, Adam et Eua. Tria uero, Gabrihel, Mychael, Seraphiel. Quatuor, lex Moysi, Psalmi Dauid, Aeuangelium, et Alfurchan.' Item: 'Nec enim simul descendit super me uerbum Dei quemadmodum simul data est lex Moysi, Psalmi Dauid, et Aeuangelium Christo,' " D 181rd.

[35] A 19vd, 19vs; the former is considerably abbreviated.

upheld by many koranic passages. For the first quotation he might have substituted 17:55, "And We preferred some of the prophets above others, and unto David We gave the Psalms," or 4:163, "We imparted unto David the Psalms." The first part of the second quotation is a paraphrase of 17:106, "And a Koran which We have divided that thou mayest recite it to the people at intervals"; on the latter part, compare, for instance, 5:66, 110; 7:157; 9:111; 35:25; 48:29.

Returning to his argument, Peter adds a few words about the nature of the salvation to which he has invited his Moslem readers, and then frames an objection which he imagines they would wish to make. The objection amounts to nothing more than a firm profession of faith in the divine revelation of the Koran and the expression of a preference not to question that faith or the validity of its tradition.[36] In reply, Peter attempts to show how inconsistent this attitude is with their eminent philosophical studies. He praises their "ingenuity and art," but marvels at "the obstinacy of superstition" which disposes them to refuse to hear anything against their laws and customs. He urges them, as "prudent according to secular science," to "consider acutely whether that custom is probable, whether it can be supported by any reason." For "no man who is rational, not so merely by nature but also by lively acumen of mind, wishes to be deceived in temporal things. He does not wish to take certain things for uncertain or uncertain things for certain."[37]

Laboring that point, Peter urges the Moslems to consider three examples. The first is the example of friends, relatives, and those "joined by the bond of love"; although it is well known that "a great many and the most grievous things of body and soul are borne patiently by friends on account of friends," he remarks, human nature dictates that a man should not err "by means of anyone else, however close or however much a friend." Next the Moslems are invited to consider whether any of the "studious

[36] D 181rd-vs. Daniel, op. cit., 17-18, quotes it in part and remarks, "There was an uncommon appreciation here of a view opposed to the Christian view and still not presented as absurd."
[37] D 181vs.

lovers of secular science" are inclined to err in such a way, or whether they do not "accept truer and more certain knowledge from the erudite or teachers." For his third example he calls up the philosophers themselves, who characteristically "worked to reach the truth of those things in which they are versed by innumerable methods of argumentation on questions proposed." It was always a cardinal requirement of the philosophical approach to truth that there be no obstructions to the inquiring mind; "on the contrary, by much arguing from opposites" the philosophers "enkindled themselves and others to praiseworthy study of all manner of assertion."[38]

What is perhaps most interesting about this entire section of the *Liber,* but especially about this last example of Peter's, is the fact that it reveals the abbot as remarkably well acquainted with and sympathetically involved in one of the major intellectual developments of his proximate milieu, namely, the rebirth of interest in philosophical speculation.[39] Like Peter Abelard, whom he received at Cluny and whose memory must still have been green, he was convinced that the religious man had nothing to fear from philosophy, but rather had in it a unique instrument for his service. Furthermore, he must have felt that the example of philosophy, a branch of learning in which the Moslems were known by him to have excelled, and in which Europeans still depended upon them to a large extent, would greatly appeal to his readers.

The rational mind, Peter continues, naturally wishes to extend itself to bring "the uncreated" into its ken. Created things are sought "in order that they may bring help or use in some way to [one's] transitory wandering," while the uncreated "gives suitable supports to living this life" and points toward "an eternal and happy life after death." As to the absolute uncreated "nature, substance, or essence," Peter asks (omitting a multitude of necessary distinctions): "Is it not that which by the common consent of all races, according to the proper term in the respective language,

---

[38] D 181vs-vd.

[39] See Haskins, *The Renaissance of the Twelfth Century,* 341-67; Richard Walzer, *Greek into Arabic* (Oxford, 1962), as background.

is believed to be God, is called God? That nature is God, who is alone uncreated, alone the Creator, alone the master of all things, alone the author and dispenser of present and eternal goods. See then, see, you to whom I write, and according to the Psalm of David (which I believe you do not discredit), 'Judge justly, sons of men' [Ps. 57:2] whether one should dispute about the creature and pass the Creator silently by, whether free faculty of speech should be accorded one seeking after infirm and fugitive goods and the tongue of one seeking and acting after the highest and everlasting Good should be stopped up."[40] Peter probably did not realize how strongly he struck in this paragraph. By presenting a philosophical defense of theology he drew attention to a bitter and persistent conflict within Islam.[41] The analogous conflict within Christendom was not posed in such exclusive terms.[42]

If he were to write a philosophical treatise, Peter points out, he would doubtless find enthusiastic readers among the Moslems. Why, then, should they refuse to listen to a theological treatise? "Is this a part of any law besides yours? . . . Direct your eyes here and there. . . . Search the laws, rites, and customs of all races, and if you can find anywhere the like of what you advance or hand out on the subject, bring it forward."[43] Emphasizing that the

[40] "Ad quid autem rem increatam et insuper omnia creantem, cunctaque creata regentem, agnoscere quaero, nisi ut et hic uiuenti congrua uitae huic subsidia donet, et post mortem hanc aeternaliter ac feliciter uiuere praestet? Quae uero est natura haec, quae substantia, uel essentia? Nonne illa, quae communi uniuersarum gentium more, iuxta proprietatem uniuscuiusque linguae Deus creditur, Deus dicitur? Est igitur natura illa, Deus ille, qui solus increatus est, qui solus creator est, qui solus rector omnium, qui solus praesentium et aeternorum bonorum auctor et largitor est. Videte igitur uos, uidete inquam uos quibus scribo, et iuxta Psalmum Dauid, cui ut credo non discreditis, 'Iuste iudicate filii hominum,' utrum de creatura disputandum sit, de creatore tacendum, utrum libera loquendi facultas dari debeat quaerenti de infimis et fugitiuis bonis, et obstrui debeat os quaerentis et agentis de summo et aeterno bono," D 182rs.

[41] Gardet and Anawati, *op. cit.*, 21-93.

[42] E. Gilson, *History of Christian Philosophy in the Middle Ages* (New York, 1955), *passim*.

[43] "Estne hoc legis alicuius, preterquam uestrae? . . . Dirigite oculos huc illucque, et . . . uniuersarum gentium leges, ritus, ac mores scrutamini, et sicubi simile quid cautum uel traditum reperire potueritis, coram producite," D 182rs.

Christian law does not adopt such a position, he quotes his patron saint, who wrote in his first Epistle, "Be prepared to render account to all who ask concerning what is in you of faith and hope" [I Pet. 3:15]. "What does a custom of this kind [as yours] indicate?" he asks. "Truth always has free expression; it does not seek corners; it disdains veiling; it flees darkness; and it seeks . . . patience from all. Only error fears to be known; is afraid of dispersion; rejoices in hiding-places; dreads like death to be led forth in public."[44] He quotes Christ's words in John 3:20-21, "All who do evil hate the light, and do not come to the light, nor are their words made clear; but whoever does the truth comes to light, as his works are manifested as done in God."

"If that custom, if that law, is of the truth," he concludes, "what does it fear to come to light in order that it may be made manifest that its deeds are in God or of God? But what long revolutions shall I vainly make about a thing which is known to all? Therefore plainly, without doubt, that custom, that law so often named, hates the light, loves the darkness, does not offer clarification, does not allow contradiction, lest its falsity be obvious, lest its wickedness, protected by a sorrowful silence, be known throughout the whole world."[45]

After those harsh words the time for proof has arrived. Peter begins with a lengthy discussion of three quotations from the Koran. The first of them is 3:18-19: "So if they dispute with thee, say: 'I have surrendered myself [lit., "my face"] to Allah, likewise those who have followed me,' and say to those to whom the Book has been given, and to the common folk: 'Have you surrendered yourselves?' If they surrender themselves, they have let themselves

---

[44] "Quid portendit mos huiusmodi . . . ? Liberam semper frontem ueritas habet, non quaerit angulos, uelari dedignatur, obscura fugit, clara cunctisque patientia quaerit. Sola falsitas agnosci timet, discuti ueretur, latibulis gaudet, produci in publicum ut mortem formidat," D 182rs-rd.

[45] "Nam si mos ille, si lex illa ueritatis est, quid timet ad lucem uenire, ut manifestum fiat, quia in Deo uel a Deo sunt facta? Sed quid frustra longos circuitus de re cunctis nota facerem? Idcirco plane absque dubio mos ille, lex illa totiens nominata odit lucem, diligit tenebras, non fert arguentem, non patitur contradictorem, ne arguatur falsitas eius, ne nota fiat orbi terrarum doloso silentio tecta nequicia eius," D 182rd.

be guided, but if they turn away—thou art only responsible for the proclamation." Because Robert of Ketton failed to number the first *sūrah* and divided the second through the sixth into fifteen, the passage is given in the Arsenal manuscript under the "fifth" *sūrah*.[46] Peter might better have used the more accurate translation in the apology of Al-Kindi.[47] The second quotation is 3:61: "If anyone dispute with thee concerning him . . . say: '. . . Let us make earnest prayer and lay the curse of Allah upon those who lie.'" It was evidently shortened from Robert's translation for the purposes of the argument; the original names specifically those who disputed with Mohammed about the nature of Christ—not, as Robert's translation states, about the Islamic law in general.[48] The third is from 29:45, misquoted from either of two versions given in the apology of Al-Kindi: "Dispute not with the People of the Book,"[49] together with a paraphrase of either 2:187: "Persecution is worse than slaughter," or 2:214: "Persecution is more serious than killing," both in Robert's translations.[50]

There follows a short general discussion of the quotations. "What kind of words are these, I ask you? . . . If I shall yield to this, it will then be necessary for me to be carried around by every wind of doctrine, and in the manner of a reed, agitated by every breeze, bending here and there, to yield to every error, to acquiesce to every sort of falsehood, to hold nothing surely, to confuse indiscriminately goods with evils, truths with false-hoods."[51] Peter is prepared to go farther and declare that they

[46] A 38v. Robert's translation is quite faulty.

[47] Missing from the Arsenal manuscript; see Muñoz Sendino, "La Apologia del Christianismo de al-Kindi," 426, ll. 28-31.

[48] A 35vd.

[49] A 161vd, which has "disceptare" for "disputare," and adds "nisi in hiis, que benigne habentur." The other version, missing from the Arsenal manuscript, has "Nolite altercari cum legem habentibus nisi benigne atque pacifice"; Muñoz Sendino, "La Apologia del Cristianismo de al-Kindi," 378, l. 33.

[50] A 30vs, and marginalia, ". . . pugnax, plusquam cedes"; A 31rd, "Guerra na[m]que plusquam cedes officit."

[51] Quae sunt queso huiusmodi uerba? . . . Si hoc concessero, necesse iam erit circumferri me omni uento doctrinae, ac more harudinis flatu quolibet agitatae hac illacque inflecti, cedere omni errori, adquiescere cuilibet falsitati, nichil certe tenere, bona malis, uera falsis indiscrete confundere," D 182vs.

attack human nature itself. If one concedes to them, he wonders, "what exactly will distinguish man from beast?" For "a beast, which is deprived of a rational soul, cannot speak out against any command. . . . Judgment is not given to the beast; it concedes to all commands." But men must be judged by a stricter law than that of beasts. "I marvel," Peter concludes, "nor do I cease to be amazed, how this could have been wrested away from skilled and learned men by any sort of cunning, that they might believe words which were allegedly sent by God, when either a negligent or a studious reader would find nothing in them but what is foolish, cruel, and senseless."[52]

Peter then takes up the quotations individually. Against the first of them he has two points to make. If he wishes to dispute with the Moslem about his faith and is countered only with that reply, he says: "Will I believe that the law which [Mohammed] delivered to your people was delivered by God? In truth, I am more than a blockhead if I agree."[53] The Moslem is apt to experience great difficulty by any stolid refusal to defend his beliefs. As far as converting others to them might be concerned, some justification for regarding the Koran as divinely revealed is essential; otherwise a stalemate will quickly be reached, which should appear undesirable to the Moslem himself. Peter then calls attention to the second part of the quotation and makes his second point: "First you make God speak in a manner of declaration and now you add words of doubt? . . . If he spoke declaratively [in the first part], why is it that everyone, learned and illiterate, does not follow your law? If he doubted that they would believe [Mohammed], why did he say that everyone would follow [it]?"[54]

Against the second quotation Peter has little to say. "Just as it is easy for you to threaten me with God's wrath unless I believe you, so also it is easy for me or anyone to threaten and imprecate

[52] *Ibid.*
[53] D 182vd.
[54] "Facis primo Deum loqui modo enuntiantis, et nunc subinfers uerba dubitantis? . . . Quod si enuntiatiue locutus est, cur omnes tam scientes quam illiterati tuam legem non secuntur? Quod si dubitabat tibi credituros, quare dixit, omnes legem tuam secuturos?" *ibid.*

you in the same way, with the same wrath of God, unless you give in to me."[55] If both the Moslem and the Christian were simply to curse and threaten one another, in other words, nothing could ever be accomplished by way of clarifying their positions or allowing reason to do its work. Confident that this matter is not open to further discussion, Peter proceeds.

Before dealing with the third quotation, he desires to clarify the term "People of the Book." Scoring its obscurity, he identifies the people in question as the Jews and Christians; "for, having trained the sight of my eyes here and there, I see no others in the world having the scripture when these things were uttered."[56] He rules out the Greeks and Romans, who developed admirable laws raising them high above bestiality, but could not be said to have possessed any scripture revealed by God.[57] It must be admitted that the point is established gratuitously, inasmuch as the Moslems always interpreted the term in precisely the same way.[58]

Confronting the first part of the quotation, Peter is perplexed. "If [Mohammed] was sure about the truth of his law, why did he prohibit his [followers] from disputing [about it]? If he distrusted it, why did he write those things which his [followers] could not defend?"[59] Peter suggests an answer. Mohammed knew that the foundations of the scriptures could not be destroyed "either by human words or reasoning . . . or by warlike force or noise of arms, or dreadful torments, or by causing whatever deaths." He pays tribute to the constancy of the Maccabees and the endurance of the first Christian martyrs. It was when faced with such constancy and endurance, he claims, that Mohammed, "destitute of all strength for resistance, took refuge in flight; he

---

[55] "Si leue tibi est iram Dei michi nisi tibi credidero comminari, ita et michi uel cuilibet facile est eandem iram Dei nisi michi adquieueris comminari pariter et imprecari," *ibid.*

[56] D 183rs.

[57] *Ibid.*

[58] Kritzeck, "Jews, Christians, and Moslems," 101-02; Arthur S. Tritton. *The Caliphs and their non-Muslim Subjects* (London, 1930), 197-228; Daniel C. Dennett, *Conversion and the Poll Tax in Early Islam* (Cambridge, 1950).

[59] "Si de ueritate legis suae confidebat, quare suos disputare prohibuit? Si diffidebat, cur ea quae sui non possent defendere scripsit?" D 183rd.

who could neither add nor oppose anything reasonable chose silence. But lest he seem to yield completely to the contrary faction, he took up arms instead of reason. . . . It is such an end, precisely that just and that rational, that your prophet Mohammed puts to disputations, O sons of Hagar; with precisely that impartial thought that he distinguishes between opposing factions; precisely that strange justice that the praiseworthy mediator offers to the centuries."[60]

As for the second part of the quotation, "words fail for refuting such absurdity, such bestial cruelty, such detestable wickedness." Peter permits himself a rare repetition of the *Summa* in attributing the words to Satan.[61] It was Satan who "knew that an incredible and very trifling sect could not otherwise stand firm for a long time" and, fearing that he would be "defrauded" if Mohammed were given the opportunity of hearing the true scriptures and "expelled from the hearts of those deceived if that were allowed admittance," made certain that the "iron . . . barrier" was created. In context the explanation is charitable, for in placing the blame upon Satan it partially exonerates Mohammed.[62]

Peter notes that "the Christian law also condemns quarrels,"[63] quoting St. Paul's words, "It is not becoming a servant of God to quarrel" (II Tim. 2: 24). They do not refer, however, to "contests . . . in the cause of truth," such as Peter's book itself, but rather to "proud and raging quarrels"; and, in any case, the principle does not lead the Christian law to hold that killing is better. "It does not say that killing is better than quarreling any more than

---

[60] "Destitutus itaque omni resistendi praesidio confugit ad fugam, et qui nil rationabile uel ponere uel obicere poterat, elegit silentium. Sed ne ex toto aduersae parti cedere uideretur, pro ratione arma assumpsit. . . . Talem, tam iustum, tam rationabilem disputationibus finem uester propheta Mahumeth o Agareni imponit, tam aequa sententia inter partes sibi aduersas discernit, tale iudicium usque ad sua uel uestra tempora seculis inauditum laudabilis arbiter profert," D 183rd-vs.

[61] D 183vs; see above, chapter IV, part 7.

[62] *Ibid.*

[63] "Quarrels" translates *lis*, which Peter preferred to *guerra*, Robert's translation of *al-fitnah*, which should perhaps be translated "persecution" in the context of the quotation.

it says that quarreling is better than killing, because it does not admit the comparison," but if a comparison were to be made, it would perforce say the opposite of the Koran, namely, that "killing is much worse."[64]

The Moslems are invited to "investigate the judgements of all peoples" in order to determine "whether human laws, which are diverse in many other things, do not agree on this one, that the offense of unjust murder suffers far greater punishment than the deviation of harmful quarreling. It is surprising if your laws, which we know to be prudent according to the flesh, do not so accord in this most just cause, for nature herself also preaches by silent words that the greater injury should be punished by the greater penalty, the greater damage condemned to the greater retribution. If this is so, then [the proposition that] killing is better than quarreling is false."[65] In Peter's opinion, there is nothing left for the Moslems to do but "lay aside such infamy" and not permit themselves "to be branded by so foul a mark," for he suspects that there lies at its root a certain distrust "about [their] own sectarian doctrine" which keeps them from "joining hands with any or the least contradictor."[66]

Having completed his discussion of the three koranic quotations, Peter makes a final appeal to the Moslems to give him a fair hearing. It is delicately worded. His first reason for making the request is a direct result of the foregoing demonstration. "Don't be the only ones," he urges, "to disagree in this from the custom of all peoples or laws. Since the greatest freedom is yours, [do

[64] D 183vd.

[65] "Disquirite uniuersarum gentium iudicia, et quicquid uspiam terrarum sol uidet scrutamini, utrum leges humanae in aliis multis diuersae, in hoc uno non conueniant, quo longe maiori paena plectitur iniustae cedis reatus, quam iniuriosae litis excessus. Mirum si et leges uestrae quos prudentes secundum carnem non ignoramus, in hac tam iustissima causa non concordant, quod natura ipsa etiam uerbis tacentibus praedicat, maiorem iniuriam maiori paena puniendam, maiorem iacturam, maiori ultione damnandam. Quod si ita est, meliorem esse cedem quam litem, falsum est," *ibid*.

[66] D 183vd-84rs.

not] put an end to all disputations and accusations. Either approve of or disprove, either receive or reject what will be said."[67]

The second reason is to repay Peter's own charity. "Because the cause of your salvation impelled me to write these things, nor has the charity which I have towards [you] . . . allowed me to keep silent, you also should owe me at least this measure of my own charity, that, even if you do not want to give in to the things which are to be said, at least you will not refuse to listen."[68] Fearing that the Moslems may be scandalized by the arguments which are to follow, Peter reminds them that in all matters of doubt "what is true cannot be declared unless what is false is first of all destroyed," and that, because it will do "no small injury" to truth if he spares falsehood "against justice," he will be obliged to speak harshly "against your lawgiver and his legislation." The Moslems are requested not to be immediately troubled and enraged, or anxious to take up their "stones and swords." He asks them to "be like us, at least in this [respect]." For Christians of his day frequently engage in friendly conversations with Jews, Peter says, and although they "hear from them many and nearly all things contrary to the Christian faith, they are not incited to fury nor aroused to their slaughter . . . but patiently hear, wisely answer." The Christians do not seek the extermination of the Jews, but "wait with equanimity should they ever chance to be converted."[69]

The same attitude is retained toward Moslem captives in the Holy Land, Peter claims; "the one faculty for returning to the only right," freedom of speech and decision, is not taken from them.[70] A precept of the Old Testament commands that blas-

[67] "Nec in hoc ab uniuersarum gentium uel legum more soli dissentiatis, maxime cum liberum uobis sit, disputationibus cunctis et allegationibus finitis, quaecunque dicta fuerint aut probare aut improbare, aut suscipere aut respuere," D 184rs.

[68] "Et quia causa salutis uestrae me ad haec scribenda impulit, nec . . . caritas quam . . . habeo, silere me permisit, debetis et uos hanc saltem huic caritati meae uicem, ut et si hiis quae dicenda sunt nolueritis adquiescere, saltem non recusetis audire," ibid.

[69] Ibid.

[70] D 184rs-rd; "freedom of speech" translates "linguae libertas."

phemers be killed;[71] but that has a different meaning for Christians, Peter insists, and the Moslems would be well advised in any case, before invoking it, to make certain that they are not blasphemers themselves. Since "every people except you of all peoples under heaven affirms that your sectarian doctrine is not of God," it would be wise for the Moslems to "put off killing for a while until it is seen, by a certain scrutiny of truth, that your prophet really was sent by God, your law really given by Him."[72]

Peter has still a third reason for requesting a hearing. He tells the Moslems of the patience with which "all the peoples of the whole earth, kings and princes, have received the messengers of Christ." They heard them, pondered their words, and finally, "illumined by the Spirit of God, ceased to resist." He cites a single example—that of "a certain kingdom in the farthest part of the West, and situated almost outside the world," called England. Its king, "Ethelbert by name, who lived almost contemporaneously with your Mohammed,"[73] showed an attitude very different from that which Mohammed recommended. Peter did not choose the example of England totally at random. Part of the *Liber* may actually have been written there, or at least the memory of his visit was still in his mind.[74] He gives the Moslems some information on the early history of the island and then, to tell Ethelbert's story, quotes a long passage from "an old history of the Angles," which is St. Bede the Venerable's *Ecclesiastical History of the English People*.[75] Peter quotes all of chapter twenty-five of Book One, except the first and last sentences and a sentence in the middle about Ethelbert's having heard of the Christian religion before from his wife Bertha.[76] There is no point in reproducing all of the text here, but a part of Ethelbert's speech to the monk Augus-

---

[71] See Lev. 24:16; cf. John 19:7.

[72] D 184rd.

[73] Ethelbert ruled from 561 to 616.

[74] See above, chapter II, part 3.

[75] *Historia Ecclesiastica Gentis Anglorum,* ed. C. Plummer (Oxford, 1946); tr. J. Stevens, revised by L. C. Lane (London, 1951).

[76] D 184rd-vs; Manitius, "Zu Petrus' von Cluni patristischen Kenntnissen," 587, lists the variants in the two texts.

tine and his companions may serve to indicate the attitude which Peter sought to praise: "Because you have come from afar into my kingdom, and, as I conceive, are desirous to impart to us those things which you believe to be true, and most beneficial, we will not molest you, but give you favorable entertainment, and take care to supply you with your necessary sustenance; nor do we forbid you to preach and gain as many as you can to your religion."[77]

"It behooves you to act in the same way," Peter tells the Moslems; "or, if you are not disposed to imitate them fully, at least in the same way to hear and approve if what they bring is suitable or salutary."[78]

[77] "Verum quia de longe huc peregrini uenistis, et ut ego michi uideor perspexisse ea quae uos uera et optima credebatis, nobis quoque communicare desiderastis, nolumus molesti esse uobis, quin potius hospitio uos benigne recipere, et quae uictui uestro sunt necessaria ministrare curabimus. Nec prohibemus, quin omnes quos potestis fidei uestrae religionis praedicando societis," D 184vd.

[78] "Decet uos hoc idem facere, aut si non ex toto illos imitari disponitis, saltim siquid commodi uel salutis uobis afferunt, audire pariter et probare," *ibid*.

☙ THE ABBOT feels that his discourse is "now hastening towards conflict," and he wishes the Moslems to know that he had the Koran translated into Latin "several years ago," has perused the translation, and is curious to know "why that prophet of yours mingled some excerpts from the Jewish law, and some from the Christian, in his Koran" and, since he showed himself to be "a great enemy" of both, "why he confirms, as though he were a Jew or a Christian, many things that he writes of [their] laws."[79]

It troubles Peter that Mohammed appears to consent to a part of the biblical revelation and yet does not accept it in full. It puzzles him that so much of both testaments is repeated with approval in the Koran. If such things were to be included as part of a merely human legislation, he allows, the ambivalence could be understood; but as part of an allegedly divine law, they call into question the very action of God. "All of what was given by Him to mortals and ordered in scripture through them is true, certain, and beyond doubt.... The Jewish and Christian scriptures . . . are to be accepted and respected not in part, as [Mohammed] does, but wholly." By way of conclusion, "If they are divine, they are not to be accepted in part, but wholly; if they are not divine, they are not to be rejected in part, but wholly."[80] Peter imagines that the Moslems will elect to acknowledge the divine authority of the biblical sources rather than risk considering the falsity of the Koran, and this admission is one on which Peter's major arguments are to turn.[81]

Peter then attempts to state the probable objection of the Moslem reader: "I do not deny that the Jewish or Christian books were divine . . . as they were written by their first authors. But by the process of ongoing time, for different reasons, those first books

[79] Ibid.

[80] D 184vd-85rs.

[81] D 185rs-rd; cf. Kritzeck, "Islam and Christian Unity," Unitas, XI (1959), 196-200; Jacques Jomier, Bible et Coran (Paris, 1959); D. Masson, Le Coran et la révélation judéo-chrétienne, 2 vols. (Paris, 1959).

perished; and the Jewish were restored by certain Jews, and the Christian by certain Christians, who, ignorant of the original truth of the first books, constructed [them as they] are now held by Jews or Christians, as they wished, both out of the variant accounts of what went before and out of the conjectures of their own hearts; and, mixing true with false and false with true, they took from them every strength of truth. For this reason I do not have faith in these books which either of these peoples use at the present time. For this reason I affirm that they were falsified or corrupted. Nevertheless, what remained true was chosen by God and given to our prophet and mixed by him into the law of our scripture."[82]

That is as strong a statement of the objection as any Moslem could be expected to require. Peter counters it by demanding proof, thanking God "that you assert that [these scriptures] were ever true, for in this particular you think with us . . . [and] with the Jews. But as for showing that they were falsified, . . . what authority, what reason do you offer by which we are compelled to agree?" The burden of proof, he says, citing Roman law, is on the accuser.[83] But because his reader is not present to answer, Peter himself offers to do so, "not slower than you [would]," by searching the books "by which you support yourselves." And "none . . . of all your scriptures is held among you to be more sublime than your celebrated Koran. . . . For it is that which you affirm was sent by God from the heavens . . . to your prophet through Gabriel." He quotes the beginnings of the first and last

[82] "Libros Iudaicos uel Christianos diuinos fuisse non nego, . . . sicut a primis auctoribus conscripti sunt. Sed noui processu temporis diuersis casibus illa prima uolumina perisse, ac postmodum a quibusdam Iudaeis Iudaicos, a quibusdam Christianis Christianos reparatos fuisse. Qui primorum librorum uelut originalem ueritatem ignorantes, tam ex uariis praecedentium relationibus, quam ex proprii cordis coniectura, libros qui nunc a Iudeis uel Christianis habentur prout libuit condiderunt, ac uera falsis, falsa ueris permiscentes, omnem eis ueritatis constantian abstulerunt. Hac de causa libris huiusmodi, quibus utraque gens instanti tempore utitur, fidem non adhibeo, hac de causa falsatos uel corruptos affirmo. Electa sunt tamen a Deo et tradita prophetae nostro, quae uera esse constabat, atque ab illo scripturae legis nostrae admixta," D 185rd.
[83] Ibid.

sūrahs.[84] "If you can bring forth from there anything said about the false Jewish and Christian books either by God or by your prophet, place it before [me]. Examine also other books, though of far inferior authority, which are read or held among you, and propose to us briefly one word, or at least one iota, signifying the aforesaid scriptures to have been corrupted by someone at some time."[85] Peter tells the Moslems that some of these books are known to him through the skill of his translators, "who have solicitously drawn out of your writings not only such things as pertain to your religion and rite, but have also gone deeply into your libraries for much that refers to your humanistic and scientific studies." In none of them Peter maintains, has he found any reference to the alleged falsification of the Bible.[86]

Unusually, Peter was ill-informed on this matter. "The plain fact is that the text of Ketton's Qur'ān which Peter claimed to have searched in vain, made clear sense of verses which assert or imply taḥrīf, the corruption of Scripture. 'And dost thou therefore expect the conversion of (the Jews) to thy religion? Definitely not. For they changed the word of God, which they had heard and known, and they did not want anything from it to be effected.' "[87] It is true that the emphasis of the Koran was on the verification of the former scriptures, but various theories of their "corruption" (Arabic *taḥrīf*), based on koranic evidence, were developed.[88] The theory of the loss of earlier sacred books was a later interpolation.[89]

Peter goes on to examine two "common rumors" about the loss

[84] For detailed comment on these quotations, see Kritzeck, "Peter the Venerable and the Toledan Collection," 198. Note the serious hiatus in the Martène-Migne text at this point.

[85] "Si aliquid de falsatis libris Iudaicis aut Christianis, uel a Deo uel a uestro propheta dictum eruere inde poteritis, coram proferte. Scrutamini et alios licet longe inferioris auctoritatis, qui apud uos leguntur aut habentur libros, et aut breue aliquod uerbum, aut saltem iota unum, corruptas a quibuslibet quolibet tempore scripturas iam dictas significans, nobis proponite," D 185vs.

[86] D 185vs-vd.

[87] Daniel, *op. cit.*, 54.

[88] Usually a distinction was drawn between *taḥrīf al-maʿnawi,* "corruption of meaning," and *taḥrīf al-lafẓi,* "corruption of words."

[89] T. P. Hughes, *op. cit.*, 61-62.

and subsequent falsification of the biblical books. Apart from indicating that they were not to be found in the Toledan Collection, he does not identify them. They were, in fact, adapted from marginal annotations to Robert of Ketton's translation of the Koran.[90] The first concerns the loss of Jewish books: "When the Jews were sent forth from the Babylonian Captivity by the indulgence of the king of the Persians, . . . they laid the divine books (those which they had kept with them while they were captives) on a donkey. . . . And because, as is the custom of a multitude going on a journey, some went faster, some slower . . . that brute animal, now lacking a guide and being frisky, as is the custom with those animals, left the journey and . . . since no one followed [it], perished, together with the Law of God which it carried."[91]

Peter has four proofs to advance for this story's falsehood. The first is based on internal evidence. He reminds the Moslems that even before the captivity the temple of Jerusalem had been destroyed and the Ark of the Covenant lost, and "none of the sacrd things except the law and the [sacred] vessels . . . remained." Therefore "how can it seem true and certain that men of the most ardent temperament, hastening to their fatherland, inflamed with all their effort toward their . . . religion, so neglected the law of God, on which all their hopes depended and because of which they alone, among all the other peoples of the earth, were glorified . . . [that] they placed it on a most valueless beast [and] left it so uncared for?"[92]

The second, and longest, proof rests on the improbability that there was only one copy of the law. Peter feels certain that the Moslems must know of the dispersion of the Jewish tribes even before the captivity. "And what people, living by a written law,

---

[90] A 28rd.

[91] "Dimissi . . . regis Persarum indulgentia a captiuitate Babilonica Iudaei . . . libros diuinos quos secum dum captiui tenerentur habuerunt, asino imposuerunt. . . . Et quia ut mos est multitudinis iter agentis, quidam uelocius, quidam tardius incedebant . . . brutum illud animal rectore iam carens, utque huiusmodi animalia solent, lasciuiens, relicto itinere, deuia secutum est . . . et . . . cum nemo sequeretur, disparuit, talique casu cum lege Dei quam ferebat periit," D 185vd.

[92] D 186rs.

has been satisfied with one and only one copy [of it]? How could only one volume of the law suffice all the numberless tribes living separately throughout many cities, villages, towns, [and] farms?" Even as he writes, Peter points out, there are "not only thousands or ten thousand, but some fifty or sixty thousand Jews" in the Christian world, and they all "daily show us the full law, all the prophets and other books of the Hebrew language. . . . Hardly twenty Jews living together among us are found without books of this kind. Is it not the same among you, too? Look about you in those parts in which you have subjected [the Jews] to your domination, and you will discover, I think, that I have not spoken false things."[93] It would have been impossible, moreover, for so many people to have learned "the doctrine of so profuse a law" unless there were many copies and many teachers. Peter asks if the Koran, for instance, is kept only in Mecca. He believes that the Moslems "will concede that the Jews were never satisfied with a single copy of their scriptures" and that the scriptures therefore could not have perished in the manner alleged.[94]

The third proof demonstrates that "the Jews, after their return from Babylon, did not lack the books of the divine law," a demonstration resting on a passage from the Book of Esdras (II Esdr. 8:1-3, 5-6) in which the prophet is described as showing the law to the Jews and reading to them from it. "Did Esdras . . . build up a false law so suddenly . . . ? Or would the people . . . hear from him a corrupted law?" The Islamic story is "again proven ridiculous and absurd."[95]

The fourth and final proof rests on the unlikelihood that any universal agreement could have been secured on such a falsification. Peter challenges the Moslems to produce the precise verses in which it can be demonstrated. "If it is a question of history . . . does not Mohammed acknowledge almost all of those things in his Koran?" He mentions a long list of items which appear both in the Old Testament and the Koran, though in the latter "with many subtractions, many changes, much admixture." It surprises

[93] D 186rs-vs.   [94] D 186vs.
[95] D 186vs-vd.

179

him that "this opinion could spring up among you, which you have not accepted from any teacher," since Mohammed "rejects nothing . . . either there or elsewhere of these things which I have listed above."[96] The argument is quite forceful even though it is not based, clearly, upon an exhaustive comparison of the biblical and koranic narratives.

Peter then closes the case. "I conclude, by necessary or [at least] probable argument," he states, "that the Jewish books were neither lost nor falsified. If Mohammed inserted things which were written [in them] . . . in his or your Law, he did not deem the rest to have been lost or falsified, nor can any of you prove what you either suspect or propound about those lost or falsified scriptures." Of course, the argument has blandly overlooked the Islamic doctrine of the uniqueness of the Koran, but it has both disposed of the story and suggested a more potent syllogism. Inasmuch as these scriptures have been proven "not partly but wholly true . . . and divine," then, Peter charges that "it is necessary for you either to accept the Jewish scriptures wholly or to reject the Koran." The Koran contains passages from the Old Testament; if the books from which they were taken are false or doubtful, then they, too, are false or doubtful. "It stands, for this reason, that . . . that law of yours, which you are accustomed to glorify as having been sent from heaven, is not only partly but wholly—in its totality—false or doubtful." If the Moslems refuse to grant that the Koran is false or doubtful, they must then hold that those passages from the Old Testament, and the books from which they were taken, are "not partly but wholly true, not partly but wholly divine."[97]

Precisely the same reasoning should force the Moslems to admit the books of the New Testament, Peter thinks. He is willing to consider, nevertheless, the story about the loss and falsification of the Christian scriptures: "At the time of the Roman emperors, who vehemently persecuted the Christians by means of exiles,

[96] D 186vd-87rs.
[97] D 187rs-rd.

proscriptions, and various kinds of deaths, who also ordered that
their books be everywhere destroyed, the Gospels, the Acts of the
Apostles, and the Epistles perished. Afterwards they were written
or repaired as the Christians wished. These [later Christians] . . .
did not take anything from the first authors of the books . . . and
did not even see them."[98]

"Is this all . . . that you pretend?" Peter asks the Moslems.
"If this is all, I shall proceed against you in the same manner as
above. I shall show in the same way of replying that what you
propose is of no strength, but very weak." He first considers the
historical accuracy of the claim. He admits that certain Roman
emperors "persecuted the Christians . . . now vehemently, then
more mildly, continuously for almost three hundred years." He is
prepared to admit that "a certain one of the last persecutors, who
was called Diocletian," who fought them "more ferociously and
longer than the others," had decreed "by public edict that throughout all of the regions subjugated to him, the churches of the
Christians should be destroyed on the most holy Paschal Day
[Easter] itself, and the books burnt."[99]

"But what is in that for you?" Peter continues. "If this edict
was promulgated by that prince through the whole length and
breadth of the Roman empire, . . . did all of the books of the
Christians perish by that single cause? Did no one . . . steal any
of all those books away, [or] pull just one from the fire? . . .
Did every sentence of the Christian religion perish? Was the love
of sacred, divine things so lacking in them that, though they
exposed their bodies to the flames, swords, and all kinds of deaths
in order to serve God's law, [yet] they could so completely neglect
that same law . . . for which they did not hesitate to die?"[100]

[98] "Romanorum . . . principum tempore, qui acriter Christianos exiliis, proscriptionibus, diuersisque mortium generibus diutissime persecuti sunt, qui et ipsa
eorum uolumina edictis publicis exuri ubique iusserunt, tam Aeuangelica quam
Apostolorum Actus uel Aepistolae perierunt. Rescripti uero postmodum sunt ac
reparati ut Christianis libuit, qui nec a primis librorum auctoribus . . . nec
libros ab ipsis conditos, utpote prius sicut dictum est succensos uiderant," D 187rd-
vs.

[99] D 187vs.

[100] "Sed in quo istud pro uobis? Etsi edictum hoc ab illo principe per imperii

For that matter, Peter reminds his readers, Christianity was by no means confined to the Roman empire. It existed in Persia, Ethiopia, India, "your own" Arabia, and "other kingdoms which the Roman power could not subjugate to itself." It is therefore impossible to believe that the Gospels and the writings of the Apostles, "as they were received from their first preachers," could have perished.[101]

Peter goes into some detail in demonstrating the transmission of the New Testament, identifying the Gospels and Epistles and tracing their history. The Moslems will have to come up with different proofs, he insists, or abandon the proposition that these books were lost.[102] And if they were not lost, there is no better reason for believing that they were falsified. Such a crime could not possibly be kept secret, Peter says, quoting a French proverb, "What two know, everybody knows."[103] He finds it beyond belief that all of the early Christians could have cooperated in such a gigantic deception. "But possibly," he goes on to suggest, permitting himself a small sarcasm, "this became known only to the Saracens and could not be known . . . to the Christians."[104]

Peter rests assured that, after this scrutiny, neither of the Islamic claims can be supported; and, unless the Moslems have something further to advance to the contrary, it will stand as established that such loss and falsification as was alleged is false. The conclusion must be the same for the New Testament as it was for the Old, with the same implications. The Koran contains matter which is also contained in the Gospels; since "nothing can

---

Romani amplitudinem promulgatum est . . . nunquid uno illo casu Christianorum uniuersa uolumina perierunt? An nemo . . . qui . . . aliquos ex tam innumeris libris absconderet, nemo qui igni subduceret . . . ? Itane ergo omne propositum Christianae religionis in eis perierat, itane amor diuinorum sacrorum in eis defecerat, ut cum corpora sua ignibus gladiis, omnisque generis mortibus pro seruanda lege Dei exponerent, ipsam legem Dei pro qua mori non differebant, sic uniuersaliter negligerent?" D 187vs-vd.

[101] D 187vd.
[102] D 187vd-88rs.
[103] The proverb has survived in many languages; see H. G. Bohn, *A Polyglot of Foreign Proverbs* (London, 1881), 128.
[104] D 188rd.

be taken from a falsified book except what is false or doubtful," the Koran becomes false or doubtful. The Moslems will consider it sinful to hold such a position, so let them acknowledge that the Christian and Jewish scriptures are true and divine: "As a result of this [demonstration], it is necessary for you to take the Jewish books as they are, as if you were Jews, . . . and, as if you were Christians, to approve of the evangelical and apostolic writings."[105]

The reader may be forgiven for wondering why Peter has belabored these points to such an extent. He himself explains the reason: "I declare you forewarned . . . that, when it will be opportune in the process of [this book], I shall attack you [with material selected] out of these [books] which you already, from necessity, hold as divine . . . and I shall assail the falsehood in which you are entangled and oppressed, above all mortals except the Jews, I think, and protected by the shield of truth, I shall, with God's help for strength, conquer."[106]

There is one last point to be made before Book One is brought to a close. "Let none of you think that the Jewish books are not [also] the Christian," Peter warns, "for the Christian accepts the law of Moses or the prophets no less than the Gospel or the Acts of the Apostles or the Epistles." The Christian "believes and confesses" that both bodies of scripture were given at various times "by the same God, the creator of all things visible and invisible." Although the Jews and Christians may "strongly disagree among themselves," nevertheless Peter wishes the Moslems to realize that the Christian "accepts the Jewish scriptures and honors them as the greatest strength and foundation of our faith."[107] Having disabused the Moslems of that notion, Peter summarizes in a few sentences the results of his refutation so far.

---

[105] D 188rd-vs.

[106] "Ea de causa uos praemonitos et praemunitos esse denuncio, quod ubi in processu propositi operis et sermonis oportunum fuerit, ex hiis quae iam necessario ut diuina tenetis uos aggrediar, et . . . falsitatem qua excaeptis Iudaeis prae cunctis mortalibus irretiti et obruti estis, ut potero impugnabo, et scuto ueritatis protectus Deo iuuante pro uiribus expugnabo," D 188vs.

[107] Ibid.

It has been proven, even from the Koran itself, that the Bible is true and divine. What will follow will prove that the Koran is not divine and that Mohammed was "neither a prophet nor a messenger of God, but a seducer and a wicked man."[108]

[108] *Ibid.*

☙ Peter the Venerable opens Book Two of his refutation with an exhortation to the Moslems to suppress the hostility which they must now feel and hear him out. He tells them that they must face the possibility that they "hold falsehood for truth, iniquity for justice, diabolical sacrilege for divine worship." He quotes Isaiah (Isa. 44:18-21) to establish the divine abhorrence of idolatry, then suggests that the Moslems could have been similarly defiled. "I have heard that you are not idolaters, and do not adore woods or stones or that sort of thing. But what . . . does it profit you not to take the creature for the Creator if God is not worshipped as He both wills and commands Himself to be worshipped? Therefore consider . . . whether what you have believed so far may be false, whether what you have thought false until now may be true. It is a property of the wise to amend errors, even if it shames; it is a property of the foolish not to correct, by silly shame, the things condemned by the world."[109]

In order that the Moslems should not think that he holds that they alone have gone astray, Peter carefully provides examples of deception on the part of both Jews and Christians. In fact, the whole human race has been ensnared by many kinds of errors since Adam.[110] In Noah's time they had all "left off divine worship" and were consequently "destroyed by avenging waters, as your Koran also says." But Noah's descendants were "not inferior to their predecessors in wickedness . . . and sprinkled the whole crust of the earth with an increase of iniquities." It was only through Moses, Peter says, that "there was distinguished . . . the one and only people chosen by God from all peoples," namely, the Jews, who were "put under precepts given by God and

[109] "Ydolatrae quidem ut audiui non estis, nec ligna uel lapides aut huiusmodi talia adoratis. Sed . . . quid prodest uobis creaturam pro creatore non suscipere, si non datur, Deum ut se colit et uult et praecipit colere? Scrutamini ergo . . . utrum quod hactenus credidistis falsum sit, quod hucusque falsum putastis uerum sit. Sapientum est etiam si pudeat emendare errata, stultotum est fatuo pudore non corrigere etiam ab orbe dampnata," D 188vd.
[110] D 189rs.

promulgated through [Moses] and disjoined from the common perdition of the wicked." Even after the law was given, many turned away from it toward idolatry, but eventually Christ was born and fulfilled the law, introducing a new testament, and "the Gospel of the Eternal Kingdom . . . was spread abroad everywhere."[111] Yet there were defections and "multiple errors" even among the Christians; but the Church, "true and the follower of truth, as soon as it sensed them, rejected them; as soon as it perceived them, condemned them."[112] The abbot has identified these instances of deception, he says, in order that the Moslems may entertain the suggestion that they, too, "could have been deceived, ensnared, could have taken darkness for light, false for true, a seducer for a prophet, and, as the Jews will do just before the end of the world, the Antichrist for Christ."[113]

Now Peter is prepared for "close combat," which he hopes will be carried out "with peace . . . not with fury; with reason, not with madness; with tranquillity, not with iniquity—lest perhaps we seem not to investigate what is true with a love of truth, but to defend what is false by a zeal for factions." He recapitulates the purpose of his book as it was set down earlier: it is an invitation to salvation, "to [that] salvation which does not pass away, but which endures to everlasting life." Once more he lists the Moslems' objections that they have not "dreamt up" or "fabricated" anything they say, but confess of God "according to what our prophet transmitted to us, who was sent by Him." Mohammed was "the last in the succession of prophets and, as it were, the seal of them all"; he was "the bearer and messenger of the divine law, not its author." So the Moslems "serve and guard . . . what was transmitted to our fathers; to them we have consecrated our souls, our bodies, our life and death."[114]

---

[111] D 189rs-rd.

[112] D 189rd.

[113] "Vt sicut dicere caeperam cogitetis et recogitetis non solum illos quos praemisi paganos, non solum Iudaeos, non solum Christianos hereticos, sed etiam uos potuisse falli, potuisse decipi, potuisse tenebras pro luce, falsum pro uero, seductorem pro propheta, et ut Iudaei circa mundi finem facturi sunt, Antichristum pro Christo suscipere," *ibid.*

[114] D 189rd-vs.

The battle lines are clearly drawn. "Hear, therefore, for the time is nigh," Peter exclaims, "to what you have consecrated your souls, your bodies, and your death. Hear whether you have placed your hope in a safe place, whether you have believed in a salutary doctrine, or in a true prophet and messenger of God." Peter wants their common assumption to be expressed at once: "A true prophet of God is to be believed; a true messenger of God is to be submitted to." What must be investigated, therefore, is "whether [Mohammed] was in fact a prophet of God, whether he was truly a messenger of God." What is needed first of all, he decides, is a definition of the terms "prophecy" and "prophet." Again he quotes St. Peter: "Prophecy came not by the will of man at any time; but the holy men spoke, inspired by the Holy Spirit" (II Pet. 1:21). His definition of "prophecy" follows: "Prophecy is the utterance of unknown things either of the past or the present or the future, not done by human invention but by divine inspiration. But the etymology of the noun pertains more to the future than to the past or present. However, because both past and present are known by the same divine virtue . . . revelation of these two times are also called 'prophecy.' " From the definition of "prophecy" comes the definition of "prophet": "A prophet is one who manifests to mortals, taught not by human knowledge but inspired by the Spirit of God, unknown things about the past or present or future."[115]

Most of the first part of Book Two is given over to an examination of the Jewish prophets, in relation to Mohammed, on the basis of this definition. A miniature of the method is presented at the start with the example of Moses. Moses prophesied about the past, Peter says, when he spoke of the creation; about the present when he spoke of the sedition of Korah; about the future when he warned Pharaoh of the ten plagues and foretold Christ.[116] Peter wonders how the Moslems will prove that Mohammed was a prophet in that way, and challenges them to produce prophecies

[115] D 189vs.
[116] D 189vs-90rs; cf. Num. 16:46ff.

in any of the three categories from the Koran, where it suited him most to prove his prophethood.[117]

Peter then assumes the method in earnest. He does extremely well with Isaiah, although he attributes to him one prophecy which is actually to be found in the Book of Ezechiel.[118] Jeremiah, Ezechiel, and Daniel are dealt with successfully along the same lines, as are Elijah and Elisha.[119] Peter cannot resist boldly challenging the Moslems to produce something similar in favor of Mohammed.

"Why did a prophet so renowned (according to you) not counsel himself, let alone anyone else, by some spark of prophecy . . . in his frequent expeditions against his enemies?" Peter asks. "Why," specifically, "when he often fled vanquished from battles, did he not know beforehand that he would be conquered by his enemies?" and "why did he not see beforehand and prevent in the battle [of Uḥud], in which he took part, a tooth of his lower teeth from being knocked out, a lip from being cut, [and] wounds on his forehead and face from being inflicted?"[120]

Once more the Moslems are urged to search the Koran for prophecies. Thinking that they may be inclined to substitute, instead, a passage from the *Fabulae Saracenorum* in which Mohammed is reported to have foretold his first successors,[121] Peter conceives a rather ingenious reply. "Listen to [Mohammed] speaking in your Koran. . . . 'Whatever you shall find written

[117] D 190rs.

[118] D 190rd-vs. The prophecy concerning Christ's baptism is from Ezech. 36:25. The distinction between "proximate" and "remote" prophecies about the future was also made by Al-Kindi, A 152vs-vd.

[119] D 190vs-91vd.

[120] "Quare ergo propheta iuxta uos tam famosus, aliqua saltem modica prophetiae scintilla in tam frequentibus suis contra hostes expeditionibus, sibi ne dicam alteri non consuluit? Quare cum sepe uictus de praeliis fugerit, se uicendum ab hostibus non praesciuit? Quare non praeuidit et praecauit in quodam suo procinctu cui ipse interfuit, unum sibi de inferioribus dentibus dentem excutiendum, labrum praecidendum, uulnera fronti et faciei suae ab hostibus inferenda?" D 191vd-92rs. The allusion, derived from Al-Kindi, A 192rs, follows an account of Elisha's predictions of the military plans of the Syrian king (IV Kings 6:8-12).

[121] A 8rs-vs; see Wensinck, *A Handbook of Early Muhammedam Tradition*, 5, 234.

for me,' he says, 'compare with the Koran; and if it does not agree [with it], then know that I am innocent of that writing and it is not mine.' Therefore compare the aforementioned writing with the Koran and see whether it is in agreement with it or in disagreement. . . . It does not agree."[122] But unfortunately for Peter's argument, the passage he quotes is not from the Koran at all; he had copied it from Al-Kindi, who made the error.[123] It actually represents one form of a celebrated Islamic tradition.[124] Guillaume calls attention to these "pseudo-prophetic *ḥadīth* portray-[ing] Muhammad warning his people against liars who will seek to mislead the community while claiming his authority for so doing."[125] It was less agreement with the Koran than "the reputation which the guarantors of the tradition bore" that became the basic principle of the science of validating Islamic traditions.[126]

Peter then discusses two koranic quotations concerning prophetic signs. The first is 6:4-5 in Robert's translation, which is a bit muddled but should read: "Not a sign of (all) the signs of their Lord comes to them but from it they have been turning away. They have disbelieved in the truth when it came to them, so one day there will come to them news of that at which they have been mocking."[127] The second is 17:61, as quoted twice by Al-Kindi: "Nothing has prevented Us sending the signs, but that the people of long ago counted them false."[128] The abbot deals with these quotations in a lengthy speech addressed to Mohammed himself. He points out, in connection with the first, that it involves an error in God's foreknowledge. The second is patently false, because Moses and Christ, for example, worked miracles and were believed.[129]

In effect, Peter contends, Mohammed is denying that he was a prophet. "Either openly declare that signs were given to you by God and remain a prophet; or, if signs were not given to you, stop being a prophet." Mohammed's insistence upon being called

---

[122] D 192rs.   [123] A 154rd.
[124] See Wensinck, *A Handbook of Early Muhammedan Tradition*, 130, 230.
[125] *The Traditions of Islam* (Oxford, 1921), 79.
[126] *Ibid.*, 80.   [127] A 49rd; cf. 3:183.
[128] A 153rd and rs.   [129] D 192rd-vs.

a prophet is in marked contrast with the humility of Amos (Amos 7:14) and John the Baptist (John 1:21) when questioned on the subject. "They were truly prophets of God, but they said they were not prophets by another understanding which does not yet reach you."[130]

At this point, so abruptly as to be almost accidental, Peter stops speaking to Mohammed and returns to the Moslems. "I cannot repeat often enough," he says, how amazing it is that Mohammed can affirm and "repeat almost *ad nauseam*" that he is a prophet of God, and yet "proclaim nothing prophetic." If the Moslems may wish to make a final suggestion of the koranic statements about heaven and hell, Peter coldly reminds them that "it was not difficult for him, and would not be for me, if I wished, to call myself a prophet" by making up "whatever I wanted about those things which are to come about after the end of the world. Nor could my lie be opposed in my lifetime." A prophet "takes the proofs of his prophecy not from the dead, but from the living." Thus Christians believe their prophets "not so much because they called themselves prophets, but because they are proven to have been prophets by evident signs, clear miracles, and the very effects of those things preached by them without any vestige of doubt."[131] Wearily remarking that this last argument should be sufficient to demonstrate Mohammed's lack of "prophetic grace," Peter braces himself and his readers for "another beginning."[132]

[130] "Qui tamen uere prophetae Dei erant, sed prophetas se non esse, alio qui ad uos nunc non pertinet . . . intellectu . . . dicebat," D 192vd.

[131] "Assumat si uult propheta credi testes prophetiae suae non ex mortuis sed ex uiuentibus, non ex hiis quae post mortem implenda promittat, sed ex hiis quae ante mortem impleta ostendat. Hoc modo, hoc tali tamque euidenti argumento credit Christianus prophetis suis, non quia tantum prophetas se dixerunt, sed quia prophetas se esse euidentibus signis, claris miraculis, ipsisque ad eis rerum praedictarum effectibus absque aliquo dubietatis uestigio comprobarunt," D 192vd-93rs.

[132] D 193rs.

A NEW CLASSIFICATION of prophecy opens the second part of Book Two. Peter distinguishes "good" prophets from "bad," and among the former those who preached "universal things" from those who preached "particular things." He exempts at once from this classification "divines, such as augurs, soothsayers, diviners, magicians, [and] fortune-tellers." The "good" prophets "are those whose life is praiseworthy, whose prophecy or prediction is true, among whose number are . . . Moses, Isaiah, Jeremiah, Ezechiel, Daniel, and many others. Among them also is Christ Himself who, though Lord of all the prophets and God, nevertheless, since He said many prophetic things, was called a prophet."[133] The "bad" prophets are those whose "life is deplorable" and whose "prophecy or prediction is false." The prophets of Baal (III Kings 18:19ff.) are cited as examples.[134]

The "universal" good prophets are those "who predicted universal things, that is, things pertaining to all. All those . . . I named above, with almost all who are called good prophets," fall into this category. The "particular" prophets are those who "predicted those things which pertain . . . to certain particular individuals who were expressly named."[135] Jonah's mission to Niniveh and Samuel's prophecies concerning his family (I Kings 9:1ff.) are mentioned among other examples of particular prophecy. Universal prophecy "ceased among the Jewish people, which alone had the cult of the divine law up to the time of Christ, . . . in John, whom we call the Baptist and you the son of Zachary (not that we deny that he was his son), for it was then unnecessary, since everything had been sent in full to those who paid attention to it. Therefore your Mohammed was not, as you say, the seal of

---

[133] "Boni sunt, quorum uita laudabilis, quorum prophetia uel praedicatio uerax. De quorum numero sunt quos supra scripsi: Moyses, Ysaias, Ihremias, Ihzechiel, Danihel, multique alii. De hiis, et ipse Christus. Qui quamuis cunctorum prophetarum Dominus et Deus sit, tamen quia multa prophetica dixit, propheta uocatus est," D 193rs.
[134] D 193rs-rd.   [135] D 193rd.

the prophets, that is, the last among the prophets, but rather John the Baptist, about whom Christ ... said, 'the law and the prophets until John' [Luke 16:16]."[136]

Peter is careful to add that particular prophecy, on the other hand, has not ceased. St. Paul, for instance, may be considered a particular prophet; his prophecy concerning apostates (II Tim. 4:3-4) has already been fulfilled, while that concerning the Antichrist (II Thess. 2:3-4) is yet to be fulfilled. Other Apostles and many of their disciples could also be so classified. In fact, particular prophecy was accorded to "an immense multitude" and is "still, perhaps, to be given to many."[137]

Peter is now free to provide more examples. Isaiah, Jeremiah, and Daniel are singled out as examples of both of the latter types of prophethood.[138] "But because I propose the Hebrew prophets to you, as if to Jews, possibly one of you will be amazed. But in order that he may cease to be amazed, let him hear what follows. The aforementioned prophets were, indeed, Jews; but, although Jews, they are also [prophets]." Peter believes there are three reasons why the Moslems must accept the Jewish prophets as their own: "First, because Ishmael and Isaac were brothers ... ; secondly, because, in addition to the fact that the line of consanguinity and language ... between you is almost common, you have also been set apart by the singular and ancient sign of circumcision as derived from the father of both [of your] peoples, Abraham ... ; thirdly, because the Jewish and Christian prophets about whom we are arguing must be accepted by you as inspired by the divine Spirit and replete with prophetic grace, as was shown by evident and invincible reasons in the previous book,

[136] "Vnde cessantibus, et in Iohanne quem nos baptistam, uos filium Zachariae dicitis, nec nos eius eum esse filium negamus, omnino inquam apud gentem Iudaicam deficientibus prophetis, quae sola usque ad Christum diuinae legis cultrix extiterat, illud tantum prophetiae genus cessauit, quod ad statum uniuersalem pertinebat, quia uniuersis ad id spectantibus plene praemissis, necessarium iam non erat. Non fuit igitur Mahumeth uester ut dicitis signaculum prophetarum hoc est ultimis in prophetis, sed Iohannes baptista, de quo Christus in Aeuangelio, iuxta uos sibi dato ait: 'Lex et prophetae usque ad Iohannem,'" D 193vd.

[137] D 193vd-94rs.   [138] D 194rs-rd.

which it would be superfluous to reconsider completely and treat
. . . as if anew if you have given solicitous hearing to the things
that went before."[139]

For these reasons, Peter concludes, the Moslem has no choice but
to accept these prophets. He betrays some impatience with them,
and says: "I shrink from reiterating the oft-spoken. But the
stylus bears all things patiently."[140]

In the following section Peter organizes his final argument.
"What do you demand of me, Ishmaelite? How shall I prove that
my prophets are yours? . . . I have already done so, clearly . . . .
Why do you accept anything taken from my books, which are far
older than yours, when I am a Christian . . . ? I take nothing from
your books." One explanation occurs to Peter: "Do you perhaps
want to become a Christian? Oh, would that you did! . . . Then
you could sing with . . . David, 'The snare is broken. We are
delivered' [Ps. 123:7]."[141] Otherwise, he insists, the Moslem position is inconsistent. "If our books lie, then the things taken from
them are false." By this line of reasoning Peter rejects the Koran,
"not certain parts of it only, but the whole of it."[142]

The alternatives are put up to the Moslems one last time: "Either
reject the Koran on account of the false things which were taken
from false scriptures . . . or admit that the Jewish and Christian

[139] "Sed quia Hebreos prophetas uobis uelut Iudeis propono, mirabitur forsitan
aliquis uestrum. Sed ut desinat mirari audiat sequentia. Hebrei quidem iam
dicti prophetae sunt, sed licet Hebrei sint, etiam uestri sunt. . . . Primo quod
Hysmahel et Ysaac fratres fuere. . . . Secundo, quod preter consanguinitatis
lineam et linguam . . . pene communem etiam singulari et antiquo circumcisionis signo uelut ab utriusque gentis patre Abram diriuato, uos ipsos ab uniuersarum gentium, aut innatis usibus aut traditis legibus secreuistis. Tertio,
quod Hebreos aut Christianos de quibus agitur prophetas ut diuino Spiritu
inspiratos, et prophetica gratia plenos a uobis suscipi debere euidentibus et
inuictis in suprascripto libro rationibus monstratum est. Quas ad integrum
reconsignare et uelut de nouo litteris tradere, si praecedentibus aurem sollicitam
adhibuistis superfluum est," D 194rd-vs.

[140] D 194vs.

[141] "Quid exigis a me Hysmaelita, unde prophetas meos tuos esse comprobem.
. . . Habeo plane, habeo multa. . . . Cur accipis aliquid de libris meis, qui longe
tuis antiquiores sunt, cum ego Christianus. . . . Nichil ego assumo de libris tuis.
. . . An forte Christianus uis fieri? Et o utinam . . . possis cantare cum Dauid
. . . , 'Laqueus contritus est, et nos liberati sumus,'" *ibid.*

[142] D 194vd.

scriptures from which they were taken are true. Since it is plain that you cannot escape from these confinements in any way whatever, I believe that you would rather choose to admit our scriptures as true than to dismiss . . . the law of your fathers. . . . If you choose this alternative, you must have faith in those scriptures."[143]

Returning to the beginning of his argument, he promises to prove with a more forceful demonstration that Mohammed was not a prophet. The demonstration is quite disappointing, for although it is obvious where Mohammed is meant to fit into the classification of prophets, nothing new is introduced to develop the argument. Instead, the Moslems are invited to produce examples of prophecies which could qualify their prophet as either universal or particular. It is strange that he should mention the former possibility, inasmuch as he had just categorically ruled it out by definition. "Do you find . . . in that whole book of yours . . . anything said by your prophet prophetically about the past . . . present . . . [or] future? Yet in this threefold distinction . . . the sum of the entire prophetic grace consists." He is absolutely confident that the only reply he will receive is silence. With as much fatigue as triumph, he states the conclusion: "[Mohammed] is therefore not a prophet."[144]

[143] "Aut propter falsa quae ex libris ut dicis falsis assumpta et libro tuo inserta sunt, Alchoran abice, aut si nolueris, Hebraicos et Christianos libros ex quibus illa sumpta sunt, ueraces fatere. Et quia non patet uspiam uia qua has angustias euadere aliter possis, credo te magis eligere, nostros libros fateri ueraces, ne quae hactenus lege paterna seruasti, cum ipso ipsius legis auctore, simul uniuersa exspirent. Quod si hanc partem elegeris, libris . . . Hebraicis et Christianis, ut scripturis propriis fidem dabis," *ibid*.
[144] D 195rd.

PETER THE VENERABLE'S *Liber contra sectam sive haeresim Saracenorum* was the first systematic refutation of Islamic doctrine in Latin. With a single exception, Peter knew none of the earlier such refutations in other languages at first hand, and was almost certainly ignorant of their existence. The single exception, of course, was the apology of Al-Kindi, which Peter was convinced would be, in its Latin translation, "of much future use to many . . . on account of the knowledge it communicates of things unknown." Even supposing that his own work was intended to supplement or even to supersede it, it is curious that Peter made no mention of this translation, on which he relied heavily in the preparation of both the *Summa* and the *Liber,* outside his *Epistola de translatione sua.* He managed to avoid repeating certain of Al-Kindi's mistakes, and the works are noticeably different. Those arguments and examples which Peter took from the *Rescriptum Christiani* were always developed and expanded.

Even apart from this translation, one is impressed with the comparatively scant direct use of the Toledan Collection in the *Liber.* There are only seven quotations from the Koran; two of them play no part at all in the argumentation, but the remaining five are central to it. Two quotations from the *Doctrina Mahumet* likewise figure in the demonstration of an important point, while the one from the *Fabulae Saracenorum* is less significant. Three Islamic traditions are quoted, one of which Peter believed to be a quotation from the Koran.

The *Liber* is quite unlike earlier Christian refutations in the respect that it does not take up in a cursory manner many points of theology, but rather a few in a greatly expanded way. The particular goals of this book's argumentation were simple, but far from trivial. They might be summed up in these terms: Peter was attempting to establish "by necessary or [at least] probable arguments": (1) that the Moslems are obliged by the Koran to regard the books of the Bible as revealed by God; (2) that, owing to inconsistencies between the Koran and the Bible, it is necessary that one or the other be abandoned; (3) that the Bible cannot be abandoned without falsifying the Koran, but the reverse is possible; (4) that it can be shown, in any case, both from the Bible and the Koran itself, (*a*) that the Koran was not revealed by God, and (*b*) that Mohammed was not, at least not by any acceptable traditional Semitic definition of the term, a prophet. There are less basic but nevertheless structurally valuable arguments against (1) the characteristic unwillingness of Moslems to engage in theological disputation and (2) those Islamic traditions concerning the corruption or loss of the books of the Bible. Although Peter endeavors to force the Moslems to return to the authority of the Bible and, indeed, invites them to become Christians, he presents almost no exposition of Christian theology as such. Far from a mere polemical trick, however, the statement of the ambivalence of the Islamic view of the Bible is perhaps the only firm basis for theological disputation between Christians and Moslems, and the value of Peter's recognition of this fact is assuredly very great.

Peter was conscious of his disadvantage in writing without benefit of hearing from his Moslem readers. Anxious to honor their "freedom of speech, the one faculty for returning to the right," he attempted to solve this problem by preserving some aspects of a dialogue, taking the Moslems' part, on occasion, with full breaks into the narrative or argumentation for expressions of doubt, scorn, or contrary opinion which they might conceivably have been moved to make at those points. A fairly long section in Book Two is addressed to Mohammed himself, and elsewhere in the *Liber* exclamations are frequently directed to him.

Several points concerning Peter's style and method of refutation deserve special mention. A fundamental and genuine good will, which a few lapses serve only to emphasize, pervades the whole of the refutation. Peter did not hesitate to call it love, and he manifested it in his unwillingness to "speak harshly against Mohammed" except for the cause of truth and in his unusual respect for his readers. He praised them as "rational not only by nature, but rational in ingenuity and art" and had some good words for their laws, "which we know to be prudent according to the flesh." When speaking to them, at any rate, he chose to regard them as heretics rather than worse, and even confided to them his disagreement with the hostility of his fellow Christians.

Peter's constant, almost tedious use of such phrases as "according to your Mohammed" and "which, I believe, you do not discredit" were intended to draw attention to his familiarity with the Koran and other Islamic books, though he had described himself as an utter "stranger to your customs and life," in order that his remarks would be seriously considered. For the same reason he appeals often to human reason, to the example of "wise men" and "the agreement of nations," to establish certain points. He was impelled to support with koranic quotations the major propositions he attacked and to provide, wherever necessary, clear-cut definitions. He showed a willingness to employ some Islamic terminology so as to accommodate what he considered acceptable in the Islamic position.

Peter's frank recognition of similarities between Islam and Christianity was important, but much of the cogency of his refutation depends upon inconsistencies which he claimed to have discovered within Islamic doctrine and in the Koran itself. Examples of such inconsistencies are the Moslems' refusal to countenance opposing claims, both a declarative and a conditional statement attributed to God in the Koran, the koranic statement on killing and strife, the incorporation of biblical elements in the Koran, and the charge of the corruption and loss of the books of the Bible. There are roughly twice as many quotations from the Old Testament as from the New in the *Liber*; the Psalms, as might have been predicted, are quoted most often.

The *Liber* represents an advance over the *Summa* in some matters of fact as well as in general attitude. Peter reveals a somewhat better knowledge of Mohammed's life and times in the refutation, doubtless because it had occasioned further study of the Toledan Collection. In the *Liber* he even seems inclined to forgive Mohammed, on the grounds on which he condemned him in the *Summa*. Among the most successful passages in the refutation are those containing the appeal to legal judgment, the example of King Ethelbert, and the establishment of Islam's debt to Judaism. The clever interposition of Mohammed's name in the various considerations of the Jewish prophets also makes the desired contrasts exceptionally vivid.

But the *Liber* is certainly not without its serious faults. Occasionally the rhetoric gets out of hand. Exclamations follow one another in rapid glissandi, and some of the arguments are set forth in disorder. There is far more repetition than is called for or effective. Indeed, parts of Book Two are almost strained, as if Peter simply does not know how to continue. The most striking example is that of the final argument. After setting down the distinctions between good and bad, universal and particular prophets, Peter suddenly breaks off and, instead of offering the new and stronger proof he had announced, lamely repeats his challenge to the Moslems to produce prophecies from the Koran.

Although there are no genuine errors in Peter's quotations from the Toledan Collection, apart from two slight changes in wording and one misrepresentation, doubtless unintentional, of a tradition as a koranic quote, he could have strengthened his arguments immeasurably had he made greater use of the translations. Even if he did not judge the alleged prophecies of Mohammed mentioned by Al-Kindi as worthy of repetition, he might have mentioned those included in the *Fabulae Saracenorum* or some of the extremely vulnerable material in the *Liber generationis Mahumet* and the *Doctrina Mahumet*. Above all, the work could have profited from a more careful scrutiny of the Koran. Peter's facile condemnations of the Koran would not appear so abrupt or anticlimactic had he discovered in it and discussed many more items at variance with Christian theology, or even had he been moved to repeat Al-Kindi's well-constructed argument concerning the production of the text.

Peter's book was not fated, as he hoped it might be, to be translated into Arabic. It did not have an influence on later Christian polemics against Islam proportionate to the success of the Toledan Collection. The entire project of which it was the final part forces us to revise our notions of European attitudes toward Islam during the period of the early Crusades, but these revisions must not be too drastic. In the last analysis, as stated before, it is the testimony of one man's intelligence and zeal and fervent conviction that the Moslems were not to be approached, "as our people often do, by arms, but by words; not by force, but by reason; not in hatred, but in love."

VI · TEXTS

Manserunt itaque ista aliquanto tempore ociosa, sed incumbente necessitate apparuerunt quæ diu vacaverant fructuosa.

PETER THE VENERABLE

1 · A NOTE ON THE TEXTS

OWING TO THE AUTHORITY and excellence of the two manuscripts upon which these editions are based, MS 1162 of the Bibliothèque de l'Arsenal in Paris (A) and MS 381 of the Bibliothèque municipale de Douai (D), I have considered it important not to depart unnecessarily from plain transcription. The sentence structure and punctuation of the manuscripts have been followed strictly. The few paragraph divisions in the manuscripts have been retained, but many new ones have been added. The orthographic peculiarities of the manuscripts have also been adhered to insofar as possible, despite the fact that there are not a few inconsistencies even within texts copied by the same scribe. The "ę" has been transcribed "æ" even in cases where "e" or "œ" would be a more usual reading, the reason for which will be clear from the texts themselves. The distinction between "v" and "u" is nearly always made by the scribes for capital letters and occasionally also for small letters; in the few instances where I have capitalized words beginning with "u," I have used "V." I have kept customary separations within certain compound words where the manuscripts call for them unless such separations would clearly lead to error or confusion. Because of scribal inconsistencies abbreviations have posed a particular problem; in general I have given the scribes the benefit of the doubt. Quotations of any kind have been placed within quotation marks and quotations within those quotations within single quotation marks. Annotation of the texts has been limited to direct quotations and indirect but specific references.

2 · *SUMMA TOTIUS HÆRESIS*
SARACENORUM

SVMMA TOTIVS heresis ac diabolicæ sectæ Sarracenorum, siue
A ɪrs Hismahelitarum, hæc est.

In primis primus et maximus ipsorum execrandus est error,
quod trinitatem in unitate deitatis negant, sicque dum in una
diuinitatis essentia trinum personarum numerum non credunt, in
A ɪrd unitate numerum euitantes, dum ternarium inquam / omnium
formarum principium atque finem, sicque rerum formatarum
causam et originem atque terminum, non recipiunt, Deum licet
ore confitentes, ipsum penitus nesciunt. Ipsi autem deuii, ipsi
uariabiles, principium uarietatis et alteritatis omnis, uidelicet binarium solum in unitate confitentur, scilicet ipsam diuinam essentiam, et eius animam. Vnde Deum pluraliter loquentem, introducit
semper Alchoran, quo nomine legem suam nuncupant, et interpre-
tatur Alchoran ex Arabico, collectio preceptorum.

Illi item cæci, Deum creatorem patrem esse negant, quia secundum eos nullus fit pater sine coitu. Christum itaque licet ex diuino
Spiritu conceptum, Dei filium esse non credunt, nec etiam Deum,
sed prophetam bonum, ueracissimum, omnis mendacii atque peccati immunem, Mariæ filium, sine patre genitum, nunquam mortuum, quia morte non est dignus, immo cum illum Iudei interficere uellent, de manibus eorum elapsum, ascendisse ad astra, ibique
nunc in carne uiuere in presentia Creatoris, usque ad aduentum
Antichristi. Quem uenientem, Christus idem gladio suæ uirtutis
interficiet, et Iudeos residuos ad legem suam conuertet. Christianos
autem, qui iam a longo tempore legem eius atque Euangelium
perdiderunt, tum propter eiusdem discessum, tum etiam propter
apostolorum atque discipulorum mortem, legem suam perfecte
docebit, in qua tunc omnes Christiani, sicut et illi primi sui discipuli, saluabuntur. Cum quibus simul et omnibus creaturis, Seraphim quem ipsi dicunt archangelum unum, sonante buccinam,
A ɪvs morietur et ipse Christus, postea / resurrecturus cum ceteris, et

ad iudicium suos ducturus, eisque auxiliaturus et pro eis oraturus, sed nequaquam iudicaturus. Deus enim solus iudicabit. Prophetæ uero et legati singuli, cum suis et pro suis intercessores aderunt, et auxiliatores. Sic enim docuit eos miserrimus atque impiissimus Mahumet, qui omnia sacramenta Christianæ pietatis, quibus maxime homines saluantur, abnegans, iam pene terciam humani generis partem, nescimus quo Dei iudicio, inauditis fabularum deliramentis, diabolo et morti æternæ contradidit.

De quo quis fuerit, et quid docuerit, propter eos qui librum istum lecturi sunt, ut scilicet quod legerint melius intelligant, et quam detestabilis tam uita quam doctrina illius extiterit sciant, dicendum uidetur. Putant enim quidam hunc Nicholaum illum unum e septem primis diaconibus extitisse,[1] et Nicholaitarum ab eo dictorum sectam, quæ et in Apochalipsi Iohannis arguitur,[2] hanc modernorum Sarracenorum legem existere. Somniant et alii alios, et sicut lectionis incuriosi, et rerum gestarum ignari, sicut et in aliis casibus, falsa quælibet opinantur.

Fuit autem iste, sicut etiam chronica ab Anastasio Romanæ ecclesiæ bibliothecario de Greco in Latinum translata, apertissime narrat,[3] tempore imperatoris Heraclii, paulo post tempora magni et primi Gregorii Romani pontificis, ante annos fere .d.tos et quinquaginta, Arabs natione, uilis genere, antiquæ primum ydolatriæ cultor, sicut et alii Arabes tunc adhuc erant, ineruditus, nullarum pene litterarum, strenuus in se/cularibus, et calliditate A ivd multa, de ignobili et egeno, in diuitem et famosum prouectus. Hic paulatim crescendo, et contiguos quosque ac maxime sanguinis propinquos, insidiis, rapinis, incursionibus frequenter infestando, quos poterat furtim, quos poterat publice occidendo, terrorem sui auxit, et sepe in congressionibus factus superior, ad regnum suæ gentis aspirare cæpit.

Cumque uniuersis pari modo resistentibus, eiusque ignobilitatem contempnentibus, uideret se hac uia non posse consequi quod sperabat, quia ui gladii non potuit, religionis uelamine, et diuini

---

[1] Acta 6:5.
[2] Apoc. 2:6, 15.
[3] Theophanis *Chronographia* (ed. C. de Boor [Leipzig, 1883-5]), 1:333, 11:209.

prophetæ nomine, rex fieri attemptauit. Et quia inter barbaros barbarus, inter ydolatras et ipse ydolatra habitabat, atque inter illos, quos utpote pre cunctis gentibus, tam diuinæ quam humanæ legis expertes, et ignaros, faciles ad seducendum esse nouerat, conceptæ iniquitati dare operam cæpit. Et quoniam prophetas Dei, magnos fuisse homines audierat, prophetam eius se esse dicens, ut aliquid boni simularet, ex parte illos ab ydolatria, non tamen ad Deum uerum, sed ad suæ quam parturire iam cæperat heresis fallaciam traducere conabatur.

Cum interim iudicio illius qui "terribilis in consiliis" dicitur "super filios hominum,"[4] et qui "miseretur cui uult, et quem uult indurat,"[5] dedit Sathan successum errori, et Sergium monachum, heretici Nestorii sectatorem, ab ecclesia expulsum, ad partes illas Arabiæ transmisit, et monachum hereticum pseudoprophetæ con-iunxit. Itaque Sergius con/iunctus Mahumeth, quod ei deerat suppleuit, et scripturas sacras tam Veteris Testamenti quam Noui secundum magistri sui Nestorii intellectum, qui Saluatorem nostrum Deum esse negabat, partim prout sibi uisum est, ei exponens, simulque apochriphorum fabulis eum plenissime imbuens, Christianum Nestorianum effecit. Et ut tota iniquitatis plenitudo in Mahumet conflueret, et nichil ei ad perditionem sui uel aliorum de-esset, adiuncti sunt Iudei heretico, et ne uerus Christianus fieret dolose precauentes, homini nouis rebus inhianti non scripturarum ueritatem, sed fabulas suas quibus nunc usque abundant, Mahumet Iudei insibilant. Sic ab optimis doctoribus, Iudeis et hereticis, Mahumet institutus, Alchoran suum condidit, et tam ex fabulis Iudaicis, quam ex hereticorum neniis confectam nefariam scripturam, barbaro illo suo modo contexuit. Quod paulatim per thomos a Gabrihele cuius iam nomen ex sacra scriptura cognouerat, sibi allatum mentitus, gentem Deum ignorantem, letali haustu infecit, et more talium, oram calicis melle liniens, subsequente mortifero ueneno,[6] animas et corpora gentis miseræ proh dolor, interemit.

Sic plane impius ille fecit, quando et Christianam et Iudaicam

A 2rs (margin)

---

[4] Ps. 65:5.
[5] Rom. 9:18; cf. Exod. 33:19.
[6] Cf. T. Lucreti Cari *De Rerum Natura*, 1:936-42.

legem collaudans, neutram tamen tenendam esse confirmans, probando reprobus reprobauit. Inde est, quod Moysen optimum prophetam fuisse, Christum Dominum maiorem omnibus extitisse confirmat, natum de uirgine predicat, nuncium Dei, uerbum Dei, spiritum Dei fatetur, nec nuncium uerbum aut / Spiritum, ut nos A 2rd aut intelligit aut fatetur. Filium Dei dici aut credi, prorsus deridet. Et de humanæ generationis similitudine uaccinus homo filii Dei eternam natiuitatem metiens, uel gignere uel generari Deum potuisse, quanto potest nisu denegat et subsannat. Resurrectionem carnis sepe replicando astruit, iudicium commune in fine seculi, non a Christo sed a Deo exercendum esse non negat. Illi tamen iudicio, Christum ut omnium post Deum maximum, ac seipsum ad gentis suæ presidium affuturum, uesanit. Inferni tormenta, qualia sibi libuit, et qualia adinuenire magnum pseudoprophetam decuit, describit. Paradysum non societatis angelicæ, nec uisionis diuinæ, nec summi illius boni quod "nec oculus uidit, nec auris audiuit, nec in cor hominis ascendit,"[7] sed uere talem, qualem caro et sanguis, immo fex carnis et sanguinis concupiscebat, qualemque sibi parari optabat, depinxit. Ibi carnium et omnigenorum fructuum esum, ibi lactis et mellis riuulos, et aquarum splendentium, ibi pulcherrimarum mulierum et uirginum amplexus et luxus, in quibus tota eius paradysus finitur, sectatoribus suis promittit. Inter ista, omnes pene antiquarum heresum feces, quas diabolo imbuente sorbuerat, reuomens, cum Sabellio trinitatem abnegat, cum suo Nestorio Christi deitatem abicit, cum Manicheo, mortem Domini diffitetur, licet regressum eius non neget ad cælos.

His et similibus non adquisitionis sed perditionis populum imbuens, a Deo plenissime auertit, et ne euangelicus / sermo ultra A 2vs in eis posset habere locum, uelut omnia quæ sunt Euangelii et Christi scientibus, cordium eorum aditum ferreo impietatis obice obturauit. Circumcisionem insuper, uelut ab Hismahele gentis illius patre sumptam, tenendam esse decreuit, et super hæc omnia, quo magis sibi allicere carnales mentes hominum posset, gulæ ac libidini frena laxauit, et ipse simul decem et octo uxores habens,

---

[7] Isai. 64:4; I Cor. 2:9.

atque multorum aliorum uxores uelut ex responso diuino adulterans, maiorem sibi uelut exemplo prophetico numerum perditorum adiunxit. Et ne ex toto inhonestus proderetur, studium
elemosinarum et quædam misericordiæ opera commendat, orationes collaudat, et sic undique mostruosus, ut ille ait, "humano
capiti ceruicem equinam, et plumas" auium copulat.[8] Qui quoniam
suadente iam dicto monacho, ac prefatis Iudeis, ydolatriam ex
toto et reliquit, et reliquendam quibus potuit persuasit, atque unum
Deum, deorum multiplicitate relicta colendum esse predicauit,
hominibus, agrestibus et imperitis inaudita dicere uisus est. Et
quia rationi eorum hec predicatio concordabat, propheta Dei
primo ad eis creditur. Dehinc processu temporis et erroris, in regem
ab eis quod concupierat, sublimatus est. Sic bona malis permiscens,
uera falsis confundens, erroris semina seuit, et suo partim tempore,
partim et maxime post suum tempus segetem nefariam igne æterno
concremandam produxit. /

A 2vd Nam statim Romano languescente immo pene deficiente imperio, permittente eo "per quem reges regnant,"[9] Arabum uel
Sarracenorum hac peste infectorum surrexit principatus, atque ui
armata maximas Asiæ partes cum tota Africa ac parte Hispaniæ
paulatim occupans, in subiectos sicut imperium sic et errorem
transfudit. Hos licet hereticos nominem, quia aliqua nobiscum
credunt, in pluribus a nobis dissentiunt, fortassis rectius paganos
aut ethnicos quod plus est, nominarem. Quia quamuis de Domino
uera aliqua dicant, plura tamen falsa predicant, nec baptismati,
sacrificio, pænitentiæ, uel alicui Christiano sacramento, quod numquam ullus preter hos hereticos fecit, communicant. Summa uero
huius heresis intentio est, ut Christus Dominus neque Deus, neque
Dei filius esse credatur, sed licet magnus Deoque dilectus, homo
tamen purus, et uir quidem sapiens, et propheta maximus. Quæ
quidem olim diaboli machinatione concepta, primo per Arrium
seminata, deinde per istum Sathanan scilicet Mahumet, prouecta,
per Antichristum uero, ex toto secundum diabolicam intentionem
complebitur. Cum enim dicat beatus Hylarius, Antichristi origi-

[8] Quinti Horatii Flacci *Ars Poetica,* 1:1-2.
[9] Prov. 8:15.

nem in Arrio extitisse,[10] dum quod ille cæpit, uerum filium Dei
Christum esse negando, et creaturam dicendo, Antichristus tandem nullo modo illum Deum uel Dei filium, sed nec etiam bonum
hominem fuisse asserendo consummaturus est, merito impiissimus
Mahumeth inter utrumque medius a diabolo prouisus ac preparatus esse uidetur, qui et Arrii quo/dammodo supplementum, et A 3rs
Antichristi peiora dicturi, apud infidelium mentes maximum fieret
nutrimentum.

Nichil quippe ita contrarium est humani generis inimico, sicut
fides incarnati Dei, per quam precipue ad pietatem excitamur, et
sacramentis cælestibus renouati Spiritus Sancti gratia operante,
illuc unde nos deiecisse gloriabatur, ad uisionem scilicet regis et
patriæ nostræ, ipso rege et conditore Deo ad nostrum exilium
descendente, nosque ad se misericorditer reuocante, iterum redire
speramus. Hanc pietatis et diuinæ dispensationis fidem pariter et
amorem, semper ab initio in cordibus hominum molitur extinguere, hanc etiam in principio adhuc nascentis ecclesiæ, si
tunc permittetur, subtilitate uersutissima, et pene hoc eodem
modo quo postea gentem istam infelicissimam seducere permissus
est, eradicare temptauit.

Dicit enim beatus Augustinus, Porphirium philosophum postquam a Christianitate miserabiliter apostatauit, hoc in libris suis
quos aduersus Christianos ædidit, retulisse, quod scilicet oracula
deorum consuluerit, et de Christo quid esset interrogauerit.
Responsum uero sibi a demonibus fuisse, quod Christus, bonus
quidem uir fuerit, sed discipulos eius grauiter peccasse, qui ei
diuinitatem ascribentes, rem quam ipse de se non dixerat, confinxissent.[11] Quæ sententia, pene eisdem uerbis, in istis fabulis inuenitur
sepissime. Quanta autem hæc diaboli subtilitas extiterit, ut de
Christo aliquid boni diceret, de quo si ex toto male / dixisset, A 3rd
nullatenus iam sibi credi sciebat, non curans quicquid Christus
putaretur, dummodo diuinitas quæ maxime saluat homines in illo
non crederetur, si quis plenius uult intelligere, legat octauum
decimum eiusdem patris Augustini librum, et nonum decimum

---

[10] Cf. S. Hilarii *De Trinitate*, vi:46.
[11] S. Augustini *De Civitate Dei*, xix:23.

De Ciuitate Dei, et primum De Consensu Euangelistarum. Ibi enim si boni ac studiosi ingenii est, coniciet pro certo, et quid diabolus tunc machinatus sit facere sed non permissus, et quid tandem occulto iudicio permittente, in hac sola miserrima gente fecerit relaxatus.

Nullo enim modo tales fabulas quales hic scriptæ secuntur, aliquis mortalium nisi diabolo presentialiter cooperante, fingere potuisset, per quas post multa ridicula et insanissima deliramenta, hoc precipue omnimodo Sathanas intendit perficere, ne Christus Dominus, Dei filius et uerus Deus, humani generis conditor et redemptor esse credatur. Et hoc est uere, quod per Porphirium tunc persuadere uoluit, sed per Dei misericordiam ab ecclesia eo adhuc tempore, Spiritus Sancti feruente primitiis, exsufflatus, tandem miserrimo homine isto Mahumet, et ut fertur a multis, arrepticio et cadente, quasi instrumento et organo sibi aptissimo usus, proh dolor, gentem maximam et quæ iam pene dimidia pars mundi reputari potest, secum in æternam perditionem demersit. Quod quare illi permissum sit, ille solus nouit cui nemo potest dicere, "Cur ita facis?" et qui "de multis etiam uocatis, paucos electos esse" dixit.[12]

A 3vs Vnde ego magis eligens contremiscere, / quam disputare, ista breuiter prenotaui, ut qui legerit intelligat, et si talis est, qui contra totam heresim istam scribere et uelit et possit, cum quali hoste pugnaturus sit agnoscat. Erit fortasse adhuc, cuius spiritum Dominus suscitabit, ut ecclesiam Dei a magna quam inde patitur ignominia liberet, quia scilicet cum omnes siue antiquas siue modernas hereses usque ad nostra tempora, respondendo confutauerit, huic soli quæ super omnes alias tam in corporibus quam in animabus infinitam humani generis stragem dedit, non solum nichil respondit, sed nec quid tanta pestis esset, aut unde processerit, inquirere saltem uel tenuiter studuit. Nam et hæc tota causa fuit, qua ego Petrus sanctæ Cluniacensis ecclesiæ humilis abbas, cum in Hispaniis pro uisitatione locorum nostrorum quæ ibi sunt, demorarer, magno studio et impensis totam impiam sectam, eiusque pessimi inuentoris execrabilem uitam, de Arabico in Latinum

[12] Matt. 20:16, 22:14.

transferri, ac denudatam ad nostrorum noticiam uenire feci, ut quam spurca et friuola heresis esset sciretur, et aliquis Dei seruus, ad eam scripto refellendam, Sancto inflammante Spiritu incitaretur. Quod quia proh pudor, iam pæne toto huiusmodi studiorum sanctorum ubique in ecclesia tepefacto feruore, non est qui faciat, expectaui enim diu, et non fuit qui aperiret os et zelo sanctæ Christianitatis moueret pennam et ganniret, ego ipse saltem, si magnæ occupationes meæ permiserint, quandoque id aggredi Domino adiuuante proposui. Semper tamen a quocumque altero melius, quam a me deterius hoc fieri, gratum haberem.

Explicit.

3 · *EPISTOLA PETRI CLUNIACENSIS AD BERNARDUM CLARÆVALLIS*

A 3vd Epistola domni Petri abbatis ad domnum Bernardum Claræuallis abbatem, de translatione sua qua fecit transferri ex Arabico in Latinum sectam siue heresim Sarracenorum.

Singulari ueneratione colendo, totis karitatis brachiis amplectendo, indiuiduo cordis mei hospiti, domno Bernardo Claræuallis abbati, frater Petrus humilis Cluniacensis abbas, salutem ad quam suspirat æternam.

Mitto uobis carissime nouam translationem nostram, contra pessimam nequam Mahumet heresim disputantem, quæ dum nuper in Hispaniis morarer, meo studio de Arabica uersa est in Latinam. Feci autem eam transferri a perito utriusque linguæ uiro, magistro Petro Toletano. Sed quia lingua Latina non adeo ei familiaris uel nota erat ut Arabica, dedi ei coadiutorem doctum uirum, dilectum filium et fratrem Petrum, notarium nostrum, reuerentiæ uestræ ut æstimo bene cognitum. Qui uerba Latina impolite uel confuse plerumque ab eo prolata poliens et ordinans, epistolam immo libellum multis ut credo propter ignotarum rerum noticiam perutilem futurum, perfecit. Sed et totam impiam sec-

A 4rs tam, / uitamque nefarii hominis ac legem quam Alchoran id est collectaneum preceptorum appellauit, sibique ab angelo Gabrihele de cælo allatam, miserrimis hominibus persuasit, nichilominus ex Arabico ad Latinitatem perduxi, interpretantibus scilicet uiris utriusque linguæ peritis, Rotberto Ketenensi de Anglia, qui nunc Pampilonensis ecclesiæ archidiaconus est, Hermanno quoque Dalmata, acutissimi et litterati ingenii scolastico, quos in Hispania circa Hiberum astrologicæ arti studentes inueni, eosque ad hoc faciendum multo precio conduxi.

Fuit autem in hoc opere intentio mea, ut morem illum patrum sequerer, quo nullam umquam suorum temporum uel leuissimam ut sic dicam heresim silendo pretierunt, quin ei totis fidei uiribus resisterent, et scriptis atque disputationibus esse detestandam ac dampnabilem demonstrarent. Hoc ego de hoc precipuo errore errorum de hac fece uniuersarum heresum, in quam omnium diabolicarum sectarum quæ ab ipso Saluatoris aduentu ortæ sunt reliquiæ confluxerunt, facere uolui, ut sicut eius letali peste dimidius pene orbis infectus agnoscitur, ita quam exsecrandus et conculcandus, detecta eius stulticia et turpitudine, a nescientibus agnoscatur. Agnoscetis ipse legendo, et sicut arbitror ut dignum est deflebitis, per tam nefarias et abiectissimas sordes, tantam hu/mani generis partem deceptam, et a Conditore suo per spur- A 4rd cissimi hominis sectam nefariam, etiam post Redemptoris gratiam tam leuiter auersam.

Specialiter autem uobis hæc omnia notificaui, ut et tanto amico studia nostra communicarem, et ad scribendum contra tam perniciosum errorem, illam uestram quam nostris diebus Deus uobis singulariter contulit doctrinæ magnificentiam animarem. Nam licet hoc perditis illis ut æstimo prodesse non possit, responsionem tamen condignam sicut contra alias hereses, ita et contra hanc pestem, Christianum armarium habere deceret. Quam si superfluam quilibet causatus fuerit, quoniam quibus resistere debeant talibus armis muniti non adsunt, nouerit in republica magni regis quædam fieri ad tutelam, quædam fieri ad decorem, quædam etiam ad utrumque. Nam ad tutelam facta sunt a Salomone pacifico arma, licet tempore suo minus necessaria.[1] Preparati sunt a Dauid sumptus, parata et ornamenta, templi diuini constructioni et ornatui deputata.[2] Sed nec illa eius tempore alicui usui profecerunt, sed in usus diuinos post eius tempora transierunt. Manserunt itaque ista aliquanto tempore ociosa, sed incumbente necessitate ap/paruerunt quæ diu uacauerant fructuosa. Nec tamen ut michi A 4vs uidetur opus istud etiam hoc tempore ociosum uocare debeo, quoniam iuxta apostolum, uestrum est et omnium doctorum uirorum, "omnem scientiam extollentem se aduersus altitudinem Dei,"[3] omni studio uerbo et scripto impugnare, destruere, conculcare. Quod si hinc errantes conuerti non possunt, saltem infir-

---

[1] II Para. 10:15-16.
[2] I Para. 22:1-6, 14-16.
[3] II Cor. 10:5, "omnem altitudinem extollentem se adversus scientiam Dei."

mis ecclesiæ qui scandalizari uel occulte moueri leuibus etiam ex causis solent, consulere et prouidere, doctus uel doctor si zelum habet iusticiæ, non debet negligere. Propono inde uobis patres omnes, et precipue patrem Augustinum, qui licet Iulianum Pelagianum, licet Faustum Manicheum, uerbis et labore suo ad fidem rectam conuertere nequiuerit, non tamen quin de eorum errore magna contra eos uolumina conderet, omisit. Sic de reliquis sui temporis et non sui temporis hereticis, sic de Iudeis, sic de paganis faciens, non solum contra eos sui temporis homines armauit, sed etiam ad nos et ad posteros omnes, maximæ ædificationis et instructionis karisma transmisit.

Si igitur reuerentiæ uestræ in his laborandi Deo aspirante uolun- A 4vd tas fuerit, nam facultas per eius gratiam deesse non poterit, re/scribite, et mittemus librum quem nondum misimus, ut per os uestrum ipsius laude repletum, spiritui nequitiæ "Spiritus benignus"[4] respondeat, et ecclesiæ suæ thesauros gazis uestræ sapientiæ suppleat.

Explicit epistola domni Petri abbatis, ad Bernardum Claræuallis abbatem.

[4] Sap. 1:6.

4 · *EPISTOLA PETRI PICTAVENSIS*

EPISTOLA PETRI PICTAVENSIS AD DOMNVM PETRVM ABBATEM

Unico et singulari patri et domno suo, domno abbati Cluniacensi D 177rs
Petro, filiorum eius exiguus Petrus, gaudere semper in Christo.

Dum semper omnia more uestro / philosophice agitis, satis D 177rd
competenter michi et patienti et multis passionibus digno, passionem legendam misistis. Gratias dulcedini uestræ, quod hac saltem
occasione, æpistolam uestram et salutationis paternæ gratiam teneo,
quibus interim absentiæ uestræ quæ michi semper grauissima
est molestiam, multo leuius fero. Verumptamen postquam intellexi
uos habere in proposito, ad Angliam ducente Domino trans-
fretare, ualde sollicitior factus sum pro uobis et pro sociis, et pro
toto itinere uestro, ac prospero ad nos reditu, omnipotenti Deo
prout ipse largitur, preces et uota supplicationis offerre. Sed et illos
quos uobis deuotiores et in sanctis orationibus noui studiosiores,
ut idem faciant deprecari studeo, et magis atque magis Christo
donante studebo. Spiritus Sanctus dirigat iter uestrum, et consilium
uestrum, et de reditu uestro ad nos plenum faciat gaudium
nostrum.

Mitto uobis capitula quæ Iohannem perdidisse mandastis, et
credo quod multo distinctius ordinata sint, quam ante. Siquidem
ita modo prænotata sunt, sicut agere cæpistis, uel si tamen uobis
uidetur deinceps acturus estis, contra illos uere inimicos crucis
Christi. Ex multa uero fiducia qua ingenium uestrum noui, siquid
addere uel mutare præsumpsi, et hoc uobis ita placuerit, maneat.
Sin autem, uestrum est corrigere quod erramus. Capitulum etiam
quod est ibi de uxoribus turpiter abutendis,[1] non uos ullo modo
scandalizet, quia uere ita est in Alchorano, et sicut ego in Hyspania
pro certo, et a Petro Toletano, cuius in transferendo socius eram,
et a Roberto Pampilonensi nunc archidiacono audiui, omnes
Sarraceni hoc licenter quasi ex præcepto Mahumeth faciunt. Volo
autem, ut sic isti confundantur a uobis, sicut confusi sunt Iudei,

---

[1] Libri secundi cap. vi, D 177vs.

215

et Prouinciales heretici. Solus enim uos estis nostris temporibus, qui tres maximos sanctæ Christianitatis hostes, Iudeos dico et hereticos ac Sarracenos, diuini uerbi gladio[2] trucidastis, et matrem æcclesiam non ita orbatam uel desolatam bonis filiis ostendistis, quin adhuc Christo propitio tales habeat qui possint "omni poscenti rationem reddere de ea quæ in nobis est spe"[3] et fide, et humiliare omnem arrogantiam et superbiam diaboli, "extollentem se aduersus altitudinem Dei."[4]

Salus et prosperitas et omne bonum uobis in primis, sociis quoque uestris et nostris, / domno Hugoni Anglico, et Iohanni qui perdidit capitula, Bartholomeo nostro, domno constabulo Godefrido, Girardo Alemanno si tamen uobiscum est, et cæteris omnibus. Ignoscite queso traditati et infirmitati meæ, quia nouit Dominus cum multum uoluissem, graui totius corporis et maxime solita pedum debilitate constrictus, non ante potui uobis hæc mittere. Scripsi enim hæc omnia etiam in maiore libro, timens ne et ipsa perdantur in uia, sicut perdita sunt capitula. Quod ualde laboriosum fuit.

Explicit epistola.

D 177vs

[2] Cf. Eph. 6:17.
[3] I Petr. 3:15.
[4] II Cor. 10:5, "omnem altitudinem extollentem se aduersus scientiam Dei."

Capitula libri primi domni Petri abbatis Cluniacensis contra sectam   D 177vs
nefandam Sarracenorum.

.i. Prælocutio ad Sarracenos, admonens et excitans eos ut patienter audiant et rationabiliter intelligant quæ secuntur. .ii. Qvam
stulte ac ridiculose dicunt Iudeos legem suam perdidisse, et modo
non nisi falsatam et mendosam habere. .iii. Qva ratione hæc illorum opinio stulta et uana esse probatur. .iiii. Quod quia similiter
Christianos Æuangelium et scripta apostolica perdidisse asserunt,
quomodo facillime refelli possit monstratur. .v. Qvod non potuisset
Christianos latere falsitas Æuangeliorum, maxime cum per uni-
uersum orbem diffusi, multaque linguarum uarietate diuisi, idem
prorsus Æuangelium omnes habeant, nec ab illa unius et eiusdem
Æuangelii ueritate aliqui hoc tempore Christiani dissentiant.
.vi. Quod si falsatum esset Æuangelium, nec tot linguarum ac
gentium homines, tamque studiosos ac sapientes hoc latere potuisset, nec seipsos ipsimet nudato mendacio falli permisissent, nec
relicta ueritate falsa pro ueris, incerta pro certis tenuissent. .vii.
Qvod ex parte illa qua Æuangelium suscipiunt, necessario eos
illud etiam ex toto suscipere debere probatur.

Capitvla libri secundi.
.i. Qvod Mahumeth dici uel credi propheta non debeat his de
causis. .ii. Qvod raptor fuerit, istudque ex sequentibus comproba-
tur. .iii. Qvod homicida insuper et parricida multorum fuerit.
.iiii. Qvod proditor fuerit, incautos et dormientes sepe iugulans.
.v. Qvod adulter nefandus extiterit, adulteria perpetrare sibi a
Deo concessum in Alchorano suo dicens.[1] .vi. Qvod insuper rem
sodomiticam atque turpissimam docuerit, præcipiens in Alchorano
suo, et uelut ex persona Dei sic loquens: "O uiri, mulieres uobis
subiectas, ex quacumque parte uobis placuerit perarate."[2] .vii.
Qvod sepissime in Alchorano suo sibimet contrarius sit, modo / ne-   D 177vd
gans, modo affirmans illud idem quod ante negauit. .viii. Qvod
legislationem eius nulla miracula commendauerunt, cum Moyses

---

[1] Cf. Kor. 33:49.   [2] Kor. 2:223, A 31vs.

antiquæ legislator et Christus Noui Testamenti conditor multis et magnis miraculis, leges quas dederunt diuinas et sanctas esse firmauerint.

Capitula libri tercii.

.i. Qvod Mahumeth miracula facere non potuisse ex supradicta eius nefanda uita probatur. .ii. Quod ipse in Alchorano suo fateatur signa sibi a Deo data non esse.[3] .iii. Qvam friuola immo quam nulla sit ratio quam ibi prætendit, quare scilicet miracula non faciat, introducens Deum sic sibi loquentem: "Nisi sciremus eos tibi non credituros, daremus tibi signa et prodigia."[4] .iiii. Quod inde etiam sibi contrarius sit, quando et prophetam se nominat, et tamen signa sibi data non esse affirmat, cum prophetia maximum signum sit. .v. Quod necesse sit eum in altero horum duorum mentiri, quia si propheta fuit signa prophetica accæpit, si signa non accæpit propheta non fuit. .vi. Quod lux ut fabula genituræ et nutrituræ ipsius habet,[5] inclusa costis Adæ, indeque costis Noæ et sic per successiones usque ad ipsum nulla unquam fuerit, sed est omnium risu dignissima. .vii. Quod eum prædixisse dicunt successuros sibi in regno, primo Abubarcharum, secundo Aomar, tertio Odmen, quarto Hali, et quædam alia, falsum esse monstretur, ex ipsius hystorici qui hoc refert relatione.[6] .viii. Quod rursus prophetam eum esse non potuisse ex Æuangelio Christi cui ex aliqua parte credunt, comprobetur.

Capitula libri qvarti.

.i. Qvod uerba Domini dicentis in Æuangelio, "Lex et prophetæ usque ad Iohannem,"[7] non de omnibus prophetis dicta sunt, sed de illis tantum qui uniuersalem mundi salutem quæ per Christum facta est, ante Christum prædixerunt. .ii. Qvod et post Iohannem uel Christum alii prophetæ fuerunt uel forte futuri sunt, qui non illa magna et singulariter salutem humanam operantia, sed quæ-

---

[3] Cf. Kor. 6:45, A 49rd.
[4] Kor. 17:61, A 153rd-vs.
[5] i.e. *Liber generationis Mahumet*, A 11rs et seq.
[6] *Fabulæ Saracenorum*, A 8rs-vs.
[7] Luc. 16:16.

dam ad quasdam proprie gentes, terras, uel personas pertinentia
prophetico spiritu prædixerunt uel fortassis prædicturi sunt, quorum exempla multa tenemus. .iii. Quod nec de istis nec de illis
Mahumeth fuerit, qui nec salutem quæ per Christum facta est,
cum longe post Christum fuerit prædixit, nec aliqua saltem
minima ad prophetiam pertinentia dixit. .iiii. Quod istud ex Alchorano eius ostenditur, in quo nichil prorsus propheticum scripsit,
cum nulla hoc habeat ratio eum scilicet aliquid alicubi prophetice
dixisse, / et hoc in illa sua iuxta illum sublimi et sola scriptura D 178rs
tacuisse, ubi cum se prophetam dicat, nulla tamen prophetica
narrat. .v. Quod tota scriptura Mahumeth nichil aliud sit quam
feces horridæ, et reliquiæ fetidæ heresum ante quingentos quam
ipse nasceretur annos ab uniuersali sacrosancta totius orbis æcclesia
dampnatarum atque sepultarum, maxime autem Manicheorum et
apocriphorum scriptorum, precipueque Thalmuth execrandi libri
Iudeorum, quas scilicet Sarraceni hereses quia ueraces hystorias
et gesta æcclesiastica non legunt nec legere sciunt, nec ipsa tempora
nec ipsas hereses fuisse aliquando audierunt, et ideo istum Sathanan quasi mira et noua dicentem, animales et miseri suscæperunt.
.vi. Exhortatio et admonitio ut saltem hoc ultimo tempore quando
iam finis sæculi prope est, ad ueram et sanctam Christianitatem
ueniant, diaboli fabulas et deliramenta respuentes, atque in crucem
Christi et mortem, in qua sola uera et tota hominum salus est,
per sacri baptismatis ablutionem credentes.

Explicivnt capitula libri qvarti.

6 · LIBER CONTRA SECTAM SIVE HÆRESIM SARACENORUM

D 178rs Incipit prologvs domni Petri abbatis Cluniacensis in libro contra sectam siue heresim Sarracenorum.

Contra sectam nefariam nefandi Mahumeth acturus, in primis omnipotentem Spiritum Dei inuoco, ut qui nulli unquam aduersus hostes suos et æcclesiæ suæ agenti defuit, michi quoque contra pessimos utriusque aduersarios agere disponenti non desit. "Locutus est" ille "per prophetas,"[1] inflammauit apostolos, perfudit exundanti chrismate orbem terrarum, et "sicut unguentum in capite usque ad ipsam oram uestimenti"[2] defluxit. Assit oro tanta eius largitas et michi ultimo suorum, et qui "continens omnia scientiam habet uocis,"[3] ad opus quod aggredior utiliter exequen-
D 178rd dum, cor scientia, os uoce, uerboque congruo repleat. Spero / autem quod inuocanti se aderit, quia benignus est. "Benignus est enim Spiritus sapientiæ,"[4] immo quod plus est non dubito, quia de æcclesia illa sum, cui Saluator promisit: "Rogabo Patrem meum, et alium Paraclitum dabit uobis, ut maneat uobiscum in æternum."[5] Sed causa forte scribendi quæritur. Quæ ne superfluus scriptor uidear, proponenda est.

Causa plane scribendi hæc michi fuit, quæ multis et magnis patribus extitit. Non potuerunt illi pati quamlibet uel paruam iacturam fidei Christianæ, nec aduersus sanam doctrinam insanientem multiformium hereticorum uesaniam tolerarunt. Cauerunt esse muti ubi loquendum erat, aduertentes immo plenissime scientes, non minus se addicendos in suptili apud Deum statera iudicii de infructuoso uel quod maius est dampnoso silentio, quam de uerbo otioso uel noxio. Ideo æpistolis, ideo libris, ideo diuersis ac robustis tractatibus obstruxerunt "os loquentium iniqua,"[6] et

[1] Symb. Nic.-Const.; cf. Luc. 1:55, 70; Heb. 1:1.
[2] Ps. 132:2. [3] Sap. 1:7.
[4] Sap. 1:6. [5] Joan. 14:16. [6] Ps. 62:12.

"omnem" iuxta apostolum, Sathanæ "altitudinem extollentem se aduersus scientiam Dei,"[7] loquente per eos Spiritu Dei, prostrauerunt, calcauerunt, destruxerunt.

Transeo antiquos ipsaque antiquitate minus famosos hereticos, Basilidem, Appellem, Marcionem, Hermogenem, Kathafrigas, Encrathitas, Montanum, cum Prisca et Maximilla feminis insanis, Nouatianum, Eunomium, multaque alia Christiani nominis monstra. Horum uesaniæ obuii restiterunt illorum temporum magni doctique homines, Agrippa, Iustinus philosophus et martyr, Theophilus Anthiocenus episcopus, Apollinaris Gerapolitanus episcopus, Philippus Cretensis episcopus, Musanus, Modestus, Hyreneus nostræ Lugdunensis Galliæ famosus episcopus et martyr, Rodon Asianus, Miliciades, Apollonius, Serapion, Yppolitus, Victorinus, Rethicius Eduorum episcopus, pluresque alii nobis ignoti. Et hos prætereo. Ad præcipuas diabolicæ impietatis pestes, quibus Sathanas maxime æcclesiam Dei inficere et uelut robustioribus machinis subuertere conatus est, uenio. Dico autem Manicheos, Arrianos, Macedonianos, Sabellianos, Donatistas, Pelagianos, omniumque ultimos, Nestorianos et Euticianos.

Horum primi Manichei, uniuersa Testamenti Veteris uolumina abicientes, prophetas respuentes, ipsum Æuangelium ex parte suscipientes, ex parte contempnentes, duo boni malique principia consti/tuebant. Deum cum gente tenebrarum pugnasse, ne uincere-   D 178vs tur partem sui frugibus, carnibus, herbis, arboribus, cunctisque huiusmodi miscuisse, liberandam paulatim post æsum talium ructibus humanis, mortem Domini phantasticam, resurrectionem falsam, multaque talia magis reticenda quam dicenda, prodigiosi, et per inanissimas fabulas aberrantes homines delirabant. Arriani fertilior aliis seges diaboli, ponentes in cælum os suum, "linguaque eorum transeunte in terra,"[8] unius ueri ac summi Dei, Patris, Filii, ac Spiritus Sancti diuinitate pro uelle abutentes. Patri tantum deitatem asscribebant, Filium ac Spiritum Sanctum creaturis connumerabant. Dicebant Filium maximum esse creaturarum, Spiritum Sanctum Filio inferiorem, sed aliis creaturis maiorem. Macedoniani et ipsi insani, cum Arrianis heresim diuidebant, Filium uerum Deum Patri-

---

[7] II Cor. 10:5.　　[8] Ps. 72:9.

que coessentialem fatentes, Spiritum Sanctum ab utriusque deitate separantes. Sabelliani omni se uelut nimis molesta Trinitatis quæstione exuentes, unam tantum deitatis personam sub tribus nominibus intelligendam esse putabant. Donatistæ ex sacris libris sub persecutione persecutoribus traditis sumpta occasione asstruebant exploso toto orbe a salute, non nisi in Affrica æcclesiam esse posse, contra Christum dicentem: "Oportebat Christum pati et resurgere a mortuis die tertia, et prædicari in nomine eius pænitentiam et remissionem peccatorum in omnes gentes incipientibus ab Ihrusalem."[9] Pelagiani gratiæ Dei qua sola saluamur superbi et pessimi inimici, suptilius aliis heresibus "acuebant linguas suas sicut serpentes, et ueneno aspidum latente sub labiis eorum,"[10] inter multiplices de hac materia blasphemias, substantiam quidem humanam a Deo, bona autem humana liberi arbitrii causa ab ipsis hominibus esse dicebant. Nestoriani horum penultimi deitatem a Christo Deo et homine remouebant, negantes esse Deum, profitentes hominem purum. Euticiani ultimi in suprascriptis, cum sint Nestorianis contrarii, non tamen minus impii, in sententia dispares, in perfidia pares, sicut illi Christum uerum Deum, sic et isti negabant uerum hominem. Dicit Nestorius: "Homo tantum est Christus"; dicit Euthices: "Deus tantum est Christus."

Et ut eo ordine quo hereses propositæ sunt, destructores quoque D 178vd heresum proponantur, / contra Manicheos primus aut pene primus libro disputationis edito egit Archelaus Mesopotamiæ episcopus. Post eum Serapion et ipse episcopus egregium librum composuit et edidit. Hiis tempore iunior, sed longe sensibus et eloquio maior magnus Augustinus succedens, libris potentibus tam contra Faustum quam contra Fortunatum Manicheorum principes editis, nefandam heresim et impugnauit, pariter et expugnauit. Contra Arrianos quantum ad scripta pertinet, primum lego ad prælia processisse armatum fide et eloquio Eustachium Anthiocenum episcopum. Qui postquam contra Arrianum dogma multa composuit, exul Constantii imperatoris præcæpto a sede et patria factus, proprium exilium gloriosa et constanti confessione moriens decorauit.

[9] Luc. 24:46-7.
[10] Ps. 139:4; cf. Ps. 13:3.

Post hunc lego et Marcellum Ancyranum episcopum multa aduersus eosdem scripsisse uolumina. Lego et Alexandrinum Athanasium non solum laboribus, non solum uerbis, sed et scriptis Arrianos urgentem, et contra Valentem et Vrsacium Arrianorum patronos integrum librum scribentem. Hylarium uero Aquitanum episcopum, uere sanctum et omni scientia doctum uirum, quis nesciat duodecim aduersus Arrianos confecesse libros? Quem lateat unus eius libellus ad Constantium imperatorem Arrianum, quem uiuenti optulit, et alius in eundem, quem post mortem eius scripsit? Est et alter, quem aduersus iam dictos Valentem et Vrsacium edidit. Scripsit et Victorinus rethor famosus contra Arrianorum magistrum Arrium libros more dialectico. Egit et de eodem contra eosdem libris duobus Didimus Alexandrinus. Optulit et apud Mediolanum Gratiano principi Maximus philosophus et episcopus insignem de fide aduersus Arrianos librum. Contra Macedonianos, suprascripti quidem libri aduersus Arrianos editi, sufficiunt. Nam sicut Patris et Filii, ita et Spiritus Sancti deitatem tam in substantia quam in maiestate, quam Macedoniani diffitebantur, commendant. Sed ut etiam libris aduersus eorum errorem specialiter dedicatis confutarentur, scripsit iam dictus Didimus de Spiritu Sancto librum unum. Composuit et Basilius Cæsareæ / Cappadociæ episcopus de eodem Spiritu Sancto uolumen. Edidit et Gregorius Nazianzenus de eadem materia librum alterum. Sed et Effrem Edessenæ æcclesiæ diaconus aliud de eodem Spiritu Sancto Syra lingua uolumen.

Contra Sabellium licet specialia opera non inuenerim, quicunque tamen resistunt Arrianis, quicunque repugnant Macedonianis, uniuersi pariter contradicunt et Sabellianis. Dico quod plus est, non solum contra ipsos agunt catholici, sed ipsis quoque Sabellianis resistunt heretici. Dicit Sabellius, unam esse personam Trinitatis, negat hoc catholicus, negat Arrius, negat Macedonius. Sufficit ergo ad condempnationem Sabellianorum, catholicorum consensus atque hereticorum. Contra Donatistas uniuersus quidem orbis cuius hostes sunt conclamat, sed speciales aduersus eos sex libros conscripsit Optatus Afer episcopus Mileuitanus. Supremo certamine eos uerbis scriptisque debellauit noster et uere noster Ipponi-

D 179rs

ensis Augustinus. Contra Pelagianos eorumque auctores Pelagium, Cælestinum et Iulianum Campanum, ultimos fere uitæ suæ annos scribendo libris insignibus dedicauit, idem qui supra maximus et summus Latinorum doctor Augustinus. Contra Nestorianos et eorum auctorem Nestorium secunda synodus Ephesina congregata est, in qua et Nestoriana heresis condempnata, et Nestorius eius auctor hereticus adiudicatus, et a Constantinopolitano, episcopatu expulsus est. Contra Euticen et ab eo dictam Euticianam heresim, nobiles tam sensibus quam stilo dignas memoria epistolas scribit sanctus et primus huius nominis papa Leo, uir magnus fide, scientia, eloquio. Huius pastorali studio sexcenti fere apud Calcedonem episcopi congregati, Nestorium cum suis, Euticem cum suis, a Christi corpore hoc est eius æcclesia præciderunt, et nisi qui supererant resipiscerent, perpetuo anathemati tradiderunt. Contra Iouinianum nuptias uirginitati æquantem, contra Eluidium perpetuam matris Domini uirginitatem negantem, contra Vigilantium sanctorum mortuorum corpora uel reliquias contempnentem, consummatæ scientiæ presbyter Ihronimus insignia more suo splendenti sermone uolumina edidit, et quantum detestandi essent

D 179rd ostendit. / Hii quidem Nestorium tempore precesserunt, sed sectam nominis sui nullam facere potuerunt.

Fecit hoc semper et facit æcclesia Dei et "uepres spinasue"[11] satis dominicis inimicas, studiosa ruricolarum suorum manu exstirpat. Non cessit quolibet tempore hostilibus iaculis indefessum robur sanctorum, sed uires uirtute, astutiam sapientia superans, et "scuto fidei"[12] suos ab hostium furore protexit, et in eorum perniciem fulminantia spicula uehementi nisu intorsit. Non potuit pati uenenosi sibilos serpentis, cælestibus oraculis præualere, nec rectæ fidei uiam ad beatam æternitatem ducentem, prauis errorum semitis ad inferos retorqueri. Hæc inquam hæc plane tota ac sola sanctis illis causa fuit scribendi, pro qua in hostes Christianæ salutis non solum uerbis librisque inuecti sunt, sed nec suis nec sibi, nec ipsi tandem uitæ propriæ pepercerunt. Hæc eadem est et michi. Nec debeo licet longe illis inferior et impar minus zelari

[11] Isa. 5:6, 9:18.   [12] Eph. 6:16.

pro æcclesia Dei, sponsa Christi, quam ipsi, cum tam michi quam illis "una" fuerit uel sit "fides, unum baptisma, unus Deus,"[13] una, quam illi iam optinent, et ad quam nos suspiramus uita æterna.

Sed forte quibusdam erroribus obuiandum est, et de quibusdam silendum. Non hæc opinio apud patres. Ostendit hoc Ypolitus episcopus, inter multa alia opera sua, scribens de pascha aduersus omnes hereses. Monstrat hoc et Barthesanes clarus olim scriptis uariis in Mesopotamia apud suos. Qui ardens ingenio et in disputatione uehemens, scripsit infinita aduersus omnes pene hereticos qui ætate eius pullulauerant. In quibus teste Ihronimo clarissimus ille est et fortissimus liber, quem Marco Antonino tradidit. Affirmat idem et Victorinus, non ille quem præmisi, sed Pitabionensis episcopus et martir. Qui Greca Latinaque lingua instructus, aduersus omnes præcædentium uel suorum temporum hereses scripsit, nullamque contra uniuersas scribens negligendam esse monstrauit. Quem utrum in scribendo imitari posteri debeant, non solum doctrina sed et martyrio quod ad extremum pro fide quam defenderat passus est, lector aduertat. Astruit hoc Epyphanius sanctus et famosus Salaminæ quæ in Cypro insula est episcopus, scribens nichilominus aduersus omnes hereses libros eosque / legendos totius D 179vs orbis æcclesiis tradens. Nulla est igitur hiis sanctorum exemplis docentibus heresis negligenda, nulla est tantis magistris instruentibus silentio prætereunda. Confutandus est omnis error, omnis prauus et fidei aduersus intellectus corripiendus, et si potest fieri, corrigendus. Exhibenda est Christo ab hiis quibus ad ipso commissa est æcclesia absque macula et ruga, ut possit audire ab illo: "Tota pulchra es, amica mea, et macula non est in te."[14]

Si ergo nulla heresis quolibet tempore orta, immunis a "gladio Spiritus, quod est uerbum Dei"[15] esse potuit, nunquid tutus ab illo Mahumeticus error erit? An forte ut nullum aut paruum Christiana lingua transibit? An forte ut innoxio uel minus noxio parcet? Et quæ unquam o lector heresis adeo æcclesiæ Dei nocuit? Quis unquam error adeo rem publicam Christianam uexauit? Quis in tantum terminos eius rescidit? Quis tanta massa perditorum numerum infernalem adauxit? Occupauit Arriana pestis maxima præ-

---

[13] Eph. 4:5-6.   [14] Cant. 4:7.   [15] Eph. 6:17.

dictarum heresum quasdam aliquandiu partes terrarum, easque
lætali haustu Sathana propinante infecit. Adiunxit nequiciæ suæ
quosdam reges Gotthorum, duosque quod maius est Romani
principes orbis Constantium et Valentem corrupit. Transiit de
solo Barbarico in Pannoniam, indeque ad Italiam transmigrauit.
Vnde pulsa, meridianam partem Galliæ, Aquitaniam dico inuasit,
sed rege Francorum Clodoueo fugante, tandem in Hyspaniis ui
bellica subactis resedit. Ibi uix centum annis exactis, ac rege Gotthorum qui genti hereticæ imperabat, ad catholicam fidem Spiritu
Dei agente conuerso, defecit.

At Mahumeticus furor ab Hysmaelitis Arabibus sumens exordium, Persas, Medos, Syros, Armenios, Ethiopes, Indos, ac reliqua
orientis regna ipsamque in tribus orbis partibus maximam Asiam
pene totam corrupit, et uel a Christianismo auertens, uel a quibuslibet antiquis erroribus ad perditi hominis sectam conuertens,
subtraxit Christo, substrauit diabolo. Hinc non miti ratione, sed
uiolenta incursione, toto fere ut dictum est armis oriente subacto,
Egyptum, Lybiam, Affricamque uniuersam prophanæ religioni
subiecit, et sic duabus mundi partibus occupatis, nec tertiam quæ
D 179vd Europa uocatur, / Hyspania peruasa Christo uel Christianis suis
integram dereliquit. Et quid dicam ultra? Nec si uniuersas a
Christi tempore per mille et centum annos diabolico spiritu suscitatas hereses numeraueris, simulque collectas uelut in statera
appenderis, adæquari huic poterunt, nec pariter omnes tantam
æternis ignibus materiem iniecisse inuenies. Quæ ergo nullam uel
paruam heresim intactam præteriit, nunquid hunc omnium errorum maximum errorem, torpens uel multa Christiana lingua
transibit?

Sed forte dicet uel cogitabit quispiam: "Illis olim heresibus
respondit æcclesia, quæ ut Iohannes apostolus ait: 'Ex nobis exie-
runt, sed non erant ex nobis.'[16] At error iste nec ex nobis exiit, nec
ex nobis fuit. Christianis enim de æcclesia hoc est Christi corpore
quolibet errore tractis uel recedentibus patres suprascripti respon-
derunt, alienos et extra æcclesiam uagantes errores, silendo con-

[16] I Joan. 2:19.

tempserunt. Quibus et hic error connumerari potest, qui nec ut dictum est de æcclesia exiit, nec se de æcclesia exisse ut aliæ hereses, erroris non heresis nomine satis ostendit. Non enim heresis dicitur, nisi exiens de æcclesia et agens contra æcclesiam."

Ad hæc ego: Fateor hoc inquam et ipse, Christianos pertinaciter contra quamlibet rectæ fidei partem agentes, iam ab antiquo usitato nomine dici hereticos, et id quod praue sentiunt uel fatentur, uocari heresim. Sed utrum Mahumeticus error heresis dici debeat, et eius sectatores heretici uel æthnici uocari, non satis discerno. Video enim eos hinc hereticorum more de fide Christiana quædam suscipere, quædam abicere, hinc ritu pagano quod nulla unquam heresis fecisse scribitur, facere pariter et docere. Nam cum quibusdam hereticis, scribente sic in Alchorano suo impio Mahumeth, Christum quidem de uirgine natum prædicant, maiorem omni homine ipsoque Mahumeth dicunt, sine peccato uixisse, uera prædicasse, mira fecisse affirmant, spiritum Dei, uerbum Dei fuisse fatentur, sed nec Spiritum Dei aut Uerbum ut nos aut intelligunt aut exponunt. Christi passionem aut mortem non solum ut Manichei phantasticam, sed nullam prorsus extitisse uesaniunt. Hæc quidem et similia cum hereticis sentiunt. Cum paganis autem baptisma / abiciunt, sacrificium Christianum respuunt, pæni- D 18ors tentiam cunctaque reliqua æcclesiæ sacramenta derident. Elige igitur quod malueris. Aut uoca hereticos propter hereticum sensum, et quo partim cum æcclesia sentiunt, partim dissentiunt, aut dic paganos propter excellentem impietatem, qua omnium heresum errores professione impia uincunt. Si hereticos dixeris, probatum est supra, omnibus hereticis uel heresibus obuiandum. Si paganos uocaueris, probo idque patrum auctoritate ostendo, non minus et illis resistendum.

Ad hoc affirmandum, redeat ad medium supra nominatus Iustinus philosophus et martir. Hic pro defendenda Christi religione plurimum laborauit, in tantum ut Antonino quoque principi et filiis eius et senatui librum contra gentes scriptum daret, ignominiamque crucis non erubesceret, et alium librum successoribus eiusdem Antonini Marco Antonino Vero, et Lucio Aurelio Commodo. Est et eius aliud uolumen contra gentes, ubi etiam de demonum

natura disputat. Item est et quartum aduersus gentes, cui tytulum
prænotauit Elegeos. Est et dialogus contra Iudeos, quem habuit
aduersus Triphonem principem Iudeorum. Sequatur hunc ad hoc
astruendum Apollinaris urbis Gerapolis quæ est in Asia episcopus.
Qui non solum imperatori Marco Antonino Vero insigne uolumen
pro fide Christiana dedit, sed et alios quinque aduersus gentes
libros conscripsit. Edidit et Lugdunensis Hyreneus contra gentes
uolumen. Scripsit et Miliciades contra gentes, Iudeosque libros
alios. Composuit et Apollonius Romanæ urbis senator sub Commodo principe ac Seuero, insigne contra paganos uolumen. Quod
rationem fidei suæ reddens in senatu legit, ac post lectionem, eiusdem senatus sententia pro Christo capite truncatus est. Successit
hiis Arnobius rethor sub Diocletiano principe, scripsitque aduersus
gentes quæ illis temporibus publice legebantur. Confecit et Methodius Tyrius episcopus libros, contra Porphirium paganum philosophum. Contra eundem et Laodicenus episcopus Apollinaris
stilum exacuit, et triginta libros condidit. Non defuit assertioni
D 18ord huic supra nominatus ac sepe nominandus magnus / Athanasius
Alexandrinus episcopus. Hic non solum contra Arrianos speciales
hostes suos scripsit, sed et aduersus gentes duos libros edidit. Sequatur hunc et Eusebius Emisenus episcopus, elegantis et rethorici
ingenii homo. Hic innumerabiles ut legitur libros confecit. Ex
quibus præcipui sunt, aduersum Iudæos et gentes. Hiis uniuersis
nulli supradictorum doctrina inferior, immo forte superior, Augustinus succedat, et libris notissimis uiginti duobus De Ciuitate Dei
editis, non tantum contra hereticos qui de æcclesia exeunt, sed et
contra paganos ac Iudeos qui in æcclesia nunquam fuerunt, contra-
que omnes omnino errores congruo tempore uerbo scriptoque
agendum esse doceat.

Siue ergo Mahumeticus error heretico nomine deturpetur, siue
gentili aut pagano infametur, agendum contra eum est, scribendum est. Sed quia Latini et maxime moderni, antiquo studio pereunte, iuxta Iudeorum uocem, uarias linguas apostolorum olim
mirantium, non nisi linguam suam nouerunt, in qua nati sunt,
cuiusmodi tantus error esset agnoscere, ne dicam tanto errori obuiare non poterant. Vnde "concaluit cor meum intra me et in

meditatione mea exarsit ignis."[17] Indignatus sum causam tantæ perditionis Latinos ignorare, et ipsa ignorantia nullum ad resistendum posse animari. Nam non erat qui responderet, quia non erat qui agnosceret. Contuli ergo me ad peritos linguæ Arabicæ, ex qua procedens mortiferum uirus orbem plusquam dimidium infecit. Eis ad transferendum de lingua Arabica in Latinam perditi hominis originem, uitam, doctrinam, legemque ipsamque Alchoran uocatur tam prece quam precio persuasi. Et ut translationi fides plenissima non deesset, nec quicquam fraude aliqua nostrorum notitiæ subtrahi posset, Christianis interpretibus etiam Sarracenum adiunxi. Christianorum interpretum nomina, Robertus Ketenensis, Armannus Dalmata, Petrus Toletanus. Sarraceni Mahumeth nomen erat. Qui intima ipsa barbaræ gentis armaria perscrutantes, uolumen non paruum ex prædicta materia Latinis lectoribus ediderunt. Hoc anno illo factum est quo Hyspanias adii, et cum domno Aldefonso uictorioso Hyspaniarum imperatore colloquium habui. Qui annus fuit ab incarnatione Domini, m.c.xli.us.

Sed forte adhuc aliquis: "Quid proderit fastidientibus cibos ingerere, quid conferet 'aspidi / surdæ et opturanti aures suas'[18] D 180vs disputatione multiplici insonare? Nam homines contra quos agere disponis, alieni sunt, barbari sunt, non solum moribus, sed et lingua ipsa, nil sibi Latinisque commune esse fatentur. Quomodo igitur audiet ne dicam exaudiet Arabs Latinum, Persa Romanum, Æthiops uel Ægyptius Gallum? Videndum est ne frustra labor insumatur, cauendum ne utili opere relicto, superfluo tempus teratur."

Ad quod ego: Poterit inquam quod scriptum fuerit in eorum linguam transferri, poterit Christiana ueritas in litteras Arabicas uel quaslibet alias commutari, sicut potuit nefandus error ad Latinorum noticiam meo studio transmigrare. Sic Latinum opus in peregrinam linguam translatum proderit forsitan aliquibus, quos ductrix ad uitam gratia Deo lucrari uoluerit. Sic ex litteris Hebraicis Vetus Testamentum, sic preter Æuangelium Mathei, ex Greco Nouum in uniuersas totius orbis linguas transfusum, mundum Deo

[17] Ps. 38:4.   [18] Ps. 57:5.

subiecit, et per Christianam fidem ad inferis reuocans cælo resti-
tuit. Sic plurima alia patrum opera et Latinus a Greco mutuauit,
et Grecus a Latino accæpit. Nec defuit inter alias multiplices orbis
linguas nobis ignotas hæc sermonum ad inuicem commutatio, de
quibus fere ut de apostolis dici possit: "Non sunt loquelæ neque
sermones quorum non audiantur uoces eorum."[19] Quod si forte
hæc de qua agitur scriptura aut interpretes non habuerit, aut
translata non profuerit, habebit saltem Christianum armarium
etiam aduersus hos hostes arma quibus aut se muniat, aut quibus
si forte ad certamen uentum fuerit, inimicos confodiat. Occurret
fortasse uolumen editum cogitationibus occultis nostrorum, quibus
scandalizari possunt, aliquam apud impios illos esse putantes pietatem, et apud mendacii ministros aliquam credentes esse ueritatem.
Iungitur huic rationi auctoritas non parua, quæ et si iure in talibus
præire debeat, nil tamen obstat, si in re proposita rationem
sequatur.

Scripserunt quoscumque præmisi et plures quos reticui, contra
hereticos, Iudæos, uel ethnicos, diuersa, magna et mira opera, nec
tamen scribentes, quibus prodesse possent aut elegerunt, aut præ-
D 18ovd scierunt. / Cumque nec elegissent neque præscissent, quorum
saluti labores proprii inseruire deberent, non tamen idcirco uel
animum a studendo, uel linguam a dictando, uel manum a scribendo uacare permiserunt. Non attendit Grecus scriptor Latino
non posse prodesse Grecitatem, non cogitauit Latinus Greco frustra
legi Latinitatem, non meditatus est quilibet quantumlibet barbarus
sed catholicus aduersus quoslibet errores agens frustra se scribendi
laborem assumere, quia non posset opus suum nisi in uarias linguas
translatum, hominibus peregrini sermonis prodesse. Nouerant,
certi erant, quod "Spiritus ubi uult spirat,"[20] sed scire non poterant,
quos, quando, uel quantum inspirat. Sciebant "non esse aliquid
neque qui plantat neque qui rigat, sed qui incrementum dat
Deus."[21] Eapropter rigando, plantando ut boni serui quod suum
erat implebant, quod Dei erat, Domino dimittebant. Hos qui sequi
uoluerit, æstimo, immo affirmo, quia non errabit. Quod si et ipse
fecero, certus sum quia non errabo. Non errabo plane, si simplici

[19] Ps. 18:4. [20] Joan. 3:8. [21] I Cor. 3:7.

oculo fecero quod meum est, et Deo ut dixi seruauero quod suum est. Non poterit certe non poterit omnino labor causa Dei assumptus euadere absque fructu, si autem conuersis profuerit, aut hostibus obstiterit, aut domesticos munierit, aut saltem horum scriptori "pax bonæ uoluntatis hominibus"[22] repromissa non defuerit. Sequatur ergo in nomine Domini diu dilati operis exordium.

In fine addo, quia noui et certus sum, insolita in talibus prolixitate me consuetas prologi metas aliquamtulum excessisse. Sed ut excusatam me lector habeat, sciat hoc importunis obiectionibus disputantium contigisse, quibus ne breuis uiderer, forte iusto prolixior aliis extiti.

Explicit prologvs.

B · LIBER PRIMUS

INCIPIT LIBER PRIMVS DOMINI PETRI ABBATIS CLVNIACENSIS ADVERVS NEFANDAM HERESIM SIVE SECTAM SARRACENORVM. /   D 180vd

IN NOMINE PATRIS ET FILII et Spiritus Sancti, unius omnipotentis et ueri Dei, Petrus quidam, Gallus natione, Christianus fide, abbas officio eorum qui monachi dicuntur, Arabibus Hysmahelis filiis, legem illius qui Mahumeth dicitur, seruantibus.   D 181rs

Mirum uidetur, et fortassis etiam est, quod homo a uobis loco remotissimus, lingua diuersus, professione seiunctus, moribus, uitaque alienus, ab ultimis occidentis hominibus in orientis uel meridiei partibus positis scribo, et quos nunquam uidi, quos nunquam forte, uisurus sum, loquendo aggredior. Aggredior inquam uos, non ut nostri sepe faciunt armis sed uerbis, non ui sed ratione, non odio sed amore. Amore tamen tali, qualis inter Christicolas et a Christo auersos esse debet, tali qualis inter apostolos nostros et illius temporis gentiles, quos ad[1] Christi legem inuitabant, extitit, tali qualis inter ipsum creatorem et rectorem omnium Deum, et illos quos dum adhuc creaturæ non creatori seruirent, a cultu simulachrorum uel demonum per suos auertit. Amauit plane ipse illos, antequam ipsi illum amarent,[2] agnouit antequam agnos-

---

[22] Luc. 2:14.

---

[1] "ad" bis.   [2] Cf. I Joan. 4:19.

cerent, uocauit dum adhuc contempnerent. Contulit bona facientibus mala, misertus est pereuntibus sola gratia, eosque sic eripuit a
miseria sempiterna. Habet hoc ab ipso æcclesia Christianorum,
ut sicut ille, ut ait Christus noster: "Solem suum oriri facit super
bonos et malos, et pluit super iustos et iniustos,"[3] sic illa et in ipso
amicos, et propter ipsum diligat inimcos.

Succædit huic Christianæ auctoritati ratio euidens, qua "omne
animal," ut ait quidam, "diligit simile sibi."[4] Probatur hoc inde,
quod cum sub hoc genere, quod est animal, uniuersæ quadru-
pedum, uolucrum uel quorumlibet talium species contineantur,
familiarius sibi est unumquodque animal in propria specie, quam
in uniuersali genere. Apparet hoc in domesticis, claret et in ipsis
D 181rd agrestibus bestiis, quæ aut semper aut sepe / ab illis quas a se
natura discreuit abhorrent, easque quas similes sibi aut con-
formes sentiunt, consectantur. Quæ si ut assolet fieri contra se
inuicem qualibet de causa felle moto concertant, redeunt tamen
cito sedato motu ad pacem, nec obliuisci quod factæ sunt, prolix-
iore tempore possunt. Cumque inter infinitas quæ ut dictum est sub
animali continentur species, etiam homo sit, et quod nulla alia
animalium species habet, etiam ratione præditus sit, longe amplius
cogitur diligere similem sibi ratione suadente, quam ille natura
trahente.

Hee sunt causæ, quibus uos Christianus, diligere, quibus uobis
salutem debet optare. Harum altera diuina, altera humana est.
In illa præcepto diuino obædit, in hac naturæ propriæ satisfacit.
Hoc modo ego de innumeris et inter innumeros seruos Christi
minimus, uos diligo, diligens uobis scribo, scribens, ad salutem
inuito. Non ad salutem filiorum hominum, in quibus iuxta
uerbum Dauid, "non est salus,"[5] quia iuxta eundem, "uana est
salus hominis,"[6] sed ad illam de qua idem: "Salus autem iustorum
a Domino, et protector eorum est in tempore tribulationis."[7]
Quæ Psalmorum uerba ea uobis de causa propono, quia Psalmos
a Deo Dauid fuisse datos, a uestro Mahumeth audio. Loquens
enim Abdiæ Iudeo, sic ait: "Vnum quidem, Deus. Duo uero,

[3] Matt. 5:45.   [4] Ecclus. 13:19.   [5] Ps. 145:3.
[6] Ps. 59:13.   [7] Ps. 36:39.

Adam et Eua. Tria uero, Gabrihel, Mychael, Seraphiel. Quatuor, lex Moysi, Psalmi Dauid, Æuangelium, et Alfurchan."[8] Item: "Nec enim simul descendit super me uerbum Dei quemadmodum simul data est lex Moysi, Psalmi Dauid, et Æuangelium Christo."[9] Inuito uos ad salutem, non quæ transit, sed quæ permanet, non quæ finitur cum uita breui, sed quæ permanet in uitam æternam. Hanc consequi, hac tempore a Deo præstituto frui mortalibus quidem datum est, sed non nisi illis qui de Deo quod est, non quod non est sentiunt, qui eum non iuxta cordis sui phantasmata, sed sicut ipse se coli et uult et præcipit colunt.

Ad ista uos: "Absit, ut aliter sentiat intellectus noster, absit ut aliter se habeat professio nostra. Nos nichil de eo somniauimus, nichil prorsus confinximus. Sentimus de ipso, fatemur de ipso, non iuxta figmenta cordis nostri, sed iuxta quod tradidit nobis missus ab ipso propheta noster. Ille cum sit ordine ultimus in prophetis, et uelut signaculum omnium prophetarum, et legis diuinæ non auctor sed lator, / non Deus sed nuntius, mandata cælestia a Deo D 181vs per Gabrihelem sibi missa, nichil plus minusue continentia accæpit, accæpta patribus nostris nobisque seruanda tradidit. Hæc seruamus, hæc custodimus, hiis animas, hiis corpora, hiis uitam, mortemque nostram dicauimus."

Et o homines, homines inquam, non solum natura rationales, sed et ingenio et arte rationabiles, utinam michi hic intellectuales uestrorum cordium aures prebeatis, utinam superstitionis obstinatione remota, quæ subinferre præparo audiatis. Audiatis ideo dico, quia quod ualde mirum est, si tamen uerum est, nullum contra morem uobis assuetum, nullum contra uestras patrias leges agere uolentem, nullum contra ritus ab ipso quem supra nominaui uestro propheta uobis traditos disputare quærentem, uos uelle audire audiui. Et non solum uos hoc a nullo uelle audire accæpi, sed ut ipsa loquendi primordia lapidibus, aut gladiis uel quolibet alio mortis genere obstruatis, uobis lege præcæptum ab oriente uestro ad occidentem nostrum, fama diffusa fatetur.

Videte igitur uiri iuxta scientiam secularem prudentes, uidete

---

[8] *Doctrina Mahumet*, A 19vd.
[9] *Doctrina Mahumet*, A 19vs; cf. Kor. 17:106.

inquam, et remoto obstinatæ uoluntatis obice, suptiliter conside-
rate, utrum mos iste probabilis sit, utrum ratione aliqua subnixus
esse possit. Non uult aliquis hominum, qui non tantum natura
rationalis, sed et uiuaci mentis acumine rationabilis est, non uult
plane in rebus temporalibus falli, non uult certa pro incertis, aut
incerta pro certis accipere, ut delusus cuiuslibet astu uel impruden-
tia, quod uerum est falsum putet, quod falsum est uerum existimet.
Non cedit in hac parte cuilibet necessitudini, nec alicui super hiis
carissimo adquiescit, non amicis, non sanguinis affinitate con-
iunctis, nec ab ipsis quibus artiori amoris uinculo iungitur con-
iugibus, se scienter decipi æquanimiter pati potest. Cumque mul-
totiens multa et maxima carni ac spiritui molesta amicorum causa
ab amicis patienter ferantur, istud tamen homini natura indidit,
ne se falli ab aliquo quantumlibet proximo aut amico, pacto
quolibet patiatur. Scrutamini uniuersa officia mortalium, et artes
ipsasquæ liberales, sed et ipsas quæ seruiles dicuntur, attendite,
D 181vd utrum aliquis studiosorum secularem / scientiam amantium, de
ipsis uel in ipsis se falli uelit, et non magis earum ueracem ac
certam notitiam ab eruditoribus siue magistris accipere.

Hoc indicato præcipue ipsius terrenæ sapientiæ studium, cui
percipiendæ cum hii qui Grece "philosophi," Latine "amatores
sapientiæ," uocantur, summo conamine inhiarent, ac pro ingenio-
rum uarietate de ipsa diuersi diuersa sentirent, laxabant libera frena
sermonibus, et pro maiori minoriue acumine rationis, in medium
quæ senserant proferentes, innumeris disputationum modis, ad
ueritatem earum rerum quæ in propositis quæstionibus uersaban-
tur, pertingere laborabant. Non obstruebant ora eorum quos
studiosos inquirendæ ueritatis credebant, immo magis de oppositis
disputando, certatim se aliosque omni loquendi genere ad lauda-
bile studium accendebant. Hic Grecorum, hic Latinorum, hic Persarum, hic Indorum, aliarumque gentium sapientibus mos hoc
propositum semper fuit, ut et ipsi, scrutandæ rerum ueritati, semper insisterent, et ad idem inquirendum, examinandum, diffi-
niendum, frequentibus studiosos collationibus animarent. Quis
iam eorum ingentem multitudinem, qui inter reliquos in inuesti-
ganda rerum ueritate maxime floruerunt enumeret? Famosa et

sollempnis est eorum notitia apud nostros, qui rerum creatarum ueritatem ac uirtutem non tacendo nec ad tacendum ora hominum obstruendo sed loquendo ac disputando, de naturæ occultis eruerunt, et quæ absque dubio certa ac uera esse reppererant, tam sui temporis hominibus quam posteris tradiderunt.

Cum igitur omnis rationabilis mens rerum creatarum ueritatem agnoscere cupiat, illiusque ueritatis agnitionem ad commoda sua conuertere optet, et quod tacendo consequi non ualet, quærendo ac disputando assequi uelit, nunquam increatæ rei uerax cognitio negligenda est, nunquid quousque qui eam non capit intelligat, inquirendum, disputandum, examinandum non est? Nonne longe acrioribus stimulis ingeri mens humana debet, ad agnoscendam increatam essentiam, quam ad inuestigandam creatam naturam? Videatur quid de hiis duobus alteri præponderet, quid magis commodis humanis inseruiat. Hoc inquam uideatur, et tunc / cuius magis D 182rs cognitioni animus humanus insistere debeat, agnoscetur. Volo plane rerum ad præsens uisibilium uim siue uirtutem agnoscere, ut in aliquo michi dum hoc mortaliter uiuo suffragentur, ut aliquod huic meæ transitoriæ peregrinationi auxilium uel commodum ferant. Ad quid autem rem increatam et insuper omnia creantem, cunctaque creata regentem, agnoscere quæro, nisi ut et hic uiuenti congrua uitæ huic subsidia donet, et post mortem hanc æternaliter ac feliciter uiuere præstet? Quæ uero est natura hæc, quæ substantia, uel essentia? Nonne illa, quæ communi uniuersarum gentium more, iuxta proprietatem uniuscuiusque linguæ Deus creditur, Deus dicitur? Est igitur natura illa, Deus ille, qui solus increatus est, qui solus creator est, qui solus rector omnium, qui solus præsentium et æternorum bonorum auctor et largitor est.

Videte igitur uos, uidete inquam uos quibus scribo, et iuxta Psalmum Dauid, cui ut credo non discreditis, "Iuste iudicate filii hominum,"[10] utrum de creatura disputandum sit, de creatore tacendum, utrum libera loquendi facultas dari debeat quærenti de infimis et fugitiuis bonis, et obstrui debeat os quærentis et agentis de summo et æterno bono. Liber ad cuncta michi poterit esse

---

[10] Ps. 57:2.

discursus loqui uolenti de uniuersis creatis, et statim ut de ipsorum creatore agere uoluero, lex Mahumetica os opturabit, aut siquid forte contra eam dixero, uix primis uerbis elapsis caput secabit? Estne hoc legis alicuius, preterquam uestræ? Estne gentis alicuius, præterquam uestræ? Estne sectæ alicuius, præterquam uestræ? Vere nullius, plane nullius. Dirigite oculos huc illucque, et ab ortu solis usque ad occasum, ab austro usque ad aquilonem, uniuersarum gentium leges, ritus, ac mores scrutamini, et sicubi simile quid cautum uel traditum reperire potueritis, coram producite. Non sic, non sic ut interim de aliis taceam lex Christiana, non sic quidam de magnis Christi apostolis iubet: "Parati," ait, "estote omni poscenti uos rationem, de ea quæ in uobis est fide et spe."[11] Quid certe, quid portendit mos huiusmodi, quid sibi uult lex talis, lex inquam talis, quæ prohibet audiri contra uos disputantem, quæ pati non potest ratione præuia contra uestros ut D 182rd cre/ditur errores agentem? Nonne uidetur uobis hoc omni plenum pudore, non cernitis hoc omnimodo refertum dedecore? Liberam semper frontem ueritas habet, non quærit angulos, uelari dedignatur, obscura fugit, clara cunctisque patentia quærit. Sola falsitas agnosci timet, discuti ueretur, latibulis gaudet, produci in publicum ut mortem formidat.

Quare hoc? Quare inquam ueritas lucem, falsitas appetit tenebras? Hæc plane causa, hæc est et nulla alia prorsus, nisi ea quam Christus noster in Æuangelio suo quod ei datum Mahumeth uester et dixit et scripsit, de bene agentibus et mala facientibus profert: "Omnis," ait, "qui male agit, odit lucem, et non uenit ad lucem ne arguantur opera eius. Qui autem facit ueritatem uenit ad lucem, ut manifestentur opera eius, quia in Deo sunt facta."[12] Certe uerba hæc, uerba ueritatis sunt. Verba sunt plane illius, quem Mahumeth uester de quo paulo ante scripsi immensis laudibus effert, quem in diuersis sui Alchoran locis, nuntium Dei, uerbum Dei, spiritum Dei fatetur, quem sine peccato uixisse, quem maiorem omni homine, etiam seipso non negat. Qui si absque peccato iuxta illum in terris conuersatus est, mendax pro certo non est. Nam si notam

[11] I Petr. 3:15.   [12] Joan. 3:20-21.

mendacii non cauisset, utique non paruus sed magnus peccator fuisset. Eius uerba sunt illa quæ præmisi: "Omnis qui male agit odit lucem, et qui facit ueritatem uenit ad lucem." Ad quid istud? Contra morem reprobum, contra legem inauditam, quæ non licere uult, quod omnibus licet, quæ agere contra se ex ratione uolentibus, auditum et aditum intercludit. Nam si mos ille, si lex illa ueritatis est, quid timet ad lucem uenire, ut manifestum fiat, quia in Deo uel a Deo sunt facta? Sed quid frustra longos circuitus de re cunctis nota facerem? Idcirco plane absque dubio mos ille, lex illa totiens nominata odit lucem, diligit tenebras, non fert arguentem, non patitur contradictorem, ne arguatur falsitas eius, ne nota fiat orbi terrarum doloso silentio tecta nequicia eius.

Attendite iam et super hiis, et recolite uerba illius uestri ut putatis prophetæ, quam friuola sint, quam eneruia, quantum omni robore ueritatis ac rationis carentia. "Siquis," ait ille Deum sibi introducens loquentem, "tecum disceptare uoluerit, dic te faciem tuam eiusque [faciei] sequaces / ad Deum conuertisse, quod agendo D 182vs tam legum scientes quam illitterati bonam legem sequentur. Sin autem, tuum est mea præcæpta gentibus solummodo patefacere."[13] Item: "Siquis tecum de lege certamen inire uoluerit, dic ei anathema, et iram Dei talibus solummodo comminare."[14] Et iterum: "Nolite disputare cum legem habentibus.[15] Melior est enim cedes, quam lis."[16]

Quæ sunt queso huiusmodi uerba? Quæ sunt huiusmodi mandata? Ergone rationalis animus in tantum asinina stoliditate sepelietur, ut more bruti animalis illius quælibet uel quantalibet onera sibi imposita patienter ferat, discæptare de hiis non audeat, inquirere utrum bona an mala, utrum utilia an noxia sint non præsumat? Si hoc concessero, necesse iam erit circumferri me omni uento doctrinæ, ac more harundinis flatu quolibet agitatæ hac illacque inflecti, cedere omni errori, adquiescere cuilibet falsitati, nichil certi tenere, bona malis, uera falsis indiscrete confundere. Quid plane hoc concesso distabit inter hominem et pecus? Quid inter humanam animum et beluinum spiritum? Plane nichil,

[13] Kor. 3:18-19, A 38v.　　[14] Kor. 3:61, A 35vd.
[15] Kor. 29:45, A 161vd.　　[16] Kor. 2:187, 214, A 30vs, 31rd.

237

quantum ad stultam obædientiam, sed rursus multum, quantum ad diuersam naturam. Non enim iam homo iumentis comparabitur, sed iure pecude stolidior iudicabitur. Non contradicit cuiuslibet imperio pecus, qui caret rationali animo, et adquiescit rationalis animus, contradicente rationis iudicio. Quia non est datum iudicium pecori, indiscrete cunctis imperantibus cedit, cui inter bonum et malum, inter uerum ac falsum discernere naturale est, hiis etiam quæ dampnanda iudicat, uilior pecude factus obædit. Miror nec mirari sufficio, quomodo hoc a peritis et ac doctis hominibus extorqueri cuiuslibet astu potuit, ut crederent uerba quæ præmisi, a Deo esse prolata, cum nichil prorsus in eis nisi stultum, nisi crudele, nisi insanum inuenire, uel negligens uel studiosus lector præualeat.

Nam quid est hoc: "Siquis tecum discæptare uoluerit, dic te faciam tuam eiusque faciei sequaces, ad Deum conuertisse?" Si ergo ut teipsum alloquar o Mahumeth, si certe michi tecum de lege tua, utrum iusta an iniusta sit discæptare uolenti, nichil aliud D 182vd responderis, nisi "te faciem tuam / eiusque faciei sequaces ad Deum conuertisse," credam te uera dixisse? Credam te uerum prophetam Dei fuisse? Credam legem quam genti tuæ tradidisti, a Deo tibi traditam esse? Vere me plusquam asinum si assensero, uere plusquam pecudem si adquieuero. In quo enim michi te ueraciter aliquid dixisse uel in modico fidem facis, si te faciem tuam ad Deum conuertisse uel a Deo auertisse asseris? Sed et quod obsecro monstrum est, quod tibi dixisse Deum adiungis: "Quod agendo tam legum scientes quam illitterati bonam legem sequentur?" Quid agendo? Si dixeris, faciem tuam te ad Deum conuertisse, propter hoc igitur tam legum scientes quam illitterati legem tuam quam bonam dicis sequentur? Sed quid rem aperte ridiculosam[17] persequor?

Hunc præcedentem, sequatur et alius uersus. Scribis enim Deum adiecisse: "Sin autem, tuum est mea præcæpta gentibus solummodo patefacere." Quid est hoc? Dixeras Deum dixisse, quod si ea quæ præmissa sunt diceres, "tam legum scientes quam illitterati bonam legem sequerentur." Quid est ergo quod addidisti: "Sin

[17] "uel ridiculam" add. supra.

autem, tuum est mea præcæpta gentibus solummodo patefacere?"
Facis primo Deum loqui modo enuntiantis, et nunc subinfers uerba
dubitantis? Enuntiantis enim modo locutus est, quando dixit
legem scientes uel sine litteris bonam legem secuturos. Dubitantis
uero, quando dixit: "Sin autem." Quod si enuntiatiue locutus est,
cur omnes tam scientes quam illitterati tuam legem non secuntur?
Quod si dubitabat tibi credituros, quare dixit, "omnes legem tuam
secuturos?"

Sed sequitur et aliud quod præmisi capitulum: "Siquis tecum de
lege certamen inire uoluerit, dic ei anathema, et iram Dei talibus
solummodo comminare." Et hoc cui non liceat? Cui plane hominum hoc non facillimum sit? Quod præciperis dicere michi, hoc
idem non prohibeor et ego dicere tibi. Sicut tibi leue est ut michi
tecum de lege tua certamen inire uolenti dicas anathema, ita michi
perfacile est, ut te mecum de lege mea agente, si adquiescere nolueris, dicam tibi anathema. Si leue tibi est iram Dei michi nisi tibi
credidero comminari, ita et michi uel cuilibet facile est eandem
iram Dei nisi michi adquieueris comminari pariter et imprecari.
Estne igitur iustum, estne rationabile, ut nulla michi auctoritate
proposita, / nulla ratione præostensa, credam tibi, adquiescam legi D 183rs
tuæ, si nichil michi aliud nisi anathema dixeris, si nichil aliud quam
iram Dei comminatus fueris? Sed quia cuius ponderis hæc tua
uerba sint, brutis etiam pectoribus patet, procædo.

"Nolite," inquit, "disputare cum legem habentibus. Melior est
enim cedes, quam lis." Et hoc infernale consilium quis non uideat?
"Nolite," inquit, "disputare cum legem habentibus." Qui sunt
legem habentes? Prout obscura hominis illius intelligere possumus,
legem habentes nulli sunt alii, quam Iudæi uel Christiani. Nam
oculorum acie huc illucque diducta, nullos alios in orbe legem
habentes, quando hæc ab illo dicta sunt, uel tunc fuisse, uel adhuc
esse uideo, quam illos quos præmisi, Iudeos scilicet aut Christianos.
Hii plane non alii legem prius accæperant, accæptam iuxta suos
libitus uel intellectus tenebant. Iudæi legem datam per Moysen,
Christiani legem datam per Christum. Nam pagani uel uestræ
stirpis Sarraceni qui uestrum Mahumeth præcesserant, legem prius
accæpisse dicendi non sunt. Nulla enim uel paganis ab aliquo lex

data fuerat, quos solus error falsis nec nunc dicendis hominum opin-
ionibus infecerat, nec Sarracenis, quia necdum legis uestræ lator ne
dicam auctor suprascriptus aduenerat. Quod siquis forte opposuerit
quasdam legum sanctiones Grecis aut Latinis uel quibuslibet aliis
gentibus traditas, sicut olim Solonis leges Grecis, sicut quorumdam
Latinorum sapientum Romanis, respondeo, legibus illis non esse
cautum uel traditum, quid de Deo crederent, quo ritu uel modo
eum colere deberent, sed tantum non mandato diuino sed hominum consilio prouisum, qualiter suam rem publicam unaquæque
gens regeret, quo ordine pacis uel belli tempore uitam transigeret,
ne si absque alicuius certæ legis limite bestiali more uiuere cona-
rentur, mala bonis, iusta iniustis passim permiscendo confunde-
rent, nec ipsi uel eorum res publica in tanta rerum perturbatione
diu persistere possent. De diuinis uero nullus apud eos sermo, nisi
qui omni auctoritate et ratione destitutus, et aut ex ridiculosis
fabulis, aut ex stultis hominum deliramentis, aut fraudulentis
demonum oraculis originem trahens, non ad ueram deitatis cogni-
D 183rd tionem, / uel cultum homines duceret, sed ydolis uel quibuslibet
rebus creatis pro Creatore ad colendum propositis ab ipsa plenissime
et omnino miserrime auerteret. Ea de causa huiusmodi homines
legem habentes dicendi non sunt, quam a Deo non accæperunt,
sed ipsi sibi ritum uiuendi uel Deum colendi prout libuit con-
fixerunt. Soli ergo Iudæi uel Christiani ante Mahumeth uel eius
tempore legem habentes dicendi sunt, quam non a se inuentam,
sed a Deo traditam, accæperunt. De hiis igitur michi uidetur dictum ab eo, "Nolite disputare cum legem habentibus."

Cur hoc ab isto dictum est, cur ne cum legem habentibus dis-
putarent, ab eo præcæptum est? Si de ueritate legis suæ confidebat,
quare suos disputare prohibuit? Si diffidebat, cur ea quæ sui non possent defendere scripsit? Sed nouerat aut ipse, aut quod pace uestra
dictum sit, qui per eum loquebatur Sathanas, legis Iudaicæ uel Christianæ tantum esse robur, tam stabile fundamentum, ut non dicam
humanis uerbis uel rationibus obrui, sed nec ui bellica, nec armo-
rum fremitu, nec tormentis dirissimis seu mortibus quibuslibet
impulsum uel in modico posse nutari. Expertus fuerat illius primæ
legis tempore Iudæorum in Machabeis constantiam, æuangelicæ

gratiæ diebus in martyribus tolerantiam, non posse præualere æternæ sapientiæ humanas rationes, inuictæ uirtuti non posse resistere
mortalium languidos et enerues conatus. Eapropter qui mundanam
sapientiam, qui humanam uirtutem legibus diuinis iam substra-
tam cernebat, quomodo sibi lite proposita de uictoria suæ partis
blandiri poterat, uel saltem primos disputationum ictus perferre?
Destitutus itaque omni resistendi præsidio confugit ad fugam,
et qui nil rationabile uel ponere uel obicere poterat, elegit silentium.

Sed ne ex toto aduersæ parti[18] cedere uideretur, pro ratione arma
assumpsit, et furiosorum more, nullum dans interroganti responsum ad lapides, fustes, uel gladios se conuertit. Hiis armatus, agentem contra se impetit, immo pene priusquam agere incipiat, uelut
ex improuiso irruens fera crudelis extinguit. Talem, tam iustum,
tam rationabilem disputationibus finem uester propheta Mahumeth o Agareni imponit, tam æqua sententia inter partes sibi aduersas discernit, tale iudicium usque ad sua / uel uestra tempora D 183vs
seculis inauditum laudabilis arbiter profert. Nam ut præmisi, hæc
eius uerba sunt.

Postquam enim dixit, "Nolite disputare cum legem habentibus,"
subdit, "melior est enim cedes, quam lis." Et quid dicam? Defi-
ciunt uerba ad tantam absurditatem, tam bestialem crudelitatem,
tam nefandam nequitiam confutandam. Vere auida humani sanguinis bestia Sathanas hoc inuenit, per hunc uelut per organum sibi
congruum hoc efflauit, cuius lingua sicut penna uel calamo usus,
tam inhumanum et immane facinus et dixit et scripsit. Sciebat
fabulosam et nugacissimam ut in suo loco probabitur sectam
aliter diu stare non posse, non ignorabat erroneum dogma uelut
aranearum telam leui negotio dissoluendum, si libera contra illud
agere uolentibus uia pateret, si prædicatoribus uerbi diuini more
antiquo aduersus eam disputare liceret. Non erat immemor olim
"in omnem terram eorum sonum exisse, et in fines orbis terræ eorum processisse uerba,"[18a] qui missi a Christo uerbum æternæ
uitæ ubique disseminauerant, et totum fere mundum ad agnitionem ueritatis perduxerant. Intelligebat nullum eorum qui per eos

---

[18] "aduersæ parti" bis.
[18a] Ps. 18:5, Rom. 10:18.

crediderant credere potuisse, nisi prius audiret quod credere deberet, nec audire hoc posset, si prædicatore careret. Nam sicut ait quidam magnus apostolus noster, "Fides ex auditu, auditus autem per uerbum Christi,"[19] non potuisset fides Christiana in hominum mentibus oriri, non audita prædicatione, nec audiri prædicatio potuisset, absque prædicatore.[20] Et quia suptilis ad fallendum et perdendum perditus angelus maximo se fraudandum lucro nouerat, sicut olim se fraudatum dolebat, si aditus audiendi sermoni Dei daretur, nec dubitabat se a cordibus decæptorum expellendum, si ille admitteretur, interposuit ferreum quem de profundo nequiciæ consilio hauserat obicem, quem nullus transgredi posset. Fecit hoc ut atrium suum heu proh dolor iam magnum in pace custodiens securius possideret, ut qui audito uerbo salutis saluari poterat, tali arte auditu subtracto, in æternum periret.

Propter hæc omnia prolatum est ab illo uestro totiens nominato uerbum tam sollempniter execrabile: "Melior est cedes, quam lis." Et litem quidem etiam Christiana lex improbat, iuxta quod præmissus noster apostolus docet: "Seruum," ait, "Dei non oportet litigare."[21] / Dampnat enim talium litium animosas contentiones, quæ fiunt non causa ueritatis inueniendæ, sed procaci studio propriæ sententiæ defensandæ. Improbat plane ut dixi Christiana sobrietas superbas ac furiosas lites, docens discipulum sapienter et modeste uel quæ proponenda sunt proponere, uel quæ obicienda sunt obicere. Non approbat tamen ut ille uester propheta cedes, nec dicit: "Melior est cedes quam lis." Vtrumque enim malum esse docet, utrumque dampnabile esse non tacet. Sed cum utrumque ipsius iudicio improbetur, magis tamen horum alterum dampnat. Non dicit, "Melior est cedes quam lis," uel "Melior est lis quam cedes," quia non recipit comparationem quod omnino malum est, adiunctum rei quæ omnino bona est, uel e conuerso. De duobus enim bonis, uel de duobus malis comparatio fieri potest, non de altero bono et altero malo, uel de altero malo et altero bono. Non igitur ut dictum est apostolus noster dicit, quod Mahumeth uester astruit, meliorem esse cedem quam litem, uel litem quam cedem,

D 183vd

---

[19] Rom. 10:17.   [20] Cf. Rom. 10:14.
[21] II Tim. 2:24.

sed cedem lite longe peiorem. Et quæ mens parum ne dicam multum rationabilis hoc uerum esse non uideat? Disquirite uniuersarum gentium iudicia, et quicquid uspiam terrarum sol uidet scrutamini, utrum leges humanæ in aliis multis diuersæ, in hoc uno non conueniant, quo longe maiori pæna plectitur iniustæ cedis reatus, quam iniuriosæ litis excessus. Mirum si et leges uestræ quos prudentes secundum carnem non ignoramus, in hac tam iustissima causa non concordant, quod natura ipsa etiam uerbis tacentibus prædicat, maiorem iniuriam maiori pæna puniendum, maiorem iacturam, maiori ultione damnandam. Quod si ita est, meliorem esse cedem quam litem, falsum est. Sed litem malam, cedem lite longe peirorem, uerum est. Quod si forte intellectus illius in eo quod dixit, "Nolite disputare cum legem habentibus," nec antiquos paganos legum quarumlibet inuentores excæpit, longe deformius et diffidentius hoc ab illo scriptum est, quando etiam cum illis quorum leges nulla diuinitatis auctoritate, nulla ueritatis uirtute subnixe coram processerant, disputare ausus non est. Quid igitur restat? Deponite tantum dedecus, neque uos tam turpi nota deinceps inuri patiamini, qua putatur in tantum uos diffidere de propria secta, in tantum eam omni rationis / robore destitutam, D 184rs ut ne dicam sponte, sed nec prouocati in publicum prodire audeatis, aut cum quolibet uel minimo contradictore disputationum manum conserere.

Et qualiter nobis uel orbi, partis uestræ siqua esse posset iustitia uel ueritas innotescet, qualiter uobis et uestris lux fidei Christianæ infulgebit, si nec uos uestra qualiacumque sint proponitis, nec nostra a nostris auditis? Et licet non ignoremus, quod uestra, uobis sufficere uideantur, quod plenam uos deitatis noticiam habere credatis, quod tam nos quam omnes alios aliarum uel alienarum legum sectatores præter uos errare arbitremini, audite tamen quæ proponenda sunt cum pace, nec in hoc ab uniuersarum gentium uel legum more soli dissentiatis, maxime cum liberum uobis sit, disputationibus cunctis et allegationibus finitis, quæcunque dicta fuerint aut probare aut improbare, aut suscipere aut respuere. Et quia causa salutis uestræ me ad hæc scribenda impulit, nec quia remotissimi et ingnotissimi eratis, caritas quam non ut erga Christianos, sed ut erga æthnicos habeo, silere me permisit, debetis et uos hanc saltem huic caritati meæ uicem, ut et si hiis quæ dicenda sunt nolueritis adquiescere, saltem non recusetis audire. Non deserat et illud tenax uestrorum ista legentium uel audientium memoria, ut quia in rebus dubiis non potest agnosci quod uerum est, nisi prius destruatur quod falsum est, necesse michi erit, et contra uestrum legislatorem, et contra ipsius legislationem uerbis materiei congruentibus agere, quia non parua ueritati iniuria fieret, si uel in sententiis uel in sermonibus contra iustitiam relator parceret falsitati.

Non igitur statim moueamini, non statim ut sic loquar insaniatis, et ad lapides ut supra dixi aut gladios concurratis. Imitamini saltem in hoc nostros, qui cum frequentem cum Iudeis quorum inter ipsos plurima multitudo subiecta moratur sermonem conserant, et multa ac pene uniuersa fidei Christianæ contraria ab ipsis audiant, non in furiam commouentur, nec uelut contra blasphemos in eorum necem insurgunt, sed audiunt patienter, respondent sapienter, neque hos ut hostes salutis suæ statim perimunt, sed æquanimiter si forte aliquando conuertantur, expectant. Hunc modum et erga innumeros ipsius uestri generis ac uestræ legis D 184rd captiuos quos in præliis sepe capere solent, conseruant, / et sola ad proprium solum redeundi facultate subtracta, linguæ libertatem non adimunt. Et ut ipsi nobis aliquid uelut ex uestra parte opponamus, quod quia forte ignoratis, ipsi opponere non possetis, legitur in lege Iudeorum quæ et Christianorum est, sed sic a nobis intellecta ut intelligenda est, Deum præcæpisse occidi blasphemos,[22] qui aliquid ad Deum pertinens uerbis uel factis impii temerare auderent. Sed non iuuat in hoc uel in modico partem uestram, quia legis illius auctorem preter paucos paganos uerum Deum esse nullus iam in orbe dubitat, quod uero secta uestra ex Deo non sit, omne preter uos uniuersarum quæ sub cælo sunt gentium genus affirmat. Iustum igitur est ut quos blasphemos creditis, interim occidere differatis, quousque indubio ueritatis examine cognoscatur prophetam uestrum a Deo missum, legem uestram a Deo datam

[22] Cf. Lev. 24:16, Joan. 19:17.

fuisse, sicut ille qui blasphemos præcipit occidi, uerus Deus probatur existere. Tali modo, tali consideratione, non furiosa sed sollicita, non præcipiti sed modesta, uniuersæ gentes totius orbis, reges ac
principes, Christi nuntios suscæperunt, suscæptos audierunt, et licet
diu multumque conati resistere, tandem rationi, tandem perspicuæ
ueritati, immo Spiritui Dei illustranti cesserunt. Inter quos ne
nimius fiam innumerabiles dimittens, regnum quoddam in ultimis
occidentis partibus ac pene extra orbem constitutum uobis propono,
ac regem ipsius Ethelbertum nomine, qui pene a uestro Mahumeth
contemporaneus extitit, in exemplum produco.

[B]rittannia prius ab antiquis Brittonibus regnum illud dicebatur, sed ab Anglorum gente nomine diriuato nunc Anglia uocatur. Gens illa ante quingentos annos de partibus Saxoniæ egressa,
magnas illius insulæ partes nam insula est magno mari oceano
circumsepta, ui bellica optinuit, atque in ea sibi regnum constituit.
Erat hæc gens antiquis ydolatriæ erroribus adhuc irretita, et cultum
Creatoris creaturæ impendens, longe ab ipso seiuncta. Misertus est
tandem benignus Conditor erroneæ gentis et per summum Christianorum magistrum Romanum dico pontificem qui Gregorius dicebatur eos a morte eripuit, et sempiternæ uitæ adiunxit. Is enim
diuino tactus Spiritu ad æuangelizandum illi genti Christi Æuangelium electos misit discipulos, in quibus primus erat uir quidam
sanctus, nomine / Augustinus, per quorum uerba et insignia opera, D 184vs
rex cum integra gente, ad fidem Christi conuersus, et Christianorum numero fideliter adiunctus est. Sed quomodo nuntios sibi
missos suscæperit, quid post causam aduentus sui redditam eis
responderit, quid egerit, qualiter se erga eos habuerit, quia ad
causam de qua agitur multum, immo ex toto pertinet audite.
Verba uero ipsa ex antiqua Anglorum hystoria excerpta hæc sunt:

"Eo tempore rex Ethelbertus in Cantia potentissimus erat, qui
ad confinium usque Humbri fluminis, quo meridiani et semptem-
triales populi Anglorum dirimunt fines imperium protenderat. Est
autem ad orientalem Cantiæ plagam Thanetos insula non modica,
id est magnitudinis iuxta consuetudinem æstimationis Anglorum
miliarium sæxcentorum. Quam a continenti terra secernit fluuius
Vuantsumu, qui est latitudinis circiter trium stadiorum, et duobus

tantum in locis est transmeabilis. Vtrumque enim caput protendit
in mare. In hac ergo applicuit seruus Domini Augustinus, et socii
eius, uiri ut ferunt fere quadraginta. Accæperunt autem precipiente beato papa Gregorio de gente Francorum interpretes centum,
mandaueruntque regi se uenisse de Roma, ac nuntium ferre optimum, qui sibi optemperantibus æterna in cælis gaudia, et regnum
sine fine cum Deo uiuo et uero sine ulla dubietate promitteret.
Qui hæc audiens, manere eos in illa quam adierant insula, et eis
necessaria ministrari, donec uideret quid eis faceret iussit. Post
dies ergo uenit ad insulam rex, et residens sub diuo, iussit Augustinum cum sociis ad suum ibidem aduenire colloquium. Cauerat
enim ne in aliquam domum ad se introirent, ueteri usus augurio,
ne superuentu suo siquid maleficæ artis habuissent, eum decipiendo
superarent. At illi non demonica sed diuina uirtute præditi uenie-
bant, crucem pro uexillo portantes argenteam et imaginem Domini Saluatoris in tabula depictam, lætaniasque canentes pro sua
simul et eorum propter quos uenerant, salute æterno Domino
supplicabant.

"Cumque ad iussionem regis residentes uerbum ei uitæ una
cum omnibus qui aderant eius comitibus prædicarent, respondit
ille dicens, 'Pulchra sunt quidem uerba et promissa, quæ affertis,
sed quia noua sunt et incerta, non hiis possum assensum tribuere,
D 184vd relictis eis quæ tanto tempore cum omni / Anglorum gente serua-
ui. Verum quia de longe huc peregrini uenistis, et ut ego michi
uideor perspexisse ea quæ uos uera et optima credebatis, nobis quoque communicare desiderastis, nolumus molesti esse uobis, quin
potius hospitio uos benigne recipere, et quæ uictui uestro sunt
necessaria ministrare curabimus. Nec prohibemus, quin omnes
quos potestis fidei uestræ religionis prædicando societis.' " Dedit
ergo eis mansionem in ciuitate Dorobernensi, quæ imperii sui
totius erat metropolis, eisque ut promiserat cum administratione
uictus temporalis, licentiam quoque prædicandi non abstulit."[23]

Sic rex iste, sic innumeri alii aliarum gentium reges, nuntios
Christi suscipiebant, suscæptos omni humanitate et honore cole-
bant. Decet uos hoc idem facere, aut si non ex toto illos imitari

[23] S. Bedæ Venerabilis *Historia Ecclesiastica Gentis Anglorum,* 1:25.

disponitis, saltim siquid commodi uel salutis uobis afferunt, audire pariter et probare.

Iam ad proposita sermo festinet, et primo contra pessimum hostem Dei adiutus Spiritu Dei ad prælium accingatur. Sed priusquam comminus manus conserere assueta ratio præliandi suadeat, præmitto quod præmittendum est, quæro quod quærendum est. Ex quo ab aliquot annis lex Mahumetica de lingua Arabica in patriam id est Latinam meo studio translata est, mirari non desino nec satis mirari sufficio, qua ratione propheta ille uester suo Alchoran quædam de Hebraica, quædam insuper de Christiana lege excerpta admiscuit, et cum magnum se pro uiribus utrique genti hostem exhibeat, uelut Iudeus aut Christianus, plurima quæ scribit, legis eorum auctoritate confirmat. Si enim hiis quæ nostra sunt credit, utique in quantum credit, nullo rationabiliter resistente nobiscum sentit. Quod si ex parte, nobiscum sentit, cur non omnibus quæ nostra sunt assentit? Si adquiescit Iudaicis uel Christianis scriptis ex parte, cur non adquiescit ex toto? Cur monstruosum se exhibet recipiendo ex scriptis nostris quod uult, et reiiciendo quod non uult? Nam lego eum introducentem in illo suo libro nomina uel gesta illorum quos litteræ Hebraicæ sonant, cerno eum nominantem quos scripturæ Christianæ memorant. De illis quasi exscerptos uideo: Noe, Abraham, Loth, Iacob, Ioseph, Moysen, Pharaonem, Dauid, et quosdam alios. / De istis: Zachariam, Elysabeth, Iohannem Zachariæ filium, Mariam, Iesum uel Christum Mariæ filium, Gabrihelem Zachariæ uel Mariæ loquentem, Iohannis exortum, Christi natiuitatem ex uirgine, et quædam alia. D 185rs

Cum igitur ut dixi quædam ex iam dictis scripturis exscerpserit, cur non aut Iudeus factus est, cuncta Iudaica suscipiendo, aut Christianus, Christiana ex integro uolumina approbando? Cur bonam dixit legem Iudaicam quam non sequitur, cur Christianum Æuangelium prædicat quod uituperat? Aut enim prauæ sunt hee scripturæ et abiciendæ sunt, aut ueraces et prædicandæ sunt. Nam longe alia lex est diuinorum uerborum quam humanorum, alia longe ratio legis diuinæ quam traditionis humanæ. Nam si in quarumlibet gentium legibus quædam iuste decreta sunt, sepe tamen contigit, quod contra regulam æquitatis aliqua uel forte plurima sanccita sunt. At non ita, prorsus non ita in lege cælesti, non sic in supernis oraculis, quolibet tempore quibuslibet datis. Etsi enim ab humanis ingeniis rationabiliter ratione utentibus uera aliqua proferuntur, potest fieri, ut quia homines sunt, quandoque raro, quandoque sepe fallantur. Vnde in Psalmis quos iam dictus propheta uester, Dauid traditos asserit legitur: "Omnis homo mendax."[24]

Illa autem æterna maiestas quæ Deus est, a quo omnis ueritas, immo qui etiam essentialiter ueritas est, sicut lux in tenebras non potest mutari, sic uel sono audibili, uel inspiratione intelligibili creaturis rationalibus loquens, nescit mentiri. Inde constat quod cuncta mortalibus ab ipso tradita et per eos scripturæ mandata, uera sint, certa sint, indubia sint. Ex hiis colligitur, quod si litteræ Iudaicæ uel Christianæ, immo ut uerius dicam, sensus earum a Deo ad homines processit, et ab illo ipsis traditus est, ut ueraces, et uelut riuus a fonte ueritatis diriuatus non ex parte ut uester propheta facit, sed ex toto suscipiendæ sunt, honorandæ sunt. Cur ergo legislator uester partim has scripturas approbat, partim reprobat, partim suscipit, partim abicit? Nam sicut dictum est, si diuinæ sunt, non ex parte sed ex toto suscipiendæ sunt. Si diuinæ non sunt, non ex parte, sed ex toto reprobandæ sunt. Aut ergo suscipiat has scripturas sicut D 185rd diuinas, ut seruet / Alchoran suum, aut si eas diuinas esse negauerit, auferat ea quæ inde assumpsit de Alchoran suo, immo iustiore assumpto consilio, auferendo falsa quæ falsis scripturis assumpserat, falsificet simul et auferat eorum causa ipsum totum Alchoran suum.

Ad hæc aliquis uestrum: "Libros Iudaicos uel Christianos diuinos fuisse non nego, sed sicut a primis auctoribus conscripti sunt. Sed noui processu temporis diuersis casibus illa prima uolumina perisse, ac postmodum a quibusdam Iudæis Iudaicos, a quibusdam Christianis Christianos reparatos fuisse. Qui primorum librorum uelut originalem ueritatem ignorantes, tam ex uariis præcedentium relationibus, quam ex proprii cordis coniectura, libros qui nunc a Iudæis uel Christianis habentur prout libuit condiderunt,

---

[24] Ps. 115:11.

ac uera falsis, falsa ueris permiscentes, omnem eis ueritatis constantiam abstulerunt. Hac de causa libris huiusmodi, quibus utraque gens instanti tempore utitur, fidem non adhibeo, hac de causa falsatos uel corruptos affirmo. Electa sunt tamen a Deo et tradita prophetæ nostro, quæ uera esse constabat, atque ab illo scripturæ legis nostræ admixta. Ista per illum legislatorem nostrum Deus inter uerum falsumque discreuit, mittendo ei per thomos ea quæ ex ipsis scripturis uera esse nouerat, non mittendo quæ falsa esse sciebat."

Et o prudentes iuxta carnem uiri, unde istud probatur? Vnde probatis inquam quod proponitis? Vnde ostenditis libros prius ueraces, a sequentibus uel Iudeis uel Christianis corruptos? Et gratias quidem Deo, quod aliquando ueraces fuisse asseritis. In hac enim parte nobiscum sentitis, in hac parte Iudæis concordatis. Sed ad probandum ut dictum est quod falsati fuerint, quam auctoritatem, quam rationem, quibus cedere compellamur affertis? Et certe iuxta legem diuinam, ac secundum illam quæ uniuersarum gentium leges aut iura scripta superat, Romanam dico, agenti probatio semper incumbit. Creditis et proponitis libros diuinos Iudaicos a Iudeis, Christianos a Christianis processu temporis casibus uariis esse corruptos. Sed quia ut absentes scribenti respondere non potestis, proponam ipse michi, nec segnius quam uos uestra quibus innitimini uolumina perscrutabor.

Et plane / nullo uestrum, ut arbitror resistente, uniuersis scripturis uestris iuxta uos sublimius et uelut uertex omnium supra memoratum Alchoran uestrum existere prædicatur. Illud enim est quod de cælis a Deo missum, et non simul sed paulatim ac per partes mense qui apud uos Ramazan dicitur, prophetæ uestro a Gabrihele traditum affirmatis. Ipsum igitur ab illo suo principio quod est, "In nomine Domini, pii et misericordis, liber hic, absque falsitatis uel erroris annexu, ueridicus,"[25] usque ad illum suum finem, in quo rursum ait, "In nomine Domini pii et misericordis, te sanctificando omnium gentium Dominum, omnium regem, omnium Deum iugiter atque suppliciter exora,"[26] ipsum inquam

D 185vs

[25] Kor. 2:2.
[26] Kor. 114:1-3, A 138rd.

summæ legis uestræ ex integro librum reuoluite, et si aliquid de falsatis libris Iudaicis aut Christianis, uel a Deo uel a uestro propheta dictum eruere inde poteritis, coram proferte.

Scrutamini et alios licet longe inferioris auctoritatis, qui apud uos leguntur aut habentur libros, et aut breue aliquod uerbum, aut saltem iota unum, corruptas a quibuslibet quolibet tempore scripturas iam dictas significans, nobis proponite. Sed non sumus adeo ignari, aut expertes litterarum uestrarum, nec lingua Arabica adeo se subducere potuit cognitioni Latinæ, ut aliquid earum rerum quæ ad causam assumptam pertinent, nos latere potuerit, et utrum litteræ uestræ in aliqua parte sui nostras falsatas esse contineant, nobis licuerit ignorare. Habet gens nostra plurimos in utraque lingua peritos, qui non tantum ea quæ ad religionem uel ritum uestrum pertinent, ex uestris litteris sollicite eruerunt, sed etiam quantum ad liberalia uel phisica studia spectat, armariorum uestrorum intima penetrarunt. Ea de causa tam ex translatis litteris iamque Latinis, quam ex ipsis Arabicis agnoscimus nec Alchoran uestrum, nec librum Abdiæ Iudei[27] nec genealogiam Mahumeth,[28] nec quælibet alia, legem uel legislatorem uestrum sonantia uolumina, scripturas Hebraicas uel Christianas, quolibet tempore, aliquo casu falsatas esse, uel in modico memorare.

Cum hæc ita se habeant, cum litteras nostras uel Iudeorum ut sepe dictum est aliquando falsatas esse libri uestri in nulla sui parte contineant, unde hæc opinio uobis? Vnde fama hæc? Quo D 185vd auctore traditio tam falsa, immo tam nulla processit? Mirum / enim et supra quam dicere possim mirum est, homines ut supra iam scripsi quantum ad temporalia et humana prudentes, quantum ad æterna et diuina tam hebetes, ut cernere non possint non esse cuilibet traditioni credendum absque examine, non esse adquiescendum famæ uulgari, absque certo et fide digno auctore. Et prorsus quidem stolidum est dubio auctori cedere, sed super omnia brutum est, absque ullo auctoris nomine inani tantum stultarum plebium fama uulgata tenere. Hæc enim iam sola superesse uidetur, qua omnino insulse immo imprudenter opinamini diuinos

[27] i.e. *Doctrina Mahumet*, A 19rs et seq.
[28] i.e. *Liber generationis Mahumet*, A 11rs et seq.

libros prius casu perditos, postmodum falsitate ueritati admixta, prout nouis scriptoribus libuit, reparatos.

Sed iam ueniat traditio famosa in medium, et quibus casibus libri totiens nominati perierint, indubia ueritate ostendat. Ac primum qualiter Iudei legem a Deo sibi datam cum propheticis et aliis coherentibus, libris amiserint, ordine congruo seruato declaret. Nam notum est orbi, Iudaica uolumina multo tempore Christiana præcessisse, æuangelica uero siue apostolica longe post ab æuangelistis et apostolis descripta. Vnde iustum est, ut eo ordine quo perierunt perisse, eo ordine quo falsata dicuntur, falsata esse probentur.

"Dimissi," aiunt, "regis Persarum indulgentia a captiuitate Babilonica Iudæi, atque ad Palestinam suam redire permissi, libros diuinos quos secum dum captiui tenerentur habuerunt, asino imposuerunt, et sic cum promiscua multitudine iter aggressi sunt. Et quia ut mos est multitudinis iter agentis, quidam uelocius, quidam tardius incedebant, diuersisque itineris necessitatibus ad plurima distracti, nunc hiis, nunc illis occupabantur, asinum diuinæ legis latorem incautius obseruarunt. Cumque primi ab ultimis longo uiæ spacio discreti, negligenter incederent, brutum illud animal rectore iam carens, utque huiusmodi animalia solent, lasciuiens, relicto itinere, deuia secutum est. Quod paulatim procedens, et nunc per plana cursitando, nunc montana conscendendo a suis segregatus cum nemo sequeretur, disparuit, talique casu cum lege Dei quam ferebat periit."[29]

Hæccine est o uiri fama, / heccine est traditio qua constat apud uos D 186rs legem Iudaicam perditam, libros propheticos amissos? Et qualiter, qualiter inquam persuaderi potuit circumspectis hominibus, Iudeos a captiuitate iam dicta redeuntes, tam incuriosos, tam desides, tam indeuotos erga sacra sua quæ sola amissis aliis omnibus eis supererant existere potuisse? Iam enim ante septuaginta annos dum captiuarentur, euersa urbe, succenso templo, archa Dei perdita, aureis, argenteis, ac æreis multi ponderis uasis quæ Deo sacrata fuerant, cum captiuato populo in Babilonem translatis, nichil sacrorum suorum redeuntibus præter legem et uasa regali dono

[29] A 28rd, marg.

sibi restituta supererat. Quomodo igitur aut uerum aut uerisimile uideri potest, homines ardentissimis animis ad patriam festinantes, et erga religionem traditam toto nisu flagrantes legem Dei de qua tota spes eorum pendebat, et de qua sola apud alios uel proximos uel remotos mundi populos gloriabantur sic neglexisse, sic animali uilissimo imposuisse, sic nec uno de tot milibus saltem sequente, incustoditam dimisisse? Et ubi erant uel quo declinauerant ministri, ubi Leuitæ, ubi qui de captiuitate redierant sacerdotes? Et si nobilium uel uulgarium multitudo mixtim uel sparsim incedens, cui seruandæ legis cura imposita non fuerat, legiferum asinum non attendens quo diuerteret subsecuta est aut præcessit, uidetur esse consequens, ut ad id electi, uniuersi pariter alias diuerterint, nec saltem unum de multo custodum numero ad seruandam legem, immo ut sic dicam, totam spem suam reliquerint? Quis enim facile equum uel iumentum quodlibet suum sic absque omni custodiæ cura negligit?

Sed esto. Sit quod non fuit, aberrauerit asinus, et in uia sequens disparuerit, amiserit stultus et iners populus asinino errore legem, perdiderit tali casu immo tanto infortunio sacra illa quæ iam dictum animal tunc ferebat uolumina, nunquid nusquam in toto orbe aliud eiusdem legis uolumen uel penes Iudeos uel penes alios aliquos remanserat? An inter tot milia Iudeorum, uel qui de Chaldea ad Syriam redibant, uel qui per plures ac diuersas orbis partes, D 186rd uel captiuati uel fugati fuerant, nullus erat qui eandem legem / in alio transcriptam uolumine haberet? Et certe si aut diuinis aut aliis ueracibus hystoriis credere non refugitis, ante illam quæ a rege Chaldeorum qui Nabugodonosor dicebatur de Iudæis facta est captiuitatem, a regibus Assyriorum decem stirpis Iudaicæ tribus in Medos et Persas, aliasque orientis gentes translatæ sunt. Nunquid tanta gens, immo tot populi quibus lex illa Dei communis erat, nullos legis tam famosæ libros secum dum transferrentur tulerunt?

Et quæ gens qualibet lege scripta uiuens, uno et solo uolumine contenta est? Quomodo innumeris gentibus per multiplices urbes, per uicos, per castra, per uillas diffuse manentibus, multamque terrarum partem occupantibus, unum tantum legis suæ uolumen

sufficere posset? An non omnes ubique gentes non solum in singulis ciuitatibus, sed pene in singulis et modicis uillis, legis cui se
deuouerunt singula aut forte plurima uolumina retinent? Nonne
ipsi de quorum lege agitur Iudei per totam Europam ac per alias
mundi partes sub Christianis manentes, non solum milleni aut
centeni, sed etiam sexageni aut quinquageni uno in loco simul
habitantes, legem integram, prophetas omnes, aliosque Hebraicæ
linguæ libros nobis nostrisque in synagogis suis cotidie ostendunt,
commodant, offerunt? Vix plane apud nos uiginti simul morantes
absque libris huiusmodi inueniuntur Iudei. Nonne simili modo et
apud uos? Scrutamini in partibus illis, in quibus eos uestro dominio
subiecistis, et me non falsa loqui ut arbitror agnoscetis.

Fuerat et iste mos eorum, dum antequam a diuersis gentium
regibus captiuarentur, adhuc quasdam partes Syriæ sibi ad Deo
concessas cum sua illa metropoli Ihrusalem incolerent, ut non
tantum in urbe illa in qua sola eis Deo sacrificare licebat, sed
etiam in cunctis aliis urbibus suis, et fere in uniuersis dicionis suæ
castellis et burgis, tam legis quam aliorum librorum uolumina
conseruarent. Nam nec aliter ut ratio consulta declarat, tam pro-
fusæ legis doctrinam discere uel memoriæ tradere maxime tanti
numeri populi possent, nisi in multis ac diuersis locis manentibus
et multitudo librorum adesset, et multorum magistrorum sollertia
non deesset. Non enim fieri poterat, ut ter tantum in anno totus
ille populus Dei præcepto ad principalem urbem ad orandum et
sacrificandum conueniens, paucissimis diebus quibus ibi mora-
batur, / lege Dei instrui, et quantalibet doctorum instantia angustia D 186vs
temporis prohibente, plene posset doceri. Habebant igitur plurima
loca, habebant plurimi in locis diuersis manentes, integrum legis
diuinæ et aliorum uoluminum corpus, sicque tam in illis Syriæ
partibus, quam in aliis per orbem diffusis regionibus lex Dei ab
innumeris conseruata, perire non poterat.

Sed quid loquor de Hebreis, quid dico de aliis gentibus, quod
leges quibus uiuunt siue a Deo traditas siue ab ipsis inuentas, non
uno in loco contineant, sed per loca aut quibus dominantur, aut
in quibus morantur diffundant? Vos, uos inquam conuenio. Alchoran uestrum traditum ut dicitis a Deo Mahumeth uestro, sola

Meccha ubi iacet continet? Nulla hoc Arabiæ alia ciuitas, nulla
Egypti, nulla Affricæ nulla orientalium ciuitatum uobis subdita-
rum, nullum earum castrum, nullus uicus, preter Meccham, Alchoran illud habet? Credo nisi monstruose pertinaces esse uelitis,
et ueritati notissimæ repugnare, tam uestro quam uniuersarum
gentium exemplo, concedetis Iudeos nullo tempore fuisse contentos
simplici scripturarum suarum uolumine, nec pro fabuloso et
mendoso immo nullo bruti animalis errore, legem Dei in illo Iudeorum a Babilone reditu potuisse perire. Affluebat enim ex diuersis
partibus orbis unde resumi non deerat facultas unde rescribi ex innumeris exemplaribus posset.

Quod quia rationabiliter negari non potest, procedat sermo ad
sequentia, et Iudæos post illum suum a Babilone reditum, libris
legis diuinæ caruisse, demonstret. Sic enim in libro Ezre, qui de
numero Iudaicorum uoluminum est, legitur: "Congregatus est
omnis populus quasi uir unus ad plateam quæ est ante portam
Aquarum, et dixerunt Ezræ scribæ ut afferret, librum legis Moysi,
quam præcæpit Dominus Israheli. Attulit ergo Ezras sacerdos
legem coram omni multitudine uirorum et mulierum, cunctisque
qui poterant intelligere in die prima mensis septimi, et legit in
eo in platea quæ erat ante portam Aquarum, a mane usque ad
medium diem, in conspectu uirorum ac mulierum et sapientium.
Et aures omnis populi erant intentæ ad librum."[30] Et uersu inter-
posito, "Et aperuit Ezras librum coram omni populo, et benedixit
Ezras Domino Deo uoce magna. Et respondit omnis populus,
'Amen.'"[31] Nunquid Ezras qui de illorum / numero captiuorum
erat, quorum ut dictum est incuria lex Dei iuxta uestrorum opinio-
nem perierat, legem falsam tam subito condiderat? Cumque
et ipse uir iustus et sapiens in eodem uolumine prædicetur, nulla-
que uel ipsi uel populo spes nisi in Domino tunc fuerit, quis sani
capitis uel suspicari audeat ab eo legem Dei corruptam, et in
totius populi conspectu ad legendum productam? Sed quia apertissime falsis diu immorandum non est, aut producantur certa indi-
cia quibus legis diuinæ liber uel ab Ezra uel a quolibet alio falsatus

D 186vd

---

[30] II Esdr. 8:1-3.   [31] II Esdr. 8:5-6.

probetur, aut ridicula et insulsa a patre mendacii procedens opinio reprobetur.

Sed iterum et iterum ad mirandum commoueor, nec satis tam prodigiosa admirari sufficio, quo Sathanæ astu hominibus ratione utentibus persuaderi potuit, ut aut crederent aut putarent libros tanto tantorum seculorum testimonio ueraces, tamque a plus-quam duobus milibus annorum ubique per orbem diffusos, cuius-libet falsatoris arte potuisse corrumpi. Quid enim? Nunquid etsi constaret iuxta uestram suspicionem ab aliquibus falsariis falsatos, constaret absque ueritatis examine ab orbe suscæptos? Itane ali-quando sensus humanus obrutus, sic ratio sepulta fuit, ut non discerneret quid susciperet, immo quod longe amplius mirandum est tantæ falsitati in uniuersis preter uos linguis et gentibus assen-tiret? Qualiter per mille fere annos dum adhuc lex illa Dei ut creditis incorrupta maneret, a nullis preter Iudeos suscæpta est, et falsata usque ad ultimos mundi terminos per uniuersos populos diffusa est? Sed quæ in uoluminibus illis falsitas notari potuit? In quibus suis partibus, in quibus uersibus primus legis illius liber qui Genesis uocatur, ueritate mutata, falsitate admixta corruptus apparet? In quibus Exodus? In quibus Leuiticus? In quibus liber Numeri? In quibus Deuteronomium? Nam in hiis quinque, sum-ma Iudaicæ legis consistit. In quibus falsati apparent Ihsu Naue, Iudicum et Ruth libri, qui prioribus quinque adiuncti Greco ser-mone Eptaticus uocantur? An forte in hystorica relatione? An in legislatione?

Si de hystoria hoc est de rebus gestis ab ipsa cæli et terræ crea-tione, usque ad eorumdem librorum finem quæstio est, nonne pene omnia ut ibi / leguntur, Mahumeth in Alchorano suo Deum D 187rs sibi fingens loquentem fatetur? Hoc de cæli et terræ creatione, hoc de Adam et Eua, de paradyso, de nemore paradysi, de arbore pro-hibita, et serpente, de expulsione a paradyso Adam et Euæ, de Chain et Abel, de Noe et archa, de diluuio, de Abraham et Iacob, de Ioseph, de Moyse et Aaron, de Pharaone et Ægyptiis, de Israhel et maris Rubri transitu, de prolixa illius populi per deserta peregri-natione, de terra Chanaan Israheli promissa et tradita, ac ut dictum est pene de omnibus quæ libri illi referunt, licet multis subtractis,

255

multis mutatis, multo insuper aggere mendaciorum admixto, illo suo barbarico ac prodigioso loquendi more plurima narrat. Si de legislatione per Moysen, et inde similiter multa subtrahens, quædam memorat. Cumque ex plurima parte Hebraicorum uoluminum ueritati attestetur, nec ut supradixi uel in modica sui parte falsata dicat, unde uobis hæc innasci potuit opinio, quam non accæpistis a magistro? Longe rectius, longe rationabilius hæc cogitare potuistis, hæc loqui debuistis. Et si nobis notæ sunt Hebraicæ uel Christianæ scripturæ, tamen ex hoc conicimus ueraces esse, quia plurima ut ibi scripta sunt in lege nobis tradita propheta noster approbat, nulla uero uel ibi uel alibi improbat.

Ex hiis omnibus quæ supra scripsi nec perditos nec falsatos Hebraicos libros fuisse, aut necessario aut probabili argumento concludo. Si quædam ut apud Iudeos scripta sunt, uelut diuino ad se facto responso suæ uestræque legi Mahumeth inserit, nec reliqua uel perdita uel falsata astruit, nec uestrum aliquis quod de perditis uel falsatis eisdem scripturis uel suspicamini uel proponitis, probare potest, constat eas absque quolibet uel minimo mendacii neuo, sicut a primis suis auctoribus editæ sunt, firmissimam summamque ut diuinas ueritatis arcem tenere. Sed nec in Alchoran uestro nec in aliis quibuslibet sectæ uestræ libris quicquam de hiis legitur, nichil aliunde a uobis unde probari possit Iudaicos libros aut perditos aut falsatos affertur.

Clarum est ergo, falsis obiectionibus ac suspicionibus longe reiectis sepe dictas scripturas non partim sed ex toto esse ueraces, certum est nullo iam resistere præualente esse diuinas. Hiis ita se D 187rd habentibus, addo quod / supra iam tetigi, necessario uos aut scripturas Hebraicas ex integro suscipere, aut Alchoran abicere. Cum enim ut iam dixi multa in illo uolumine sicut in Iudaicis libris habeantur, si falsati dicuntur, quæ aut inde sumpta, aut sicut ibi posita sunt, falsa omnino uel dubia esse probantur. Quod si falsa uel dubia in illa uestra lege scripta sunt, cuncta prorsus quæ liber ille continet, aut falsa aut dubia sunt. Nam nec ex falsatis libris aliquid potuit sumi nisi falsum et dubium, nec sicut ibi aliquid poni, nisi falsum aut dubium. Sed constat ut sepe dictum est plurima aut inde sumpta, aut quantum ad sensum pertinet, sicut ibi leguntur, in Alchorano posita. Constat igitur hac ratione legem illam illam inquam legem uestram, quam de cælis missam gloriari soletis, non solum ex parte sed totam ex integro falsam uel dubiam. Quod si falsum uel dubium Alchoran uestrum uel dicere uel credere refugitis, urgente uos undique certa quæ nec fallit nec fallitur ueritate, fateri cogemini libros illos unde a Mahumeth uestro plurima uel sumpta, uel quantum ad sententiam sicut ibi leguntur legi uestræ inserta sunt, non ex parte sed ex toto ueraces, non ex parte sed ex toto diuinas.

Hoc concesso, non solum Iudaica uolumina absque ulla mendacii nota, ut diuina suscipietis, sed hac eadem per omnia ratione, etiam Christianos libros pariter admittetis. Nam et de illis ut supra memoraui, plurima eidem legi uestræ a iam dicto uestro legifero admixta sunt, et pene toti illius uoluminis corpori ipsius inserta. Quæ si ut ex falsatis libris assumpta, reprobanda sunt, cum eis modo quo supra, et omnia illa quibus adiuncta fuerant, condempnanda sunt. Quod si et istud uitatis, simili immo eadem qua prius rationis conexione, libris Christianis eandem quam Iudaicis auctoritatem confertis. Et licet hoc negari non possit, licet breui compendio Christianos libros ueraces et diuinos esse claruerit, ueniat tamen et in medium procedat opinio, qua et ipsi perditi, qua falsati, a uestris aut omnibus aut quibusdam traduntur.

"Romanorum," inquiunt, "principum tempore, qui acriter Christianos exiliis, proscriptionibus, diuersisque mortium generibus diutissime persecuti sunt, qui et ipsa eorum uolumina edictis publicis exuri ubique iusserunt, tam Æuangelica quam Apostolorum Actus uel Æpistolæ perierunt. / Rescripti uero postmodum sunt ac reparati ut Christianis libuit, qui nec a primis librorum auctoribus, utique longa annorum serie interposita illis succedentes quicquam accæperant, nec libros ab ipsis conditos, utpote prius sicut dictum est succensos uiderant."[32] D 187vs

Et hoc est totum? Hoc est inquam totum quod prætenditis, hoc est totum ac solum unde euangelica uel apostolica scripta perisse, unde falsata esse asseritis? Si hoc est totum, eadem qua supra contra uos uia incedo, eodem respondendi modo, quæ proponitis nulla-

[32] Hunc locum non locavi.

257

rum uirium immo prorsus eneruia esse ostendo. Fateor quidem Romanos principes, qui toti Europæ, qui toti Affricæ, qui maximis Asyæ partibus cum adiacentibus uel in oceano, uel in Tyrreno mari insulis dominabantur, trecentis annis pene continue Christianos ubique iam diffusos nunc acrius, nunc remissius, persecutos esse. Fateor quendam ex ultimis persecutoribus qui et Diocletianus uocabatur, qui et ferocius et diuturnius aliis eos aggressus est, publico sanxisse edicto ut per uniuersas sibi subditas regiones, ipsa paschali sacratissima die Christianorum æcclesiæ subuerterentur, librique incenderentur.[33] Hoc certe ut dixi uelut pro parte uestra faciens, fateor.

Sed in quo istud pro uobis? Etsi edictum hoc ab illo principe per imperii Romani amplitudinem promulgatum est, si ex parte uel fortassis ex toto quantum ad æcclesiarum euersiones spectat impletum, si et hii qui inuenti sunt libri combusti sunt, nunquid uno illo casu Christianorum uniuersa uolumina perierunt? An nemo in tot tantisque populis Christianis per maximum illud imperium diffusis extitit, qui audito regio edicto aliquos ex tam innumeris libris absconderet, nemo qui igni subduceret, nemo qui seruaret? Et certe quod probari ex hystoriis ueracibus potest, uix in tam famoso et diffuso regno uix erat ciuitas, uix municipium, uix uillæ aliquæ, quæ non haberent Christianorum multitudinem admixtam paganis. Inter quos per urbes singulas, episcopi, presbyteri, diaconi, clerique non modicus numerus Christianis populis præsidebant, et sacros Christianæ legis libros cum aliis sibi creditis cælestibus sacris ac sacramentis, summa et singulari cura seruabant. Itane ergo omne propositum Christianæ religionis in eis perierat, itane D 187vd amor diuinorum sacrorum in eis / defecerat, ut cum corpora sua ignibus gladiis, omnisque generis mortibus pro seruanda lege Dei exponerent, ipsam legem Dei pro qua mori non differebant, sic uniuersaliter negligerent?

Et quid de Persis ac Medis, quid de Æthiopibus et Indis, quid de ipsa uestra Arabia, quid de aliis regnis quæ sibi Romana potentia subiugare non potuit dicetis? Nam cum in omnem iam terram discipulis Christi ubique clamantibus sonus æuangelicæ prædica-

---

[33] Cf. Eusebii Pamphili *Historia Ecclesiastica*, VIII:2.

tionis exisset, nullumque pene orbis angulum Christianis per omnes gentium linguas diffusis lateret, perierunt uel perdita sunt etiam apud illos Christiana uolumina? Periit Æuangelium? Perierunt apostolica scripta? Nullusne populus, nullæ linguæ, nulla Christianorum regio Christianos libros sicut eos a primis suis prædicatoribus accæperat ne possent perire seruauit? Sed seruatum est, seruatum est plane ab innumeris gentibus Christianis ut ab æuangelistis traditum est Æuangelium, seruata per successiones certissimas apostolica scripta, et usque ad tempora moderna transmissa.

Et ut de remotioribus minusque nobis cognitis mundi partibus taceam, habet Latina æcclesia a Petro, habet Greca a Paulo, habet Europa tota ab utroque sibi tradita Æuangelia, sibi commissa apostolica scripta. Hii cum summi et præcipui in discipulis Christi fuerint, alter edoctus ab illo corporaliter, alter inuisibiliter, incipientes a Ihrosolimis usque ad ultimos occidentis terminos, aliquando simul, aliquando separatim, nunc per se, nunc per suos, Æuangelium Christo uerbo prædicauerunt, scriptumque posteris tradiderunt. Petrus Æuangelium Marci, quod ipse probauerat, Paulus Æuangelium Lucæ, quod ille in partibus Greciæ scripserat. Nec defuit Iohannes alter ex discipulis Christi, ab eo dum adhuc cum hominibus moraretur electus et doctus, suum quod scripserat Æuangelium minoris Asiæ Christianis populis tradens. Sed nec Mathei quod prior scripserat Æuangelium cismarinis partibus et populis a iam dictis apostolis traditum perire potuit, quod festinanter ubique transcriptum atque diffusum, multorum populorum sollertia conseruauit. Hæc sibi ab apostolis iam dictis mox et sicut scripta fuerant tradita, præter innumeras alias, omnium mundi æcclesiarum Romana æcclesia caput, per succedentes nobisque ex scriptis notissimos apostolicos pontifices / a Petro incipiens usque D 188rs ad hæc nostra tempora custodiuit, falsumque prorsus et inane esse quod perisse a uestris aut creduntur aut dicuntur ostendit.

Sic et de apostolicis scriptis a Luca iam dicto Apostolorum Actus, a Petro æpistolæ duæ, a Iohanne tres cum Apochalipsi sua, a Paulo partim de Italia partim de Grecia scribente, æcclesiisque per diuersas urbes mittente, æpistolæ quatuordecim primis in

Christum credentibus traditæ sunt, et tam in Romana quam in cæteris urbibus per sibi succedentes fidelium generationes usque ad nos summo ut dictum est studio conseruatæ. Restant de nouo Christianorum canone duorum apostolorum Iacobi et Iudæ æpistolæ duæ, hoc est una Iacobi et alia Iudæ. Hec licet in Asia maiore scriptæ, cum oriente uestro nostrum quoque occidentem eodem pene tempore penetrarunt, aliisque statim adiunctæ ab eisdem quos nominaui, eo quo cætera studio sunt conseruatæ. Inde ad manus nostras cunctorumque fidelium nunc uiuentium deuenerunt, seruandæ a nobis ac posteris nostris quamdiu cælum imminet terræ.

Hiis ita præmissis, quid restat? Quid restat plane, nisi hoc? Nam necesse est eos qui ex uestris credunt uel opinantur libros Christianos perisse, aut certa ratione ostendere perditos, aut cædentes præmissis tam probabilibus causis, fateri a Christianis esse seruatos. Iam si constat quod non perierint constat quod nec falsati fuerint. Cum enim sicut ipso frequenter cotidiano usu experimur, etiam a paucis condictum secreti cuiuslibet mysterium, leuitate humana impellente diu tectum manere nequeat, uerumque sit prouerbium Gallorum nostrorum, "Quod sciunt duo sciunt omnes," qua arte, quo modo libri per orbem diffusi, tantaque tantorum ut dictum est sollertia conseruati, falsari potuerunt? An totus simul Christianus orbis tam prophanæ falsificationi assensit? An corrumpi sic uniuersaliter libros suos Christiana ubique sapientia passa est? Nullusne ex tantis Christicolarum populis, primis librorum suorum corruptoribus restitit?

Si enim corrupti sunt, primo ab uno, siue a paucis uel forte a multis sibi inuicem consentientibus corrupti sunt. Nam quomodo id aliter fieri potuisset, nisi corruptio hæc a paucis cæpisset? Cæpit ergo corruptio hæc a paucis, / quia nec aliter ut dixi subripere potuisset uel fortassis a pluribus. Sed nunquid a totius orbis populis? Nunquid simul uniuersi aut libros quos accæperunt corruperunt aut corruptoribus primis cesserunt? Itane omnes aut per se falsando, aut falsatoribus subito uel paulatim cædendo, æternam salutem suam quam solam libri illi prædicant, prodiderunt? An posset fama tam generalis falsitatis occultari, cum ut præmissum est, uix aliqua secreta etiam a paucis, interpositis ipsis fidei sacra-

D 188rd

mentis possint celari? An forte et totus mundus tunc falsitati assensit, et totus nunc nec tenuem famam tam uniuersalis falsificationis accæpit? Omnia plane monstra, cuncta portenta exsuperat, orbem terrarum libros suos corrupisse, et corruptos nescisse.

Sed forte hoc ad solos Sarracenos peruenit, et ad solos Christianos peruenire non potuit. Fortassis alienorum librorum uel perditio uel corruptio eis patuit, quæ tantis temporibus Christianos latuit. Aliena Sarracenis nota sunt, propria Christianis ignota sunt. Sed quid ultra? Quid ultra uel inanissimis nugis uel nugacibus hominibus respondendum est? Quod sine tegmine friuolum et falsum cernitur, quid tantopere stilus persequitur? Claudat modo quo supra ea quæ præmissa sunt ratio, nec eneruia uelut fortia diutius insectetur. Aut proba quicunque hoc asstruis uel opinaris certis rationibus libros Christianos falsatos, aut si non habes quid e conuerso afferas, crede ueraces, crede diuinos. Nam nec uniuersaliter potuere falsari, Christianorum nemine reclamante, nec si falsati essent, latere potuisset Christianos omnes in orbe, quod quantum ad infinitos Christiani nominis populos factum esset ab orbe.

Hiis quæ de Hebraicis libris iam dixi adiungo, non posse uos falsare Æuangelium nostrum, nisi pariter falsificetis et Alchoran uestrum. Nam si falsum est Æuangelium, illa quæ ut in Æuangelio leguntur, sic in Alchorano habentur, falsa uel dubia sunt. Quod si illa falsa uel dubia sunt, et totus liber cui illa admiscentur, falsus uel dubius est. Clarum est enim, quia de libro falsato nichil assumi potuit, nisi falsum aut dubium. Quod si legem illam uestram falsam aut dubiam credere uel dicere nefas putatis, Æuangelium uel æuangelicas scripturas ueraces esse et diuinas ratione cogente inuiti siue spontanei affirmatis. Affirmatis uero, / si D 188vs admixtas uestro Alchorano æuangelicas sententias ueras esse dicitis. Nam, ut sepe iam dictum est aut reprobatis ipsis, liber cui insertæ sunt reprobatur, aut approbatis pariter approbatur. Hac ratione cogimus uos et credere et fateri Hebraicos ut præmissum est libros cum nostris id est Christianis esse ueraces pariter et diuinos. Veraces, quia iam claret eos neuo mendacii expurgatos, diuinos, quia teste legislatore uestro, et lex Hebraica Moysi data est, et

Æuangelium Christo a Deo traditum est. Hac consequentia necesse est uos quantum ad diuinum canonem spectat, prorsus ut Hebreos Hebraicos libros suscipere, et ut Christianos æuangelica siue aposto-lica uolumina probare.

Ea de causa uos præmonitos et præmunitos esse denuncio, quod ubi in processu propositi operis et sermonis oportunum fuerit, ex hiis quæ iam necessario ut diuina tenetis uos aggrediar, et sicut ex concessis fieri ratio disputandi suadet, falsitatem qua excæptis Iudæis præ cunctis mortalibus irretiti et obruti estis, ut potero impugnabo, et scuto ueritatis protectus Deo iuuante pro uiribus expugnabo. Sed quia euangelica et apostolica scripta nostra dixi, Iudeorum uero uolumina nostra esse non scripsi, nemo uestrum æstimet Hebraicos libros Christianos non esse, quia non minus suscipit Christianus legem Moysi uel prophetas, quam Æuangeli-um, aut apostolorum gesta, uel epistolas. Ab eodem enim Deo cunctarum rerum "uisibilium et inuisibilium" Conditore[34] utrius-que gentis canonicas scripturas diuersis temporibus utriusque populis traditas Christianus et corde credit ad iustitiam, et ore confitetur ad salutem. Et licet hii inter se ualde dissideant, suscipit tamen Christiana uniuersitas intellectu quo debet Iudaica scripta, et ea ut maximum robur ac fidei nostræ fundamentum honorat.

Hæc interim dicta sint ad probandum o Sarraceni, ex ipsa lege uestra cui creditis litteras Hebraicas aut Christianas ueraces esse ac diuinas, nec earum ueritati obuiare posse humana figmenta, quas non solum ueritas inuicta commendat, sed et ipse qualiscunque legislator uester sacras esse modo quem præmisi confirmat. Quod autem sepe dicta lex uestra omni prorsus ueritate destituatur, ipse-que ille, ille plane ille nec propheta fuerit, nec Dei nuntius, sed seductor et prophanus, sequencia declarabunt.

EXPLICIT LIBER .I.us.

[34] Symb. Nic.-Const.

INCIPIT LIBER SECUNDUS.

IAM QVIA O HYSMAELITE præmissis quæ præmittenda erant, con- D 188vd
tra summum religionis uestræ robor agendum est, continente
ut præmonui gladios, seponite lapides, aperite aures, et siquid prudentiæ saltem humanæ in uobis est, deposito pertinaci ac
puerili uincendi studio, intentis animis quæ secuntur audite. Vtile
poterit hoc esse uobis, et si gratia uestri misereri uoluerit summe necessarium, ut intente scrutemini, sollicite perquiratis, perquirendo
aduertatis, cui uosipsos, cui salutem uestram non dico tantum hanc
fugacem et transitoriam, sed illam quæ huic succædit æternam, cui
inquam corpora et animas uestras credideritis, ne forte iuxta
famosum prophetam Ysaiam, sit mendacium in manu uestra, ne
forte pro ueritate falsitatem, pro iustitia iniquitatem, pro cultu
diuino diabolicum sacrilegium teneatis. Dicit ille loquens de
ydolatris sic: "Nescierunt neque intellexerunt. Obliti enim sunt
ne uideant oculi eorum, et ne intelligant corde suo. Non recogitant
in mente sua, neque cognoscunt neque sentiunt ut dicant. Medieta-
tem eius (hoc est arboris) combussi igni, et coxi super carbones
eius panes, coxi carnes et comedi, et de reliquo eius ydolum faciam?
Ante truncum ligni procidam? Pars eius cinis est. Cor insipiens
adorauit illud, et non liberauit animam suam, neque dixit: 'Forte
mendacium est in dextera mea.' Memento horum Iacob et Israhel,
quoniam seruus meus es tu."[1]

Potest hoc idem et uobis contigisse. Ydolatræ quidem ut audiui
non estis, nec ligna uel lapides aut huiusmodi talia adoratis. Sed
quid? Quid inquam quid? Quid prodest uobis creaturam pro
Creatore non suscipere, si non datur, Deum ut se colit et uult et
præcipit colere? Scrutamini ergo, nec longeuo iam errore imbuti
scutari dedignemini, utrum quod hactenus credidistis falsum sit,
quod hucusque falsum putastis uerum sit. Sapientum est etiam
si pudeat emendare errata, stultorum est fatuo pudore non corrigere etiam ab orbe dampnata. Et ut pertinacem et perdentem uos

[1] Isai. 44:18-21.

263

D 189rs uerecundiam / si datum fuerit, erroneæ saltem multitudinis con-
templatione, a uestris cordibus abigatis, nec solos uos errasse suspi-
cemini, propono tam de alienis quam de nostris exempla, qui
multiplicibus errorum monstris ut a uia ueritatis recederent, ab
hoste pulsati non cesserunt, immo innumeris per deuia errantibus
et pereuntibus, soli a præostenso rectæ fidei tramite non recesserunt.

Videte, disquirite sollicite præterita secula, et quot, quantis
quam multiplicibus errorum laqueis ab ipso primo mortalium
parente, angelo apostata qui Sathanas dicitur instigante, usque ad
hæc uestra tempora genus humanum implicitum fuerit si sapitis
attendite. Vltus est Deus in sceleratos, qui tempore patriarchæ
Noe fuerant, ut etiam Alchoran uestrum fatetur,[2] et totam illam
progeniem quæ a cultu diuino recesserat, terramque uniuersam
non toleranda iniquitate repleuerat, ultricibus undis extinxit. Successit dehinc exsiccatis terris, donoque diuino securitate reddita
soboles priorum, nequicia præcedentibus non inferior, et cultu
diuino abiecto, immo ut uerius loquar nec cognito Creatoris honorem creaturæ contulit, indeque ad ydolatriam progressa, tam
religione prophana quam uita nefanda, iniquitatum cumulis terræ
superficiem uniuersam respersit. Excæpti sunt paucissimi iusti,
sola Dei gratia ab uniuersali perditorum massa discreti, et sic rara
luce in densis et ubique diffusis impiorum tenebris lucente, prin-
ceps tenebrarum orbem totum iuxta Æuangelium quod Christo
nostro datum Mahumeth uester scripsit, heu usque ad Moysi
tempora, ut atrium suum diuturna et mortifera pace possedit.[3]

Illustrata est dehinc lege diuina per iam dictum prophetam
Moysen, una et sola de cunctis gentibus a Deo electa gens, et omnibus aliis in erroris iam antiqui tenebris derelictis, præcæptis a
Deo datis, et per ipsum promulgatis subiecta est, et ab impiorum
communi perditione seiuncta. Non destitit tamen prophanus et
pertinax hostis, etiam post legem datam gentem illam a cultu
diuino auertere et dampnatæ ac relictæ ydolatriæ nequitiisque ne-
fandis, et actibus execrandis gentilium artibus dolosis temptando,
illiciendo, seducendo rursum adiungere. Miserta est tandem per-

[2] Kor. 54:9-13, 71:1-28.
[3] Cf. Rom. 5:14.

euntis hominis benigna deitas, et / ad auxilium miserorum ueritas $\quad$ D 189rd
orta de terra, hoc est Christus de uirgine natus processit, et cælesti
lumine suo tenebris paulatim discussis, orbem perfundens, Æuangelium regni æterni cuius ipse ut suo loco probabitur rex erat,
ubique diffudit. Cernitis in gentes uniuersas diffusum Æuangelium
eius, et fidem Christi in cordibus uniuersorum Iudeis ex toto et
uobis ex parte excæptis feruere.

Non defuerunt tamen nomini Christiano multiplices exorti in
cordibus Christianorum errores, quos uerax et ueritatis sequax
æcclesia Dei statim ut sensit reppulit, statim ut aduertit dampnauit.
Ad quid istud, in hoc huius libri principio? Vt sicut dicere cæpe-
ram cogitetis et recogitetis non solum illos quos præmisi paganos,
non solum Iudæos, non solum Christianos hereticos, sed etiam uos
potuisse falli, potuisse decipi, potuisse tenebras pro luce, falsum
pro uero, seductorem pro propheta, et ut Iudæi circa mundi finem
facturi sunt, Antichristum pro Christo suscipere. Et ne ultra res
differatur, iam non eminus iacula emittenda, sed comminus
manus conserendæ sunt, cum pace tamen ut supra dixi, non cum
furore, cum ratione non cum insania, cum æquitate, non cum
iniquitate, ne forte non uideamur ueritatis amore inuestigare quod
uerum est, sed studio partium defensare quod falsum est.

Dixi superiori et proximo libro: "Inuito uos ad salutem non
quæ transit, sed quæ permanet, non quæ finitur cum uita breui, sed
quæ permanet in uitam æternam."[4] Hanc consequi, hac tempore a
Deo præstituto frui, mortalibus quidem datum est, sed non nisi
illis, qui de Deo quod est, non quod non est, sentiunt, qui eum non
iuxta cordis sui phantasmata, sed sicut ipse se coli et uult et præcipit
colunt.

Ad ista uos respondistis: "Absit ut aliter sentiat intellectus noster,
absit ut aliter se habeat professio nostra. Nos nichil de Deo somniauimus, nichil prorsus confinximus. Sentimus de ipso, fatemur de
ipso, non iuxta figmenta cordis nostri, sed iuxta quod tradidit
nobis missus ab ipso propheta noster. Ille cum sit ordine ultimus
in prophetis, et uelut signaculum omnium prophetarum, et legis
diuinæ non auctor sed lator, non dominus sed nuntius, mandata

[4] D 181rd.

265

cælestia a Deo per Gabrihelem sibi missa, nichil plus minusue
continentia accæpit, accæpta patribus nostris nobisque seruanda
tradidit. Hæc seruamus, hæc custodimus, hiis animas, hiis corpora,
D 189vs / hiis uitam mortemque nostram dicauimus."

Audite ergo quia iam tempus est cui animas uestras, cui corpora,
cui uitam mortemque uestram dicastis. Attendite si tuto in loco
spem uestram constituistis, si doctrinæ salubri si uero prophetæ
Dei et nuntio credidistis. Prophetam eum uocatis, nuntium Dei
dicitis. Concedimus quod uero Dei prophetæ credendum est, quod
uero Dei nuntio adquiescendum est. Sed uideatur ut dixi, utrum
uere Dei propheta fuerit, utrum uere nuntius Dei sit. Ad quod
aduertendum, quid prophetia sit, quid dicatur uidete.

Ait priums et summus in apostolis Christi apostolus Petrus,
cuius nomen cum toti orbi notum sit, uos ignorare non credimus,
cuius ex parte uitam, cuius mortem, cuius in urbe orbis capite
quæ Roma uocatur sepulchrum, ut arbitror non ignoratis: "Non
uoluntate," inquit, "humana allata est aliquando prophetia, sed
Spiritu Sancto inspirati locuti sunt sancti Dei homines."[5] Ex hiis
illius apostoli uerbis sic recte uel describere uel diffinire prophetiam possumus. Prophetia est rerum ignotarum aut de præteritis,
aut de præsentibus, aut de futuris non humana inuentione sed diuina
inspiratione facta prolatio. Sed nominis æthimologia magis ad
futura respicit, quam ad præterita uel ad præsentia. Quia tamen
eadem uirtute diuina qua reuelantur futura nota quandoque fiunt
et præterita et præsentia, horum etiam duorum temporum reuela-
tio uocatur prophetia. Ex prophetiæ diffinitione et prophetam
possumus diffinire. Propheta est, qui res ignotas aut præteriti temporis aut præsentis uel futuri, non humana cognitione edoctus, sed
Spiritu Dei inspiratus mortalibus manifestat.

Prophetiam præteriti temporis retexuit Moyses, quando dixit in
principio creasse Deum cælum et terram, creasse lucem, fecisse
cælum firmamentum et illud medium posuisse inter aquas supe-
riores et inferiores, produxisse ex terra herbam uirentem et pro-
ferentem semen, et lignum pomiferum faciens fructum, fecisse
solem lunam, ac reliqua astra, tam ex aquis pisces et uolatilia

[5] I Petr. 1:21.

266

quam ex terra quadrupedia, et reptilia produxisse, creasse tandem
hominem ad imaginem et similitudinem suam, ac dedisse ei
comparem similem.[6] Hæc uerba prophetica fuerunt, non de præsenti uel futuro tempore, sed de præterito, quæ propter hoc maxime se probant esse prophetica, quia ut quidam magnus de nostris
ait: "De illo tempore / locutus est homo quando non erat homo."[7] D 189vd

Probatur idem ex præsentis temporis prophetia esse propheta,
sicut legitur in uno ex quinque libris Moysi, qui Numeri dicitur.
Absortis enim ultione diuina maximo hiatu terræ rebellibus, Moysi
Chore, Dathan, et Abyron cum tabernaculis suis et uniuersa substantia, eaque de causa murmurantibus contra ipsum Iudeis, eumque occidere molientibus, fugit ille ad tabernaculum Domini.
Cumque iaceret coram Deo prostratus in terra, dixit ad Aaron
fratrem suum, summum tunc Dei pontificem: "Tolle thuribulum,
et hausto igne de altari, mitte incensum desuper pergens cito ad
populum, ut roges pro eis. Iam enim egressa est ira a Domino, et
plaga deseuit."[8] Præsentis ergo temporis prophetia tunc eius
Spiritus illustratus est, quando in tabernaculo Dei prostratus iacens,
quid in remota et diffusa multitudine agZeretur agnouit. Statimque
sequitur eadem scriptura: "Quod cum fecisset Aaron, et cucurrisset
ad mediam multitudinem, quam iam uastabat incendium optulit
thimiama. Et stans inter mortuos ac uiuentes pro populo deprecatus
est, et plaga cessauit. Fuerunt autem qui percussi sunt, quatuordecim milia hominum et septingenti, absque hiis qui perierant
in seditione Chore."[9] Hoc idem ut dixi de præsentis temporis est
prophetia.

De futuro autem tempore quis ex facili eius prophetica uerba
enumeret? Præsciuit et prædixit indicante sibi Deo decem famo-
sis plagis Ægyptum percutiendam, non simul sed separatim, non
una die, sed pluribus et diuersis diebus, nunc per aquas uersas in
sanguinem, nunc per ranas implentes omnia, nunc per sciniphes,
nunc per muscas diuersi generis, nunc per grauissimam animalium
pestem, nunc per puluerem Ægyptum operientem, nunc per
grandinem igni mixtam, nunc per locustam operientem super-

---

[6] Gen. 1-2.   [7] Hunc locum non locaui.
[8] Num. 16:46.   [9] Num. 16:47-49.

ficiem terræ, nunc per tenebras horribiles et palpabiles, nunc per mortes primogenitorum, quando in tota terra Ægypti non erat domus, in qua non esset mortuus. Secuta est maxima et ultima dans cunctis plagis præcedentibus finem plaga, hoc est Pharaonis ipsius in mare submersio, et totius exercitus eius nullo euadente perditio.[10] Præsciuit et prædixit iam dictorum rebellium terribilem interitum, præsciuit et prædixit prophetam a Deo in Israhel suscitandum, quem qui non audiret exterminaretur de populo suo, / præsciuit et prædixit quam plurima alia per totum Pentatheucum suum, hoc est per quinque quos supra nominaui libros suis in locis digesta. Hæc uniuersa singillatim antequam fierent prophetico Spiritu plenus Moyses iam dictus prædixit, seque uere prophetam Dei esse, ipsis uerborum effectibus declarauit. Hoc idem ante ipsum quidam, ut Enoch, Noe, Iacob et Ioseph, post ipsum plurimi, ut Samuhel, Dauid, Ysaias, Helyas, Helyseus, Ihremias, multique alii orbi notissimi.

D 190rs

At Mahumeth uester o Agareni, unde propheta a uobis probabitur? An quia quæ erant prius ignota mortalibus reuelauit præterita? An quia quæ alios latebant, indicauit præsentia? An quia quamlibet parua et uilia præsensit et prædixit futura? Vnde hoc inquam ei, ut propheta dicatur? An quia ipse sepe in Alchorano suo se prophetam nominat? Si prophetam se nominat, ostendat quid propheticum dixerit, quid propheticum fecerit. Ostendite et uosipsi michi, qui eum prophetam creditis, qui eum prophetam dicitis, unde propheta præteritorum, unde propheta præsentium, unde propheta rerum futurarum appareat. Reuoluite sepe nominatum Alchoran uestrum, scrutamini totum textum illius uestræ cælestis ut putatis scripturæ. Relegite ac recensete ab illius libri prima azoara hoc est oraculo, quod intitulatur "De Boue octoginta quinque uerborum,"[11] ac transitum facientes per azoaram "De gente Ioachim ducentorum uerborum,"[12] ac per alias per totum nefandi illius operis corpus diffusas, usque ad azoaram centesimam uigesimam tertiam,[13] quæ in ultimo posita libro illi finem imponit, cursum celerem continuate. Probate ex iam dicta

[10] Exod. 7:14.   [11] Kor. 2.   [12] Kor. 3.   [13] Kor. 114.

illa uestra sublimi scriptura eum saltem unum et solum uerbum propheticum protulisse.

Et ubi magis si propheta fuit eum se ostendere prophetam decuit, quam in libro cælitus ut scribit per thomos allato, sibique a Deo per Gabrihelem transmisso? Vbi se magis ostendere prophetam debuit, quam in libro cui super omnia inheretis, cui totam fidei uestræ summam credidistis, cui salutem uestram, cui ut supra scripsi, corpora uestra et animas deuouistis? Quæ causa esse potest, ut Deus eum prophetam nominet, et a Deo ut dicit propheta uocatus nulla prophetica prædicet? Quis unquam præcædentium prophetarum a Deo propheta dictus est, ipse tamen nulla prophetica / locutus est?

D 190rd

Non sic Moyses ut supra dixi noster, non sic Ysaias, cuius pene totus liber nil nisi propheticum sonat, nil nisi aut de proximo aut de longinquo uentura prænuntiat. De proximo, sicut illud quod regi Iudeorum Ezechiæ egrotanti, ac iam de uita desperanti, ait: "Hæc," inquit, "dicit Dominus: 'Ecce ego adiciam super dies tuos quindecim annos, et de manu regis Assyriorum eruam te, et ciuitatem istam, et protegam eam.' "[14] Quod et factum est. Nam et sospitati redditus, annis postea quindecim superuixit, et de manu regis Assyriorum erutus est, tam ipse quam regia ciuitas eius Ihrusalem, interficiente Deo sub unius nocturnæ horæ spacio de regis blasphemi exercitu, centum octoginta quinque milia, et a Deo protectus est, nullo regum, nulla gentium aduersus eum toto uitæ ipsius tempore præualente. Sic et pro quibusdam aliis ab eo prædictis, et proxime expletis, Dei propheta fuisse probatus est.

De longinquo, sicut Babilonis a Persis et Medis facta et ab ipso prædicta uastatio, sicut soluta a rege Cyro facta ante annos septuaginta a rege Chaldeo captiuitas, cuius etiam Cyri nomen suptili prophetiæ oculo ante annos fere trecentos, et præsciuit et prædixit, sicut post multa tempora iam dictæ Babilonis omnimodam ut nunc cernitur destructionem, quam et in solitudinem redigendam, et pro hominibus monstruosorum animalium et uenenatorum serpentium habitaculum futuram non tacuit. Rursum de longinquo Christi natiuitatem, cum dixit: "Ecce uirgo concipiet et pariet

[14] Isai. 38:5-6.

filium,"[15] quod uerum esse ipsi quoque affirmatis, baptismum salutare quod ab ipso traditum est Iudeis et gentibus, cum Deum introducens loquentem, ait: "Effundam super uos aquam mundam et mundabimini ab omnibus inquinamentis uestris, et ab uniuersis ydolis uestris mundabo uos,"[16] Christi miracula cum ait: "Tunc aperientur oculi cæcorum et aures surdorum patebunt, tunc saliet sicut ceruus claudus et aperta erit lingua mutorum,"[17] Christi passionem ubi dicit: "Sicut ouis ad occisionem ductus est, et tradidit in mortem animam suam, et cum sceleratis reputatus est."[18]

Et quid hiis plura de tanto propheta eloquar? Quæcunque de Christo, quæcunque de Christianorum sacramentis, quæcunque de Iudeorum reprobatione et gentium uocatione, quæcunque de statu post ipsum præsentis seculi et fide futuri prouenisse cernitur, tam clare Spiritu Dei illustratus prædixit, ut iuxta cuiusdam sapi-

D 190vs entis olim uerba, magis / uideatur præterita texere quam futura prædicere.

Sic post Ysaiam et Ihremias, cui postquam a Deo dictum est, "Prophetam in gentibus dedi te,"[19] prophetam Dei se uere esse, multis non tantum post mortem, sed etiam dum adhuc uiueret indiciis declarauit. Post mortem, ex septuaginta annorum numero quo toto tempore ut iam dictum est Iudei Babilonica captiuitate detenti sunt, cuius captiuitatis relaxatio ut supra scripsi ab Ysaia prædicta est, sed numerus annorum ab eo expressus non est, quem quia a solo Ihremia expressum, ac post mortem eius impletum et legimus et scimus, prophetico cum hoc Spiritu prædixisse, indeque uere eum prophetam Dei fuisse clarum est. Sic et qaundo ab Ysaia prædictam illam Babilonicam desolationem etiam ipse prædixit, sic et quando de Christo et eius genitrice prælocutus est, "Faciet Dominus nouum super terram, femina circumdabit uirum,"[20] et multa in hunc modum.

Ante mortem, cum regem Chaldeorum ad Syriam uenturum, cum per principes suos Ihrusalem obsessurum, ac post annos paucissimos eam capturum, et Iudaicum populum legis diuinæ contemptorem captiuaturum et præconatus est, et ut prædixerat im-

---

[15] Isai. 7:14.   [16] Ezech. 36:25.   [17] Isai. 35:5-6.
[18] Isai. 53:7, 12.   [19] Jer. 1:5.   [20] Jer. 31:22.

pleta contemplatus est. De quibus propheticis uerbis et illud fuit, nam uniuersa recolligere et ad medium deducere refugio, ne forte ista lecturis plus nimio prolixus uidear, illud inquam de similibus extitit, quod regi Sedechiæ ab ipso ad secretum colloquium euocatus, atque interrogatus, "Estne uerbum a Domino?" respondit, "Est. In manu regis Babilonis traderis."[21] Cumque ille subiunxisset uereor, "Iudeos qui transfugerunt ad Chaldeos, ne forte tradar in manibus eorum et illudant michi," respondit ille, iam secundo pro re simili euocatus: "Non te tradent. Audi queso uocem Domini, quam ego loquor ad te et bene tibi erit, et uiuet anima tua. Quod si nolueris, iste est sermo quem ostendit michi Dominus: 'Ecce omnes mulieres quæ remanserunt in domo regis Iudæ, educentur ad principes regis Babilonis. Et omnes uxores tuæ et filii tui educentur ad Chaldeos, et non effugies manus eorum, sed manu regis Babilonis capieris, et ciuitatem hanc comburet igni.' "[22] Noluit rex, uel timuit consilio prophetico adquiescere, et expertus est quicquid prædixerat illi propheta.

Sic Ihzechiel ut multos et multa præteream de eadem Sedechiæ captiuitate licet longe positus in Chaldea, quæ in Iudæa / futura D 190vd erant, et quæ iam pene fiebant, absens corpore, præsens Spiritu prædicens, ait: "Nunquid qui dissoluit pactum effugiet? Viuo, ego dicit Dominus Deus, quoniam in loco regis qui constituit eum regem, cuius fecit irritum iuramentum et soluit pactum quod habebat cum eo in medio Babilonis morietur."[23] Et in sequenti prophetiæ serie: "Et omnes," inquit, "profugi eius cum uniuerso agmine gladio cadent, residui autem in omnem uentum dispergentur, et scietis quia ego Dominus locutus sum."[24] Hæc ut propheta ille præfatus est, sic omnia contigerunt, rege Sedechia ab hostibus capto, et captiuato, ac deinde in Babilone mortuo, cunctisque profugis eius cum uniuerso agmine gladio cadentibus, residuisque in omnem uentum dispersis.

Sic et Danihel ex toto libri sui textu tam de proximo quam de longinquo futura prædicens, se clare Dei prophetam esse indicat. De quo ipsius prolixo uolumine hæc pauca excerpsi. Ait ille cui-

[21] Jer. 37:16.   [22] Jer. 38:19-23.
[23] Ezech. 17:15-16.   [24] Ezech. 17:21.

271

dam regi Chaldeo qui Nabugodonosor dicebatur, et sub cuius ipse degebat imperio somnium sibi proponenti, et interpretationem postulanti: "Domine mi, somnium hiis qui te oderunt, et interpretatio eius hostibus tuis sit. Arborem quam uidisti sublimem atque robustam cuius altitudo pertingit ad cælum et aspectus illius in omnem terram, et rami eius pulcherrimi, et fructus eius nimius, et esca omnium in ea, subter eam habitantes bestiæ agri, et in ramis eius commorantes aues cæli, tu es rex qui magnificatus es, et inualuisti, et magnitudo tua creuit et peruenit usque ad cælum, et potestas tua in terminos uniuersæ terræ. Quod autem uidit rex uigilem, et sanctum, descendere de cælo, et dicere: 'Succidite arborem, et dissipate illam, attamen germen radicum eius in terra dimittite, et uinciatur ferro et ære in herbis foris, et rore cæli conspergatur, et cum feris sit pabulum eius, donec septem tempora commutentur super eum.' Hæc est interpretatio sententiæ Altissimi, quæ superuenit super dominum meum regem. Eiicient te ab hominibus, et cum bestiis feris erit habitatio tua. Et fænum ut bos comedes, et rore cæli infunderis. Septem quoque tempora mutabuntur super te, donec scias quod dominetur Excelsus super regnum hominum, et cuicunque uoluerit det / illud. Quod autem præcæpit ut relinqueretur germen radicum eius id est arboris, regnum tuum tibi manebit, postquam cognoueris potestatem esse cælestem. Quam ob rem rex consilium meum placeat tibi, et peccata tua elemosinis redime, et iniquitates tuas misericordiis pauperum, forsitan ignoscet delictis tuis."[25]

D 191rs

Cum hæc uniuersa prophetico illustratus Spiritu prædixisset, post unius tantum anni spacium impleta esse non tacet. "Omnia," inquit, "hæc uenerunt super Nabugodonosor regem. Post finem mensium duodecim in aula regis Babilonis deambulabat rex et ait: 'Nonne hæc est Babilon magna quam ego ædificaui in domum regni, in robore fortitudinis meæ, et in gloria decoris mei?' Cum adhuc sermo esset in ore regis, uox de cælo ruit: 'Tibi dicitur, Nabugodonosor rex: Regnum transiit a te, et ab hominibus te eicient, et cum bestiis feris erit habitatio tua. Fænum quasi bos

[25] Dan. 4:16-24.

comedes, et septem tempora mutabuntur super te, donec scias quod dominetur Excelsus in regno hominum et cuicunque uoluerit det illud.' Eadem hora sermo completus est super Nabugodonosor. Ex hominibus abiectus est, et fænum ut bos comedit, et rore cæli corpus eius infectum est, donec capilli eius in similitudinem aquilarum crescerent, et ungues eius quasi auium.

"Igitur post finem dierum ego Nabugodonosor oculos meos ad cælum leuaui, et sensus meus redditus est michi, et Altissimo benedixi, et uiuentem in sempiternum laudaui et glorificaui, quia potestas eius potestas sempiterna, et regnum eius in generatione et generationem, et omnes habitatores terræ apud eum in nichilum reputati sunt. Iuxta uoluntatem enim suam facit, tam in uirtutibus cæli, quam in habitatoribus terræ, et non est qui resistat manui eius, et dicat ei: 'Quare fecisti?' In ipso tempore sensus meus reuersus est ad me, et ad honorem regni mei decoremque perueni. Et figura mea reuersa est ad me, et optimates mei et magistratus mei requisierunt me. Et in regno meo restitutus sum, et magnificentia amplior addita est michi. Nunc igitur ego Nabugodonosor laudo et magnifico et glorifico regem cæli, quia omnia opera eius uera, et uiæ eius iudicia, et gradientes in superbia potest humiliare."[26]

Sic et regi Balthasar iam dicti regis successori, cum ab eo de scriptura parietis / consultus esset respondit, quod de instanti hoc D 191rd est eadem qua loquebatur nocte futurum erat. Sic multa maxima et mira tam de proximo quam de longinquo ut dixi tempore propheta ille prædicens, se uere Dei nuntium, se uere Dei prophetam rerum prædictarum effectibus declarauit.

Sic et tempore Roboam filii Salomonis regnantis super duas tribus Iudaici populi, ueniens quidam uir Dei uere propheta cuius nomen reticetur, ad quendam alium regem ydolatram, decem eiusdem gentis tribubus imperantem, dum eum super altare sacrificantem ydolis inuenisset, ait: "Altare altare, hæc dicit Dominus: 'Ecce filius nascetur domui Dauid, Iosyas nomine, et immolabit super te sacerdotes excelsorum, qui nunc in te thura succendunt, et ossa hominum incendet super te.' Deditque in die illa signum dicens: 'Hoc erit signum quod locutus est Dominus: Ecce altare

---

[26] Dan. 4:25-34.

scindetur, et effundetur cinis qui in eo est.' Cumque audisset rex
sermonem hominis Dei quem inclamauerat contra altare in
Bethel, extendit manum suam de altari dicens: 'Apprehendite
eum.' Et exaruit manus eius quam extenderat contra eum, nec
ualuit rex eam retrahere ad se. Altare quoque scissum est, et effusus est cinis de altari, iuxta signum quod prædixerat uir Dei in
sermone Domini. Et ait rex ad uirum Dei: 'Deprecare faciem
Domini Dei tui, et ora pro me ut restituatur manus mea michi.'
Orauit uir Dei faciem Domini, et reuersa est manus regis ad eum,
et facta est sicut prius fuerat."[27] Ecce quam magna propheta hic
et de longe post futuro tempore, et de instanti prædixit. De longe
post futuro, cum post ducentos ad minus annos nasciturum regem
etiam nominat dicens: "Ecce filius nascetur domui Dauid Iosyas
nomine." De instanti, cum dicit: "Hoc erit signum quod locutus
est Dominus: 'Ecce altare scindetur, et effundetur cinis qui in
eo est.'" Altare enim statim ut loqui cessauit, scissum est, et effusus
est cinis eius.

Sic Helyas, sic Helyseus, sic innumeri alii, quos præ multitudine,
piget referre, plurima et magna prædixerunt, quorum ueracem
in omnibus prophetiam res absque diminutione, ut prædictum fuerat implere docuerunt. Et ut aliqua, etiam de hiis
quos nominaui prophetica proferam, impletum est quod Helyas
ydolatræ populo comminans prædixerat: "Viuit Dominus, si erit
D 191vs (hoc est non erit) ros aut pluuia / nisi iuxta oris mei uerbum."[28]
Nam triennio ac sex mensibus omni rore ymbreque suspenso,
tandem ad preces eius et cælum dedit pluuiam, et terra dedit fructum suum. Impletum est et illud, quod cuidam regi Iudeorum
prophetice prædixerat: "Quia," inquit, "misisti ad consulendum
Beelzebub Deum Accharon quasi non esset Deus in Israhel, a quo
posses interrogare sermonem, idcirco de lectulo super quem ascen-
disti non descendes, sed morte morieris."[29] Impletum est et aliud,
quod quidem non ipse sed filii prophetarum de ipso non semel
tantum sed bis Helyseo eius discipulo dixerunt: "Nunquid nosti
quia hodie Dominus tollet dominum tuum a te?" Quibus ille

---

[27] III Reg. 13:2-6.   [28] III Reg. 17:1.   [29] IV Reg. 1:6.

bis interrogatus bis respondit: "Et ego noui. Silete."[30] Quod impletum esse et currus igneus et equi ignei magistrum et discipulum diuidentes, ipseque Helyas per turbinem raptus in cælum ostenderunt.

Quid et de Helyseo? Duplicem in se spiritum Helyæ fieri poposcerat, sed licet res illa, teste eodem propheta ad impetrandum esset difficilis, quod postulauerat impetrauit. Sed quando eius propheticus Spiritus, et mens rerum tam præsentium quam futurarum sollicita indagatrix, et ueracissima pronuntiatrix explicabitur? Spoponderat ille leproso regis Syriæ principi purgationem a lepra, cumque ut curari posset Iordanicis fluentis intingui mandauerat. Obædierat ille, licet prius de imperatis indignans, consilio seruorum et obædientia mandato prophetali exhibita, salutem concupitam meruerat. Tactus est pestifera et miseris mortalibus nimium assueta cupiditate Gyezi puer eius, et quod gratis a Deo per prophetam datum fuerat, multo argenti ac uestium precio uemundare nisus, lepram principis iam curati simul cum opibus illicite concupitis, leprosus ipse subito factus sibi protinus uendicauit. Non latuit hoc licet absentem prophetam, nec se hoc latuisse reuerso ad se puero indicauit. Ait enim illi: "Vnde uenis Gyezi?" Qui respondit: "Non iuit seruus tuus quoquam." Et ille: "Nonne," ait, "cor meum in præsenti erat, quando reuersus est homo de curru suo in occursum tui? Nunc igitur accæpisti argentum et accæpisti uestes, ut emas oliueta et uineta, et oues et boues et seruos et ancillas. Sed et lepra Naaman adherebit tibi et semini tuo in sempiternum." Subditque scriptura: "Egressus ab eo leprosus quasi nix."[31] Ecce non fallax sed uerax propheta, non falsus sed uerus / D 191vd nuntius Dei curandum leprosum et presciit et prædixit et factum est, auarum seruum lepra curati hominis respergendum et presciit et prædixit, et factum est.

Quid simile o Agareni tot tantisque tam maximis prophetis, uester ille, ille plane, ille uester propheta saltem de re qualibet uili et modica aut præsciit aut prædixit? Proponatur liber eius, reuoluatur Alchoran eius sublimis illa et cælestis iuxta uos ut

---

[30] IV Reg. 2:3, 5.   [31] IV Reg. 5:25-27.

dixi scriptura, nulla azoara excæpta per uerba singula replicetur, procedat ille ad publicum tantorum propheta populorum, et se aliquid ut dictum est uile uel modicum prophetice prædixisse, ex libro quem suis reliquit ostendat.

Sed redeat adhuc Helyseus: "Rex Syriæ," ait quædam Hebraica et Christiana scriptura, "pugnabat contra Israhel consiliumque iniit cum seruis suis dicens: 'In illo loco et illo ponamus insidias.' Misit itaque uir Dei Helyseus ad regem Israhel dicens: 'Caue ne transeas per locum illum quia ibi Syri in insidiis sunt.' Misit itaque rex Israhel ad locum quem dixerat ei uir Dei et præoccupauit eum et obseruauit se ibi, non semel neque bis. Conturbatumque est cor regis Syriæ pro hac re. Et conuocatis seruis suis ait: 'Quare non indicatis quis proditor mei sit apud regem Israhel?' Dixitque unus seruorum eius: 'Nequaquam domine mi rex, sed Helyseus propheta qui est in Israhel indicat regi Israhel omnis uerba quæcunque locutus fueris in conclaui tuo.' "[32] Audistis? Præsciebat et predicebat Spiritu prophetico plenus propheta regi Israhel Syrorum insidias, nec uspiam oculum illum inuisibilem aliquo astu hostium acies effugere poterat. Penetrabat suptilis ille et perspicax prophetæ intuitus remota terrarum profunda uallium, abdita siluarum, intererat secretis propheticus auditus consiliis, claustris uel portarum repagulis repelli non poterat, cubiculis regalibus non deerat, cuncta quæ hostiliter et callide longe positi aduersarii machinabantur, regi suo propheta nuntiis semper intercurrentibus indicabat.

Quare ergo propheta iuxta uos tam famosus, aliqua saltem modica prophetiæ scintilla in tam frequentibus suis contra hostes expeditionibus, sibi ne dicam alteri non consuluit? Quare cum sepe uictus de præliis fugerit, se uincendum ab hostibus non præsciuit? Quare non præuidit et præcauit in quodam suo procinctu cui ipse / interfuit, unum sibi de inferioribus dentibus dentem excutiendum, labrum præcidendum, uulnera fronti et faciei suæ ab hostibus inferenda?[33] Sed quid? Expecto o Hysma-

D 192rs

[32] IV Reg. 6:8-12.
[33] *Rescriptum Christiani*, A 151vs.

elitæ aut a uobis aut ab ipso proferri ex iam dicto Alchoran hoc est lege uestra aliquid, prophetam uestrum prophetice prædixisse, ne dicam aliqua ex prædictis ut ab eo prædicta sunt contigisse. Quid enim ex prædictis ab eo prouenire potuit, de quo clarum est quod nichil prædixerit?

Sed forte opponet uestrum aliquis et producet ad medium uelut magnum quiddam scripturam aliam, genealogiam eius, actus quosdam ipsius et prælia continentem. In qua legitur eum prædixisse duodecim de gente propria uel familia quæ Chorais dicebatur, singillatim sibi inuicem succedentes se mortuo principaturos, ex quibus tres primos nominasse scribitur: Eubocaram, Aornar, et Odmen.[34] Sed nec sic nec sic prodesse poterit parti suæ diabolica fraus, nec pro splendore tenebras, pro lucis angelo Sathanan fuligineum ingerere præualebit.

Et quis nobis o Agareni quos causa assumpta cogente totiens nomino, ad probandum hunc de quo agitur prophetam Dei non fuisse, quis inquam aptior ad hoc probandum inueniri poterit, quam ipse quem Dei prophetam dicitis? Si plane ipse se negauerit prophetam, nunquid ipso resistente eum dicetis prophetam? Hoc quomodo? Audite, et si aliquis in uobis rationabilis intellectus superest, aduertite. Et ne diutius uos protrahens plus nimio suspensos teneam, audite ipsum loquentem in Alchoran uestro, cui scripturæ ab aliquo contradici nefas putatis: "Quicquid," ait, "inueneritis pro me scriptum, conferte illud cum Alchoran, et si ei non concordauerit, scitote quia innocens sum ab illa scriptura, et non est mea."[35] Conferatur ergo scriptura iam dicta cum isto Alchoran, et uideatur utrum concors cum illa, aut discors ab ipsa sit.

Dicit illa ut iam dictum est eum prædixisse duodecim uiros de stirpe uel gente sua quæ Chorais uocabatur principatui suo post se singillatim principaturos, quorum primos tres ut præmissum est nominat. Hoc quidem scriptura illa, ab alio quam ab ipso edita. Ipse uero non alius e contra: "Quicquid inueneritis pro me scriptum, conferte illud cum Alchoran, et si ei non concordauerit,

[34] *Fabulæ Saracenorum*, A 8rs-vs.
[35] *Rescriptum Christiani*, A 154rd.

D 192rd scitote quia innocens sum ab illa scriptura, / et non est mea." Non
concordat autem cum Alchoran, quoniam totus ipsius libri textus,
nichil ab eo prophetice dictum sonat, nichil de futuris eum prædixisse scribit. Nulli ergo magis ut iudicia tam æcclesiastica quam
Romana, immo tam diuina quam humana fatentur, et ratio ipsa docet, nulli inquam magis quam de se confesso credendum est. Post-
ponantur igitur, et tantæ dignitatis quantum ad uos libro, unde-
cunque occurentia scripta subponantur, quia teste Mahumeth uestro, siqua scriptura ut eius utar uerbis non concordauerit Alchoran
suo, innocens est ab illa, et non est eius.

Nonne ista o uiri sufficiunt ad comprobandum eum non esse prophetam? Sed succedant hiis alia, et impium immo perditissimum,
hominem ab omni prophetica gratia etiam ipso fatente procul
exclusum declarent. Introducens enim uelut poetico figmento
nequam et mendax homo Deum sibi loquentem, sic in Alchoran
ait: "Tu quidem nequaquam ad eos cum Dei miraculis manifestis
uenies, quoniam ea uelut odiosa atque contraria reiiciunt, et ueritati ad eos uenienti contradixerunt."[36] Et rursum: "Nisi sciremus
eos tibi non credituros [sicut nec aliis crediderunt], daremus tibi
signa et prodigia."[37] Quid dicam? Quis digne mirari, quis effari,
quis congruis uerbis irridere tantam hominis stultitiam immo in-
saniam potest?

Et ut ad ipsum de quo agitur uerba conuertam: Hæccine tot
causa est o Mahumeth, qua sine miraculis missus a Deo ad homines
uenisti, quoniam ea uelut odiosa atque contraria reiecturi erant, et
ueritati ad eos uenienti contradicturi? Hæccine inquam causa est,
qua signa et prodigia tibi data non sunt, quia præsciebat Deus
eos tibi non credituros, sicut nec aliis crediderunt? Si hoc tibi a
Deo ut dicis dictum est, falsa est plane, falsa est absque dubio
præscientia Dei. Quomodo enim iuxta hæc quæ proponis falsa non
est præscientia Dei, si præsciuit homines tibi etiam cum signis et
prodigiis misso non credituros, cum sine miraculis signis et prodigiis, nugacissimis fabulis tuis populi multi crediderint, sectæ
nefariæ adquieuerint, infernali doctrinæ tuæ seipsos, nil morati

[36] Kor. 6:4-5, A 49rd.
[37] Kor. 17:61, A 153rd, 153vs.

subdiderint? Et cui hoc commentum tuum, cui plane non appareat enerue, fragile, testeum?

Elige certe elige de duobus quod malueris. Aut dic Deum in prescientia sua errasse, dic mentitum esse, quod tibi non credituros, homines etiam cum signis et prodigiis dixerit, cum tibi Arabes, Persæ, Syri, Ægyptii, / multaque pars Afrorum etiam sine mira- D 192vs culis crediderit, aut si fateri uereris Deum errasse, Deum mentitum esse, aufer falsa, aufer blasphema de libro tuo, immo quod sanioris consilii est, dampna ut erroribus, ut mendaciis, ut blasphemiis respersum totum Alchoran tuum.

Sed quid est et illud, quod postquam Deum inducis tibi loquentem quod præmisi, "Nisi sciremus eos tibi non credituros," addis, "sicut nec aliis crediderunt?" Qui sunt isti alii quibus homines non crediderunt? An forte Moyses? An forte ipse Christus? Non occurunt alii, non occurunt plane alii, de quibus hoc te sensisse, de quibus hoc te dixisse conicere possim. Sunt hii summi et soli legislatores in orbe, Moyses Iudeorum, Christus uniuersarum gentium. Moyses uenit cum signis et prodigiis, Christus multo magis cum signis et prodigiis. Credidit Moysi uisis signis et prodigiis Iudeorum populus, credidit Christo eiusque apostolis uisis maximis et innumeris miraculis mundus. Qui sunt ergo de quibus dixisti: "Sicut nec aliis crediderunt?" Istis enim miracula facientibus crediderunt a Deo inspirati homines, tibi sine signis uana et falsa loquenti a te decæpti crediderunt homines. Falsum est ergo oraculum tuum, quo tibi a Deo dictum finxisti, nec illis credidisse, nec tibi credituros homines.

Sed redeo ad illud quod probare proposui tuo te testimonio prophetam non esse. Quando enim signa tibi a Deo data non esse affirmas utique te prophetam negas. Quid enim insignius prophetia, quod signum maius prophetia? Quid enim rectius signum, quid prodigium, quid miraculum uocatur, quam aut præterita quantum ad homines ignorata referre, aut præsentia reserare, aut futura prædicere? Cum ergo de præclaris quæ a Deo dantur signis prophetia sit, cum tibi signa a Deo data non esse prædicas, prophetam utique te esse negas. Aut igitur profitere signa tibi a Deo data esse et propheta permane, aut si tibi signa data non sunt,

279

propheta esse desine. Vrget enim undique te coartans ratio, ut si sicut dictum est, signa tibi esse data, negaueris prophetam te pariter diffitearis. Si data tibi dixeris, necesse est ut Deum mendacii arguas, necesse est ut quod mendaciter scripsisti, corrigas. Et quia monstruosa uerba tua et hactenus inaudita pene obstupescere me cogunt, quis o miser ex uniuersorum collegio prophetarum sic se dixit prophetam ut tu, sic se uoluit credi prophetam ut tu?

D192vd   Vitabant illi ut ueri et humiles serui Dei / gloriam magni nominis, et cum uere Dei prophetæ essent prophetas se dicere salua quantum poterant ueritate refugiebant. Vnde quidam ex ipsis, qui Amos uocabatur, dicentibus sibi, "Noli prophetare in Bethel, neque stilles super domum ydoli," respondit, "Non sum propheta et non sum filius prophetæ, sed puer armentarius ego sum, uellicans sichomoros."[38] Et Iohannes quem propheta uester baptistam nominare refugit, sed Zachariæ filium dicit, multaque tam ipsum quam parentes eius in Alchoran suo laude extollit, dicentibus sibi inuidis Iudeorum sacerdotibus et Leuitis "Propheta es tu?" respondit, "Non sum."[39] Qui tamen uere prophetæ Dei erant, sed prophetas se non esse, alio qui ad uos nunc non pertinet quamdiu infideles estis intellectu, salua ueritatis suæ professione dicebant. Reliquerunt tamen in libris suis de quibus dubitari non posset signa prophetica et quæ prædicebant aut impleta ipso suo tempore demonstrabant, aut implenda ut apud posteros postmodum claruit declarabant.

At uester ille, et quod satis admirando frequentare non possum ille, prophetam se dicit, Deum in scriptis suis se uocantem prophetam introducit. Et cum pene usque ad nauseam se Dei prophetam dicat, affirmet et replicet, nichil de futuris loquitur, nichil propheticum sonat, nichil a se non solum prædictum uel impletum ostendit, sed nec implendum prædicit. Taceo illa quæ de paradyso uoluptuosa uel de inferno phantastica promittit, in quibus ante non potest apparere propheta, quam ab illis qui in paradyso uel in inferno fuerint probentur impleta. Non fuit ipsi nec esset michi si uellem difficile me uocare prophetam, non esset difficile scribere,

[38] Amos 7:13, 16.
[39] Joan. 1:21.

et scripto inducere Deum me uocare prophetam, non esset difficile prædicare me hominibus Dei prophetam. Possem fingere quæ uellem, de hiis quæ post finem mundi et post rerum occasum aut futura sunt, aut non, nec possem de mendacio argui, in hac uita, prædicendo ea que futura sunt, aut non, post hanc uitam.

Sileat ego commentum diabolicum et sicut supra dixi, fragile, enerue, ac testeum, quia propheta credi non potest, prædicendo ea quæ post mundi huius finem futura sunt, nisi se probet prophetam in hiis et ex hiis quæ ante mundi finem sunt. Assumat si uult propheta credi testes prophetiæ suæ non ex mortuis sed ex uiuentibus, non ex hiis quæ post / mortem implenda promittat, sed ex hiis quæ ante mortem impleta ostendat. Hoc modo, hoc tali tamque euidenti argumento credit Christianus prophetis suis, non quia tantum prophetas se dixerunt, sed quia prophetas se esse euidentibus signis, claris miraculis, ipsisque ad eis rerum prædictarum effectibus absque aliquo dubietatis uestigio comprobarunt. D 193rs

Aut ergo talibus indiciis te o Mahumeth ostende prophetam, aut si hoc non potueris desine te o dampnate atque dampnande uocare prophetam. Et licet quæ præmisi sufficere possint ad demonstrandum longe te esse a prophetica gratia aggrediar tamen uelut ab altero exordio ista legentibus ostendere, te non esse prophetam.

Prophetarum uel qui fuerunt uel qui dicuntur, alii boni, alii mali. Bonorum alii prædicentes uniuersalia, alii particularia, alii de eisdem simul uniuersalia et particularia. Malorum alii fallaces, alii ueraces. Sunt preter hos, qui non prophetæ sed uulgari nomine diuini dicuntur, ut augures, arioli, aruspices, magi, sortilegi. Prosequatur ergo stilus eo ordine singulorum distinctiones, ut proposite sunt.

Boni sunt, quorum uita laudabilis, quorum prophetia uel prædicatio uerax. De quorum numero sunt quos supra scripsi: Moyses, Ysaias, Ihremias, Ihzechiel, Danihel, multique alii. De hiis, et ipse Christus. Qui quamuis cunctorum prophetarum Dominus et Deus sit, tamen quia multa prophetica dixit, propheta uocatus est. Testatur hoc Æuangelium, quod ei datum ipsi o Sarraceni fatemini, sicut ibi de illo a turbis dictum legitur, "Propheta magnus surrexit in nobis,"[40] et sicut ipse de seipso, "Non capit perire prophetam extra Ihrusalem."[41] Qui tam uitæ quam prædicationi suæ uerax ut decebat testimonium ferens in eodem Æuangelio Iudæis secum altercantibus, ait: "Quis ex uobis arguit me de peccato?"[42] Nullus enim eum de peccato arguere poterat, qui sine peccato erat. Istud quidem de uita. Sed et de prædicatione quid? "Si ueritatem dico, quare uos non creditis michi?"[43] Nam nichil nisi quod uerum erat, ueritas proferre poterat. Est igitur ipse cum aliis bonis prophetis, et etiam super alios bonus propheta.

Sed mali prophetæ qui sunt? Quorum uita reproba, quorum prophetia uel prædicatio falsa. Tales erant tempore Helyæ, illi qui in libro Regum Israhel et Iuda leguntur, quadringenti quinqua-
D 193rd ginta prophetæ Baal, et item quadringenti / lucorum. Quos idem Helyas oblatum Deo sacrificium, igneque cælesti absumptum, suo iussu a populo comprehensos ad torrentem Cyson multo zeli diuini ignitus feruore pertrahi fecit, et ut pessimos ydolatras interfecit.[44]

Bonorum prophetarum ut dixi qui uniuersalia, hoc est ad uniuersos pertinentia prædixerunt, hii sunt ex parte, quos supra nominaui, cum cunctis pene aliis qui boni prophetæ dicuntur, quorum ut præmisi uita laudabilis est, et prædicatio uerax. Ad uniuersos enim pertinet, quod ab illis de Christo prædictum est, qui ut ait in Æuangelio magnus quidam iustus: "Positus est in ruinam et in resurrectionem multorum."[45] Cuius uita, cuius prædicatio, cuius miracula, cuius mors, cuius resurrectio, cuius a cæli egressio, et ad ipsos regressio, credentibus ad uitam, incredulis ad mortem facta sunt. Ipsius tandem in fine seculi, uniuersale et ultimum iudicium, perpetuas sedes toti mortalium massæ, ante tremendam maiestatem eius ui diuina collectæ distribuet, pro meritis singulorum unumquemque aut igni perpetuo tradens, aut uitæ secum sempiternæ restituens. Hoc modo et cuncta reliqua quæ in uerbis illis uel libris propheticis leguntur, ad omnes non ad quosdam pertinentia, siue in bono siue in malo accæpta, illos respiciunt, quos uniuersales prophetas nomino.

Particulares illos dico, qui non illa quæ ad uniuersos pertinent

[40] Luc. 7:16. [41] Luc. 13:33. [42] Joan. 8:46.
[43] *ibid.* [44] III Reg. 18. [45] Luc. 2:34.

prædixerunt, sed qui ea quæ ad quosdam populos, uel quæ ad quasdam nominatim expressas personas pertinebant, prophetico Spiritu
prælocuti sunt. De quibus est Ionas, qui ad gentilem tantum
Niniuitarum populum a Deo missus est, licet illa eius missio uni-
uerarum gentium uocationem præsignauerit, licet quod mersus
in mare, quod uoratus a pisce, quod in eius uentre, manens illesus,
quod incolumis et a belua et a mari euadens, actu non uerbo, salua-
tricem Christi mortem, eiusque a morte cunctis miraculis præfe-
rendam resurrectionem prophetauerit.

De istis est et Samuhel, qui non uniuersalia sed quædam ad quosdam specialiter pertinentia prædixit, ut Heli sacerdoti de hiis quæ
peruentura erant posteris domus eius, ut Sauli primo regi Hebreo-
rum, prius de asinabus Cis patris sui perditis et inuentis, post de
regno eius ad proximum et emulum transferendo, ac de quibusdam aliis, uel ad solam gentem Iudaicam uel ad quasdam certas
personas pertinentibus causis. / De hiis et ille eiusdem temporis   D 193vs
propheta, qui eius a scriptura sacra non expresso proprio nomine
uocatur uir Dei, et qui post multa quæ iam dicto Hely uentura
prædixerat, id etiam addidit: "Hoc," inquit, "erit tibi signum
quod uenturum est duobus filiis tuis, Ofni et Finees: In die una
morientur ambo."[46] Quod et factum est.

De hiis est et ille, quem eadem scriptura tacito nomine prophetam nominat, et quem cuidam regi Israhel de rege Syriæ uictoriam
consecuto inducit loquentem: "Vade et confortare et scito, et uide
quid facias. Sequenti enim anno, rex Syriæ ascendet contra te."[47]
Rursus eidem regi alter sine nomine propheta: "Hæc," ait, "dicit
Dominus: 'Quia dixerunt Syri, "Deus montium est Dominus, et
non Deus uallium," dabo omnem multitudinem grandem hanc in
manu tua, et scietis quia ego sum Dominus.' "[48] Quod et sicut prædictum fuerat septima statim die impletum est. Nam inito Hebrei
contra Syros prælio percusserunt de ipsis centum milia perditum,
in die una. Fugerunt et qui reliqui erant in ciuitatem, et cecidit
murus super uiginti quinque milia hominum qui remanserant.
Hæc a iam dictis prophetis prædicta non fuerunt uniuersalia, sed

[46] I Reg. 2:34.   [47] III Reg. 20:22.   [48] III Reg. 20:28.

aut de singulis gentibus, aut de certis personis, et de propriis ipsa-
rum prouentibus præostensa.

De hiis est et magnus Helyas, de hiis ipso quantum ad miracula
spectat non inferior Helyseus. Quorum alter ut supra dixi regi
Ochoziæ mortem minatus est, illeque ut prædictum fuerat mortuus
est, alter alteri regi qui Ionas dicebatur, frequentes de rege Syriæ
triumphos prædixit, quod et sic contigit, et quædam similia ab ipsis
quibusdam prædicta, et ut dictum fuerat, adimpleta.

Sunt igitur hii quos præmisi, multique quos reticui de illorum
numero, quos quia non ea quæ ad omnes sed quæ ad quosdam
spectant prophetico prædixerunt Spiritu, particulares dico prophetas. Sed distinguendum est inter hos et illos, et caute ac sollicite
aduertendum, uniuersales hoc est ad uniuersos pertinentia prædicentes, iam a Christi tempore nec potuisse nec deinceps usque ad
mundi finem esse posse prophetas. Nam quicquid ad communem
mortalium uel ipsius mundi statum aut defectum, quicquid ad
religionem ueracem aut fallacem, quicquid ad debitos et uniuersales bonorum aut malorum fines spectat, totum a iam dictis qui
uniuersales dicuntur prophetæ prædictum, et ab ipsis ad doctrinam
D 193vd et memoriam posterorum litteris traditum est. / Quod ex maxima
iam parte impletum, ex toto in seculi fine implendum seruatur.

Vnde cessantibus, et in Iohanne quem nos baptistam, uos filium
Zachariæ dicitis, nec nos eius eum esse filium negamus, omnino
inquam apud gentem Iudaicam deficientibus prophetis, quæ sola
usque ad Christum diuinæ legis cultrix extiterat, illud tantum
prophetiæ genus cessauit, quod ad statum uniuersalem pertinebat,
quia uniuersis ad id spectantibus plene præmissis, necessarium iam
non erat. Non fuit igitur Mahumeth uester ut dicitis signaculum
prophetarum hoc est ultimis in prophetis, sed Iohannes baptista, de
quo Christus in Æuangelio, iuxta uos sibi dato ait: "Lex et prophetæ usque ad Iohannem."[49] Prophetæ plane illi, qui ad omnes pertinentia prædicerent, non illi qui aliqua personalia prophetarent.

Illos enim qui personarum aut temporum uarios euentus post
Iohannem baptistam prophetico Spiritu sepius prædixerunt, in

[49] Luc. 16:16.

diuersis temporibus ac diuersis mundi partibus frequenter habuit
et experta est æcclesia Christi, sicut Paulum apostolum qui multa
de futuris et impleta et implenda prædixit. Impleta, ut in uobis et
in Iudæis, quando dixit: "Erit tempus cum sanam doctrinam non
sustinebunt," et in eodem uersu, "A ueritate auditum auertent, ad
fabulas autem conuertentur."[50] Nam claret orbi preter uos et ipsos
quod tam uos quam ipsi ut suo loco probabitur, a ueritate auditum
auertistis, et ad fabulas hunc conuertistis, a ueritate Christiana uos
ad fabulas Mahumeth, Iudæi, ad fabulas Thalmuth. Implenda uero
prædixit, quando reuelandum hominem peccati, "Filius perditionis
qui aduersatur et extollitur supra omne quod dicitur Deus aut quod
colitur,"[51] eumque in templo Dei sessurum, quem nos Antichristum dicimus, scripsit.

Sic et alios ex apostolis sic plurimos ex aliis eorum discipulis qui
et prophetæ dicti sunt et prophetas se esse rerum prædictarum
effectibus se ostenderunt. De talibus et ille fuit, qui Agabus uocabatur, qui zona Pauli Ihrusalem euntis suos pedes alligans, ait:
"Virum cuius hæc zona est, sic alligabunt in Ihrusalem."[52] Qui
breui tempore elapso cum urbem illam adisset, captus a Iudæis
alligatus a tribuno, flagellatus a Romanis, ueridicum fuisse prophetam illum ostendit. Et quis huiusmodi prophetarum numerum,
qui post Christum inter Christianos tam uita quam prophetia
splenduerunt explicet?

Si loquerer fidelibus et Christo credentibus, pateret campus im-
mensus. Quando enim / uel a me uel a quolibet explicari posset D 194rs
tanta prophetarum non uniuersalia ut præmisi sed singularia ut dixi
a Christo usque ad nostra tempora prædicentium numerositas?
Si eorum singillatim nomina uel numerum qui in parte huius
propheticæ gratiæ claruerunt ex ueracibus gestis collecta retexere
uellem, fidem dictis ut arbitror adhibere refugeretis. Quomodo
enim prophetis Dei credere possetis, qui necdum Deo ipsi creditis?
Sed scio hunc esse intellectum uestrum, hanc esse professionem
uestram, uos uero Deo et in uerum Deum credere. Sed utrum hoc

[50] II Tim. 4:3-4.
[51] II Thess. 2:3-4.
[52] Acta 21:11.

uerum sit, subsequens et uos per Dei Spiritum deuincens ratio declarabit.

Interim rem propositam sermo rationi famulans prosequatur. Erat autem sermo ille, erat ratio illa, qua de uniuersalis prophetiæ modo distinctione præmissa, de sequenti hoc est singulari uel personali prophetiæ modo iuxta propositam partitionem agebatur. De illo inquam, plane prophetiæ modo, quo singularia ut dixi prædicuntur, non quo uniuersalia prophetantur. Nam ille ut sic loquar uniuersalis prophetiæ modus, ab ipsa pene primi hominis creatione, exortus est, sed in Iohanne ut dixi consummatus est. Particularis uero aut personalis et ante Iohannem et post, multis datus est, et adhuc fortasse pluribus dandus. Hac gemina discretione prophetice gratiæ descripta, ad uniuersales simul et particulares prophetas sermo redeat, et qui sint ex scriptis declaret.

De istorum numero rursus Ysaiam produco, qui sicut uniuersalia prædixisse præostensus est, sic quod etiam singularia ad quasdam gentes, uel personalia ad quasdam personas pertinentia prædixerit probandum est. Ad quasdam gentes, ut illud, quod contra Babilonem, quod contra Moab, quod contra Damascum, quod contra Ægyptum, quod contra Ydumeos, quod contra Arabiam, quod contra Tyrum, ut lectio libri eius indicat prophetauit. Ad quasdam personas, ut illud, quod de rege Assyriorum Sennacherib, quod de rege Iudeorum Ezechia, quod de quibusdam aliis sicut ibi diffusis legitur prophetauit.

Sequitur hunc et suprascriptus Ihremias, qui modo eodem sicut multa ad uniuersos pertinentia prædixit, ita et singularia uel personalia pleraque non tacuit. Singularia quarundam gentium ut ea quæ contra Palestinos, ut ea quæ contra Moab, ut ea quæ contra filios Ammon, ut ea quæ contra regna Asor, ut ea quæ contra Ælam, ut ea / quæ contra Babilonem, prophetico plenus Spiritu prophetauit. Personalia, sicut quando regem Sedechiam a Chaldeis capiendum et captiuandum prædixit, sicut quando Ananiæ cuidam falso prophetæ sic minatus est: "Non," inquit, "misit te Dominus, et tu confidere fecisti populum istum in mendacio. Idcirco hæc dicit Dominus: 'Ecce emittam te a facie terræ. Hoc anno morieris. Aduersus Do-

D 194rd

minum enim locutus es.' "⁵³ Sic et quando quibusdam duobus ait:
"Hæc dicit Dominus exercituum Deus Israel, ad Ahab filium Culiæ
et ad Sedechiam filium Amasiæ, qui prophetant uobis in nomine
meo mendaciter: 'Ecce ego tradam eos in manu Nabugodonosor
regis Babilonis, et percutiet eos in oculis uestris.' "⁵⁴

De hiis uniuersalibus simul et personalibus est et Danihel, qui
ut longe supra premisi utroque charismate plenus, et quæ ad omnes
et quæ ad quosdam solummodo pertinebant, sepe præfatus est.
Ad omnes, ut quando somnium regis Chaldei, cuius idem rex
immemor factus fuerat, recitans, quid præsignaret prædixit. Vi-
derat ille statuam cuius caput aurem, cuius pectus et brachia
argentea, cuius uenter et fæmora ærea, cuius crura ferrea, cuius
pedes partim ferrei, partim fictiles, præsignabunt maxima mundi
regna, sibi inuicem successura, uarios habitura processus pariter
et prouentus. Quæ per mutuas sucessiones in tantum sui diutur-
nitatem protenderent, donec percussa lapide absciso de monte
sine manibus, deficiente mundo finirentur et ipsa. Rursus ea quæ
ad omnes, ut ultima pars prophetiæ eius indicat, quæ siquis uestrum
legerit inueniet. Quæ uero ad quosdam, ut ea quæ ab ipso prædicta
sunt regi Nabugodonosor, ut et illa quæ regi Balthasar. Est igitur
Danihel ut duo supramemorati, non uniuersalis tantum, uel personalis tantum, sed simul uniuersalis et personalis propheta.

Sed quia Hebreos prophetas uobis uelut Iudeis propono, mirabitur forsitan aliquis uestrum. Sed ut desinat mirari audiat sequentia. Hebrei quidem iam dicti prophetæ sunt, sed licet Hebrei
sint, etiam uestri sunt. Sed dicetis: "Nostri quomodo? Quid enim
Arabs ad Hebreum? Quid Hysmahelita ad Iudeum?" Et multum
plane. Primo quod Hysmahel et Ysaac fratres fuere, licet ille de
Agar ancilla, iste de libera Sara. Secundo, quod preter consanguinitatis lineam et linguam tam in notis / litterarum quam in D 194vs
æloquio pene communem etiam singulari et antiquo circumcisionis
signo uelut ab utriusque gentis patre Abram diriuato, uos ipsos ab
uniuersarum gentium, aut innatis usibus aut traditis legibus secreuistis. Tertio, quod Hebreos aut Christianos de quibus agitur pro-

⁵³ Jer. 28:15-16.
⁵⁴ Jer. 29:21.

phetas ut diuino Spiritu inspiratos, et prophetica gratia plenos a uobis suscipi debere euidentibus et inuictis in suprascripto libro rationibus monstratum est. Quas ad integrum reconsignare et uelut de nouo litteris tradere, si præcedentibus aurem sollicitam adhibuistis superfluum est.

Quod si forte, aut ut rerum de quibus agitur instantium contemptores negligenter audistis, aut communi que pene omnes preter studiosos occupat desidia lecta uel audita obliuioni letargicæ tradidistis replico breuiter, quæ supra diffusius dicta si tanta uobis salutis uestræ cura est, recolligere poteritis. Ex quibus prophetas Iudaicos aut Christianos de quibus longus sermo processit, uestros etiam esse uosque eisdem ut uestris credere debere, si remota ut suprascripti perspicuæ ueritati renitens obstinatio fuerit, omni fugata nubium caligine ratio indubia declarabit. Et quid dico declarabit? Immo iam declarauit, et nisi infidelibus loquerer, et hiis qui a Deo prorsus alieni sunt, sepe dicta iterare refugerem. Sed ferat stilus omnia patienter, et hereticis aut æthnicis hominibus salua fidei et ueritatis constantia morem gerat.

Quid exigis a me Hysmaelita, unde prophetas meos tuos esse comprobem, unde ex uerbis ipsorum uelut a te concessis contra te pugnem? Habeo plane, habeo multa. "Quæ?" Audi. Cur accipis aliquid de libris meis, qui longe tuis antiquiores sunt, cum ego Christianus, tu hereticus ut dixi aut æthnicus sis? Quid michi et tibi? Nichil ego assumo de libris tuis, quare tu furaris aliquid de libris meis? An æmularis mea? An forte Christianus uis fieri? Et o utinam. O utinam plane, utinam relicto errore stulto, mortifero, carente omni ratione, destituto omni ueritate, euanescente per inania phantasmatum, et inaudita nugarum, ad Deum uerum conuertaris, Christum Dei uirtutem et sapientiam agnoscas, et a nefandi et turpissimi hominis laqueis erutus, possis cantare cum Dauid rege et propheta cui Psalmos a Deo datos nequam ille scripsit: "Laqueus contritus est, et nos liberati sumus."[55]

D 194vd   Hoc si dissi/mulas, dimitte michi mea, serua tibi tua. Nichil meis libris intersero de Alchoran tuo, nichil scriptis tuis admisceas de

[55] Ps. 123:7.

Æuangelio meo. Relinque michi Moysen meum, dimitte prophetas meos, noli mixturam prodigiosam et a nullo rationabili
animo færendam conficere, ut uel infernalibus scriptis cælestis
oraculi uerba interseras, uel ea nefandarum admixtione fabularum
et undique circumposito aggere mendaciorum deturpes. Et qua
ratione immo qua insania de falsis ut credis et prædicas Hebraicis
aut Christianis libris, quædam illi tuo ut æstimas de cælis misso
Alchoran miscuisti? Qua mente, Iudaica ut putas uel Christiana
mendacia ueraci scripturæ tuæ inseruisti? Nam si libri nostri
mendaces sunt, et quæ inde excerpta sunt falsa sunt. Quod si excerpta falsa sunt, et scripta quibus inserta sunt, falsa sunt. Sed
uerum est, quia inserta sunt Alchoran tuo. Certum est igitur, quia
falsitate illi admixta, falsum est et ipsum Alchoran tuum. Nec in
parte tantum, sed in toto falsum. Nam etsi forte aliqua ibi uera
sunt, falsorum admixtione corrupta sunt, nec iam fide digna sunt.

Nunquid non ita se habent uniuersarum gentium iudicia? Vbi-
que per orbem lex ista uiget. Si uel in uerbo uno falsus testis in-
uentus fuero, nec in ueris audiar, nec in ueris fidem merebor. Hac
iustitia reprobo Alchoran tuum, hoc æquitatis iudicio non eius
aliquas partes, sed ex integro condempno totum Alchoran tuum.
Elige tibi ut longe supra posui de duobus alterum. Aut propter
falsa quæ ex libris ut dicis falsis assumpta et libro tuo inserta sunt,
Alchoran abice, aut si nolueris, Hebraicos et Christianos libros ex
quibus illa sumpta sunt, ueraces fatere.

Et quia non patet uspiam uia qua has angustias euadere aliter
possis, credo te magis eligere, nostros libros fateri ueraces, ne quæ
hactenus lege paterna seruasti, cum ipso ipsius legis auctore, simul
uniuersa exspirent. Quod si hanc partem elegeris, libris sepe iam
nominatis, hoc est Hebraicis et Christianis, ut scripturis propriis
fidem dabis. Hiis de causis Hebreos tibi prophetas proposui, et proponam sicut Hebreo Christum, et Christi discipulos ut Christiano.
Vnde cum probare aliquid intendo, sicut ex concessis, sicut ex hiis
quibus iam adquiescis, ut ratio / docet, exempla produco.   D 195rs

Et quoniam iam communes nobis uobisque o Agareni libri
iam dicti facti sunt, ad cæpta sermo recurrat, et qua de causa tot
prophetarum exempla coram produxerit indicet. Mahumeth legis-

latorem uestrum, prophetam uel Dei nuntium non fuisse, ex superioribus plene quidem probatum est, sed adhuc ob maiorem euidentiam ista lecturis conferendam, iuxta præmissas diuisiones probandum est. Nam ut supra scripsi, prophetarum uel qui fuerunt uel qui dicti sunt, alii boni, alii mali. Bonorum alii prædicentes uniuersalia, alii particularia, alii de eisdem simul uniuersalia et particularia uel personalia. Quos nominatim ad medium deduxi, et quæ de tripertita propheticæ gratiæ distributione gratia quemque contigerit, singillatim expressi. Hoc ea de causa, ut tu quicumque Mahumeth prophetam nominas, quicumque eum prophetam affirmas, ostendas, et aut auctoritate aut ratione probes eum aut de uniuersalibus esse prophetis, uniuersale aliquid, aut de particularibus particulare aliquid, aut de personalibus personale, aliquid prædicendo, fuisse prophetam.

Sed quid frustra laborem insumerem? Quid in uanum certarem? Inuitaui et inuito, prouocaui et prouoco ut respondeas, qua ui, qua ratione, quo figmento ueraci uel fallaci, hominem hunc o tu Arabs prophetam esse credis, prophetam esse dicis. Prædixitne aliqua ad uniuersalem mundi salutem pertinentia unde uniuersalis iuxta præfatam diuisionem dici possit propheta? Prædixit aliqua, unde particularis ad quosdam non ad omnes pertinentia prædicens possit dici propheta? Prædixit aliqua, unde non ad quosdam pluraliter, sed ad quosdam personaliter, uera aliqua priusquam fierent prophetizans, possit probari propheta? Sed quid errori tuo pertinacius militans, et saluti tuæ contrarius, quæ salutis sunt refugis, quæ perniciosa sequeris? Dic, dic iam, siquid habes. Ostende Mahumeth tuum ex aliqua prædictarum diuisionum parte, aut prophetam esse uniuersalem, aut particularem, aut simul utrumque, aut personalem, hoc est non ad uniuersos, uel ad multos, sed ad quosdam pertinentia prophetantem.

Sed quid agis? Quid me suspensum tenes? Dic siquid habes, et iustificeris. Hæc quidem uerba Dei sunt, sed et post ipsum et cum ipso, / etiam mea sunt. Siquid magnum, siquid saltem uile uel modicum prophetico Spiritu dictum uel scriptum ex Alchoran tuo totiens et usque ad tedium nominato proferre potes, profer, enarra. Inuenisne ut supra iam dictum est in toto illo libro tuo iuxta te

D 195rd

sacro, iuxta nos execrando, aliquid ab illo tuo propheta prophetice dictum de præteritis, aliquid de præsentibus, aliquid de
futuris? Nam in hac ut præmissum est trina distinctione totius
propheticæ gratiæ summa consistit. Nam quæcumque prophetice
prædicuntur, aut sunt ut dictum est de præteritis, aut de præsentibus aut de futuris, siue sint illa quæ dicuntur uniuersalia, particularia, uel personalia, uel instanti tempore, uel prope, uel longe
post futuro prædicta. In quibus ergo propheticæ gratiæ diuisionibus
tam suptiliter et diligenter exquisitis, prophetam tuum o Arabs
contra quem ago inuenire poteris?

Sed refugio obicere, quæ iam obieci. Nam nec uniuersalem, nec
particularem nec personalem eum esse prophetam probaui, nec de
præteritis aliqua reuelasse, nec de præsentibus aliqua demonstrasse,
nec de futuris aliqua prophetasse ostendi. Si hæc ita se habent,
non est hic tuus uel alicuius ut dicebas propheta. Sed ut ex præmissis colligitur, nichil prorsus propheticum dixisse uel scripsisse
legitur. Non est igitur propheta.

EXPLICIT LIBER SECVNDVS DOMNI PETRI CLVNIACENSIS ABBATIS CON-
TRA SECTAM SARRACENORVM.[56]

[56] "Desunt duo libri quos inuenire non potui," in marg.

INDEX